CYBER-CRIME

Hong Kong University Press thanks Xu Bing for writing the Press's name in his Square Word Calligraphy for the covers of its books. For further information, see p. iv.

CYBER-CRIME

The Challenge in Asia

Edited by

Roderic Broadhurst and Peter Grabosky

香港大學出版社

Hong Kong University Press

Hong Kong University Press
14/F Hing Wai Centre
7 Tin Wan Praya Road
Aberdeen
Hong Kong

ISBN 962 209 735 9 (Hardback)
ISBN 962 209 724 3 (Paperback)

British Library Cataloguing-in-Publication Data

Secure On-line Ordering
http://www.hkupress.org

Printed and bound by Lammar Offset Printing Ltd., Hong Kong, China.

Hong Kong University Press is honoured that Xu Bing, whose art explores the complex themes of language across cultures, has written the Press's name in his Square Word Calligraphy. This signals our commitment to cross-cultural thinking and the distinctive nature of our English-language books published in China.

"At first glance, Square Word Calligraphy appears to be nothing more unusual than Chinese characters, but in fact it is a new way of rendering English words in the format of a square so they resemble Chinese characters. Chinese viewers expect to be able to read Square Word Calligraphy but cannot. Western viewers, however are surprised to find they can read it. Delight erupts when meaning is unexpectedly revealed."

— Britta Erickson, *The Art of Xu Bing*

Contents

Lists of Tables and Figures

Page no.

List of Tables

List of Figures

Foreword

For two principal reasons, this very useful book is highly representative of the valuable work done by the University of Hong Kong's Centre for Criminology. So much so that the book is almost emblematic of the centre. First, the subject-matter of the book, cyber-crime, is one to which the centre has devoted much attention as one of the great problems of today. Secondly, the book, like the centre itself, draws on and co-ordinates the learning and experience of persons from academia, industry and law enforcement throughout Asia and the Pacific Rim.

As a matter of form, this book can be described as a collection of essays. Between them, the essays cover the emerging trends and key issues which Asian and the Pacific Rim jurisdictions face in their efforts to combat computer-related crime. Discussed are crimes committed with computers (such as online fraud), crimes committed against computers (such as hacking) and crimes in which computers are incidentally involved (as, for example, where the records of illegal activities are stored in computers).

In the course of my opening address at the centre's Second Asia Cyber-Crime Summit in November 2003, I ventured to observe that in no other field of criminal activity are international borders more porous than they are in cyber criminal activity, and that this presents the family of nations with a unique challenge. This book makes a significant contribution to the means by which that challenge can be met. In addition to the need for international and transnational co-operation on an unprecedented scale, cyber-crime has given rise to a need, which this book brings out and explains, for closer co-operation between the public and private sectors.

This book is suitable for use as a textbook in advanced criminology courses. Over and above that, it deserves a wide readership in academic, business, government and professional circles.

The Hon Mr Justice Bokhary PJ,
Hong Kong Court of Final Appeal.

Acknowledgements

This collection is the work of many hands. First we would like to thank all of the contributors for their patience, and for their prompt attention to our editorial entreaties.

We would also like to thank the Centre for Criminology of the University of Hong Kong, and its sponsors for hosting the two Asia Cyber-Crime Summits that provided the inspiration for this book. The partnerships between industry, law enforcement and the university that ensured the success of these meetings continued to aid us in the preparation of this volume. We are especially grateful for the wonderful support and assistance given to us by the officers of the Hong Kong Police Technology Crime Division. We are also grateful to Venetia Somerset, Bronwyn McNaughton and Yeung Oi Yan for their masterful editorial contributions, encouragement and support.

Finally we would like to extend our appreciation to Hong Kong University Press and in particular Dennis Cheung for bringing this book to life.

If, despite the efforts of those above, there are any shortcomings in the book, they remain ours alone.

Roderic Broadhurst
Hong Kong

Peter Grabosky
Canberra

January 2005

Contributors

Roderic Broadhurst is an Associate Professor, Department of Sociology, and Senior Fellow, Centre for Criminology, the University of Hong Kong. He is the current Chair of the Hong Kong Society of Criminology, Associate Fellow of the Australian Institute of Criminology and associate editor of the Australian and New Zealand Journal of Criminology. His research interests include violence, repeat offending, professional delinquency, organised crime and crime in developing countries. Recent work includes editor of *Bridging the GAP: A Global Alliance Perspective on Transnational Organised Crime*, Hong Kong Police (2003), and contributions to the journals *Forensic Science International* and *Criminal Behaviour and Mental Health*. He was co-convenor and proceedings editor of the First and Second Asia Cyber-Crime Summits held in April 2001 and November 2003 at the University of Hong Kong. (broadie@hkucc.hku.hk)

Peter Grabosky is a Professor in the Research School of Social Sciences, Australian National University, and a Fellow of the Academy of the Social Sciences in Australia. His general interests are in harnessing non-governmental resources in furtherance of public policy. His publications include *Cyber Criminals on Trial* (with Russell Smith and Gregor Urbas, 2004); *Electronic Theft* (with Russell Smith and Gillian Dempsey, 2001); and *Crime in the Digital Age* (with Russell Smith, 1998). He was previously Deputy Director of the Australian Institute of Criminology. Other appointments include Russell Sage Fellow in Law and Social Science at Yale Law School (1976–78), Visiting

Professor, Institute of Comparative Law in Japan, Chuo University (1993), Visiting Expert, the United Nations Asia and Far East Institute for the Prevention of Crime and the Treatment of Offenders (1995), and Visiting Professor, Chinese People's Public Security University (1996). He was Rapporteur for the Workshop on Crimes Related to the Computer Network at the Tenth United Nations Congress on the Prevention of Crime and the Treatment of Offenders, Vienna, 2000. He is past president of the Australian and New Zealand Society of Criminology, and in 2000 was elected Deputy Secretary-General of the International Society of Criminology. (Peter.Grabosky@anu.edu.au)

Simon Bronitt is a Reader in Law and Director of the National Europe Centre at the Australian National University in Canberra. His scholarly interests lie in the field of criminal law and procedure, evidence, criminal justice and criminology. His research takes a broad interdisciplinary and comparative perspective, which is reflected in his recent book, Bronitt and McSherry, *Principles of Criminal Law* (Law Book Co, Sydney, 2001). He is a State Editor of the *Criminal Law Journal* and an Associate of the Australian Institute of Criminology.

Jeffrey G Bullwinkel graduated from Duke University with a Bachelor of Arts degree (cum laude) and received his law degree from New York University (cum laude). He is a member of the New York State Bar. He is presently Microsoft Corporation's Director of Corporate Affairs for the Far East Region, including Greater China, Japan, and Korea. Based in Hong Kong, he oversees a broad range of the company's activities in the region relating to the protection of intellectual property rights, as well as initiatives focused on building a safer and trustworthy computing environment. He also participates actively in industry associations devoted to increasing international protection of trademarks and copyright works, including the International Intellectual Property Association, the International Anti-Counterfeiting Coalition, the Quality Brands Protection Committee and the Business Software Alliance. In addition, he is an active member of the American Chamber of Commerce in Hong Kong. He has served as chairman of the Chamber's Intellectual Property Committee since January 2002 and was elected to the Board of Governors in December 2002. Prior to joining Microsoft, he was a federal prosecutor with the Office of International Affairs, Criminal Division, United States of America Department of Justice and, was responsible for matters relating to international criminal law enforcement, including negotiating bilateral treaties and multilateral conventions on international cooperation in criminal matters, and providing advice on international law to the Office of the Attorney General.

Chan Keen Wai was formerly the Director of Infocomm Security at the **Infocomm Development Authority** (IDA) of Singapore. **Clement Leong** is a senior consultant at IDA. The IDA develops, promotes and regulates info-communications in Singapore, with the aim of establishing Singapore as one of the world's premier infocomm capitals. To nurture an internationally competitive infocomm industry, the IDA offers a comprehensive range of programmes and schemes for both local and international companies. For more information, visit www.ida.gov.sg

Ivan S K Chiu obtained his BA (Hons) from Hong Kong Baptist University, and his MA and MPhil in Social Science from the Hong Kong University of Science and Technology. His main research interests are risk, reliability, safety and security in respect to science and information technology policy, cultural and the social psychology of online education. His publications (in Chinese) include, 'The Difficulty of Taking the Initiative in Online Teaching in Hong Kong' (2002) and 'The Difference of Risk Perception among the Educated Youth in Hong Kong and China: The Issue of Using Computers' (2002). He is also a manuscript reviewer for the *Journal of Risk Analysis*. (ivanchiusk@sinaman.com).

CISC (Centre for Information Security and Cryptography, Department of Computer Science & Information Systems, Faculty of Engineering, the University of Hong Kong) represents a coordinated effort to promote academic research and industrial collaboration with a mission of becoming a centre of excellence, in the University of Hong Kong and in the Asia-Pacific region. Research interests of CISC include computer security technology, cryptographic systems, network and Internet security, Public Key Infrastructure (PKI) systems, and most recently, the study of e-crime. **K H Pun, Venus L S Cheung, Lucas C K Hui, K P Chow, W W Tsang, H W Chan,** and **C F Chong** are colleagues of CISC

Peter Csonka is currently a Senior Counsel at the International Monetary Fund's Legal Department, which he joined in December 2002. Born in Hungary and educated in France, he is a lawyer by training (LLM). In 1986–91 he was an Assistant Professor in criminal law at the Faculty of Law of Miskolc (Hungary) and conducted research at the University of Pau (France). He also practiced law as a Junior Prosecutor during this period. He then joined the Council of Europe (Strasbourg, France), where he worked until December 2002 as Deputy Head of the Economic Criminal Law Division (Directorate General of Legal Affairs). He was in charge of legal drafting, policy and assessment-related issues in the area of economic criminal law, including cyber-crime and money laundering.

Pavan Duggal is an Advocate of the Supreme Court of India. He is the Founding President of Cyberlaw Asia, and has undertaken pioneering work in the field of convergence law. He is also President of Cyberlaw Asia, Asia's first organisation committed to the passing of dynamic cyber-laws in the Asian continent and President of Cyberlaws.Net, which is the Internet's unique online consultancy dedicated exclusively to cyber laws. He is a member of the Nominating Committee, Membership Advisory Committee and a member of the Membership Implementation Task Force of the Internet Corporation for Assigned Names and Numbers. He is a member of the WIPO Arbitration and Mediation Centre Panel of Neutrals and member of AFACT Legal Working Group of UN / CEFACT and a consultant with International Trade Centre, UNCTAD / WTO, Geneva. As a practicing advocate he has been a counsel in many path-breaking cyber law cases. He was the counsel for the complainant in the case that led to India's first cyber-crime conviction and he represented the plaintiff-company in India's and Asia's first 'Cyber Defamation' case. He was also counsel in the first Indian case for damages under India's Information Technology Act, 2000. He is the author *of Cyberlaw — The Indian Perspective.*

Miriam Gani is a Lecturer in the Faculty of Law at the Australian National University. She teaches criminal law and legal method and her principal research areas are cyber-crime, stalking, terrorism and statutory interpretation. She is currently participating, with several faculty colleagues, in a major project funded by the Australian Research Council. The project involves, in part, examining Australia's legislative response to terrorism.

Michael Jackson is a Lecturer in the Faculty of Law, the University of Hong Kong, where his teaching includes criminal law and cyber-crime. He writes mainly in the field of criminal law and is the author of *Criminal Law in Hong Kong* and a contributing author to *Archbold Hong Kong*. He was a member of the Criminal Law and Procedure Committee of the Law Society of Hong Kong from 1996–2003, and has practised criminal litigation both in New Zealand and in Hong Kong. (mjackson@hkucc.hku.hk)

Laurie Lau is a PhD candidate at the Cyberlaw Research Unit, Department of Law, University of Leeds. He was a Resident Graduate Scholar (2002–03) at the David C Lam Institute for East-West Studies, Hong Kong Baptist University. At present, he is a part-time lecturer in criminal justice studies at the University of Hong Kong. His research interests are: computer-related crimes, computer fraud, computer forensic evidence and cyber-policing issues. He has also presented conference papers in Europe and Asia. Currently he is a member of the executive committee of the Hong Kong Society of Criminology. (laurie.lau@alumni.cityu.edu.hk)

Julie Shannon is a doctoral student and an Assistant Lecturer in International Relations in the School of Political Science at the University of New South Wales. She holds an MA in International Relations from the University of New South Wales and a BA in Philosophy from the University of Sydney, and her interests include regional institutions and human security in East Asia. She has also provided research and programme management assistance for the Asia-Australia Institute's regional programmes and has recently been involved in programme preparation for the Research Institute for Asia and the Pacific training of East Timor's Environmental Protection Unit.

Masao Tatsuzaki is Assistant Director. Foreign Affairs Division, Security Bureau, National Police Agency, Japan. Previously he was Assistant Director, Security System Planning Office, Community Safety Bureau, National Police Agency (2001–03). He holds a Bachelor of Law from the University of Tokyo (1993) and LLM from Cornell Law School (1998). He is an Attorney at Law (New York), and has passed the Japan Bar examination.

Nicholas Thomas is a researcher at the Centre of Asian Studies, the University of Hong Kong. His main focus is the China-ASEAN project, which provides briefing reports on events in Southeast Asian countries to the Central Policy Unit of the Hong Kong SAR Government, and organises roundtables and meetings between Southeast Asian and Chinese scholars and policymakers. Prior to assuming this position, he worked as a Research Fellow at the Asia-Australia Institute, University of New South Wales. This involved academic research on East Asia as well as the design and management of 'Track Two' meetings between Australian and East Asian policy-makers. He has published articles, chapters and books on East Asian regionalism, human security, and Hong Kong politics. His most recent book is *Re-Orienting Australia-China Relations: 1972 To The Present*, Ashgate Publishing (UK), 2004.

Keiji Uchimura is a Professor in the Applied Technology Department, National Police Academy (Japan). He was previously Staff Officer of the First Criminal Investigation Division at Keishicho (Metropolitan Police Department) from 1997–98, and was Assistant Director in the Investigative Planning Division, Criminal Bureau, Keisatsucho (National Police Agency) from 1998–2001. From 2001–03 he completed an MSc in Criminology and Criminal Justice at Cardiff University in the UK while on secondment from Keisatsucho.

Gregor Urbas, PhD, is an academic lawyer based in Canberra, Australia. He was a researcher in the Sophisticated Crime and Regulation Program of the Australian Institute of Criminology and in the intellectual property legislation section of IP Australia, and is currently a Lecturer in the Law Faculty of the Australian National University teaching in criminal law, evidence and intellectual property. He is also a part-time Research Officer for the Law Council of Australia and has published on cyber-crime, intellectual property piracy, DNA evidence and criminal justice policy.

Georgiana Wong is a senior executive of an international computer firm with 20 years of experience in information technology. Her extensive knowledge in IT business applications and the rapid growth of Internet usage has prompted her to pursue research studies in the area of computer crime and cyberspace governance. Georgiana holds a Master of Social Science in Law and Public Affairs and a Bachelor of Arts in English Literature from the Chinese University of Hong Kong as well as a Master of Science in Computing (University of Ulster) and Master of Business Administration (University of Macau). She is an independent researcher and has co-authored with Dr Kam Wong several papers on cyberspace studies in the PRC and Hong Kong.

Kam C Wong is currently an Associate Professor of Law and Criminal Justice, University of Wisconsin (Oshkosh) and received his JD from Indiana and PhD (SUNY – Albany). He teaches police and homeland security related subjects. Previously, he was Director of the Chinese Law Program (1997–2002) in the Chinese University of Hong Kong. Professor Wong is currently involved with two research projects: *The Impact of USA PATRIOT ACT, on Society* and *Police Reform in Modern China*. His publications have appeared in many international criminal justice and law journals, including the *British Journal of Criminology, Georgetown Journal of Law and Public Policy, Columbia Journal of Asian Law, Australian Journal of Law and Society, International Journal of the Sociology of Law* and others. Professor Wong is an editor of *Police Practice and Research: An International Journal*, and an Advisory Board Member of the *International*

Journal of Comparative Criminology. He was the former vice-chair of the Hong Kong Society of Criminology and is an associate fellow of the Center for Criminology, the University of Hong Kong. He was President (2002–03) of the Asian Association of Police Studies and serves on the Advisory Board for the Yale in China Legal Program.

Abbreviations

ACCORD	ASEAN and China Cooperative Operations in Response to Dangerous Drugs
APCERT	Asia Pacific Computer Emergency Response Teams
APEC	Asia-Pacific Economic Cooperation
APG	Asia-Pacific Group on Money Laundering
APIG	All Party Internet Group
ASEAN	Association of South East Asian Nations
ASEANAPOL	ASEAN Association of National Chiefs of Police
ATM	automatic teller machine
B2B	business to business
B2C	business to consumers
BSA	Business Software Alliance
CA	Certification Authority (Singapore)
CBI	Confederation of British Industry
CBI	Central Bureau of Investigation (India)
CCA	Controller of Certification Authorities (Singapore)
CNNIC	China Internet Network Information Center
CD	compact disk
CERT	computer emergency response team
CICP	Centre for International Crime Prevention
CID	Criminal Investigation Department (Singapore)
CISC	Center for Information Security and Cryptography
CMA	Computer Misuse Act (Singapore)

CMC	computer-mediated communication
CND	Commission on Narcotic Drugs
COE	Council of Europe
CPC	Chinese Communist Party
DESK	Digital Evidence Search Kit
DNS	domain name system
DVD	digital video disk
ECOSOC	Economic and Social Council
ECSG	Electronic Commerce Steering Group
ETA	Electronic Transactions Act (Singapore)
ETSI	European Telecommunications Standards Institute
EU	European Union
FATF	Financial Action Task Force
FBI	Federal Bureau of Investigation (USA)
FIRST	Forum of Incident Response and Security Teams
HKCERT / CC	Hong Kong Computer Emergency Response Team Co-ordination Centre
HKP	Hong Kong Police
HKSAR	Hong Kong Special Administrative Region
I^2R	Institute of Infocomm Research (Singapore)
IASP	Internet Access Service Providers (Singapore)
ICC	International Chamber of Commerce
ICP	Internet content provider
ICT	information and communication technology
ID	identification
IDA	Infocomm Development Authority (Singapore)
IFPI	International Federation of Phonographic Industries
IIPA	International Intellectual Property Alliance
Interpol	International Criminal Police Organisation
IP	Internet protocol / intellectual property
IPEG	Intellectual Property Rights Working Group
IPR	intellectual property rights
IRC	Internet Relay Chat
IRD	Inland Revenue Department (Hong Kong)
IRT	Incident Response Team
iSec	Infocomm Security Division (Singapore)
ITU	International Telecommunication Union
IWP	Internet Watch Foundation
KISA	Korean Information and Security Agency

MAS	Monetary Authority of Singapore
MCCOC	Model Criminal Code Officers Committee (Australia)
MII	Ministry of Information Industry (PR China)
MLA	mutual legal assistance
MLAT	mutual legal assistance treaty
MPA	Motion Picture Association
MPS	Ministry of Public Security (China)
MPT	Ministry of Posts and Telecommunications (Japan)
NCFC	National Computing and Networking Facility of China
NCIS	National Criminal Intelligence Service
NICC	National Infocomm Competency Centre
NIRT	National Incident Response Team (Japan)
NISC	National Infocomm Security Committee (Singapore)
NPA	National Police Agency (Japan)
NPC	National People's Congress (China)
NSO	non-state organisation
PCCW	Pacific Century CyberWorks
PC-CY	Committee of Experts on Crime in Cyber-Space
PKI	Public Key Infrastructure
PKU	Peking University
POP	problem-oriented policing
R&D	research and development
RIPA	Regulation of Investigatory Powers Act (UK)
SCCP	Sub-Committee on Customs Procedures
SCMP	*South China Morning Post*
SingCERT	Singapore Computer Emergency Response Team
SITF	Singapore Information Technology Federation
SOMTC	Senior Officials Meeting on Transnational Crime
TATF	Telecoms Action Task Force
TCD	Technology Crime Division (HK Police)
UNAFEI	United Nations Asia and Far East Institute for the Prevention of Crime and the Treatment of Offenders
UNCITRAL	United Nations Commission on International Trade Law
UNDCP	United Nations Drug Control Program
USTR	United States Trade Representative

WAP	wireless applications
WIPO	World Intellectual Property Organization
WITSA	World Information Technology and Services Alliance
WTO	World Trade Organization

1

Computer-Related Crime in Asia: Emergent Issues

Roderic Broadhurst and Peter Grabosky

The rapid development of computer connectivity and the role of the Internet in the emergence of new e-commerce markets have increasingly attracted the attention of national governments and international agencies. Hyperbole aside, the astonishing reach of these tools has changed the way a large part of the world communicates and does business. It may be too early to evaluate claims that this medium ushers in an irresistible phase of a global 'information revolution' and, with it, a 'new economy'. However, we can be certain that with the erosion of traditional barriers to communication, our concepts of time and place have irrevocably changed and the process of 'globalisation' has accelerated.

The convergence of computing and communications and the exponential growth of digital technology have brought enormous benefits to modern society. Along with these new benefits, however, come greater risks. As never before, and at negligible cost to themselves, lone offenders can inflict catastrophic loss or damage on individuals, companies, and governments from the other side of the world. With these developments has come the awareness that 'information security' is no longer a matter for the technical and computer specialist, but for millions of people who now engage these new media every day for business, communications and leisure. The continued prosperity of industrial nations, and the economic development of the world's less affluent societies, seems likely to depend increasingly on electronic commerce. To the extent that public confidence in e-commerce is jeopardised by criminal activity, so too will economic well-being be threatened.

The new opportunities created in 'cyberspace' have also enhanced the capacity for criminal enterprises to operate more efficiently and effectively both domestically and across borders. In Asia and other parts of the world an evolving role for both individual offenders and criminal networks has emerged to exploit criminal opportunities in the e-commerce / new economy environment. The extremely rapid development of digital technologies and e-commerce in Asia, coupled with the expansion of the Internet and other forms of connectivity, has occurred at such a pace that law enforcement agencies in many jurisdictions have been unable to respond effectively. The traditional notion of information security with an emphasis on system and data protection no longer captures the scope of the risks and threats now unleashed by digital and wireless connectivity. In the chapters to follow the contributors address the wide range of problems and issues now faced in policing and regulating cyberspace and cyber-crime in Asia. The role of public and private law enforcement is crucial in curtailing criminal activity and ensuring the digital 'highways' are not lawless or hazardous but safe for all who wish to travel them. The term 'cyber-crime' is of course a misnomer, for what is described and discussed in the following pages includes computer-related crime: illegal behaviours with an obvious terrestrial dimension. As digital technology becomes more pervasive and interconnected, ordinary crime scenes are bound to contain some form of digital evidence.

Criminality and Computer Crime

With governments, industries, markets and consumers increasingly dependent on computer connectivity, they are prone to an array of threats. The most notable have been the widely publicised computer 'viruses', which have increased in both virulence and velocity since 2000. The beginning of 2004 saw the development of increasingly complex malicious code in the form of the 'MyDoom' or 'Norvag' worm. It apparently combined the effects of a worm, spreading rapidly across the Internet, with that of a distributed denial of service attack, where computing power is directed at a target system with a view to shutting it down. In other words, infected computers were remotely 'commandeered' and directed against the target computer. The implications of such activity for infrastructure protection are ominous (Semple 2004).

Many of these risks appear to mimic traditional criminal exploitation, albeit often executed with unprecedented ease, speed and impact across jurisdictions. Law enforcement has truly entered the digital age. The tasks of identifying cyber-criminals and bringing them to justice pose formidable challenges to law enforcement agencies across the globe, and require a degree and timeliness of cooperation that has been until only recently regarded as difficult, if not impossible, to achieve.

As rational choice theories of criminal behaviour have gained increasing credence and the significance of pathological theories (defects of individual personality and socialisation) has declined, the perception has arisen of organised crime as essentially operating like any profit-seeking enterprise. Until the American scholar, E H Sutherland, coined the term 'white-collar' crime in 1939, the connection between business, politics and crime groups was a neglected part of criminological theory. He drew on the fundamental idea that criminal behaviour is learned through 'differential association'; that is, primary relationships that justify and support illegal conduct.

That criminal behaviour itself need not depend on social deviance is a fact that makes distinguishing good or bad behaviour from good or bad people one of the natural conundrums of policing. It also ensures that risk profiling, despite actuarial sophistication, is much more difficult than is often assumed. Thus while underlying motives are important at the individual level, at the macro level diverse criminal motives are in reality governed by opportunities — opportunities that are perceived to present low risk and high profit to the criminal or deviant enterprise.

The 'situational crime prevention' model is the criminological perspective most applicable to understanding crime and the control of opportunity-driven criminal groups or enterprises. Drawing on the work of 'situational crime prevention' criminologists such as Marcus Felson (1998) and Ron Clarke (1992; Newman & Clarke 2003), Grabosky argues that computer-related crime, like crime in general, may be explained by the conjunction of three factors: motivation, opportunity, and the absence of capable guardianship. Motives will vary depending on the nature of the crime in question, but include greed, lust, revenge, challenge and adventure.[1] Offenders tend to be generalists rather than specialists in choice of crime. Although offender profiling requires a flexible approach, there is increasing evidence of greater offender interest in financial rewards.

The convergence of these three factors in time and place — the motivated offender, a suitable target, and the absence of capable guardians — accounts for the amount of crime experienced. Crime prevention strategies based on this idea focus on strengthening the role of guardians (for example, neighbourhood watch, police telephone hotlines, CCTV) and reducing opportunity by target-hardening high-risk property (installing more effective anti-theft devices) and educating the public about the proper use of digital technology. A fourth factor, crucial to the success of a criminal act, is the extent to which the motivated offender has access to the resources (both social and technical) that allow the act to take place. It is through a network of relationships that the various resources necessary to complete a criminal transaction are mustered; coupled with the opportunities provided by the absence of capable guardians, this is what gives criminal groups their sustenance.

Computer-Related Crime in Asia

Criminal opportunities are expanding globally with the rapid proliferation and penetration of digital technology.[2] A number of jurisdictions have reported substantial increases in computer-related crime following the passage of laws designed to control computer-related offences. Valeri (2001) suggests that the mixed trends in computer-related crime within the European Union reflect the partial success of longstanding regional efforts to address computer crime; this is also to an extent reflected by those jurisdictions in Asia with a longer 'history' of a formal legal response.

The relative novelty of computer crime has meant that most policing agencies have only recently developed specific measures for recording them. The advent of computer-related criminal laws and associated prosecutions and the establishment of computer emergency response teams (CERTs) and dedicated technology crime units within policing agencies, coupled with the development of crime-victim awareness and consumer advocacy, have prompted jurisdictions at the forefront of the digital revolution to begin recording the incidence of illegality in cyberspace. However, in many jurisdictions cyber-crimes, if reported, may not be differentiated from other commercial crime, fraud reports or criminal damage statistics or other categories. Thus the extent of computer-related crimes, even when reported, remains unclear.

Police statistics about reported crime often tell us more about the activities and priorities of police than they do about the extent of crime. This is because in many traditional crimes, victims do not report them to the authorities. This is undoubtedly also the case with computer crime. Replicated random surveys of crime victims in many jurisdictions over the past 30 years have shown there are various reasons why victims of crime do not report to police. These include, for example: the belief that police cannot (or will not) do anything; the offence was trivial or the victim felt the matter was better dealt with privately; reporting the case was too troublesome; or fear of reprisal or further trouble if they did report the incident (see for example Newman 1999; Alvazzi del Frate 1998).

Nevertheless, despite these limitations it is instructive to explore the available data from several Asian jurisdictions where some official records of reported computer crime are available.

We take as an example the work and capabilities of the Hong Kong Police, who have recognised the increased interdependence of global markets and have responded to the general risks to Hong Kong's commerce and financial services. The Hong Kong Police Commercial Crime Bureau's Technology Crime Division (TCD) was established in 2001 and its predecessor, the Computer Crime Section, was established in 1993. Headed by a senior superintendent with a team of 66 officers, TCD deals with computer crime investigations, computer forensic examinations, and support to force-wide investigation units both at scenes of crime and during their investigations. The TCD is divided into three sections Operations, Forensic Investigations and Intelligence, and has a mission that broadly reflects the scope of public policing now required:

- Maintaining a professional investigation capability
- Broadening the investigation capability within the Force
- Developing accredited computer forensics
- Proposing changes in laws and policies
- Prevention and education
- Intelligence management, and liaison with industries and professionals
- Liaison with overseas law enforcement agencies and international law enforcement cooperation

In 2000, TCD conducted computer forensic examinations in 91 crime cases and in 2001 the number of examinations increased by 159 cases. The amount of computer data examined grew from 1100 gigabytes in 2000 to 4800 gigabytes in 2002 and in the first eight months of 2002, 128 cases and 3400 gigabytes of data were examined. In the same year a state-of-the-art Computer Forensics Laboratory was established, enabling each of its computer forensics examiners to handle, at any one time, three to four cases involving 'stand-alone' computers, or 600 gigabytes of data on any networked computer. (See Table 1.1.)

Cases reported under 'other' are mostly personal identification (ID) and password theft usually involving the fraudulent obtaining of access to Internet, phone and other services. While six cases of e-banking fraud were reported in 2002, all involved the 'misuse of passwords' and obtaining services without payment. Customer passwords, and not the bank system, were the actual target of offenders. Notably, Internet obscenity cases that totalled 32 cases in 1999 have since rapidly declined with only one case reported in 2001.

Table 1.1 Computer-related crimes reported in Hong Kong

Reported cases	*1995*	*1996*	*1997*	*1998*	*1999*	*2000*	*2001*	*2002*	*2003*
Hacking / cracking[a]	4	4	7	13	238	275	114	164	403
Criminal damage	2	4	3	3	4	15	27	16	16
Online deception	0	0	2	1	18	29	65	64	103
E-theft and other	8	13	8	17	57	49	29	30	66
All	14	21	20	34	317	368	235	274	588

Note: a. Unauthorised access or access to a computer with criminal or dishonest intent.

The general decline in cases reported in 2001 was thought to be due to the successful prosecution of hacking, obscenity and copyright breach offences and consumer and business security awareness. Another possibility for the rapid increase in reported computer crime in 2000 and 2001 was the widespread upgrading of computer networks and personal computers as a result of the 'millennium bug' fear and the consequent wider application of intrusion-tracking software and other security measures. Another less dramatic source of the drop in reported cases was the general reduction in the use of dial-up Internet connections and subsequent fewer cases of password and ID theft to gain free access. Although simple hacking cases have decreased, there are now increases in complex hacking, theft and criminal damage offences.

Other Asian Countries

Japan

In his chapter Masao Tatsuzaki of the National Police Agency of Japan describes the current status of cyber-crime in Japan, the law enforcement response, and the imperative of international cooperation. Cyber-crime is increasing in Japan, as elsewhere. Child pornography and Internet fraud are prominent, and fraud involving Internet auctions has risen sharply; government systems have been the target of attack, and viruses are common. To respond to these threats, the National Police Agency (NPA) established a Cyber Force: a mobile technical assistance unit that assists prefecture police in the course of their investigations. In 2000, 560 cases were reported, of which 87% were 'access' offences and 50% involved obscene materials. Keiji Uchimura's chapter outlines the Japanese approach to the interception and surveillance of Internet and other communications so necessary to combat the activities of Boryokudan and millennium sects such as the Aum Shinri

Kyo. He stresses the tensions between public police and the limitations of the 'Tachiainin' system (telecom enterprise technical staff) that mandates due process supervision of such interceptions.

Singapore

The chapter by Chan Keen Wai and Clement Leong from Singapore's Info-communications Development Authority of Singapore (IDA) outlines the Republic's efforts in both developing an information society and fostering information security. The emphasis in Singapore is that computer security and crime prevention is everybody's responsibility. In 2000 a special computer response group was created and merged with the Commercial Affairs Bureau of the Finance Department. In the first (financial) year of operation, 75 computer investigation cases were reported. In the same year 191 computer-related offences were recorded and, of these, 82% involved intrusion offences; most (64%) involved global roaming services.

Korea

The Korean Information and Security Agency (KISA) is the most active agency responsible for cyber-crime control in Korea and is a reflection of the nation's rapid acceptance of information technology. KISA has helped developed a comprehensive package of legislation and programmes designed to ensure a secure e-commerce environment hostile to cyber-criminals. Korea was one of the first countries to criminalise spamming and advocates a vigorous public education programme centred on a 'Prevention Day' on the 15th of every month. Of the 2000 incidents reported by KISA in 2001, 33% comprised 'spam' mail; 11% were virus or 'cracking' offences, 9.1% obscenity offences, and 43.5% were personal information and privacy intrusions. Korea's pioneering responses to the ubiquitous menace of 'spam' include efforts to both criminalize this conduct and to stress the critical role of consumer awareness. However, 'spammers' from outside Korea's borders still operate with relative impunity. KISA estimated that on average 41 'spam' mails were received per person per day in Korea in July 2003 and unless spamming was addressed this was likely to flood email systems to extinction. KISA notes that many 'relay servers' were sourced from schools and that improving information security in that sector along with requiring ISPs to register bulk mailers may stem the flood of unsolicited commercial email. According to a KISA survey

56% of 'spam' involved sexually explicit material, 19% other illegal products, 14% was fraud style emails, and 11% other forms of advertising (Broadhurst 2004).

China

The Information Security Supervision Bureau of the Ministry of Public Security of PR China estimates that in 2002 there were approximately 48.8 million Internet users, nearly 30 million computers and 150 000 websites in China. Just fewer than 5000 computer crimes were reported in 2001, up from about 2900 in 2000 and around 400 in 1999. By mid-2002 the bureau had reported just over 3000 cases. It estimated that by year's end it would handle 350 cases of system intrusion and over 800 cases of damage to computer systems.[3] The number of cases identified by the bureau was thus seen to be growing at an overwhelming rate, although many cases went unreported or unnoticed. Most offenders were younger people (aged 18–30) with most attacks mounted from Net or cyber-cafés with offenders hiding their identities by connecting through a http or Sock proxy, by fake IP addresses or by employing cryptography or steganography. Consequently, stronger measures have been taken in the registration and monitoring of cyber-cafés, with many being closed or reorganised.

At present, the bureau labours without specific laws and with no explicit definition of computer evidence or procedures to retrieve evidence. Although current regulations (Regulation of Security and Protection of Computer Information Systems of the People's Republic of China 1994; Management Regulation of Security and Protection of Computer Information Networks Connected with the Internet 1997; and the Criminal law of PR China 1997) relating to cyber-crime are complex, they lack the detail to enable successful enforcement, while emergency response and case reporting measures have yet to be fully developed. Being implemented are basic policies that seek to place prevention as the priority, along with the protection of crucial computer systems while strengthening education and propaganda about information and computer security. More needs to be done to develop the local information security industry and to improve the level of cooperation with foreign police in the pursuit of cross-border cases.

Thailand

Although no specific computer crime statistics are available for Thailand, the Royal Thai Police have set up an Internet Hotline.[4] In its first eight months, 3640 incidents were reported. Over half related to pornographic websites (39% Thai and 23% foreign languages) and a further 15.5% related to pornographic products or prostitution. About 10% related to intellectual property piracy or other illegal products, 3.5% to gambling sites and 7.5% to national security. Several new laws are being worked on (Electronic Transaction, Signatures and Fund Transfer Laws, Computer Crime, Data Protection and National Information Infrastructure Laws) by the newly restructured (November 2002) Ministry of Science and Technology. The *Electronics Transaction Act* B.E. 2544, which provides electronic transactions and signatures, came into effect in April 2002, and the computer-crime law now in draft follows the framework of the Council of Europe's Cyber-crime Convention. ThaiCERT was established in April 2001 and at present the Royal Thai Police, the Special Investigations department of the Ministry of Justice and the National Electronic Computer Technology Centre are responsible for dealing with all aspects of cyber-crime in Thailand.[5]

Indonesia

Indonesia, one of the largest countries in the region, has an Internet service that is estimated to serve about 7.5 million users via 170 ISPs. Internet banking began in 1998–99, and the most prevalent cyber-crime is the misuse of payment cards. Website defacing of the major banks and government departments have been reported, as well as cases of cyber-squatting and typo-pirating. At present there is no legal framework, although draft cyber-crime, electronic and personal data protection laws are being drawn up. A significant lack of relevant human resources among law enforcement and IT professionals is acknowledged.[6]

Philippines

Since the infamous Trojan type 'I love you' virus was launched from the Philippines in May 2000, the passage of the *Electronic Commerce Act* in June 2000 penalised hacking or cracking and piracy offences. Since the passage of the new law, there have been ten cases of hacking as well as cases involving cyberspace defamation, pornography, gambling, and the sale of firearms and drugs. The National Bureau of Investigation (Anti-Fraud and Computer Crimes Division) along with the Intellectual Property Office, the National Telecommunication Commission and the Department of Trade and Industry, has overall responsibility for addressing computer-related crime. A comprehensive cyber law is under study with proposals to criminalise intentional unauthorised access, computer sabotage, domain squatting, spamming, and the illegal distribution of copyright products. The Philippines National Police have limited capacity and generally lack technical capability, trained investigators and developed domestic and regional cooperation mechanisms.[7] Weak banking laws make the Philippines an ideal 'staging' post of money laundering via wire or electronic transfer.

The position of Uzebekistan, Kazakhstan and Mongolia is considerably less developed than the countries reported above, although all are in the process of developing both laws and infrastructure to enable e-commerce. Vietnam, Laos, Cambodia, Myanmar and North Korea have yet to enter the digital age, although the North Korean government may be developing an information warfare capability.

Transnational Policing and Cyber-Crime

Cyber-crime is often transnational crime, and efforts to address it therefore need to adopt a transnational approach. The focus here is on the development of international and multilateral efforts aimed at addressing increasing threats posed by various computer-related crimes and the associated investigative, evidentiary, legal and procedural problems. A simple but effective response is the need for expedited (e-mail) requests for mutual legal assistance (MLA); a number of nations are moving towards compulsory disclosure of cryptographic keys subject to judicial oversight (Grenville-Cross 2003).

The transnational nature of cyber-crime reflects the process of globalisation, which has intensified over the past two decades. By globalisation, we mean the general shift of economic forces towards multinational and interdependent markets coupled with a decline in the capabilities of individual states to assert independent jurisdiction over such markets. The pace of this process, characterised by the expansion and transnational flow of capital coupled with 'real-time' communications, undermines the power of states to control (or protect) both markets and populations from external forces. The revolution in information and communication technology (ICT), particularly digital technology, has accelerated the impact of transnational capital flows and production such that traditional concepts of time, distance and place have fundamentally changed. The emergence of e-commerce, as well as the social dimension of the Internet and associated 'cyber-crimes', is a striking example of the challenges to the independent capability of nation-states to regulate social and economic order within their territories. As significant has been the shift in the form of economic management, because by the 1990s most of the largest economies in the world were transnational corporations and not nation-states. Braithwaite (2000) argues that the influence of transnational corporations and the numerous hybrid private-public international regulators (for example the Basle Commission on Banking Supervision) serve to reduce the dominance of the regulatory role of states.

Radical versions of globalisation go further and suggest that the nation-state system of international relations no longer provides an effective methodology for regulating either domestic or transnational activity, especially international trade. In either version of globalisation, so-called 'sub-state' actors, such as large commercial institutions, play a crucial role in the emergence of what Sheptycki (2000) terms a transnational-state-system. In this system, new configurations of actors and power emerge and transnational organisations (both licit and illicit) will flourish due to the diminishing sway of the state (Lizee 2000: 165). The roles of multinational agencies such as Interpol and the United Nations have never been more essential. Yet within Asia (and globally) the results fall far short of creating a seamless web of bilateral or multilateral agreements and enforcement that would ensure a hostile environment for cyber-criminals. The compatibility of criminal activity with these global changes is illustrated by the expansion and convergence of the profitable business of smuggling of humans, narcotics or other illicit commodities with the development of communication infrastructure and trade.

Given the context just described, what may eventuate in the absence of the rule of law in transnational environments is 'governance without governments' (Rosenau 1992). While there now exist international conventions and treaties expressly designed to inhibit serious criminal networks or offenders operating across borders, the reach of these instruments is limited by the speed and scale of domestic ratification and consequential enabling laws. Nevertheless, they provide a moral climate hostile to some forms of transnational crime and seek to harmonise laws and evidentiary processes that enable cross-border investigations to take place as well as other cooperative undertakings.

The UN Convention Against Transnational Organised Crime (the TOC Convention) was introduced in December 2000 in Palermo, Italy.[8] The TOC

Convention significantly extends the reach of the 1988 Vienna Convention Against Illicit Traffic in Narcotics and Psychotropic Substances. The TOC Convention establishes several offence categories: participation in an organised criminal group, money laundering, corruption and obstruction of justice as well as protocols in respect to trafficking in women and children, illicit manufacturing and trafficking in firearms, and smuggling of migrants. Serious crime is defined broadly (conduct attracting punishment of four or more years' imprisonment). The basis of the framework is one that yields such flexibility in the definitions of both organised and transnational crime that it may serve as a generic legislative model across diverse common law and continental systems. In addition, the TOC Convention expressly refers (Art. 29 (2)) to methods for combating the misuse of computers and telecommunications networks. Provisions for training and materials, especially assistance for developing countries, place obligations on capable states.

As well as the innovations provided by the TOC convention, the Council of Europe's Convention on Cyber-crime, discussed in Peter Csonka's chapter, was completed in November 2001. It specifies a variety of computer-related offences.[9] The convention is designed to deal with the special problems of cyber-crime and the inevitable transnational character of many of the offences involved. Upon ratification, the convention will provide law enforcement agencies with the basis for investigating and preserving vital evidence in the cross-border dimension so characteristic of those forms of crime that exploit new information and communication technology. In dealing with ICT crime, law enforcement is at a disadvantage because of the remarkable speed in which cyber-crimes unfold against the typically 'low-speed cooperation' offered by traditional forms of mutual legal assistance. Although requests for law enforcement assistance are now routinely undertaken on an officer-to-officer basis via encrypted e-mail, this novelty should be available to judicial officers in the future. It is now conceivable that 'letters rogatory' and associated instruments may in the near future arrive by secure encrypted e-mail, as already do many of the communications between law firms.

These developments are mirrored by the increasing transnational activities of corporate and private security. Indeed, given the role of (self-) regulatory[10] approaches by corporations, especially multinational enterprises, the role for transnational private policing is already significant and widespread (Johnston 2000). For example, private security is the major provider in the payment card industry, intellectual property investigations and airline security. The sheer volume of potential global cyber-crime activity compels police partnerships with banks, telecommunication providers and corporations.

Partnerships also raise real issues of shared intelligence in environments of trust. Thus the mobilisation of so-called 'private police' and non-government organisations in partnership with public police are essential if cyber-crime is to be contained. Crime exploits the 'gaps' in the sovereign state system of international relations and, unless it is recognised that in communities of 'shared fate', coordinated forms of regulatory endeavour (free, for example, from unduly strict or pedantic definitions of 'dual criminality') may be the only means to curtail cyber-crime and its inevitable cross-border dimension. To fail to recognise that we share a 'common fate', that problems belong to others and not ourselves alone, undermines the very basis of mutual legal assistance — reciprocity.

Regional Coordination and Cooperation

As noted by Jeff Bullwinkel in his chapter, although cyber-crime has drawn increasing attention at both national and international levels in Europe and North America,[11] rather less is known about the nature and extent of the problem in the Asian region. Gregor Urbas provides a comprehensive overview of the current status of Asian jurisdictions in the development of domestic laws to address computer-related crime and the protection of intellectual property. Bullwinkel provides a detailed review of the international effort to manage the impacts of cyber-crime.

Regional efforts have begun, notably through ASEAN and the APEC forum. Such developments have yet to evolve into fully institutionalised forms of cross-border legal cooperation or significantly influence the response of states within the region.[12] However, the 'Interpol Asia and South Pacific Working Party on IT' is active, and nine countries within the Asia-Pacific region participate in the Cyber Crime Technology Information Network System formed by the National Police Agency of Japan.[13] There are now significant regional forums for police and other law enforcement officials and there is routine exchange of consular police liaison officers.

In recent papers, both Keiichi Aiziwa (2001) and Yasuhiro Tanabe (2004) of the United Nations Asia and Far East Institute for Crime and the Treatment of Offenders (UNAFEI), have argued that existing MLA Treaties including extradition are inadequate. Key problems relate to dual criminality, reciprocity, and the non-political nature of the predicate offence in order for formal cooperation to take place — states must mutually agree that the conduct is outlawed. The Council of Europe approach is innovative because it requires requested states to assist regardless of dual criminality. The treaty places emphasis on preserving evidence and reducing procedural delay while promoting the role of 24/7 agents (24-hour, 7 days a week contact or liaison). Michael Jackson outlines the approach and scope of Hong Kong's arrangements for facilitating mutual legal assistance, extradition and evidence collection (see also Luk 2001; Blanchflower 2003).[14]

The various measures now operating within the European Union, notably the Council of Europe Convention, the establishment of EUROPOL and a European Judicial Network, provide examples of greater law harmonisation and fewer opportunities for transnational criminals to exploit jurisdictional and legal loopholes between nations.[15] European initiatives in international crime provide sound examples of the way forward in regional cooperation, but may not serve as a model for the development of countermeasures in the vastly different socio-cultural and economic circumstances found in Asia (Khoo 2003). Nonetheless, it is abundantly clear that cyber-crime, and not just the traditional concerns about narcotics and piracy, is a matter of significant concern. Thus 'international law enforcement' has shifted from a peripheral to a central role within otherwise domestically focused law enforcement agencies. In addition, the lines between the policing function and national security appear less distinct, and considerable overlap now routinely occurs between the agencies countering threats such as cyber-crime, low-intensity warfare and terrorism. Thus, importance is attached to intra-agency cooperation within jurisdictions and the need to improve and maintain these to enhance MLA at the regional and international levels.

While ASEAN[16] has provided a limited pan-Asian approach, it does form a basis for developing a wider regional forum for considering matters of MLA. Its approach, even given the developing nature of the region, mirrors the methodology of the European Union. The sheer cultural and economic diversity of Asia makes the process of multilateralism fraught with difficulty (Khoo 2003). Yet understanding the different capacities and perspectives of how each state could contribute was an essential first step. The endorsement in October 2000[17] of the action plan of the ASEAN and China Cooperative Operations in Response to Dangerous Drugs (ACCORD) in partnership with the United Nations Drug Control Program (UNDCP) illustrate within our own region the quickening of MLA responses to transnational crime such as cyber-crime. ASEAN has conducted four ministerial meetings on problems of transnational crime (Manila 1997, Yangon 1999, Singapore 2001, Bangkok 2003). These meetings oversee the work of the Annual Senior Officials Meeting on Transnational Crime and consider the deliberations of ASEANAPOL meetings of the ASEAN National Chiefs of Police and their cooperative efforts to combat transnational crime.

Julie Shannon and Nick Thomas provide an overview of the role of 'human security' models in dealing with complex threats posed by cyber-crime. They suggest that over-reliance on the state, especially the public police, to address cyber-security issues would expose both markets and society to frequent low level, but costly, risks. Consequently the role of public-private police partnerships in the market-place and the emergence of civil society on the Internet, combined with public awareness, may be the only viable means to contain cyber-crime among ordinary users.

Internet Security and the Public

Internet connectivity is now estimated to reach over 50% of the populations of the most developed nations in the Asian region and an increasingly significant number of people in the less developed nations have on-line access.[18] China, for example, in 2003 had nearly 50 million Internet users, and about 30 million computers regularly connect to the Internet. Internet penetration was reported to reach 19% of households in cities such as Beijing, Shanghai, Guangzhou and Shenzhen. Chinese households were connected for an average of 9.6 days a month and web surfing accounted for 61% of activities online, followed by e-mail (19%) and Internet messaging (10%).[19] This was low compared to the 45–48% connected to the Internet estimated for cities like Hong Kong and Singapore and the high rates of participation reported for Japan, Taiwan, and Korea. However by the end of 2002, in the People's Republic of China (PR China) about 57 million or 5–6% of households had access to the Web (about 33 million computers online) and by the year 2006 it is expected that 200 million (15% of the population) or 25% of households will be connected (Neilsons / Netrating 2002).[20] In short, China will become one of the largest populations of computer and Internet users[21] when compared to the most developed countries such as the United States (166 million with Internet access), United Kingdom (29 million), Japan (51 million) and Germany (32 million). The striking challenge that this rapid uptake in connectivity poses for e-governance is addressed later in the chapter by Wong and Wong. In China, the growth of M-commerce and WAP (wireless applications) access to the Internet is also likely to grow faster and pose similar risks to commerce.[22] Mobile phone users are now estimated to number 198 million and may reach the astonishing figure of 500 million mobile / land phones by 2006.

Among the Asian tiger economies / 'little dragons' (Hong Kong, Singapore, Taiwan and Korea) and Japan, Internet access has already reached between

40 and 60% or more of households. Many of those households and business have also adopted broadband access. Both the speed and utility of connectivity have been enhanced by developments in data compression, while telephone line connectivity may present less of a barrier to data transmission. This is especially the case with the large data files needed to transmit digital images (movies, books and music). In contrast to such astonishing developments are the Asian Central Republics and ASEAN's least developed economies: in Laos, Cambodia, Mynamar and Vietnam, Internet access is less than 1–2% of the population. The gap between the digital 'haves' and 'have nots' could not be greater.

E-commerce customers and businesses are most concerned about threats to the integrity of financial transactions as well as violations of privacy. Ivan Chiu's research on the attitudes of Chinese users and their concerns about privacy and risk provide an example of the universality of this issue. Risk of card fraud, the ability to track purchases and delivery, and legitimacy of online merchants were more important than convenience, lack of sales support and the personal touch (Lisker 2001; Valeri 2001). The UK National Consumer Council reported that many consumers cited concerns about releasing credit card details as the major reason for considering e-commerce risky. Internet shopping was regarded as the most unsafe of all methods (survey undertaken in August 2000, cited by Valeri 2001). Based on research reported by a payment card enterprise, Lisker (2001) showed that fraud involving Internet services has tended to cluster around 'adult' or pornographic content sites,[23] online services, and direct marketing activities. He also notes a significant trend towards the use of online payment methods and it was forecast that 52% of all payment card transactions would be conducted remotely by 2005.[24]

The exponential growth of computer usage and Internet connectivity is expected to continue unabated, but it is also evident that this increased connectivity will be highly structured and unevenly distributed. The gap between wealthy and poor, the computer literate and illiterate, will also significantly widen, both within and across nations.[25] Access constitutes an important indicator of both national and individual potential for growth. It attracts attempts, enlightened or otherwise, at governance of this new arena for markets and social relations. The fundamental issue of how to regulate and police this new arena, 'cyberspace', is the basic focus of the chapters that follow. The contributors cover the international or multilateral implications of cross-national cooperation through to the role of the private and public sectors in information technology security, and the forensic issues involved in the investigation of computer-related crime.

Responding to Computer-Related Crime

The expansion of computer connectivity and the associated risks to data privacy, new modes of criminal opportunity, and other nuisances present special difficulties to law enforcement agencies. Moreover, the increasing take-up and connectivity (via TV) of digital technology means that cyber-crime is becoming a core business rather than a specialised function of law enforcement. Most significantly, attacks are instantaneous and often remote, disregarding national sovereignty.

However, digital technology also affords new opportunities for individual citizens to communicate efficiently with police. An example is the Internet Fraud Complaint Center, which operates in the United States and receives online information from members of the public relating to questionable online activity. Personnel at the centre evaluate these communications and refer them to the appropriate agency or jurisdiction At the international level, Interpol has stressed financial and high-technology crime — two of Interpol's top five priorities (along with drugs, terrorism. people smuggling and organised crime).

The threat of cyber-crime and the capacity to respond to it will vary dramatically across nations. Nearly half of Interpol's member countries lack the infrastructure for online communication (Noble 2003). The UK response to this challenge was to establish a National High-Tech Crime Unit and along with the G8 network (with its 17 members) for 24/7 or round-the-clock liaison in cyber-crime matters. There remains, however, a need for enhanced mutual legal assistance, for speedier processes for extradition, for consistent evidential standards, and for improved liaison between police and industry.

The scope of criminal activities, and associated law enforcement and their social consequences, are expanded upon in the next chapter by Peter Grabosky. A typology of computer-related crime comprises the following: conventional crimes in which computers are instrumental to the offence, such as child pornography and intellectual property theft; attacks on computer networks; and conventional criminal cases in which evidence exists in digital form.

The kinds of criminality encompass the following (by no means exhaustive) list:

- Interference with lawful use of a computer: cyber-vandalism and terrorism; denial of service; insertion of viruses, worms and other malicious code
- Dissemination of offensive materials: pornography / child pornography; online gaming / betting; racist content; treasonous or sacreligious content
- Threatening communications: extortion; cyber-stalking

- Forgery / counterfeiting: ID theft; IP offences; software, CD, DVD piracy; copyright breaches etc
- Fraud: payment card fraud and e-funds transfer fraud; theft of Internet and telephone services; auction house and catalogue fraud; consumer fraud and direct sales (e.g. virtual 'snake oils'); on-line securities fraud
- Other: Illegal interception of communications; commercial / corporate espionage; communications in furtherance of criminal conspiracies; electronic money laundering

The offences are diverse, but many are traditional crimes executed with new technology. Thus the appropriate response is guided by new technological disciplines. Lucas Hui and colleagues in their chapter present an example of cooperation between police and universities when they discuss a new forensic tool developed jointly by the Hong Kong Police and the Center for Information Security and Cryptography at the University of Hong Kong. The Digital Evidence Search Kit, or DESK, enables investigators to search for patterns in both Chinese and English, as well as to identify codified or deleted files. The technology permits inspection of the suspect's machine from a connected computer, while locking the suspect's machine to preserve file integrity. They stress the vulnerability of computers, especially via e-mail services, and note that system security is closely related to the capabilities of system administrators and auditors.[26]

Forensic computing and evidence preservation protocols are essential to effective investigation and prosecution, especially given the trans-border nature of evidence collection (Chan 2001; Pollitt 2003).[27] In most cases it is unlikely that a computer expert will be available at the crime scene and the risks of contaminating the evidence are high. Consequently, as with other types of crime, the emphasis is on following the traditional chain-of-evidence rules and ensuring that command and control assigns the relevant expertise promptly to the task at hand. Frequently this will require drawing on expertise in the private sector or academia.

Criminal Networks and IT Crime

Striking illustrations of the practicality of social network theories (Castells 1996) in understanding the impact of global communications on criminality are the behaviour of computer viruses. The way in which computer viruses (for example the 'I Love You' bug and the 'Code Red' worm) may spread, within days, to virtually every computer network and terminal around the world shows how connections facilitate behaviour. Little imagination is required to extend the ideas behind these dramatic phenomena to the actual and potential networks of social relations that enable illicit commodities to move across borders and to be distributed to consumers. Organised crime 'is a social phenomenon, a network of relationships based on reciprocal benefits that extends to the heart of society and of institutional and economic life'. Nor is it simply a problem of the criminal law but one of 'civil law, economic regulation, industrial management, and fiscal policy' (Jamieson 2001: 386).

There is growing evidence to show that digital technologies have greatly enhanced the effectiveness of forgery and counterfeiting, especially of ID documents, payment cards and bank and securities instruments. IP and other copyright infringements have now become lucrative targets for organised criminals, while smuggling (humans, endangered species, narcotics, precursors, disc stampers, and arms) and traditional customs avoidance are assisted by the application of encrypted communications and the use of sophisticated forged documentation.

Apart from the use of digital technology to improve forgeries and instruments of deception, organised crime groups appear to have used IT to assist in online gaming (and gaming scams), pornographic sites and advance fee and other deception offers via e-mail or websites. The major area of risk is forged payment cards and related ID theft to obtain goods including via online transactions. The Hong Kong Police Organised Crime and Triad Bureau report few cases of systematic triad involvement in online fraud; traditional activities of protection, debt collection and vice are still dominant. Nevertheless, China's 'opening up' policy and its rapid development as a market economy have allowed foreign criminal groups to establish relationships with local groups and to invest directly or indirectly in licit or illicit business. This infiltration of foreign syndicates has helped to enhance the size and reach that serious criminal groups have in many cities and towns across China. Local criminals have shifted activities, once typically based on 'black markets' and commodity theft, into lucrative intellectual property offences, trafficking, vice and gaming. The most insidious aspects have been the criminal investment in factories (both licit and illicit) including state-owned enterprises through the corruption of officials. Chinese police, once reluctant to develop arrangements with their counterparts, now actively seek the cooperation and assistance of overseas colleagues and support arrangements for shared intelligence and capacity-building (Zheng 2003).

Although there is little novelty in the criminality involved, its scale and scope make contemporary cyber-crime of a different kind from crimes of the past. In future, organised crime may be expected to recruit IT specialists, intimidate corporate insiders to obtain access to IT systems, and use anonymisers and encryption in furtherance of cyber-crime. Such a global problem demands a global solution. In addition, the nature of telecommunications has changed: there are no more monopolies, geographically confined. Now a single communication can pass through many providers in different countries with different legal systems. Remote attacks are now possible. Whether they are the work of a 14-year-old, a terrorist, a foreign intelligence service or an organised criminal may not be immediately apparent; all must be investigated.

Digital footprints are fragile or ephemeral, so swift action is often required. This becomes very difficult when an attack transits multiple jurisdictions with different regimes for preserving evidence. Traditional methods of law enforcement are therefore no longer adequate. A slow formal process risks losing evidence, and multiple countries may be implicated. Following and preserving a chain of evidence is a great challenge. Even 'local' crimes may have an international dimension, and assistance may be required from all countries through which an attack has been routed. Examples include the case of Mafiaboy, whose distributed denial of service attacks in February 2000 was a watershed event: the seriousness of the threat and the vulnerability of e-commerce became apparent. The investigation of Mafiaboy was a textbook example of close cooperation between the FBI and the Royal Canadian Mounted Police; only rapid and close collaboration between the two police services could have achieved such a result.

Among the challenges faced by investigators is the enormous increase in storage capacity in today's computers, and the challenge to effective and efficient searches that this entails. Almost every case will soon require computer forensics, and evidence will be located in multiple places. The challenge faced by investigators will be one of *information management* (Pollitt 2003).

The Role of Public and Private Security

Digital technologies have greatly facilitated the commission of such traditional offences as intellectual property theft, piracy, counterfeiting and forgery.[28] Generic problems of forgery and counterfeiting were the focus of Interpol's efforts illustrated by a recently established Universal Classification System for Counterfeit Payment Cards secure website. This secure site provides up-to-date information on trends and techniques with respect to the forgery of payment cards and fraud. Apart from illustrating how Interpol's unique clearing house function[29] can be adapted to meet new problems it shows that, with fiscal and technical support from the payment card industry, the law enforcement community can be better trained and equipped. This cooperation strengthens police capacity to respond to the theft of payment cards and other computer-related crimes that reduce the integrity of the market and limit the social benefits of Internet communications. It takes little imagination but considerable endeavour[30] to see that a rapid application of this model to many global and transnational crimes would help fulfil repeated recommendations for more practical support for cross-national cooperation in law enforcement.

As well as serving as an example of how international agencies can assist with essential tasks, such as secure shared intelligence, this example also clarifies the role of private non-state actors in the prevention of crime. Private investigation has grown significantly in recent years, and there is now much closer cooperation between the private IT security sector and law enforcement. Cooperation is paramount but there is still a degree of mutual suspicion and uncertainty about what form this cooperation should take. These matters are discussed with emphasis on the way individuals and private industry can contribute to their own security, since commercial and computer crime is generally an area of weak policing.

The active cooperation of the private sector is essential in assisting police investigations. Given corporate victims' reluctance to report cyber-crime attacks, Len Hynds (2003), Director of the UK National High Tech Crime Unit, has proposed a new initiative: confidentiality contracts between police and victim. Such contracts can serve to harness intelligence that would otherwise be lost because of non-reporting. He also observed that police should begin to appreciate the mindset of corporate executives and that the police may have a role in collecting and sharing business intelligence.

The FBI has also stressed that critical infrastructure protection is a current priority in the United States. This is particularly challenging, given that most elements of critical infrastructure such as power generation, telecommunications, transport, and institutions of the financial system are owned by the private sector. The need for cooperation between law enforcement and the private sector is obvious. To help bridge the public–private gap, the FBI has introduced its Infraguard Program with over 4000 members (Iden 2003).

Reinforcing the essential need for industry self-help, Li (2001) cited recent survey data from the United States that shows 70% of organisations experienced unauthorised use of their computers but, of these, only 44%

reported the intrusion to the police. Among the most frequently cited reasons for not reporting intrusions was the fear of negative publicity and / or giving a competitor an advantage. He also stressed the neglected observation that a significant threat arises within the victim organisation from employees and other insiders and this risk may be higher than the more widely publicised attacks by outsiders.

Effective control of cyber-crime, however, requires more than cooperation among institutions of public and private security. The role of the communications and IT industries in designing products that are resistant to crime and that facilitate detection and investigation cannot be understated. No less an entity than Microsoft has now committed itself to reducing the vulnerability of its products (Charney 2003).

Copyright and the Internet

The problems of protecting various forms of intellectual property (IP), specifically music, motion pictures, games and computer software, are heightened in the Internet environment. Significantly, as digitised versions of these products become available, Internet access is rapidly becoming the preferred means for obtaining them. Consequently, the illegal or unauthorised access to relevant Internet sites is perceived as both a motive and source of increased risk to IP holders. Given that IP piracy has traditionally been widespread within the Asian region, it had been thought that only an unlikely radical change in community attitudes could impact on the volume of 'illegal' sales. While community sentiment, at least in Hong Kong, has shifted away from pirated products, this was assisted by a multi-level enforcement approach that incorporated vigorous and sustained investigation and prosecution with the full cooperation of the relevant industries. The inclusion of copyright offences as part of Hong Kong's Organised Crime Ordinance provided better legal prescription and aided customs agents in cooperation with private sector counterparts to substantially improve IP protection Tsang (2001).

In Hong Kong and other jurisdictions, however, non-actionable cases were typically linked to overseas or cross-border events. Although IP piracy is often touted as a problem restricted to wealthy multinational corporations and not a significant local or Asian issue, it is apparent that IP piracy can also be fatal to indigenous IP holders, as Malaysian, Thai, Mandarin and Cantonese artists have lamented. Typically in Hong Kong and other jurisdictions, government willingness to address legal loopholes, including extradition, and provide police with resources is still a critical factor since the deterrent value of punishment and the associated publicity is a crucial part of any multi-level approach.[31]

Poon (2003) observed how digital technologies facilitate IP and copyright infringements. He noted that there were many websites in Hong Kong for downloading pirated content. In response to this challenge, Hong Kong Customs has a forensic special interest group, a computer analysis and response team, an anti-Internet piracy team, and a computer forensics support team with its own lab. The three most pressing problems they face are limits of territorial jurisdiction, impediments to the acceptance of digital evidence, and the fact that many offenders commit their offences from overseas. Poon concluded that to meet these challenges will require active dialogue with industry, improved forensic skills, and better technical means for the collection, preservation and presentation of digital evidence.

Copyright, however, is primarily a private right and the IP holder or industry has the responsibility to be active and vigilant in the protection of such rights.[32] As many commentators note, piracy is sustained by public demand and the need for education and raising respect for IP are also important factors. Given the relatively low investment required to set up activities such as optical disk piracy, even rigid inspection and raids may merely force them underground and / or displace activities to weaker jurisdictions. More resources may not be enough because of public demand encouraged by low prices. Efforts by governments[33] and consumers to encourage better pricing of legitimate products and fund public education are seen as positive measures.

China has suffered heavily from piracy despite a strong policy to crush illegal operators. Although 115 underground optical disk manufacturers had been closed before 2001, the problem continued as offenders had actively countered government schemes that encouraged reporting of illegal operations. The ready supply of unemployed workers provided IP 'pirates' with an ample sales force and distributive network, and modifications to the criminal law were necessary to criminalise this conduct.[34] He also noted that considerable quantities of pirated good were imported from neighbouring countries. The pressure on IP pirates in Hong Kong had led to the displacement of factory-style operations to China and, unless the financiers are targeted, the underground industry is destined to continue.[35] Malaysian police, who have also been concerned with targeting the financial sources of piracy production,[36] have observed a similar displacement effect. Nevertheless, it is apparent that targeting optical disk 'stampers' and the introduction of mandatory laser recorded codes would be the most helpful strategically.

Industry is responding with impressive resort to additional remedies, as a recent successful civil action in PR China on behalf of the motion picture industry illustrates. The Motion Picture Association (MPA) achieved resolution of two civil actions in relation to DVD piracy in the Beijing Second Intermediate People's Court, and six cases in the People's Courts of Shanghai, in 2003. The terms of the settlements included: ceasing further replication and destroying all copies; making formal apologies; the payment of penalties averaging US$10 000 per case; and an agreement to pay increased penalties if unauthorised replication recurs.[37]

The Role of Law and Comity Between States

Many nations and regional bodies such as the Council of Europe have addressed these issues and laws exist that criminalise unauthorised access and unlawful use of computers, but such laws are neither universal nor uniform.[38] In India, the recently passed *Information Technology Act 2000* is instructive, and provides a variation on the approach adopted by the Europeans. The Act aims to facilitate e-commerce governance, and specifically recognises electronic evidence and signatures. The Act creates two levels of cyber-crime: infringements and offences. Infringements (eight types are specified) focus on improper use of computers and impose no fines or criminal punishment, although compensation can be ordered via non-judicial civil compensation mechanisms. Offences, however, include hacking, destruction of data, unauthorised access, misrepresentation / fraud, and the publication of offensive material and are dealt with through normal criminal proceedings. The law creates special prosecutors and courts to deal with special offences and requires police, prosecutors and judges to be technologically literate.[39]

Law enforcement agencies are now compelled to respond to cyber-crime through technological adaptation (retooling) and legal innovation. Consensus is the best strategy, for the suppression of computer-related crime entails a mixture of law enforcement, technological and market-based solutions. We argue, however, that a strict enforcement agenda is usually not feasible because of the limited capacity of the state. It is also feared that over-regulation could stifle commercial and technological development. Those sceptical of a heavily interventionist approach also argue that the marketplace may at times be able to provide more efficient solutions to the problems of computer-related crime than the state. Even if they were increased, police resources could never be enough. Without political will, public support (especially awareness of the potential threat) and the cooperation of industry in the context of a global response, policing is unlikely to bring timely relief. Given pressures on government to reduce public expenditure, the challenge is to enhance policing capacity, especially between nations. As one practitioner observed:

> The most important need in the battle against cyber-crime is to develop close cooperation and personal relationships among law enforcement agencies and technical experts around the world ... A custom-made liaison mechanism is needed ... a mechanism by which countries can investigate offences and obtain evidence quickly and efficiently, or at least not lose important evidence in cross-border law-enforcement.[40]

An underlying concern among many observers is the effect of 'crime displacement', that is, as some jurisdictions effectively enforce laws, criminal activities will shift to jurisdictions of low capability — the vulnerable 'weakest link'. Comity thus can only be assured if wealthy states and affected industries are prepared to extend aid to those states or agencies less capable. If a single theme emerges as dominant, then the role of mutual legal assistance in developing universal or global measures to suppress computer-related crime is perhaps the most evident.

The capacities of the state are nevertheless limited, and constructive ways of mobilising private industry to help are necessary. The nature of the public–private interface must be flexible and responsive to the changing environment. Effective cooperation ultimately relies on shared objectives and the benevolence of all parties. A frequently cited need is for the education and training of law enforcement personnel, including prosecutors and judges. Considerable deficits characterise the technical and computing capacities of police and others, and it is often difficult to retain trained agents. A critical factor is the need to cultivate multidisciplinary approaches that require a broader educational preparation than previously necessary. Education, that all-purpose solution for technical and social ills, however, had not been developed or effectively targeted in respect to 'high-tech' crime, and long-term shortages in the relevant skills might have been foreseen. Support for specialised education within law enforcement agencies, and more generally in the public higher education system, is urgently required. This is one ready avenue by which the private and state sector might effectively contribute to long-term solutions to the numerous problems arising from the criminal exploitation of Internet and information technology.

Conclusion

With properly funded international law enforcement agencies, established mechanisms for common threat assessments and joint intelligence, more comprehensive forms of mutual legal assistance might be effectively activated. Many commentators express concern about the failure to address the 'weakest links' in the supposedly seamless security chain necessary to prevent and reduce serious criminal groups. Short and long-term policing assistance, sensitively deployed via regional security coordination, can give enormous help to vulnerable developing countries, countries in transition and those traumatised by conflict.[41] To help train, specialise and equip the law enforcers of these at-risk states will benefit them, their communities and all of us. The remarkable effects on morale that are produced by sound leadership, adequate equipment, best practices and practical training should not be underestimated. Some law enforcement agencies in the Asian region are critically short of specialised personnel in the forensic sciences, ICT, law, accounting and investigations, crime prevention and intelligence analysis. In addition, basic training is often rudimentary and leadership (command and control) training limited or military in nature. Endless lists of shortages in materiel are evident, from the most basic items such as radios and vehicles, mortuaries and armouries to the more advanced such as comparison microscopes or advanced electronics and decryption.

A number of policy and programme initiatives are suggested, from increasing regional-level coordination and cross-jurisdictional exchanges in personnel, intelligence and training to the creation of joint task forces and other operational collaborations. Many of these are already taking place and need to be expanded as rapidly as possible while continuing to evolve common methods among stronger and wider law enforcement networks. The technically advanced, highly capable policing agencies must provide more direct and strategically relevant assistance to hard-pressed neighbours; they must be triggered not by particular cases but by the mutual benefits of long-term collaboration. They must focus this 'police aid' on the priorities of the evolving regional and international security entities and by systematically undertaking the essential preparatory work in the field.

Despite the muscular image of police, much of modern policing revolves around the intelligent management of information. Police are now 'knowledge' rather than 'craft' workers and this is increasingly so as the full impact of the 'information age' is realised. High-order research and analytical skills and communication skills are increasingly needed along with traditional skills and discipline. Shortages in specialities such as forensic computing, law and accounting, as well as statistical evaluations and communications, are now widely encountered. Training and retaining agents will be a major challenge, and reliance on in-house or short-term training will no longer serve the need for professionalism and continuous learning. There are an estimated 5 million police officers in Asia; around 5% of these are graduates but many are barely literate. If we are to address the myriad problems faced by modern policing and invest in prevention and intelligence, then due recognition must be given to investment in knowledge and the research that feeds it.

In conclusion, controlling crime involving digital technology and computer networks will require a variety of new networks: networks between police and other agencies within government, networks between police and private institutions, and networks of police across national borders. Over the past five years, considerable progress has been made within and between nations to develop the capacity of police to respond to cyber-crime. But the pace of technological change will continue unabated, and the adaptability of cyber-criminals will continue to pose challenges for law enforcement. The extent of transnational law enforcement cooperation achieved thus far, laudable though it may be, can only be regarded as a beginning.

2

The Global Cyber-Crime Problem: The Socio-Economic Impact

Peter Grabosky*

This chapter discusses current and emerging forms of computer-related illegality. It reviews 11 generic forms of illegality involving information systems as instruments or as targets of crime, and discusses in general terms the costs imposed by computer-related crime, and attempts to control it within and across nations.

It will suggest that much computer-related illegality lies beyond the capacity of contemporary law enforcement and regulatory agencies alone to control, and that security in cyberspace will depend on the efforts of a wide range of institutions, as well as on a degree of self-help by potential victims of cyber-crime. The ideal configuration may be expected to differ, depending on the activity in question, but is likely to entail a mix of law enforcement, technological and market solutions. These themes are explored in greater detail in two books (Grabosky & Smith 1998; Grabosky, Smith & Dempsey 2001).

Before we begin to review the various forms of criminality involving information systems as instruments and / or as targets, and the most appropriate means of controlling them, let us first look at the questions of motivation and of opportunity.

Motives and Rationalisations of Computer Criminals

The motives of those who would commit computer-related crime are diverse, but hardly new. Computer criminals are driven by time-honoured motives, the most obvious of which are greed, lust, power, revenge, adventure, and the desire to taste 'forbidden fruit'. The ability to make an impact on large systems may, as an act of power, be gratifying in and of itself. The desire to inflict loss or damage on another may also spring from revenge, as when a disgruntled employee shuts down an employer's computer system, or to ideology, as when one defaces the web-page of an institution that one regards as abhorrent. Much activity on the electronic frontier entails an element of adventure, the exploration of the unknown. The very fact that some activities in cyberspace are likely to elicit official condemnation is enough to attract the defiant, the rebellious, or the irresistibly curious. Given the degree of technical competence required to commit many computer-related crimes, there is one other motivational dimension worth noting here. This is, of course, the intellectual challenge of mastering complex systems.

None of the above motives is new. The element of novelty resides in the unprecedented capacity of technology to facilitate acting on these motives.

Alongside motives are the justifications or excuses that offenders will put forward to rationalise or justify their activities. These will, of course, vary with the offence in question but might include blaming the victim (as when one maintains that the CIA deserves to have its website defaced); claiming that the activity was harmless (the hacker who claims to have been just looking, and didn't take anything); arguing that the victim could afford it (my piracy of Microsoft product won't effect Bill Gates' wealth); or suggesting that the practice is so widespread as to be legitimate (everybody takes music off the Web).

Rationalisations in turn may be paralleled by legal defences and, in the event of conviction, evidence in mitigation of sentence. Not all of these rationalisations are believable and, indeed, not all are genuinely believed by the offender. They may include the claim that the offence occurred by accident, it was in furtherance of legitimate research, or resulted from personal stress or from Internet addiction. These and other excuses are discussed more fully in Smith, Grabosky & Urbas (2004).

Increasing Opportunities for Computer-Related Crime

Recent and anticipated changes in technology arising from the convergence of communications and computing are truly breathtaking, and have already had a significant impact on many aspects of life. Banking, stock exchanges, air traffic control, telephones, electric power, and a wide range of institutions of health, welfare, and education are largely dependent on information technology and telecommunications for their operation. We are moving rapidly to the point where it is possible to assert that 'everything depends on software' (Edwards 1995). The exponential growth of this technology, the increase in its capacity and accessibility, and the decrease in its cost, has brought about revolutionary changes in commerce, communications, entertainment, and education. Along with this greater capacity, however, comes greater vulnerability.

Statistics on computer use and connectivity are notoriously evanescent. They are out of date before they appear in print. But the following data give a general sense of the growth and penetration of digital technology in recent years.

Internet use in general and the volume of electronic commerce are increasing exponentially. Worldwide, approximately 605 million people were online as of September 2002, up from 254 million in January 2000. Of that 605 million, roughly 187 million are from the Asia-Pacific region (Nua.com 2002). Internet users worldwide are expected to double to 1.05 billion by 2006.

China had over 45 million regular Internet users as of July 2002, a fourfold increase in little more than two years. Chinese may well become the dominant language on the Internet by the end of this decade.

E-commerce revenue is estimated to reach US$6501 billion worldwide in 2006, a tenfold increase from 2001, while over this time Asia-Pacific e-commerce will expand over 20 times to US$894 billion (Reuters 2002). By 2005, business-to-business Internet commerce in the Asia / Pacific region will account for 28% of the worldwide total (Pastore 2001).

Not only does the increasing connectivity increase the number of prospective victims of computer-related crime, it also increases the number of prospective offenders. Let us look now at the various forms that cyber-crime may take.

The Varieties of Computer-Related Crime

The variety of criminal activity that can be committed with or against information systems is quite diverse. Some of these are not really new in substance; only the medium is new. Others represent new forms of illegality altogether. The following generic forms of illegality involve information systems as instruments and / or as targets of crime. They are not mutually exclusive, nor is the following list necessarily exhaustive.

Theft of telecommunications services

The 'phone phreakers' of three decades ago set a precedent for what has become a major criminal industry. By gaining access to an organisation's telephone switchboard (PBX), individuals or criminal organisations can obtain access to dial-in / dial-out circuits and then make their own calls or sell call time to third parties (Gold 1999). Offenders may gain access to the switchboard by impersonating a technician, by fraudulently obtaining an employee's access code, or by using software available on the Internet. Some sophisticated offenders loop between PBX systems to evade detection. Additional forms of service theft include capturing 'calling card' details and on-selling calls charged to the calling card account, and counterfeiting or illicit reprogramming of stored value telephone cards.

It has been suggested that up to 5% of total industry turnover has been lost to fraud (Schieck 1995: 2–5; Newman 1998). Costs to individual subscribers can also be significant. In one case, computer hackers in the United States illegally obtained access to Scotland Yard's telephone network and made £620 000 worth of international calls for which Scotland Yard was responsible (Tendler & Nuttall 1996).

A Chinese citizen was jailed for 11 years in March 2002 for fraudulently leasing telephone trunk lines from state-owned Shanghai Telecommunications, then billing US customers for Internet-routed calls to Vietnam. During one week in July 2001, he managed to steal services worth 2.3 million yuan (*SCMP* 2002).

The proliferation of Internet services has also made them an attractive target for theft. Recently in India, a computer engineer was charged with allegedly stealing 100 hours of Internet time from a client (*The Hindu* 2000). A number of hackers in Thailand were reported to have succeeded in accessing customer accounts at a Singapore ISP and to have used them freely (BizAsia 2000).

Communications or data storage in furtherance of criminal conspiracies

Just as legitimate organisations in the private and public sectors rely on information systems for communications and record-keeping, so too are the activities of criminal organisations enhanced by technology.

There is evidence of telecommunications equipment being used to facilitate organised drug trafficking, child pornography and terrorism. The use of information technology by Osama bin Laden and his associates was noted months in advance of 11 September 2001 (Associated Press 2001; Kelley 2001). The use of encryption technology may place some criminal communications beyond the reach of law enforcement.

The use of computer networks to produce and distribute child pornography has become the subject of increasing attention. Today, these materials can be imported across national borders at the speed of light (Grant, David & Grabosky 1997). The more overt manifestations of Internet child pornography entail a modest degree of organisation, as required by the infrastructure of IRC and WWW, but the activity appears largely confined to individuals.

By contrast, some of the less publicly visible traffic in child pornography appears to entail a greater degree of organisation. Although knowledge is confined to that conduct which has been the target of successful police investigation, there appear to have been a number of networks that extend cross-nationally, use sophisticated technologies of concealment, and entail a significant degree of coordination.

Illustrative of such activity was the Wonderland Club, an international network with members in at least 14 nations ranging from Europe, to North America, to Australia. Access to the group was password protected, and content was encrypted. Police investigation of the activity, codenamed 'Operation Cathedral' resulted in approximately 100 arrests around the world, and the seizure of over 100 000 images in September 1998.

Information piracy, forgery, and counterfeiting

Digital technology permits perfect reproduction and easy dissemination of print, graphics, sound, and multimedia combinations. The temptation to reproduce copyrighted material for personal use, for sale at a lower price, or indeed for free distribution, has proved irresistible to many. According to the *Straits Times* (8 November 1999) a copy of the James Bond film *The World is Not Enough* was available free on the Internet before its official release.

When creators of a work, in whatever medium, are unable to profit from their creations, there can be a chilling effect on creative effort generally, in addition to financial loss. But the victims of piracy are not always large companies. Musicians, authors and small software developers all suffer. In recent years, one popular Chinese rock band released two CDs, each of which was pirated on the Internet before it was available for legitimate purchase (McDonald 2000). Rampant piracy can stifle the growth of information technology and the economic development on which it is based. It has been suggested that globally, one in three compact disks (CDs) sold is a counterfeit copy (White House 2000).

The emergence of new technologies such as digital video disks (DVD) creates new opportunities for piracy. An estimated 43 million illegal video CDs and 3.5 million conventional videocassettes were seized worldwide as long ago as 1998 (Europe Information Service 1999).

The following estimates from the Business Software Alliance (BSA) indicates a high prevalence of piracy in some Asian countries.

Table 2.1 Top ten countries by piracy rate (%)

	1999	*2000*	*2001*	*2002*
Vietnam	98	97	94	95
China	91	94	92	92
Indonesia	85	89	88	89
Ukraine / Other CIS	90	89	87	89
Russia	89	88	87	89
Lebanon	88	83	79	74
Pakistan	83	83	83	80
Bolivia	85	81	77	74
Qatar	80	81	78	76
Bahrain	82	80	77	76

Source: BSA 2002, 2003a

Digital technology also permits perfect reproduction of documents such as birth certificates or other papers that may be used to construct a false identity for use in a variety of subsequent criminal activities, as well as the counterfeiting of currency and other negotiable instruments. Identity-related crime has become a serious problem around the world, and Southeast Asia is renowned as a centre for document forgery.

Dissemination of offensive materials

Content considered by some to be objectionable exists in abundance in cyberspace. This includes, among much else, sexually explicit materials, racist propaganda, online gambling sites, and instructions for the fabrication of incendiary and explosive devices. What is significant here are the differences across the world in what various sovereign states deem to be offensive. What is treasonous in one country may be celebrated in another; what is blasphemous in one country may fail to raise an eyebrow elsewhere. In Laos, for example, authorities forbid the online promotion of activities that might disturb the peace and happiness of the Lao People's Democratic Republic. This includes distribution of news stories that the government considers harmful or misleading (Nua.com 2000).

The world may in some sense be described as a global village, but differences in values persist. Indeed, there may be profound differences in a single country about what is offensive and what is not. As one might imagine, this will pose significant impediments to international cooperation.

Stalking

Telecommunications systems can also be used for harassing, threatening or intrusive communications, from the traditional obscene telephone call to its contemporary manifestation in 'cyber-stalking', in which persistent messages are sent to an unwilling recipient (Ogilvie 2000). Messages may be sent directly by the offender, or the offender may incite others to send the offending communication.

Malaysian Police reported a number of incidents in 2001 where women's personal information had been posted on the Internet. In one case, a man in Malaysia allegedly dialled into a Singapore-based website and posted a sex-for-hire ad that included the telephone number of his estranged wife. She subsequently received obscene telephone calls from Singapore, Thailand and Brazil (Reuters 2001). A similar case in Thailand, in which a man posted the telephone number of a student on a bulletin board, and alleged that she was a prostitute, resulted in a conviction for defamation (*ABC News* 2002).

One man in Delhi is reported to have logged on to an Internet chat room using the identity of a woman. The offender allegedly used suggestive language, and disclosed the woman's telephone number. She subsequently received harassing telephone calls, one from as far away as Kuwait. The offender was located through the IP address used in contacting the chat room and was subsequently arrested (Duggal 2001).

One former university student in California used e-mail to harass five female students in 1998. He bought information on the Internet about the women using a professor's credit card and then sent 100 messages including death threats, graphic sexual descriptions and references to their daily activities. He apparently made the threats in response to perceived teasing about his appearance (Associated Press 1999). Similar cases have been reported in Hong Kong (Lo 2000).

Extortion

Computer networks may also be used in furtherance of extortion. The *Sunday Times* (London) reported in 1996 that over 40 financial institutions in Britain and the United States had been attacked electronically over the previous three years. The victims were reported to have paid significant amounts of money to sophisticated computer criminals that threatened to wipe out computer systems (*Sunday Times*, 2 June 1996). The article cited four incidents between 1993 and 1995 where companies, convinced that the extortionists could crash their computer systems, paid out £42.5 million to avoid the execution of the threat (Denning 1999: 233–4).

One case, which illustrates the transnational reach of extortionists, involved a number of German hackers who compromised the system of an ISP in South Florida, disabling eight of the ISPs ten servers. The offenders obtained personal information and credit card details of 10 000 subscribers and, communicating via electronic mail through one of the compromised accounts, demanded that US$30 000 be delivered to a mail drop in Germany. Cooperation between US and German authorities resulted in the arrest of the extortionists (Bauer 1998).

The Asian region is by no means immune to extortion. One hacker reportedly launched a denial of service attack against a Korean company, and demanded 100 million Won to desist. Electronic mail can also be used for sending threatening letters in furtherance of extortion. Early in 2000, a Hong Kong ISP discovered unauthorised alterations to its web-page. It subsequently received a message demanding that several thousand US dollars be deposited in a Russian bank account in order for the attacks to cease (Lo 2000).

Electronic money laundering and tax evasion

For some time now, electronic funds transfers have assisted in concealing and in moving the proceeds of crime. Emerging technologies will greatly assist in concealing the origin of ill-gotten gains. Legitimately derived income may also be more easily concealed from taxation authorities. It was alleged that nearly US$70 billion has been transferred from Russian banks through the small Pacific island nation of Nauru via the Internet (Seneviratne 2000).

Large financial institutions will no longer be the only ones with the ability to achieve electronic funds transfers transiting numerous jurisdictions at the speed of light. The development of informal banking institutions and parallel banking systems may permit central bank supervision to be bypassed, but can also facilitate the evasion of cash transaction reporting requirements in those nations which have them. Traditional underground banks, which have flourished in Asian countries for centuries, will enjoy even greater capacity through the use of telecommunications. The Asia-Pacific Secretariat of the Financial Action Task Force has advised that increased use of new technologies such as Internet banking and smart cards is making money laundering easier (Infosec.com 1998).

With the emergence and proliferation of various technologies of electronic commerce, one can easily envisage how traditional countermeasures against money laundering and tax evasion may soon be of limited value. I may soon be able to sell you a quantity of heroin, in return for an untraceable transfer of stored value to my 'smart-card', which I then download anonymously to my account in a financial institution situated in an overseas jurisdiction which protects the privacy of banking clients. I can discreetly draw on these funds as and when I may require, downloading them back to my stored value card (Wahlert 1996).

Electronic vandalism, and terrorism

As never before, industrial society is dependent on complex data-processing and telecommunications systems. Damage to, or interference with, any of these systems can have catastrophic consequences. Whether motivated by curiosity or vindictiveness, electronic intruders cause inconvenience at best, and have the potential for inflicting massive harm (Schwartau 1994; Hundley & Anderson 1995; Denning 2000).

While this potential has yet to be fully realised, experience to date gives some indication of the scope of risk. The 'Melissa' virus, the 'Love Bug' virus (which appears to have originated in the Philippines) and the 'Anna Kournikova' virus have disrupted computer systems around the world in recent years. It was reported that about 85% of computers in China were infected with a computer virus during 2003 (BBC 2003). The Sobig.F worm, which struck in August of that year and spread with unprecedented speed, was estimated to have quickly infected one-third of the nation's computers (Mail Utilities 2003).

The distributed denial of service attacks against Yahoo, Amazon.com and other commercial sites in early 2000 illustrated the vulnerability of systems to the mischief of a mere teenager acting alone. Such attacks not only threaten public confidence in electronic commerce, they also pose risks to nations' critical infrastructure.

In March 2000, an Indonesian student residing in Australia gained access to a computer in Singapore and altered a number of files. After subsequently relocating to Singapore, he was prosecuted under the *Singapore Computer Misuse Act* (Tan 2000). In China, financial institutions such as banks and securities firms have also been targeted by hackers (Kwan 1999; Yeang 2001). Authorities there have expressed concern about the vulnerability to hacking of hospital records, with consequent threats to public health (Chan 1998). In September 2002, supporters of the Falun Gong movement were reported to have hacked into a national satellite TV system and disrupted normal programming (Associated Press 2002).

In 1996, intruders were reported to have inserted user IDs of over 100 government officials on a Singapore government website (Goh 1996). In Malaysia, a Perak State government website was hacked into in 1997, giving rise to concerns that changes to website content might create a negative image for the state (*New Straits Times* 1997). It was reported that the content of Malaysia's Parliamentary website was erased late in 2001 (Yeang 2001).

In March 2001, hackers based in South Korea caused the crash of a website at the Japanese Ministry of Education in protest against a newly approved history textbook (BBC 2001). Korean computers were themselves targets of nearly 600 attacks in 1999, approximately half of them originating in foreign countries (McCardle et al. 2000: 12). Recent attacks on websites in Hong Kong, Singapore, Myanmar and Malaysia have also been reported (Goh 1996; Lee 2000; McCardle et al. 2000; Yeang 2001). Long-simmering tensions between India and Pakistan are reflected in a number of recent hacking incidents, and attempts have also been made to disrupt the computer systems of the Sri Lankan government (Associated Press 1998; Joseph 2000).
Readily available programs that break into networks and Internet accounts can be easily downloaded from the Internet. Such technology appears to have been used by 12 youths in Singapore who were arrested for breaking into a website of the University of California in 1997 (LeBlond & Lin 1997).

Defence planners around the world are investing substantially in information warfare — a means of disrupting the IT infrastructure of defence systems (Institute for the Advanced Study of Information Warfare 2001). McCardle and colleagues (2000: 9) report that Chinese military computer systems have been the subject of malicious attack. Whether the intruder is bent on rampant destruction or electronic vandalism, or is merely taking a look around, intrusions and attempted intrusions often occupy the energies of systems administrators.

Sales and investment fraud

As electronic commerce becomes more prevalent, the application of digital technology to fraudulent endeavours will be that much greater. The use of the telephone for fraudulent sales pitches, deceptive charitable solicitations, or bogus investment overtures is increasingly common. Online auctions are an increasing source of consumer complaints; in Japan, consumer hotlines reported nearly a threefold increase from 1999 to 2000 (*Nikkei Weekly* 2001).

In addition, cyberspace now abounds with a wide variety of investment opportunities, from traditional securities such as stocks and bonds, to more exotic opportunities such as coconut farming, the sale and leaseback of automatic teller machines, and worldwide telephone lotteries. Indeed, the digital age has been accompanied by unprecedented opportunities for misinformation. Fraudsters now enjoy direct access to millions of prospective victims around the world, instantaneously and at minimal cost. In 1999, a man in Australia posted false financial information on the Internet, causing the price of a particular company's shares on the US NASDAQ to double. The offender sold his own shares in the company at a handsome profit, before the information was repudiated and the price of the shares fell (Australian Associated Press 2000).

Classic pyramid schemes and 'Exciting, Low-Risk Investment Opportunities' are not uncommon. The technology of the World Wide Web is ideally suited to investment solicitations. In the words of two staff of the US Securities and Exchange Commission, 'At very little cost, and from the privacy of a basement office or living room, the fraudster can produce a home page that looks better and more sophisticated than that of a Fortune 500 company' (Cella & Stark 1997: 822).

As the Internet becomes increasingly a medium of commerce, it will become increasingly a medium of fraud. Japan's experience of complaints related to online auctions, and of individuals' credit card details being published on the Internet (*Nikkei Weekly* 2001) are similar to those of other countries. Trust is the fundamental basis of society and of commerce. If cyberspace becomes widely regarded as a jungle, electronic commerce, and the economic development that depends on it, will suffer.

Illegal interception of telecommunications

Developments in telecommunications provide new opportunities for electronic eavesdropping. From activities as time-honoured as surveillance of an unfaithful spouse, to the newest forms of political and industrial espionage, telecommunications interception has increasing applications. Here again, technological developments create new vulnerabilities. The electromagnetic signals emitted by a computer may themselves be intercepted. Cables may act as broadcast antennas. Existing law may not prevent the remote monitoring of computer radiation.

It has been reported that the notorious American hacker Kevin Poulsen was able to gain access to law enforcement and national security wiretap data prior to his arrest in 1991 (Littman 1997). In 1995, hackers employed by a criminal organisation attacked the communications system of the Amsterdam Police. The hackers succeeded in gaining police operational intelligence, and in disrupting police communications (Rathmell 1997). More recently, the unauthorised access to Microsoft source code in October 2000 indicates the vulnerability of companies to industrial espionage (Associated Press 2000).

Electronic funds transfer fraud

Electronic funds transfer systems have begun to proliferate, and so has the risk that such transactions may be intercepted and diverted. Valid credit card numbers can be intercepted electronically, as well as physically; the digital information stored on a card can be counterfeited. In 1999, seven Hong Kong teenagers were arrested for using stolen credit card numbers on the Internet to purchase computer products worth more than HK$1 million (Lo 1999). In Malaysia, criminals attached a device to an ATM and captured credit card and PIN details for use in counterfeiting credit cards (Dato' 2000). Hackers broke into a leading Thai retail website, stole the credit card information of 2000 customers, and posted it on the Internet (McCardle et al. 2000: 10). More recently, Japanese Internet users are reporting that their phone and credit card numbers are being published on the Internet, making them even more vulnerable to criminal exploitation (*Nikkei Weekly* 2001).

A decade ago, the financial controller of a Hong Kong company made false computer entries and shifted HK$2.6 million in company assets to his personal accounts (Cook 1993). In Singapore that year, counterfeit ATM cards were used to steal about S$95 000 (Tan 1994). According to one report, a bank in Singapore was defrauded of A$18.7 million over the course of two years between 1995 and 1997 (Leung 1999). It has been suggested that the assets of the national bank of a small country in the Asia-Pacific region came close to being the subject of an illicit electronic transfer. Individuals too can suffer. One customer of a Hong Kong bank lost up to HK$900 000 stolen from online accounts (Bowman 2001). The European Union Bank, which operated exclusively on the Internet, collapsed in 1997 leaving depositors stranded.

In December 1998, two brothers in China manipulated a bank's computer to transfer US$31 000 into their accounts (Yeang 2001). In January 2001, two Indian IT specialists were arrested allegedly attempting to hack into the information systems of the State Bank of India (*Bloomberg News* 2001). Similar cases have been reported elsewhere in Asia.

The above forms of computer-related crime are not necessarily mutually exclusive and need not occur in isolation. Just as an armed robber might steal an automobile to facilitate a quick getaway, so too can one steal telecommunications services and use them for purposes of vandalism, fraud, or in furtherance of a criminal conspiracy. Computer-related crime may be compound in nature, combining two or more of the generic forms outlined above. The various activities of Kevin Mitnick, as described in Hafner & Markoff (1991) are illustrative.

In addition, a number of themes run through each of these forms of illegality. Foremost among them are technologies for concealing the content of communications. Encryption technologies can limit access by law enforcement agents to communications carried out in furtherance of a conspiracy, or to the dissemination of objectionable materials between consenting parties (Denning 1999).

Also important are technologies for concealing a communicator's identity. Electronic impersonation, colloquially termed 'spoofing,' can be used in furtherance of a variety of criminal activities, including fraud, criminal conspiracy, harassment, and vandalism. Technologies of anonymity further complicate the task of identifying a suspect (Froomkin 1995).

Beyond the aforementioned reluctance of victims to report, the technologies of secrecy and anonymity noted above often make detection of the offender extremely difficult. Those who seek to mask their identity on computer networks are often able to do so, by means of 'looping', or 'weaving' through multiple sites in a variety of nations. The Hong Kong extortion case noted above involved messages transiting sites in Canada, France and the United States (Lo 2000). Anonymous remailers and encryption devices can shield one from the scrutiny of all but the most determined and technologically sophisticated regulatory and enforcement agencies. Some crimes do not result in detection or loss until some time after the event. Considerable time may elapse before the activation of a computer virus, or between the insertion of a 'logic bomb' and its detonation.

The Size of the Problem

The cost of cyber-crime

The task of accurately estimating the cost of cyber-crime is futile. Monetary estimates of the cost of computer-related crime should be regarded as broadly indicative at best. First, a great deal of computer-related crime never reaches official attention. Victims may be unaware that they have become victims, or may for a variety of reasons choose to keep their misfortune to themselves. For example a business, which falls victim to a form of electronic fraud, may conclude that the immediate financial loss would be outweighed by the damage to its commercial reputation, should its misfortune become public knowledge. Moreover, the likelihood of recovering its losses may be minimal. In addition, there may be a concern that publicising a successful crime may encourage imitative or 'copy cat' behaviour. So it is that an unknown but presumably very large proportion of computer-related crime never reaches official attention in the first place.

Of those incidents that do reach official attention, law enforcement agencies may be disinclined to take further action or may lack the capacity to do so. Because the definitional boundaries of what constitutes cyber-crime, and how it might be counted, will vary across jurisdictions, there can be no standard statistical database on known offences.

In addition, there may also be temptations on the part of various interests to either overstate or understate the volume and the seriousness of computer-related crime. Those perpetrators of computer-related crime who are given to boasting may seek to exaggerate their exploits. Victims may be tempted to inflate the extent of their losses in order to lobby for stricter laws and penalties. Moral entrepreneurs who object to specific types of online content may seek to overstate the nature and the severity of the content in question. Law enforcement agencies seeking greater powers or material resources may be inclined to invoke the spectre of catastrophe. And purveyors of information security products and services may wish to increase the size of their market.

This is not to suggest that computer-related crime is a non-problem. Rather, estimates that one does encounter from time to time should not be accepted uncritically, and certainly should not be given the status of absolute truth. And there are some adverse impacts of computer-related crime, such as violations of privacy, which are arguably unquantifiable.

Those offences that are detected can be difficult to cost. It may be instructive to look at cost on three dimensions. There can be direct out-ofpocket losses sustained by victims; costs in lost productivity while systems are 'down'; costs involved in repairing and securing information systems which have been subject to attack; and the costs of economic opportunities forgone when individuals avoid e-commerce because of lack of trust. Some of these losses are more readily measurable than others.

According to the BSA, Asia-Pacific regional dollar losses due to software, music and data piracy increased from US$4.1 billion in 2000 to more than US$4.7 billion in 2001, accounting for almost half of the revenue losses worldwide. The industry is quick to note that the economic costs of piracy also include lost jobs, smaller tax revenues, and lower economic growth (BSA 2003b)

Data from just one country are illustrative of the magnitude of the problem. In August 2000, a Malaysian Copyright Task Force raided a factory, seizing 100 CD stampers, 200 000 counterfeit CDs and 20 PCs, worth an estimated US$480 million (Smith & Urbas 2001: 58). This is by no means a recent phenomenon. In the ten years before 1996, an estimated RM 888 569 in pirated goods was seized in Malaysia (Farinordin 1996).

Estimates of job losses attributable to piracy will vary from country to country. The Malaysian government has recognised that the Malaysian software industry and the development of its Multimedia Super Corridor (MSC) would be threatened by uncontrolled counterfeiting (Kasim 1996). Industry estimates of the costs of software piracy in Malaysia in 1996 were RM 92 million (Farinordin 1996).

Estimates suggest that the economic impact of virus attacks on information systems around the world amounted to US$12.1 billion in 1999 and US17.1 billion in 2000 (Business Wire 2000; Computer Economics 2002). The person who pleaded guilty to releasing the Melissa virus of 1999 admitted to causing US$80 million in damage, the highest point on the scale of United States sentencing guidelines. Estimates of the full losses attributable to the Melissa virus ranged up to US$393 million in lost productivity (*Bloomberg News* 1999).

The distributed denial of service attacks against Yahoo and Amazon.com in February 2000, apparently the work of a lone Canadian teenager, illustrate the damage that can be inflicted by concerted effort. The Yahoo site was offline for approximately three hours, depriving users of services and costing the company from US$200 000 to US$500 000 in lost revenues from advertising and sales (Krochmal 2000; see also http://www.icsa.net/html/communities/ddos/index.shtml).

The 'I Love You' virus released from the Philippines in May 2000 may have entailed lost productivity amounting to billions of dollars around the world. It was estimated that two-thirds of the Fortune 500 companies took their mail servers down at the time (Masterson 2000).

But quantification can still be deceptive. What appears to be a trivial matter may in fact be the tip of a very big iceberg. A classic illustration was provided by Stoll (1991) whose pursuit of a US$0.75 accounting error in a computer account led to the discovery of an international espionage ring.

Some attempts are being made to develop a systematic overview of the incidence of crime in cyberspace. Surveys are conducted periodically by major accounting firms, and by specialised organisations such as the Computer Security Institute in the United States. Turnbull (2000) reports the results of a recent survey that found a third of companies in Hong Kong had detected security breaches in the previous 12 months. National and multinational organisations are also moving to establish databases of risks and remedies.

The International Chamber of Commerce (ICC) has opened a new division to assist 7000 member companies around the world to protect themselves against computer-related crime. In addition to identifying how and where attacks occur, the chamber seeks to provide security information to members. The new ICC cyber-crime unit is developing a database on criminal activities in cyberspace, and will facilitate information exchange between the private sector and law enforcement (ICC 2001).

There are, however, more hidden costs. To the extent that every legitimate move one makes in cyberspace is potentially traceable, this can have a chilling effect on individual expression, and may discourage full use of digital technology.

Privacy

Digital technology poses significant threats to personal privacy. Whether by accident or by design, personal details may become accessible to the world, or to particular institutions or individuals that one would prefer remain ignorant of one's affairs. And governmental responses to cyber-crime may themselves jeopardise privacy.

In 1998, a hacker broke into the computer network of a Japanese company, and published the names, bank account numbers, and other personal details of the company's customers on a website (*Daily Yomiuri* 2000).

Governments have always been inclined to encroach on individual privacy.

Today, law enforcement and security agencies around the world are seeking and obtaining greater powers to intercept electronic communications.

In democratic societies where the rule of law tends to prevail, these powers are generally subject to a degree of judicial oversight. In Great Britain, the *Regulation of Investigatory Powers Act* (RIPA) provides for monitoring and interception of electronic mail. In the United States, a system called 'carnivore' assists the scanning and capture of e-mail packets. In addition, a globally integrated communications intelligence system known as 'ECHELON' operated by the United States, Great Britain, Canada, Australia and New Zealand, permits the systematic collection and analysis of telecommunications content (Campbell 1999, 2000; Whitaker 1999).

Governments have been joined, if not surpassed, by large commercial organisations that would exploit, legally or otherwise, the increasing volume of personal details that accumulate in cyberspace. The use of a credit card for purchases now leaves an electronic trail. Technologies of data manipulation that permit merging of databases and matching of individual identities now facilitate the aggregation of data from disparate sources (Clarke 1998). The term 'data mining' is commonly used to refer to such practices. The linking of disparate data is facilitated by the existence of identification numbers, which are common in most industrial societies; the nine-digit Social Security Number in the United States is a classic example Through the collation of disparate personal details, the whole becomes greater than the sum of its parts.

Technologies may facilitate electronic eavesdropping by individuals as well. A recently identified but commonly available technology allows the originator of an e-mail message to see what the recipient wrote when it is forwarded on to another user. A few lines of JavaScript can be embedded in an e-mail message and thereby direct the recipient's mail to be returned to the original sender. It only works, however, if the recipient's e-mail program is set to read JavaScript (Evans 2001).

Of course, a great deal of personal information may be disclosed by accident. Medical records of thousands of patients have appeared on the Internet (Grabosky, Smith & Dempsey 2001: Ch. 10). Whether at the hands of the government or the private sector, by design or by blunder, the loss of one's private life is often accompanied by a decline in spontaneity, creativity, and a diminished sense of self.

Lost productivity

The unauthorised use of IT resources by the employees of both public and private sector organisations can entail significant losses in productivity. Whether the errant employee engages in behaviour as relatively innocuous as sending personal e-mail or reading the newspapers, or in conduct more questionable such as visiting pornographic sites on the Web, this may be regarded as theft of an employer's time. One company, for example, analysed the websites visited by its employees and found that 20 people had visited more than 1000 sexually explicit sites each in less than a month. Another company found that 15% of websites visited by its employees contained sexually explicit material. In a survey of executives conducted by PC World, 20% of the 200 companies surveyed had disciplined staff for misusing Internet access; the most common offences involved visits to pornographic websites, shopping, using chat lines, gambling, and downloading illegal software (Denning 1999: 360–1).

The epidemic of unsolicited commercial e-mail, colloquially referred to as 'spam,' has taken a significant toll. According to one estimate, spam accounts for 15 billion e-mail messages per day, and some US$20 billion in lost productivity per year (Blackman 2003).

The costs of controlling cyber-crime

At the outset, it is important to recognise that cyber-crime has no universal definition. What is, and is not, cyber-crime varies over time and space, depending on what the authorities in a given jurisdiction define as criminal. And so the cost of controlling cyber-crime will be a function of what authorities in a given country define as cyber-crime. A country, which defines online depictions of naked people as criminal, is likely to devote more resources to the suppression of this content than one that does not.

Among the considerations that may contribute to a nation's priorities for cyber-crime control will be the capacity of state law enforcement or regulatory agencies, and the existence and capacity of quasi-regulatory institutions that exist outside the public sector. These might include the software and publishing industries, telecommunications carriers and ISPs, those who deal in IT security products and services, and concerned citizens. In some countries there may be institutions in the private sector with the capacity to prevent, detect and investigate computer-related crime. Indeed, the expertise residing within these organisations may exceed that which exists within law enforcement agencies.

The cost of securing the national infrastructure and of providing a safe and secure platform for electronic commerce — the costs of *preventing* cyber-crime — may be formidable, but the costs of inaction will be even greater.

The limited availability of law enforcement resources in the face of the widespread threat of cyber-crime means that states will be required to determine

- What kinds of behaviour in cyberspace they should even attempt to control
- The amount of resources they choose to devote to policing cyberspace
- The burdens they wish to impose on non-state actors by enlisting them for co- production or devolving responsibility on them for self-defence

Some governments may be tempted to share the burden of policing cyberspace by sharing or delegating responsibility to other institutions or interests. This raises the question of who ultimately will bear the cost of this co-production.

Internet service providers, for example, may be asked to retain detailed records of their subscribers' transactions for an indefinite period. Because this would require considerable storage space, it would significantly increase the cost of providing Internet services. This cost would either be prohibitive for the ISP, or passed on to the consumer of Internet services. In any event, this could significantly limit the citizen's uptake of digital technology. The Netherlands recently imposed legal requirements on its ISPs to install expensive network-monitoring equipment. An estimate of the cost for a medium-sized ISP was around US$600 000, and an increase in the cost of Internet access of up to 25% (Evers 2000). China requires Internet cafés to install software to block restricted websites and record user activities (BBC 2002).

The responsibility for exercising some degree of control in cyberspace can be shared with other traditional institutions in society. Parental supervision of their children's online activities may be a more feasible strategy than state surveillance. In addition, there may well be market solutions, in the form of information security technology, which can contribute to the enhancement of security and prosperity in cyberspace.

Some governments may respond to some manifestations of cyber-crime in the belief that they can eliminate it completely. Other governments, recognising that their powers are not unlimited, may respond in a manner that creates a hostile climate for the target behaviour, and thereby achieve partial success. Other governments will respond symbolically, with verbal denunciation but no enforcement activity. The challenge facing societies today is to exploit the benefits of digital technology while minimising the downside risk.

The Challenge of Controlling Computer-Related Crime

Controlling contributing factors

Motives

Recall from the earlier discussion that crime can be explained in part in terms of the supply of motivated offenders. Motives, whether on the part of individuals or in the aggregate, are very difficult to change. Training in computer ethics is important, but its impact will be marginal at best. For this reason, the most strategically advantageous approaches to computer-related crime will be concerned with the reduction of opportunities, and with the enhancement of surveillance.

Opportunities

The most effective way of eliminating opportunities for online crime is simply to pull the plug. This is, of course, unrealistic; the affluent nations of the world are now highly dependent on information technology. For the poorer nations, IT is probably a necessary, if not sufficient, path to economic development. Thus the challenge lies in managing risk so as to achieve the maximum benefits that flow from new technologies, while minimising the downside. A merchant could scrutinise every credit card transaction so as to drastically reduce the risk of fraud, but in the process drive away legitimate customers. At a higher level, nations around the world are in the process of forging policies on where to draw the line on such fundamental questions as the balance between the citizen's privacy and the imperatives of law enforcement, and freedom of expression versus the protection of certain cultural values.

There are many technologies, which reduce the opportunity to commit computer-related crime. Given that so much computer-related crime depends on unauthorised access to information systems, access control and authentication technologies have become essential. Sophisticated advice and products for computer crime prevention are provided by one of the world's growth industries of today, namely computer security.

Denning (1999) offers a comprehensive inventory of technologies for reducing opportunities for computer crime. She describes technologies of encryption and anonymity, which permit concealment of the content of communications (such as a consumer's credit card details), or of the identity of the communicator (not all participants in discussion groups on reproductive health wish to disclose their identities). Denning also outlines technologies of authentication, from basic passwords, to various biometric devices such as fingerprint or voice recognition technology, and retinal imaging, which greatly enhance the difficulty of obtaining unauthorised access to information systems.

Virus detectors can identify and block malicious computer code; blocking and filtering programs can screen out unwanted content. A rich variety of commercial software now exists with which to block access to certain sites (Venditto 1996).

Surveillance

The third basic factor that contributes to computer-related crime is the absence of adequate surveillance. Capable guardianship has evolved over human history, from feudalism, to the rise of the state and the proliferation of public institutions of social control, to the post-modern era in which employees of private security services vastly outnumber sworn police officers in many industrial democracies.

Technology can also enhance surveillance. Denning (1999) describes various technologies for detecting attempted intrusions into information systems. Alarms can indicate when repeated login attempts fail because of incorrect passwords, or when access is sought outside of normal working hours. Other anomaly detection devices will identify unusual patterns of system use, including atypical destination and duration of telephone calls, or unusual spending patterns using credit cards.

Market forces can also enhance surveillance. A market is currently emerging for ISPs specialising in content suitable for family consumption, guaranteed to be free of sex, violence, and vilification.

Market forces may also generate second-order controlling influences. As large organisations begin to appreciate their vulnerability to electronic theft or vandalism, they may be expected to insure against potential losses. It is very much in the interests of insurance companies to require appropriate security precautions on the part of their policyholders. Indeed, decisions to set and price insurance may well depend on security practices of prospective insureds. Subcontractors may also be required to have strict IT integrity programmes in place as a condition of doing business.

Citizen co-production can complement activities undertaken by agencies of the state. Grassroots concern about the availability of undesirable content has given rise to the private monitoring and surveillance of cyberspace. In the Asia-Pacific region, an NGO website known as 'Kids.ap', supported by UNESCO, contains information that aims to eradicate child pornography and the activities of child molesters via the Internet. http://www.kidsap.org/ (visited 14 April 2001). And the motion picture, music and software industries have developed considerable capacity to detect piracy, to assist governments in investigation and prosecution, and to undertake private civil action against offenders. The policing of terrestrial space is now very much a pluralistic endeavour, and so too is the policing of cyberspace. In cyberspace today, as on terrestrial space two millennia ago, the first line of defence will be self-defence — in other words, minding one's own store.

Legislative issues

It is becoming increasingly apparent that the economic well-being of nations depends on their integration into the global economy. As cyberspace becomes the dominant medium for commerce, it becomes increasingly important that there be a secure legal platform for electronic commerce.

For any jurisdiction to protect itself against computer-related crime, a basic legislative foundation is required. This will involve the substantive criminal law, the law of search and seizure, and the law of evidence. Because of the global nature of cyberspace and the transjurisdictional nature of much computer offending, a degree of harmony and consistency, if not uniformity, is desirable across nations.

The laws of some countries are relatively elastic, able to embrace new circumstances without having to be amended. Other legal systems are quite rigid, necessitating amendment for new forms of crime. In the common law world, for example, fraud means obtaining something of value by means of deception. Deception entails the involvement of the mind of a human victim. Where fraud is carried out against an electronic system (such as an ATM), new legislation may be necessary. Similarly, the law of theft or damage in some countries may extend only to tangible items. That is, it may not be a crime to steal or to damage property in digital form.

Most basically, the substantive criminal law should provide for the following:

- Unauthorised access to a computer or computer system
- Interference with lawful use of a computer or a computer system
- Destruction or alteration of data within a computer system
- Theft of intangible property
- Obtaining value by deception (including electronic systems).

Similarly, the laws of evidence and procedure should accommodate search and seizure in an electronic environment, and should permit the admissibility of electronic evidence in judicial proceedings.

Jurisdictions such as Hong Kong have undertaken systematic reviews of their legislative requirements with respect to the prevention and control of computer-related crime (Hong Kong Security Bureau 2000).

Extra-territorial issues

One of the more significant aspects of computer-related crime is its global reach. While international offending is by no means a uniquely modern phenomenon, the global nature of cyberspace significantly enhances the ability of offenders to commit crimes in one country that will affect individuals in a variety of other countries. This poses great challenges for the detection, investigation and prosecution of offenders.

Two problems arise in relation to the prosecution of telecommunications offences which have an inter-jurisdictional aspect: first, determination where the offence occurred so it can be decided which law to apply and, second, obtaining evidence and ensuring that the offender can be located and tried before a court. Both these questions raise complex legal problems of jurisdiction and extradition (see Lanham et al. 1987; Tan 2000). If an online financial newsletter originating in the Bahamas contains fraudulent speculation about the prospects of a company whose shares are traded on the Tokyo Stock Exchange, where has the offence occurred?

Even if one is able to decide which law is applicable, further difficulties may arise in applying that law. In a unitary jurisdiction, such as Singapore, where there is one law and one law enforcement agency, determining and applying the applicable law is difficult enough. Criminal activities committed from across the globe, however, pose even greater problems. Sovereign governments are finding it difficult to exercise control over online behaviour at home, not to mention abroad. A resident of Bangkok who falls victim to a telemarketing scam originating in Albania, for example, can expect little assistance from law enforcement agencies in either jurisdiction. As a result, regulation by territorially based rules may prove to be inappropriate for these types of offences.

Extraterritorial law enforcement costs are also often prohibitive. The time, money and uncertainty required by international investigations and, if successful, extradition proceedings, can be so high as to preclude attention to all but the most serious offending. Moreover, the cooperation across international boundaries in furtherance of such enforcement usually requires a congruence of values and priorities that, despite prevailing trends towards globalisation, exists only infrequently.

Other issues which may complicate investigation entail the logistics of search and seizure during real time, the sheer volume of material within which incriminating evidence may be contained, and the encryption of information, which may render it entirely inaccessible, or accessible only after a massive application of decryption technology.

Traditionally, the jurisdiction of courts was local. That is, courts could only entertain prosecutions in respect of offences committed against local laws where there existed a sufficient link between the offence and the jurisdiction in question. There is, however, always the possibility that legislatures will confer extraterritorial jurisdiction for some crimes. Some common examples include offences committed on the high seas, counterfeiting offences, crimes committed by members of the defence forces, and, recently in Australia and elsewhere, sexual relations between Australians and children overseas who are under 16 years of age.

In rare circumstances, a nation's laws may apply to acts committed overseas by foreign nationals. Recent war crime prosecutions in Australia involved defendants resident elsewhere at the times the alleged offences were committed. These circumstances are, to say the least, most unusual. But in a shrinking world where the financial burdens of extradition are unlikely to decline, they may become more common.

To the extent that international computer-related crime is amenable to international enforcement, it will require concerted international cooperation. Past performance in the context of other forms of criminality would suggest that this cooperation is unlikely to be forthcoming except in the relatively infrequent types of illegality where there is widespread international consensus about the activity in question (such as child pornography, or fraud on a scale likely to destabilise financial markets), and about the desirability of suppressing it. In many instances, extradition is likely to be more cumbersome the greater the cultural and ideological distance between the two parties. At the best of times, international extradition can be expensive.

There are nevertheless examples of extradition between countries following successful investigation of computer crime. In January 2000, Canadian authorities returned a suspect in a fraud case to officials of the Public Security Bureau in Beijing (People's Daily Online, 2000). In August 2001, Thai authorities agreed to a US request to commence extradition proceedings against a US national, but reserved the right to prosecute him first after discovering child pornography downloaded from the Internet in his possession (*Bangkok Post* 2001).

Even so, this would assume a seamless world system of stable sovereign states; such a system does not exist today, nor is it likely to exist in our lifetime. Law enforcement and regulatory vacuums exist in some parts of the world, certainly in those settings where the state has effectively collapsed. Even where state power does exist in full force, the corruption of individual regimes can impede international cooperation.

Nevertheless, some excellent progress has been made in furtherance of international harmonization of laws relating to computer crime and its investigation. For an example of movement toward consistency in legislative response, one may look to the Council of Europe's Draft Convention on Cyber-crime. This draft convention contains general sections relating to the substantive criminal law, search and seizure of electronic data, jurisdiction, and mutual assistance. Measures to be taken at national level with regard to the substantive criminal law included the adoption of measures to criminalise illegal access to computer systems; illegal interception of, or interference with, data; the production, sale or procurement of 'hacking' tools or software; computer-related fraud and forgery; offences relating to child pornography; and offences relating to copyright infringement. http://conventions.coe.int/ (visited 8 October 2000).

In addition, the work of the United Nations (including its affiliated Institutes such as UNAFEI), the G8, the OECD, the Council of Europe and Interpol are other examples of international cooperation. In our region, one may look to the Interpol Asia and South Pacific Regional Working Party of IT crime, established in 1995.

Such international efforts at capacity building are essential for, issues of trans-border criminality aside, many law enforcement agencies as we know them lack the capacity on their own to control computer-related crime which occurs entirely within their own jurisdiction. This arises from a number of factors, not the least of which is resource constraint. In most countries around the world, police are being asked to do more with less. The broad sweep of the criminal law and the abundance of criminal activity mean that police must often choose which matters to pursue and which to ignore. This is even more the case with transnational electronic crime than it is with domestic offending.

Another fundamental issue, at least at the present historical moment, is the difficulty faced by police services around the world in retaining expert computer crime investigators. Very attractive opportunities exist in the private sector for persons with forensic computing skills. A competent police officer may well be able to double or triple his or her salary in the private sector, whether working for one of the big multinational accounting firms or for a large financial institution. Whether this 'brain drain' will continue indefinitely, or slow down as the supply of highly computer literate individuals in both public and private sectors catches up with demand, remains to be seen. For the time being, however, police will not be able to go it alone. They will remain dependent on private and non-profit institutions to help combat crime in cyberspace.

In general, this division of labour will include elements of self-protection by prospective victims of telecommunications-related illegality; market-based commercial solutions; self-regulatory initiatives by the targets of regulation; traditional law enforcement or regulatory intervention by the state; and third party 'co-production' of surveillance by private individuals and citizens' groups.

Conclusion

Total control of cyber-crime may be achievable, but only at great cost. Most new technologies are accompanied by a downside risk. The advent of the internal combustion engine has led to millions of deaths and injuries, and massive property damage, not to mention deterioration in environmental quality. The advent of the telephone has greatly enhanced the efficiency of communications among criminals and the photocopier made counterfeiting and forgery easier. Our response has been not to forgo or to discard these technologies but rather to regulate their use or to design them in a manner that will reduce their exploitation for criminal purposes.

So we build safer cars, with cleaner engines. We design safer roads, and impose speed limits, which we employ police to enforce. In so doing, we accept that these solutions will not be perfect. We seek an optimal solution, one that would maximise the benefits and minimise the costs.

Every country must decide for itself what kind of future it seeks, and what kinds of behaviours are acceptable. In these undertakings, contradictions and tradeoffs are inevitable. For the most part, prosperity is very difficult to achieve without a degree of economic freedom. Conversely, state control over the economy and information is difficult, if not impossible to achieve without sacrificing a degree of prosperity.

The control of computer crime is about tradeoffs. The reduction of opportunities to commit cyber-crime, if carried out solely through the curtailment of connectivity, would be counterproductive. Where the economy is not already linked with global forces, it will become increasingly so. 'Pulling the plug' will only impede commerce. The Hong Kong Inter-Departmental Working Group on Computer-Related Crime observed the risk of overkill that can arise from excessive regulation of information technology in a free market economy (Hong Kong Security Bureau 2000).

Responsibilities for the control of computer crime will be similarly shared between agents of the state, information security specialists in the private sector, and the individual user. In cyberspace today, as on terrestrial space two millennia ago, the first line of defence will be self-defence — in other words, minding one's own store.

3

Cyberspace Governance and Internet Regulation in China

Kam C Wong and Georgiana Wong

Computer-mediated communication (CMC) in the new information age has brought people closer together in a virtual world, transcending geographical distance, time zones, social gaps and cultural barriers. The introduction of CMC, however, raises new concerns about criminality as it accentuates aspects of traditional criminality. Computers and the Internet facilitate traditional criminality as they bring about new deviance. As currently used, the term 'computer crime'[1] generally refers to three kinds of criminal activity involving the computer: crimes committed with computers, attacks on networks or computer systems, and crimes where information technology is incidental to the offence.

The study of cyberspace governance and Internet regulation in the People's Republic of China (PRC or 'China'), both in law and social science, is just beginning. There was little computer crime research in China prior to 2000.[2] What there is now suffers from a lack of valid and reliable primary data and independent and objective secondary analysis. For example, at present computer crime is not reported separately in annual PRC police reports.[3] No independent computer crime victimisation survey is conducted by universities.

The research presented in this chapter is a first attempt to study cyberspace governance and Internet regulation in China with indigenous PRC data and from a Chinese perspective. In particular, it investigates the nature and extent of computer-related crime and reports on the effectiveness of legal and other measures addressing computer-related crime.

The Internet in China

IT development in China and the emergence of computer crime

Since the 1990s, China's information technology industry has become 'a strategic industry and a new area for the growth of China's economy in the 21st century'.[4] The immediate past PRC President Jiang Zemin, an engineer and Minister of the Electronics Industry (1985), considered IT indispensable for the four modernisations in China.[5] Many leading Chinese economists viewed the Internet as instrumental in China's economic transformation, particularly since accession to the World Trade Organisation (WTO).[6]

This chapter will describe with statistics and demonstrate with examples the origins and development of the computer and Internet in China, from 1987 to the present.[7] It will analyse how the PRC government and political leadership perceive and react to the social and political problems raised by the introduction of the computer and the Internet into China.

The origin and development of the Internet in China

In September 1987, China's first e-mail was sent through the Chinese Academic Network. In October 1990, the Chinese Internet domain name was officially registered as 'CN' in DDN-NIC, a network centre of ARPANET. Since then, 'CN' has been used for China e-mail communication worldwide.

In 1993, the Institute of High-Energy Physics established the first direct Internet link to China. In the following year, China's National Computing and Networking Facility of China (NCFC), a part of the Chinese Academy of Sciences, was formally connected with the Internet in the United States. This move was formally endorsed and enthusiastically supported by the Sino-American Federation of Science and Technological Cooperation and the National Science Foundation of the United States.

Since 1993, the PRC government has experimented with conducting government business by the Internet. It launched a number of Golden Projects, for example 'Golden Agriculture' to facilitate agricultural information exchange, 'Golden Shield' to promote police information-sharing (local versus national, domestic versus foreign, government versus citizens), and 'Golden Tax' to make electronic tax collection possible.

In 1999–2000, the PRC government formally launched the e-government on the Web project.[8] Since then, PRC government agencies have adopted the Internet as an integral part of their open government and efficient administration strategy to legitimise the political authority and rationalise the administrative process.

Disparate growth and impact of the Internet

The number of Internet users in China is the largest among nations in the Asia-Pacific region. There are 68 million users with 25.72 million computers linked to the Internet and a total bandwidth of 18 599M. Table 3.1 gives a summary of the annual growth in the number of Internet users, computer hosts, the 'CN' domain name 'WWW' websites, and total bandwidth from 1997 to mid-2003.[9]

Table 3.1 CNNIC statistics on the development of China's Internet, 1997–2003

Year	*June 2003*	*2002*	*2001*	*2000*	*1999*	*1998*	*1997*
Internet users	68 000 000	59 100 000	33 700 000	22 500 000	8 900 000	2 100 000	620 000
Computer hosts	25 720 000	20 830 000	12 540 000	8 920 000	3 500 000	747 000	299 000
'CN' domain names	250 651	179 544	127 319	122 099	48 695	18 396	4 066
'WWW' websites	473 900	371 600	277 100	265 405	15 153	5 300	1 500
Total bandwidth (M)	18 599	9 380	7 597.5	2 799	351	143.2	25.4

Source: CNNIC

The following observations can be made of the PRC authorities' concerns about the development of the computer and Internet trends in China:[10]

1. *The PRC authorities are concerned with harnessing an ill-understood, runaway electronic media, for beneficial use.* The PRC experienced exponential computer and Internet growth in the last decade. According to the latest China Internet Network Information Center (CNNIC) survey, there was a total of 68 million Internet users in China as of 30 June 2003, compared with only 620 000 users in October 1997. This is a 109-fold increase. This exponential growth rate is projected to continue.
2. *The PRC authorities are much concerned with the destabilising impacts of the computer / Internet in Chinese society.*[11] As noted above, the Internet is becoming more and more popular with the public. It facilitates the free

flow of information from abroad and the unrestricted exchange of ideas at home. It breeds independent thought and promotes divergent views.[12] It also allows cultural pollution from abroad (e.g. pornography) and political propaganda by foreign countries (e.g. Voice of America), facilitating organised dissent in the process (e.g. the Falun Gong).[13]

3. *The PRC authorities are most concerned with the corrupting influence of the Internet on the impressionistic younger generation.* Internet users are becoming younger by the year; for example, users below age 18 surged from only 2.4% in 1999 to 17.1% in mid-2003. A study of Internet crimes in Hexi, Tianjian, between January and July 2001 indicated that 75% of offenders were below the age of 18.[14] The CPC strongly believes that failure in setting and directing the behaviour of this age group will lead to serious social and political problems in the future.
4. *The PRC authorities are increasingly concerned with the negative educational impact of the Internet on the less educated.* The falling level of education among Internet users makes for a population more vulnerable to temptation; a less educated Internet population means more potential for criminality on the Net.
5. *The PRC authorities are increasingly concerned with the impact of the Internet on less developed regions of China.* The Internet is spreading from economically more developed, for example Guangzhou, to less developed parts of China, for example Jilin. The eastern, southern and northern regions remain the top three in terms of Internet usage. The increasing popularity of the Internet has been moving from large cities to rural areas gradually in the past six years. For example, Internet usage in places like Beijing is dropping while Jilin, Heilongjiang, Jiangsu and Zhejiang are catching up very rapidly. The sights and sounds of advanced economic development in parts of the less well developed regions of China are likely to cause discontent, disaffection and disorder.
6. *The PRC leadership is fearful of the loss of ideological, cultural and social control over the masses.* CNNIC data show that more and more people can afford to pay for their own computers and related services. As more and more people start using private computers at home, the government has increasingly had less ability to monitor and control what they write and read.
7. Finally, *the PRC authorities are concerned with Internet security, particularly with e-commerce and e-government.* As revealed by CNNIC data, increasingly the public is relying on the Internet to conduct their personal affairs, for example commercial activities. The future development and growth of e-commerce and e-government hinges on computer security.

From these we can see why the PRC political leadership is much concerned with the inappropriate, abusive and illegal use of the Internet: political instability at a national level, cultural corruption at a personal level, moral hazards especially for youth and security problems in relation to e-commerce.

Nature, Prevalence and Distribution of Computer Crime

In the PRC, cyber-crime has been grouped into five major categories by an Internet information security official:

1. Using a computer to make, copy and spread pornographic materials. This category accounted for more than 50% or 2000-odd cases of all computer-related crime under investigation in 2001.
2. Committing economic crime via the Internet, for example theft, blackmail and illegal pyramid sales activity.
3. Spreading computer viruses and mounting hacking attacks. Six hundred cases were uncovered in 2001, representing an increase of 58% over the previous year.
4. Infringement of citizens' personal and democratic rights, such as personal attack and libel through the Internet. In 2001, 186 criminal investigations were mounted, representing a rise of more than three times over the previous year.
5. Using the Internet to jeopardise national security, for example the Falun Gong.

Another way to define and classify computer criminality is with reference to the PRC Criminal Law, for example, according to the structure of Part Two, Specific Provisions, of the Criminal Law (1997):[15]

- Endangering national security
- Endangering public security
- Disrupting the order of the socialist market economy
- Infringing a citizen's personal and democratic rights
- Property violation
- Obstructing the administration of public order
- Impairing the interests of national defence
- Embezzlement and bribery
- Dereliction of duty
- Servicemen's transgression of duties.

Case examples

The first computer-related crime in China was officially reported in 1986 as a regular theft since there was no computer crime legislation at the time. The case was uncovered in Shenzhen on 22 July 1986 when a Hong Kong merchant realised that a deposit of RMB20 000 (equivalent to US$2400) was missing from his bank account. A similar crime was reported at a different branch of the bank two months later. A computer operator of the bank, Mr Chen, succeeded in transferring the bank's money to his designated account through unauthorised access to the depositors' database.[16] In March 1988, a mini-computer operator, Mr Tse, and his gang managed to transfer a sum of RMB870 000 from the Agricultural Bank in Szechuan for their personal use while working on the bank's computers. Between late 1989 and June 1990, another computer operator, Mr Fong, a bank employee in Zhejian, was successful in withdrawing RMB1.61 million in cash from the bank deposit accounts by abusing his access privilege in the course of his duty.[17] The earliest cases recorded were mostly related to banking systems and financial services.[18]

Statistics

According to the Supervision Bureau for Public Information Security (Zhongguo Gongan Gonggong Xinxi Wangluo Anquan Jianchaju) of the Ministry of Public Security (MPS), China has recorded an increasing amount of cyber-crime: it has grown from roughly 100 cases in 1998 to 4500 cases in 2001.[19] A yearly breakdown of the figures is set out in Table 3.2.

Table 3.2 Statistics of cyber-crime in China, 1998–2001

Year	*2001*	*2000*	*1999*	*1998*	*Total*
No. of cyber-crime cases under investigation	4500	2700	400	100+	7700+
Annual Growth Rate	67%	575%	300%	–	–

Source: MPS

These cyber-crime statistics were published on 11 April 2002 in a working conference of the Supervision Bureau for Public Information Security held in Beijing. This set of data does not provide a complete picture of the current status of Internet crime in China: the magnitude of 'dark figures' of computer crime has yet to be ascertained. On closer inspection, we find that pornography is considered the top computer crime problem, followed by economic crime and national security breaches. Together, they contribute to 38% of all the Internet crimes reported.

Research

There was little independent research on computer crime in China before 2000. In 2000 Jiang Ping, now one of the very few computer crime and security experts in China, pioneered the first 'scientific' study of the causes of, and remedy for, computer crime in China.[20] Jiang's data, valuable though they obviously are in providing a rare glimpse of the nature, prevalence and distribution of computer crime in China, suffer from a number of methodological problems, which detract from their potential scientific use. For example, they are somewhat dated (1996–99) and deal with a small number of cases (183) drawn exclusively from newspapers. Thus Jiang's data should be cited with these caveats in mind and used carefully. Jiang's study can best be described as exploratory and tentative.

Jiang's study is based on 183 'typical' cases of computer-related crimes reported in PRC newspapers between 1986 and 1999.[21] His analysis of the 'crime commission environment' of 183 cases with sufficient detail is set out in Table 3.3. The figures show that more than 90% (169) of reported computer crime cases were committed over the network.

Table 3.3 Jiang's analysis of computer crime cases, 1989–99

Environment in which commissioned	Stand-alone computer	Intranet	Extranet	Internet
No. of crimes	14	123	8	38
% of 183 cases	7.65	67.21	4.37	20.77

Source: Jiang Ping

Jiang further summarised his findings[22] from all 183 cases as follows.

1. Most crimes are in the finance sector: 54.05% are related to financial systems. This is followed by 32.97% related to business enterprises. In China, computer crime is commercial crime.
2. Most offenders are young IT professionals with access through their jobs to computers, for example computer operators (59.85%), IT system administrators (31.39%), or computer programmers (3.65%). In China, computer crime is an occupational opportunity.

3. The majority of offenders are educated. The majority of the principal offenders are college graduates (40.42%), college students (19.15%) or postgraduate students (10.64%). Fewer than a third (29.79%) of the total have only completed high school education level or below. In China, computer crime is a crime of the elites.
4. Most cases were committed by insiders and resulted from a breach of trust. In China, computer crime is white-collar crime.
5. Most cases resulted from a lack of internal control over computer use. In China computer crime is often committed by an employee.
6. Most computer crimes are committed by males (91.4%). In China computer crime is a male crime.

Cyberspace Governance in China

Cyberspace policy

The Chinese government wants to use the Internet primarily as an instrument of economic reform, social development, cultural revival and political control. The PRC leadership has recognised that IT, with its speed, efficiency and cost-effectiveness, is a powerful tool to spur, leverage, and in time transform China's nascent economic development. For example, according to Zeng Peiyan, the Minister in charge of the State Development Planning Commission, IT will help China to achieve and sustain an economic growth rate of around 7% in 2002 and beyond.[23]

The PRC leadership and government officials are also keenly aware that the Internet has the potential to change the availability of information to the masses and, in the process, change their values and beliefs. With the introduction of the computer and spread of the Internet, the CPC and the PRC government find it increasingly difficult, if not impossible, to control people's access to information by way of computers. From a political point of view, the PRC political leadership has good reasons to adopt proactive measures to regulate uncontrolled information made available in cyberspace. Of most concern is the fact that free Internet access threatens national security, social stability, ideological dominance and Chinese Communist Party (CCP) leadership.[24]

On 12 July 2001, the CPC Central Committee held a special meeting at Zhongnanhai to discuss policy issues pertaining to IT development, cyberspace governance and Internet control. The legal system policy meeting was attended by the senior leadership and key CCP Political Bureau members such as then President Jiang Zemin, Chair of National People's Congress Li Peng, Premier Zhu Rongji, Vice-President Hu Jintao, Minister of Public Security Li Ruihuan, and Wei Jianxing. Professor Cheng Chengxi, a researcher at the Law School of the Chinese Social Science Academy chaired the landmark meeting. Cheng raised and discussed three salient cyberspace governance and control issues with the political bureau leadership: the importance of Internet development and the corresponding need for regulation and control in China; the need to learn cyberspace governance and Internet regulation lessons from foreign countries; and proposals for the establishment of an Internet legal and regulatory system in China.

As a matter of state policy, 'the net is to be tightly controlled and strictly regulated to forestall against any inappropriate and non-approved use'.[25] The national strategies of Internet control are:

- To perfect regulation and control of the Internet through legislation
- To promote civilised (*wenming*) use of the Internet
- To enhance international cooperation in Internet control
- To train and educate party leaders and government officials in the use of the computer and the Internet

Computer crime theory

PRC cyber-crime control and Internet regulation follows traditional crime control strategies and methods, that is, a 'comprehensive control scheme' (*zonghe zhili*). Comprehensive crime control theory calls for the integration of multiple control measures such as economic, political, legal and social sanctions, by different control agents, for example government and communal, and at various levels of government such as central, provincial, municipal, community and family. Control measures include public education, legal punishment, administrative regulation and individual rehabilitation. The comprehensive crime control policy echoes Western crime control theory, for example Felson's 'routine activities theory', and methods, for example Goldstein's 'problem-oriented policing' (POP) approach.[26]

Comprehensive crime control in China is built around prevention, with education as a key component. It resembles POP, which treats crime as the manifestation of larger and more enduring problems in the community to be resolved by the police working with the local community.

The policy of a comprehensive approach to crime control was established ten years ago.[27] On 5 September 2001, the Central Committee of the CCP and the State Council called for improving public security through comprehensive control of crime.[28] The key elements of the comprehensive crime control policy are summarised as follows (emphasis added):

1. To vigorously develop crime *prevention networks at the grassroots level* in parallel to law enforcement with harsh punishment while keeping crime prevention in a primary role. Education in moral and legislation to the youth is emphasised.
2. To strengthen the crime prevention infrastructure and extend *comprehensive control to different hierarchies*, from cities, rural areas, to streets.
3. To reinforce a *total scheme of comprehensive control in communities*, coordinate efforts in crime fighting, crime prevention, and crime control by local authorities with appropriate provision in rules and regulations.
4. To hold *responsible bodies strictly accountable* to ensure effectiveness of comprehensive control in maintaining social order and public security.[29]

Computer crime legislation

Before 1997 there was no law against computer crime. All computer-related crimes were prosecuted under traditional PRC criminal law provisions. The Criminal Law of PR China was substantially revised with effect from 1 October 1997[30] but there is still no separate category or section on computer crime. There are, however, three provisions dealing with computer-related crime under Chapter VI of the Criminal Law of the PRC:

1. Article 285: 'Whoever, in violation of state regulations, invades the computer information system in the fields of state affairs, national defense construction or sophisticated science and technology shall be sentenced to fixed-term imprisonment of not more than three years or criminal detention.'
2. Article 286: 'Whoever, in violation of state regulations, cancels, alters, increases or jams the functions of the computer information system, thereby making it impossible for the system to operate normally, if the consequences are serious, shall be sentenced to fixed-term imprisonment of not more than five years or criminal detention; if the consequences are especially serious, he shall be sentenced to fixed term imprisonment of not less than five years. Whoever, in violation of state regulations, cancels, alters or increases the data stored in or handled or transmitted by the computer information system or its application program, if the

consequences are serious, shall be punished in accordance with the provisions on the preceding paragraph. Whoever intentionally creates or spreads destructive programs such as the computer viruses, thus affecting the normal operation of the computer system, if the consequences are serious, shall be punished in accordance with the provisions of the first paragraph.'

3. Article 287: 'Whoever uses computers to commit the crimes such as financial fraud, theft, embezzlement, misappropriation of public funds and theft of State secrets shall be convicted and punished in accordance with the relevant provision of this law.'

In brief, Art. 285 deals with unauthorised access, Art. 286 with contamination of data, and Art. 287 with the use of the computer as an instrument of crime.

Regulatory measures and framework

Until very recently, criminal law was not the dominant means of combating computer crime and abuse in China. From the beginning, PRC authorities have used administrative regulation and police supervisory measures to control them. For example, on 5 April 1995 the Ministry of Public Security issued a notice calling for concerted efforts to curb the use of computers to duplicate, spread and sell pornographic materials.

Generally, administrative regulations on computer security can be grouped into three major categories: network monitoring and control, network information system security protection, and domain name registration. Together with criminal law, these regulations provide a framework for the Chinese government to monitor and control information flow on the Internet, keep track and watch over Internet users and regulate and supervise Internet service providers.

Regulations providing for computer network monitoring and control

China began to regulate the Internet in earnest in 1996. On 1 January 1996, the PRC government called for a crackdown on the abusive use of the Internet, for example promoting pornography and spreading anti-government information.[31]

On 1 February 1996, China's State Council issued Order 195, 'Provisional Regulations of the PRC for the Administration of International Networking of Computer Information Networks', a first of its kind, a prototype for PRC Internet regulations. The order provides that Internet users are required to register with the MPS within 30 days and to report subsequent changes if they cancel or switch accounts to a different ISP. Another regulation, the 'Internet Content Regulation' of 2000, requires Internet content providers (ICPs) to keep 60-day records of online user activity, including the user's log-on time, Internet account, Web address and other information, to facilitate government control and secure users' accountability. The Internet Content Regulation specifically provides: 'The ICPs are prohibited from providing information related to anti-government, obscenity and anti-social stability, and intruders will be punished according to the actual situations.' [32]

In brief, this category of computer regulation allows for the monitoring of Internet information flow, tracking of Internet usage and establishment of Internet oversight responsibilities.

Regulations on network information system security

The 'Safety and Protection Regulations for Computer Information Systems' (18 February 1994) put the burden of securing the nation's computers from abusive use and attacks on individual organisations, which are required to establish fail-safe internal procedures against unauthorised access and illegal use of computers.

In 2000, the PRC authorities promulgated a host of Internet security regulations, including the 'Regulations on State Secrets Administration for International Networking of Computer Information Systems', issued by the State Bureau of Secrecy and effective from 1 January 2000 ('Regulations on State Secrets Administration') and the 'Decision of the Standing Committee of the National People's Congress Concerning Maintaining Internet Security', adopted on 28 December 2000 ('Internet Security Decision').

The Regulations on State Secrets Administration was promulgated to protect state secrets and secure international computer information systems. The regulations are based on the Law of the People's Republic of China on the Preservation of State Secrets. The Internet Security Decision lists numerous criminal acts involving computer systems and the Internet. It provides that such computer criminality should be dealt with — investigated and punished — in accordance with the Criminal Law of the PRC. It further provides that, if the Internet is used to commit illegal but not criminal acts, violators will be punished in accordance with the 'Regulations on Public Order Administration Penalties'. If an act does not constitute a crime but is in violation of administrative regulations, administrative penalties will be imposed. Finally, if the Internet is used to violate the lawful rights and interests of individuals, violators are exposed to civil liability. On 3 April 2001, 'Measures for Managing Business Operations in Providing Internet Services' was jointly issued by the Ministry of Information Industry, MPS, Ministry of Culture and General Administration of Industry and Commerce. These measures prohibit service providers and Internet users from engaging in any illegal behaviour that jeopardises computer network security and information security.

In brief, this category of regulations is designed to address a wide spectrum of computer system and Internet security problems, from stealing state secrets to the proliferation of encryption. These regulations provide for a means to track down Internet abusers as they fortify computer systems and networks from computer viruses and hacking attacks.

Regulations on registration of domain name

Throughout the 1970s and 1980s, the computer network expanded as technology became more sophisticated and accessible. In 1984, the domain name system (DNS) was introduced, giving the world domain suffixes such as .edu, .com, .gov and .org, and a series of country codes. This system made the Internet much more manageable. Without it, users would have to remember the Internet protocol (IP) address — a long series of numbers — of every Internet site they wanted to visit.[33] CNNIC is the only authorised body for providing domain names registration, administration and dispute resolution in China.

To establish an orderly environment for Chinese character domain names, the MII released a new regulation, 'China Internet Domain Name Regulations',[34] in September 2000 to streamline the protocol for Chinese domain name registration. Under the regulation, no organisations or individuals can engage in domain name registration without first seeking approval from the Telecom Administrative Bureau of the MII.[35] This category of regulations in effect provides for Internet censorship by controlling who can and cannot regulate Internet website operators.

Regulations for the protection of intellectual property and facilitation of e-commerce

China has joined all major international intellectual property rights conventions and has enacted a vast array of laws and regulations to discharge its treaty obligations, including regulations protecting computer software copyright, Internet intellectual property rights, and e-commerce transaction integrity. With China's entry to the World Trade Organization (WTO) and in reaction to international business competition,[36] intellectual property rights regulations are expected to grow substantially within the coming two or three years.

Table 3.4 A brief chronology of China's intellectual property protection

April 1963	The *Trademark Control Act* supplants PRC's 'Provisional Trade Mark Registration of 1950' and is repealed in 1982.
July 1979	A US–China Agreement on Trade Relations marks the beginning of the current PRC intellectual property protection regime. Both sides stipulated that they would offer reciprocal protection of patents and copyrights.
June 1980	China accedes to the World Intellectual Property Organisation (WIPO)
August 1982	The *Trademark Law of the People's Republic of China* replaces the *Trademark Control Act* 1963 Act (detailed Implementing Regulations follow in 1983, 1988). Based on first-to-file system; registration is valid for ten years after approval, with a ten-year renewal option. The 1988 revisions introduce protection for service marks.
March 1984	The *Patent Law of The People's Republic of China* (Implementing Regulations are issued in 1985) mandates registration of consumer products and licensing contracts; infringement penalties can be twice the profit earned though violations based on first-to-file system.
March 1985	China accedes to the Paris Convention for the Protection of Industrial Property.
May 1989	A US–China Memorandum of Understanding on the Enactment and Scope of PRC Copyright Law stipulates that copyright legislation will include computer programs as a specific category; and expands patent protection without specifying industries or time limits.
October 1989	China accedes to the Madrid Agreement for International Registration of Trademarks.
June 1991	China extends protection to computer software, and to literary, artistic, and scientific works.
June 1991	A 'Computer Software Protection Regulation' (followed by 'Software Registration Procedures' issued in 1992*)* protects published software registered after the enactment date, leaving all existing software in China in the public domain.
January 1992	A US–China Memorandum of Understanding on Intellectual Property Rights results in China pledging to extend copyright protection to foreign owners of software, books, firms, sound recordings and other mediums previously unprotected.
September 1992	'Regulations for the Implementation of International Copyright Treaty Provisions' provide further amendments to the Copyright Law and extends protection to 'applied art' (jewelry, watches, toys, furniture etc.) which are subject to registration requirements.

Table 3.4 *(continued)*

October 1992	China accedes to the Berne Convention for the Protection of Literary and Artistic Works.
October 1992	China accedes to the Universal Copyright Convention.
February 1993	A 'Supplementary Provisions Concerning the Punishment of Crimes of Counterfeiting Registered Trademarks' is issued.
June 1993	China accedes to the Convention for the Protection of Producers of Phonograms Against Unauthorized Duplication of their Phonograms (Geneva Convention).
December 1993	An 'Unfair Competition Law' protects unregistered trademarks, packaging and trade designs and prohibits unfair competition by monopolies and cartels in control over prices.
January 1994	China accedes to the Patent Cooperation Treaty.
July 1994	The 'Copyright Implementing Regulations' makes copyright infringement a criminal offence; violators can be sentenced to prison for up to seven years or executed in severe cases.
February 1995	In a US–China IPR Enforcement agreement, China undertakes to markedly reduce piracy, improve border enforcement, and open its markets to US computer software, sound recordings and motion pictures.

Source: Cheng-China Huang 'A Brief Chronology of China's Intellectual Property Protection' (n.d.), http://www.american.edu/ted/hpages/ipr/cheng.htm (visited 15 January 2004)

Law enforcement

MPS established the Supervision Bureau for Public Information Security in September 1998 to conduct Internet policing.[37] At present, the MPS has set up in each of the 26 provinces, autonomous regions and municipalities directly under the central government's corresponding Supervision Bureau for Public Information Security to direct and coordinate cyber-crime suppression efforts locally and nationally. For example, Shanghai, one of the largest and most progressive municipalities in the nation, established its own Internet police (*wangluo jingcha*) in June 2001. The structure and function of the Shanghai Internet police mirror that of the MPS and of other provinces. Its major functions are: to guide, coordinate, inspect and supervise the computer and Internet safety of CCP and government organs; to protect and secure financial, communication and critical infrastructure; to investigate and deal with computer hackers; and to study and formulate policies in the prevention of computer crime.[38]

The Supervision Bureau for Public Information Security boasted a clearance rate of 89% (6889 cleared versus 7700 reported cases) between 1998 and 2001.[39] In view of fast-growing computer crime rates, especially by young people, the MPS has focused on monitoring, regulating and controlling Internet cafés and other electronic amusement shops as a major enforcement strategy. Since 1999, there have been increasing numbers of reported criminal activities that involve Internet cafés that, for example, include pornography,[40] gambling,[41] fraud, and infringement of copyright. Many parents and teachers are worried that illegally operated Internet cafés might expose teenagers to unhealthy social relationships, corrupting moral influences and harmful physical health risks.[42] For example, a 17-year-old student died of heart failure in an Internet café as a result of prolonged computer game sessions.[43] Adverse publicity regarding Internet cafés resulted in angry public outcries that led to stern government or police actions. For example in late 2000 more than 20 000 Internet cafés and 12 000 computer game shops were suspended by police during a public order campaign that aimed to enforce the regulation of the Internet services market.[44] Since then all Internet cafés must have a valid licence, and this is strictly enforced. The Measures for Managing Business Operations in Providing Internet Services of 2001 specifically prohibits those younger than 18 years from visiting Internet cafés without a responsible guardian. It further restricts teenagers' visits to Internet cafés between the hours of 8 a.m. and 9 p.m. during national holidays. A three-month strict enforcement campaign was conducted between April and June of 2001 to curb illegal or irregularly operated Internet cafés. During the campaign, more than 56 800 Internet cafés were inspected nationwide, with 2000 Internet cafés shut down and 6000 units suspended for a variety of illegalities and irregularities.[45]

Cyber-crime prevention through education

Chinese leaders believe in using education to prevent crime. In the computer crime area, the focus is on promoting public awareness of the impact and effect of the harm from computer crime and educating users on the protocols and ethics of proper Internet use. Apart from cracking down on Internet crime, it is crucial to induce 'healthy Internet' practices among the younger generation. According to Vice-Premier Li Lanqing, 'Supervision over culture-oriented entertainment business needs to be strengthened to provide a healthy social atmosphere for young people.' Places of entertainment, including Internet cafés, are under strict supervision to prevent gambling, prostitution, drug trafficking and other crimes.[46]

Studies in China have shown that young people absorb 90% of their learning, including social knowledge, rules of the game, life philosophy, and concept of value, through mass communication media, including electronic media such as the Internet. To promote healthy, ethical, moral and responsible use of the Internet, the CCP organised a host of activities through the China Communist Youth League to educate young people on proper computer and Internet use; for example, issuing the 'National Youth Civilised (use of) Internet Pact' (*Quanguo qingshaonian wangluo wenming gongyue*).[47] The PRC government also organised many seminars to inform the public, especially parents and teachers, about how young people think, act and communicate with computers and through the Internet. The major issue is how to communicate and teach the younger generation traditional Chinese morals and contemporary Communist social responsibilities in the Internet age. Ultimately all agreed that the young Internet-bound generation should be imbued with a stronger sense of social responsibility as Chinese nationals while exercising their new-found freedom as Internet citizens.[48]

Management control

The Chinese government thinks it is important to control computer crime and Internet abuse, not only through law and by way of punishment but also with good management of computer use and a secure Internet environment. In a symposium on Internet security and management, Yang Zhenquan, vice-director of the Information Office of the State Council, commented that Internet security through effective management is a worldwide trend. '[With] no security and effective management, there will be no healthy development of the Internet to speak of, not to say the legal rights and overall interests of websites and social public to be undermined, that's a consensus view reached by the International community.'[49]

Proper computer management as an effective crime prevention measure covers a wide spectrum of areas, including taking all reasonable and prudent steps to achieve both personnel security, for example hiring trustworthy computer operators; and physical security such as securing computer facilities; enhancing operations security, and establishing firewalls.

The biggest threat to computer security is people. In fact empirical studies and police data indicate that it is the internal staff of the victimised organisations that commit most computer crimes. Developing a sound personnel security programme, including employee selection processes and staff training, will contribute much to the prevention and detection of computer crime and abuses.

In addition to personnel security, physical security is vital in preventing people from gaining unauthorised access to a computer facility. Lastly, the Chinese government hopes that computer users and organisations will take steps to secure their computer operations from external intruders, for example by building firewalls, and preventing internal abuse, for example by adopting access codes.

To facilitate proper management of computer security, the PRC has promulgated a number of laws and regulations assigning responsibilities and providing for best practices, including 'Management Measures on Internet Security Protection', 'Provisional Implementation Measures on Internet Management', and 'Provisional Regulations on the Management of Computer Information System Security'.

Technology control

One of the most effective ways to prevent computer crime and control Internet misuse is through technology. Conversely, design weaknesses and program flaws in an IT system might expose computers to hackers from without, and abusers from within. Fighting computer crime thus requires advanced technical know-how. Here China is at a distinct disadvantage. Thus far, China imports most of its IT, under licence. The imported IT often comes with less than perfectly secure design features and software programs. As a result, China's computer security experts and public security personnel have to keep playing a catch-up game to secure Chinese computer systems and users from people or organisations that are knowledgeable about, and intent on, exploiting the technical flaws inherent in imported computer technology, including foreign intelligence agencies.

As countermeasures, China established uniform national security standards for information technology and communication networks, based on international conventions and norms.[50] For example, as of 1997, China had established through legislation 13 national standards and six military standards in information security technology.

In this section we have seen how the Chinese government, following the theory of comprehensive crime control, attempts to prevent (*fang*), combat (*da*), and regulate and control (*zhi*) cyber-crime with different kinds of measures: legislation, education, management and technology. In the next section we will discuss the impact and effectiveness of such a comprehensive control approach to cyberspace governance and Internet regulation in China.

Impact and Effectiveness of Comprehensive Control of Computer Crime

The overall effectiveness of such comprehensive control in preventing and reducing cyber-crime must be assessed according to its stated goals and objectives.

Preventing corrupting influence on youth

In preventing (actually limiting) the corrupting influence of the Internet on young people, the comprehensive approach measures have to a large extent been successful. On this front, the PRC's concern and approach is similar to that of other countries. In fighting against Internet vice, the Chinese government adopts a highly conservative traditional approach. It draws no distinction between vice in the street and vice on the box. Gambling and pornography are considered immoral, evil and corrupting for the public. While the battlefield is now a virtual one and the instruments deployed include advanced technology, the control strategy is one and the same — patient education and severe punishment. People, especially young people, must be made to understand right and wrong and to distinguish moral from immoral.

The 'Civilised Use of the Internet Pact' is a national youth campaign for moral and civilised use of the Internet by young people and is vigorously pursued as a long-term strategy. Unlike the United States, China is able to promote the campaign through mass education, heavy punishment and strict enforcement with relative ease. The China Communist Youth League's work with various local communities gets personal commitment and active participation from youth in its fight against Internet crime.[51]

One major criticism of this educational approach is that the campaign is 'top-down' imposed by the central authority and carried out by government officials. Young people have little say in the conception and implementation of the campaign, which affects their personal interests and freedom on the Internet. In short, young people feel alienated.

Interestingly, some US officials support the idea of having young people learn and practice 'cyber-ethics'.[52] Like the Chinese, the US Department of Justice initiated the Cybercitizen Partnership Program[53] to teach young people the right ways to use the Internet. The department maintains a cyber-ethics web-page to provide information, generate discussion and raise awareness.[54]

On the enforcement front, strict licensing requirements, restrictive opening hours and persistent Internet café raids are having an impact on public access to Internet vice by targeted and at-risk youth groups. The introduction of safe Internet cafés is another proactive measure to reduce young people's exposure to any corrupting influences, bad associations and tempting criminal opportunities by offering the Internet as a healthy place to work and play. In this respect, the Chinese government is applying Felson's 'routine activities' theory in a textbook like manner: attempting to remove the motivated offender, reduce crime opportunity and provide for guardianship as the means of preventing Internet crime.[55] There is much more work to be done in the days ahead, as noted in the teleconference jointly held by eight government agencies in early May 2002. A special control programme is being planned to clean up the Internet further.[56]

Preventing people from accessing anti-government information

Until very recently, China was a closed society. The communist leadership is now greatly concerned with the adverse impact of the free flow of information on the dominance of communist ideology and the legitimacy of CCP rule. It is concerned to prevent people from being exposed to capitalist propaganda that is polluting the culture, for example by spreading a decadent lifestyle; it opposes Western ideas and ideology that subverts CCP rule, such as criticism over the handling of the 4th of June incident or the Falun Gong, and it fears the promotion of human rights, which might alienate the people. China has been doing its utmost to control communication in and out of China, especially via electronic channels.[57] For example, in December 1999, China Democracy Party founder Wang Youcai was sentenced to 11 years in prison for subversion. Two of his crimes were sending e-mails to exiled Chinese dissidents in the United States and accepting overseas funds to buy a computer.

However, China's effort to censor the flow of information is never very successful. *VIP Reference*, an electronic magazine based in Washington, was able to bypass the Chinese Internet censorship system by way of e-mail. The group managed to distribute its pro-democracy magazine throughout China with a mass e-mailing to about 250 000 addresses compiled from publicly available e-mail lists.[58] Unlike objectionable websites that contain pornography and gambling content, this kind of ad hoc information dissemination arriving 'on the fly' from abroad is so unpredictable that the PR China government finds it hard to prevent until after the fact. Since millions of e-mails are exchanged each day, the MPS does not have the resources or capacity to monitor more than a fraction of the information coming into China each day. Moreover, technology is changing so rapidly that it is impossible to filter out all suspicious or objectionable websites or materials. The best the PRC law enforcement officials can hope for is individual monitoring based on intelligence or profiling, and imposing severe punishment in the hope of a deterrent effect. Overall, the strategy of the PRC authorities in controlling objectionable Internet information through censorship at its source is not working. The CCP is left with indoctrinating the people on political and ideological correctness and educating them about patriotism, in other words combating free competition in the marketplace of ideas and ideals.

As long as China still benefits politically, economically, socially and culturally from the use of the Internet, it is politically unlikely and technologically not feasible for the PR China government to curb all external websites and cleanse them of unwholesome content.

Providing for a safe Internet environment

In building a secure Internet environment for e-commerce and protecting networks from attack, the effectiveness of the PRC comprehensive control scheme is not apparent. From our earlier discussion on Internet legislation and administrative regulation, a *comprehensive* legal framework that appears to protect network security and e-commerce does not exist. In terms of technological measures, China is not well equipped, and is poorly resourced to deal with the myriad of security concerns that afflict the e-commerce community and are demanding attention.

Conclusion

China's economy cannot prosper without IT. On the other hand, the Internet changes the availability, flow and content of information to millions of Chinese people, in the process transforming their values and affecting their interests in unpredictable and uncontrollable ways. Given such a reality, Chinese leaders strongly believe that cyberspace must be governed and policed through a comprehensive control scheme. Through the combination of legislation, education, management and technological measures, China attempts to develop a unique model in cyberspace governance and Internet regulation. Internet development in China had been so rapid and dynamic that it has outpaced the PRC's traditional legal and regulatory systems. The Internet-related regulations put forth thus far tend to be driven by events, and develop in a piecemeal and a reactive mode. Following accession to the WTO, legislation on e-commerce, dealing with issues such as digital signatures and encryption, is urgently needed.[59]

From a technological perspective, China needs to speed up research and development on crucial IT products such as encryption, firewalls and routers, to overcome weaknesses in imported and off-the-shelf IT and communication security technology. As long as China has to rely heavily on imported technology, it will not be able to secure its computer networks from foreign computer attacks.

Human resources are a key to effective and efficient cyberspace governance and Internet regulation. China needs to put substantial investment into training more technically competent and ethically disposed computer professionals to provide for proper and effective security management and control of computer systems and networks.

Cyber-crime is an emerging problem in China, the impact of which has yet to be completely accounted for, much less fully realised. The Internet knows no borders. Cyber-crime, in its virtual world, very often needs to be tackled by the joint efforts of various countries. Seeking international cooperation — in setting standards, exchanging information, coordinating law enforcement — is crucial if China is to prevent and control computer crime in the future.

Finally, the study of cyberspace governance in China is just beginning and current circumstances call for more scientific research by scholars, researchers and computer professionals.

4

Cyber-Crime and E-Business in China: A Risk Perception Perspective

Ivan S K Chiu*

With the rise of the information and network society, computers have become a vitally important tool in every aspect of society throughout the world. The influence of computers in our lives ranges from simple tasks such as creating documents and graphics and printing reports to complicated functions such as transferring money, and equipment control information.[1] In countries all over the world, more and more computers are being used, and China is no exception.[2]

The Internet, in turn, has come to assume an important role in computing. Its influence is so widespread that it is an almost indispensable part of daily life. The Chinese government accepts this with both optimism and trepidation. Although the Internet can help link China to the rest of the world and facilitate commercial activities, keeping China apace with communication and information technology, it also opens doors to the risks of cyber-crime. Many Chinese companies now use the Internet for electronic business (e-business). E-business is defined as electronic forms of commercial activities conducted over the Internet (Sterrett & Shah 1998: 43; Turban & King 2003: 3). With China's entry into the World Trade Organization, expectations are that the role of e-business in China will increase, but its development is placed at risk by the equally widespread development of cyber-crime; consumers may consider e-business to be risky and therefore may not be willing to accept it as a reliable method of conducting business.

The Current Development of e-Business in China

At the end of April 2002, more than 56 million people in China were able to access the Internet at home, the largest Internet population in the Asia-Pacific region and, after the United Sates, the second largest Internet population in the world. The figure represented only about 5% of households in China[3] but the Internet uptake is growing rapidly, as illustrated by a China Internet Network Information Center (CNNIC) survey, which indicated there were 68 million Chinese Internet users[4] by June 2003.

The CNNIC survey, probing characteristics of websites in China, also showed that as of 31 December 2002, only 8.7% of websites were commercial, and 78.8% were enterprise websites.[5] Among the commercial websites, only 68.5% were involved in e-business; of these 24.4% were involved in business to consumers (B2C), 16.4% in business to business (B2B), 13.4% in online games, 4.9% in online hotel reservation, 3.5% in online stock trading, 3.1% online booking, and 1.9% online auctions and 0.9% in other business.[6] Among the enterprise websites, only 22.9% were involved in e-business, of which 7.5% were B2C, 7.3% were B2B and 8.1% were online tender.[7]

In 2002, a study by British market research company Taylor Nelson Sofres showed a big increase in B2C in Asia and the Pacific region (Sanchez 2002: 1). From such sources, it was difficult to conclude whether or not e-business websites were well developed in China, although potential markets for e-business in China seem to be bright.[8] Nonetheless, many impediments such as cyber-crime could hinder the development of e-business in China. In a study by MasterCard International, about 65% of respondents expressed concern for privacy, which is related to the issue of risk, as a hindrance to using e-business (Lisker 2001: 236).

The present study therefore reviews the relationship between perception of the risk of cyber-crime among Chinese Internet users, and e-business, particularly in B2C transactions, in China.

Cyber-Crime

Donn Parker (1976, 1983, 1998) and David Carter (1995) identify three types of cyber-crime. First, cyber-crime is where computers become the focus of unlawful activity. For example, the behaviours of hackers / crackers are acts of cyber-crime because they illegally enter computers, steal data and / or damage them.[9] Second, cyber-crime is where computers are used to commit an offence; for example, for disseminating pornography. Third, cyber-crime is where computers are used to store evidence about an offence (Casey 2000: 16–17; Herrera 2001: 167–8).[10] In this discussion, the term 'cyber-crime' refers to the first situation.

Cyber-crime can be responsible for seriously undermining an economy by causing huge losses to companies, even though the exact figure may be difficult to determine. Part of the reason for incomplete figures is that a company that has become a cyber-crime victim may not be willing to make a police report for fear of denting its own image.[11] Nevertheless, a survey conducted by the FBI of the United States and the Computer Security Institute reported that computer crime in 2002 resulted in losses of US$20.1 billion.[12] Findings from another survey that cooperated with the FBI pointed out that only 35% of victim companies were willing to admit they suffered from cyber-crime. The victims, however, contributed to a loss of at least US$37.78 billion in 2001 — a disastrous increase over the 2000 figure.[13] Reports suggest that hackers / crackers have contributed to financial losses of US$150–200 billion worldwide since 1999.[14]

The risk of cyber-crime poses a new challenge to society (Williams 2001: 152–3). As pointed out by Turnbull, cyber-crime can be committed at any time, anywhere, and authorities charged with investigating it need to spend more time and effort, compared to traditional crimes, to locate and detect the offenders.[15] Police and security officers, for example, need to learn how to locate electronic evidence and deal with cross-border issues in tracing suspected hackers / crackers.[16] The risk of cyber-crime has become a global issue and is now affecting almost all countries. In Australia, 67% of respondents said they had been victims of computer- and cyber-crime (Smith and Urbas 2001).[17] The risks of cyber-crime are so serious that in 1999 former US President Bill Clinton allocated US$1.46 billion to improve government computer security.[18] International cooperation to combat the risks of cyber-crime (Bullwinkel 2001: 87; Shehu 2001: 120–2) is progressing.

The risks of cyber-crime not only fall on the governments and e-business companies but on individual Internet users as well. In commenting on a survey on cyber-crime conducted in 2001 by the Confederation of British Industry (CBI) and other parties, including PricewaterhouseCoopers, the director-general of the CBI, Digby Jones, said cyber-crime could hinder the growth of e-business because it caused people to be afraid of possible financial loss.[19] His remark may reflect the attitudes of some people towards e-business. As presented in 2001 by the Australian Internet Industry Association and Deloitte Touche Tohmatsu, hackers / crackers launched 5 million attacks a day, or 2 billion attacks a year. This means that on average, hackers / crackers launched 35 attacks on the same company every day.[20] The Australian Computer

Emergency Response Team concurred; recording a sharp increase in the numbers of computer security incidents reported from 1816 in 1999, to 8197 in 2000.[21] According to figures reported by China's Ministry of Public Security, 1000 cyber-crimes occurred in China in 1999 (NA 2000: 1). With such security concerns, what do Chinese Internet users think about e-business? Do they regard it risky, thus posing a personal threat? Before looking at the security risk perception among Chinese Internet users towards e-business, I briefly review the idea of security risk perception.

Security Risk Perception

The reliance of all kinds of social systems on computers is so complete that computer breakdowns or failures may cause a serious social malfunction. Employees may be unable to receive their salary, social benefits or bank interest. Companies may be unable to conduct their normal business because they cannot perform normal accounting, payroll, inventory and other data-processing functions. The effect is not limited to individual companies but may extend to business partners; the business partner may in turn be affected, and so the chain reaction continues.[22] All of us, experts and lay people alike, as individuals or collectively, have to face the risk of computer failure (Starr 1969: 1234–5).

Computer failure is not the only risk. With the Internet's rise, the chance of a slip-up in security while conducting a business transaction or sending data is very real. Personal data can be easily and unintentionally disclosed to others, such as through communicating software like ICQ, AOL or Microsoft NetMeeting. Cyber-thieves may be able to access a personal or security number without the individual knowing it, and use it to commit a crime; for example, a credit card number may be used to make an unauthorised purchase of goods. With the perception that transmitting personal data by Internet is unsafe, many computer users take measures to minimise the risk. One precaution is in the selection of computer software, some of which can be easily accessed unlawfully. A recent instance of security concerns was illustrated when the Beijing government selected Linux rather than Microsoft products.[23]

Survey on Risk Perception at Peking University

In this chapter, findings on computer risk perceptions come from two surveys; one conducted by the author using a sample of students at Peking University,

Beijing, (PKU), the other a half-yearly survey conducted by the CNNIC examining the relationship between cyber-crime and the development of e-business, and perceptions on the risks of using the Internet in China.

In the PKU survey, educated youth were targeted with 250 questionnaire-based face-to-face interviews taking place between 4 October and 19 November 2001. The sample was divided into computer major, and non-computer major, students. Questionnaires were distributed in university dormitories and computer laboratories and, to safeguard the confidentiality of respondents, all original and back-up photocopied questionnaires were destroyed after analysis.[24]

In all, 202 questionnaires were completed, 90 from postgraduate students, and 112 from undergraduates: a response rate of 80.8%. Of the respondents, 55.4% were computer majors, 44.6% non-computer majors, 60.9% were male,[25] 39.5% were in the 20–25 age group, another 39.5% were below 20, 43.6% had been using computers for one to three years, 63.9% regarded their computer skills as average; 34.8% normally used computers more than 30 hours a week.[26]

The CNNIC is one of five organisations that provide Internet protocol (IP) addresses and domain names to either end users or Internet service providers in China. China connected to the Internet in 1994 and in June 1996 began to offer an Internet service to commercial and private users. In June 1997, the Chinese government institutionalised regulation of the Internet by setting up the CNNIC to control Internet use, especially the IP addresses and domains. Up to July 2003, the CNNIC had conducted 12 surveys on Internet usage in China.[27] The CNNIC survey of January 2002 is used as it enables a fair comparison with the PKU survey, both being conducted at a similar time.

The CNNIC twice-yearly surveys on the use of the Internet in China target mainly two groups of potential respondents: householders with a fixed telephone line, and high school students living in school. Householders are further divided by province. Respondents were approached at random by telephone, both in urban and rural areas. The confidence level was set at 95%. For students, 120 high schools were randomly selected, with 50 students randomly selected from each school. The confidence level was also set at 95%.[28]

Findings

Findings of the research are presented below; first, showing the opinions of respondents on hackers / crackers and, secondly, showing the security risk perceptions of respondents, together with their e-business behaviour. Findings are then compared with those from the CNNIC's survey, whether appropriate and possible, and differences are discussed.

View on hackers / crackers

While few respondents had first-hand experience of hackers / crackers, they were seen as posing a threat to society. In addition, respondents described the likely effects of an intrusion or 'invasion' by hackers / crackers on themselves as serious or moderate.

As can be seen from Table 4.1, most respondents had rarely experienced an invasion from hackers / crackers. The finding was, however, different from the CNNIC result, which found that 63.3% of respondents had had their computers invaded in the previous year (CNNIC 1/2002).

Table 4.1 Personal experience of hackers / crackers

	Very often	*Sometimes*	*Rarely*	*Never*	*No Idea*
Personal experience of hackers / crackers	7 (4.2%)	15 (8.9%)	75 (44.6%)	62 (36.9%)	9 (5.4%)

Note: In Tables 4.1, 4.2, 4.3 and 4.5 the first number is the number of respondents (n), with percentages in brackets. Due to rounding, the sum of the percentage in some of the items may not equal 100%.

In Table 4.2, while respondents had rarely experienced an intrusion, most agreed that hackers / crackers posed a threat to society and the effects were moderate to serious (see Table 4.3). The survey found a much lower experience of hackers / crackers than among the CNNIC sample. Results suggested that Peking University students share the belief, along with other Internet users, that hackers / crackers pose a threat to society and that any intrusion would be serious. This, in turn, affected security risk perceptions towards e-business.

Table 4.2 Threat of hackers / crackers to society

	Strongly agree	*Agree*	*Disagree*	*Strongly disagree*	*No opinion*
Do you agree that hackers/crackers pose a great threat to society?	15 (7.5%)	91 (45.3%)	70 (34.8%)	6 (3.0%)	19 (9.5%)

Table 4.3 Self-description on the effects of invasion by hackers / crackers

	Very serious	*Serious*	*Moderate*	*Minor*	*None*
Effect of hacker / cracker intrusion	9 (9.3%)	37 (38.1%)	35 (36.1%)	11 (11.3%)	5 (5.2%)

Perceptions of security risk

Most respondents (78.6%) had installed firewall software to protect themselves from risks when surfing the Internet. This suggested that risk perception among the university respondents was high and matched the CNNIC survey, which found that 64.6% of respondents had installed firewall software as the main method of Internet risk protection (CNNIC 1/2002).

Table 4.4 shows that most respondents send their personal or important information by using encrypted e-mail or via the Internet with encryption. (Encryption is a kind of secure format for sending information to and from computers. The use of encryption increases the security of personal or important information from interception from unauthorised persons during data transfer.) The result matched the CNNIC findings that 45.0% of respondents were satisfied with the protection of their personal privacy over the Internet (CNNIC 1/2002) and suggests that many feel uncomfortable about Internet security.

Table 4.4 Sending personal or important information (n and %)

Sending personal or important information	*Very often*	*Sometimes*	*Rarely*	*Never*
In e-mail, without encryption (secure format)	50 (25.8%)	39 (20.1%)	49 (25.3%)	56 (28.9%)
In e-mail, with encryption (secure format)	29 (15.3%)	69 (36.5%)	54 (28.6%)	37 (19.6%)
Via the Internet, without encryption (secure format)	27 (14.2%)	51 (26.8%)	62 (32.6%)	50 (26.3%)
Via the Internet, with encryption (secure format)	17 (9.2%)	73 (39.5%)	49 (26.5%)	46 (24.9%)
In a computer that is not yours, via e-mail	24 (12.5%)	38 (19.8%)	70 (36.5%)	60 (31.3%)
In a computer that is not yours, via the Internet	23 (12.0%)	37 (19.4%)	70 (36.6%)	61 (31.9%)

Figures also suggest that Chinese Internet users have a high perception of risk for their computers or their data, and that most had installed firewall software. To protect their personal data, they tended to use encryption during data transmission. In short, they were worried about the security of their computers and their data. So, how did the perception of high security risk affect e-business behaviour?

E-business behaviour

From Table 4.5, about half of respondents agreed that purchasing from e-business websites was a widespread practice. In Table 4.6, although the respondents agreed that e-business was widespread, most surfed e-business websites only occasionally or not very often. In the CNNIC survey, 49.8% of respondents sometimes accessed e-business.

Table 4.5 Agree that purchasing from e-commerce websites is a widespread practice in your society

	Number	*%*
Strongly agree	24	12.0
Agree	85	42.5
Disagree	69	34.5
Strongly disagree	10	5.0
No opinion	12	6.0

Table 4.6 reveals that the PKU respondents occasionally or never made purchases through e-business, although 13% did sometimes or often. In the CNNIC survey, 68.4% of respondents had not purchased goods or services through e-business during the previous year. The figures suggest that users did not purchase goods or services from e-business websites very often but that, among the computer literate (such as the PKU students), some were willing to try.

Table 4.6 Proportion visiting and purchasing from e-business websites

	Visiting Number	*%*	*Purchasing Number*	*%*
Very often	22	11	9	4.7
Sometimes	26	13	16	8.3
Not very often	64	32	32	16.6
Occasionally	83	41.5	64	33.2
Never	5	2.5	72	37.3

Security was the main concern in using e-business. Table 4.7 shows that most respondents preferred to pay by cash on delivery. The CNNIC survey found that 42.8% preferred paying this way. Moreover, if bills were more than RMB1000, 73.3% would want to pay by cash on delivery of goods, showing concerns about security when paying for purchases online.[29]

Table 4.7 Preferred method of payment for online purchases

	Number	*%*
Online payment	7	5.8
Mail the cheque to the company	7	5.8
Deposit to the specific bank account	11	9.1
Cash on delivery	93	76.9
Others	3	2.6

Respondents considered security (47.5%) and convenience (30.5%) as their main concerns in choosing a particular e-business payment method. Overall, figures from both surveys suggested that Internet users in China are still not happy about adopting e-business despite its convenience. Most still go to traditional shops and, for those willing to deal with e-business, they tend to regard it as a security risk due to concerns about hackers / crackers. Although not all respondents had experienced invasions, they considered that the theft of personal information was a risk in e-business, and they tended to choose cash on delivery payment method instead. The suggestion is that current e-business fails to offer a sense of security to customers and, therefore, is hindering the development of e-business in China.

Implications

Implications of the risks of using e-business among Chinese Internet users are of concern to three interests: business, consumers, and the Chinese government.

The PKU study shows that Chinese Internet users still regard e-business as a risky activity. Those who conduct e-business with consumers (i.e. B2C) have to bear in mind that success of e-business in China depends on how acceptable it is to consumers. A study (BCS SocioTechnical Group 2003: 27) has pointed out that companies using e-business should take information such as the educational level and cultural background of consumers into consideration. The perception of risk among Chinese Internet users towards e-business is unlikely to see a great change in a short time. To have successful e-business in China, the proprietors of e-business need to spend time and effort in convincing consumers it is secure. They could also use other business strategies to win support of their targeted consumers. For example, they could guarantee prompt delivery of goods (McKinsey 2001: 35), or they could, as in the case of Eguo.com, set up offline stores to supplement their online e-business (Murphy 2001: 36).

Given the views of Chinese Internet users on the risks of e-business, the Chinese government has three possibilities open to it. First, it could work hand in hand with e-business to combat cyber-crime by developing legislation to protect the safety of computer information and Internet security (Urbas 2001: 64). Regulation can help combat cyber-crime and help foster the development of e-business in China.

Second, the government could help promote e-business indirectly. At present, the central and local governments have created their own homepages and introduced and explained their functions and their place to the world. They also use the Internet to disseminate public information and announcements. The central government could go further and create a secure digital or e-governance project to show that using the Internet is safe and reliable in China.[30] Once this is set up, the efficiency of the Chinese government would be improved and more Chinese people could experience an online solution that will help them better accept e-business.

Third, the Chinese government could facilitate the running of e-business in China, as State Councillor Wu Yi stated: 'promotion of trade facilitation is the shared goal of customs departments and the business community' (*Asiainfo Daily China News*, 14 August 2001). Such an e-commerce approach could help reduce the time to complete custom procedures (although it cannot reduce perceptions of the risk of B2C among Chinese Internet users), and help e-businesses reduce their operational cost and demonstrate the usefulness of secure Internet transactions.

The development of e-business in China could be beneficial to Chinese society. Nonetheless, the perception of a high security risk arising from the threat of cyber-crime has undoubtedly hindered development. The perception among the PKU respondents is affected by whether or not they have an accurate understanding and appreciation of the problem of cyber-crime and e-business. Their understanding and appreciation, in turn, depends on whether they have received accurate information on the issue. The ability and willingness to learn is affected by the interaction between humans and their environment (Morgan 1981). Even though not all people agree on a causal relationship between perception and behaviour, the more knowledge people have about cyber-crime and e-business, the more options are available to them and this can only facilitate the development of e-business. E-business could flourish in China by focusing on increasing knowledge among about the cyberworld, both in business and in criminal activity, through the support of appropriate educational programmes in schools, the workplace and the mass media.

5

Governance in the Digital Age: Policing the Internet in Hong Kong

Laurie Yiu Chung Lau*

The early predictions of anarchy on the Internet have not come to pass, at least not in Hong Kong or in many other parts of the world. In Western countries such as the United Kingdom, the discourse over policing the Internet has shifted from legal regulation to the broader issues of governance and victimisation. In Hong Kong, however, much of the discourse concerning the Internet still focuses on issues of law enforcement and the investigation of crimes, what Wall (2001a) has called 'the maintenance of order'. This chapter explores the roles of public and privately funded bodies involved in 'policing' the Internet in Hong Kong, the dichotomy of private and public policing, and the governance of cyberspace in Hong Kong. Which of these agencies regulate what in Hong Kong? Who, if anyone, has control over cyberspace? How is control achieved? How and why do Hong Kong's policing of the Internet differ from that in the United Kingdom?

Hong Kong, Economic City

Hong Kong is an economic city, an international centre of financial and commercial flows between East and West. Its geographical location has made it a trading centre since the nineteenth century and over the years, Hong Kong people have themselves developed a reputation for their entrepreneurial skills and business savvy. Domestically, Hong Kong people are financially literate in a fashion rare in other societies. They develop a reputation for risk-taking, openness to new ideas and absorbing new technologies at a fast pace. It is in this climate that the Internet has taken root and grown in Hong Kong.

The late 1990s witnessed the boom of e-commerce in Hong Kong: dot.com stock prices rocketed and attracted many local and overseas blue-chip investors. For example, the initial public offering of the Tom.Com shares in Hong Kong led to half a million local residents queuing up on busy streets to apply for shares. As H Lau of Celestial Asia Securities Holding said, 'Two years ago, no one knew what a dotcom was. Today, there are literally hundreds of players, all looking to be the next big thing.'[1] Similarly, when in April 1999 Richard Li (son of Li Ka Shing, Hong Kong's richest tycoon) announced that he was going to turn a small telecom equipment distributor into Asia's premier Internet company (Pacific Century CyberWorks or PCCW), he sparked frenzied buying on Hong Kong's stock market.[2] At that time, ideas rather than concrete business plans were capital, carrying a money value and meriting financial investment. For a few years, this cyber-bubble seemed as though it would only expand and never burst. Local media in Hong Kong recounted each remarkable story of the local technological companies, each instance of wonderful cyber-entrepreneurship. The prevailing view was that if one was not on the Internet bandwagon, then one was missing out. As in the United Kingdom, there was a frenzied rush to take part in cyberspace business. When the Internet bubble did eventually burst, however, there were serious financial consequences. The scenario was remarkably reminiscent of Tulipmania and the South Sea bubble. In Hong Kong, the share price of PCCW dropped to just over 10% of its highest value and, just as ordinary members of the public had participated in the dot.com success, so now they bore its losses.

Public understanding of cyber-crime

The Hong Kong media tend largely to write on the good news about new technology businesses rather than the bad. By contrast, the UK media coverage has covered both sides of the story, cyber-entrepreneurship heroism as well as cautionary tales of the downside of technological advancement. As a result, stories about cyber-criminality (such as fraud and child pornography) have received a wider coverage and debate in the United Kingdom than in Hong Kong. Overall, the UK public is better informed about such issues.

There are a number of factors contributing to this absence of a Hong Kong discourse on the darker side of the Internet. One is the Hong Kong press. The Hong Kong media are primarily market-driven, reflecting the culture and ethos of the society. Ever since the mid-1980s, the interests of the Hong Kong mass media have largely been dictated by the market (so-called 'market-driven journalism').[3] This is the result of the corporatisation of many local newspapers. There are needs to attract public funds and minimise owners' risks. A few big newspapers dominate the market and block new entries, making the survival of other smaller, family-owned newspapers difficult.[4] Big media firms are far more able to win the price war between newspapers and media groups. A few of the most popular Chinese language newspapers now dominate the market and set the rules of the game. They have been able to exert immense influence over matters such as output level, technology, and styles of news reporting.[5] Consequently, news and opinion formation are dominated by a few corporations, effectively narrowing channels for debate and the dissemination of information. As Lee had argued: 'They can use their financial power to ward off potential challengers and elbow weaker competitors out of the market by raiding creative talents, fixing prices through price wars ... Moreover, they can harass their critics with legal action.'[6]

'Yellow' tabloid journalism aimed at the mass market has thrived in this market-driven environment. Bureaucratic controls of the press in Hong Kong have been weak, partly because of the government's laissez-faire policy but also because control of the press raises issues of political censorship to which the Hong Kong public (especially after 1997) is sensitive.

There is, however, another factor that has contributed to the relative lack of serious investigative journalism in Hong Kong. Hong Kong had been a British colony for 154 years until its sovereignty reverted to Mainland China on 1 July 1997. From the 1840s onwards, Hong Kong was a trading port. Socially, politically, and economically, the majority Chinese population was governed by a small community of European elite. In the early days, those Chinese appeared to have come to Hong Kong attracted partly by its liberal trading regime and partly by the desire to escape poverty and oppression in China. Later, in the 1950s and 1960s, waves of refugees from China occurred. Hong Kong today, therefore, is a society with little historical continuity.[7] This has had an enormous impact on the territory from the socio-political, socio-cultural and socio-economic standpoint. According to Lau and others, the Chinese who came to Hong Kong saw it principally as a stepping stone to another life, probably in America, Britain or Taiwan. Their normative orientation was, Lau says, short-term and materialistic, valuing social stability above political participation and securing their families' longer-term futures.[8]

One consequence of this 'ethos of the Hong Kong Chinese' was a low rate of participation in political and civic affairs. Fatalism may also have played its part, since the exclusion from the political sphere of all but a small circle of Chinese elite provided them with no opportunity to influence civic affairs.

One legacy has been the lack of lively public debate around controversial issues. Thus while the character of the media discourages critical journalism of the Internet, this civic apathy discourages public debate about such issues as the Internet and its impact on public and private life. Public understanding of cyber-crime is limited and discussion of how it should be policed is virtually non-existent.

Understanding the impact of cyber-crime in Hong Kong

To some, the term 'cyber-crime' signifies no more than behaviour ordinarily regarded as harmful in everyday life, but which is carried out via the computer.[9] They may be right — the concept is still largely a media invention with little or no foundation in law.[10] Indeed, the law is struggling to get to grips with this phenomenon, and one issue it has to face is whether cyber-crime is simply ordinary crime committed by virtual means, or whether it is qualitatively different.

Poorly understood as it may be, the word 'cyber-crime' nevertheless frequently invokes a panic response from media, policymakers, politicians, academics and the public alike. In Hong Kong, the media provide ad hoc reports on cyber-crime from time to time but responses to these reports vary, from major to little or no reaction. The strongest reaction has tended to come from the publicly funded police organisation (principally the Hong Kong Police, or HKP) and a few politicians. Local media report and repeat what these two groups have said but there is little independent, in-depth analysis of either the phenomenon itself or reactions to it. There is also little or no response from academia, and even less from the established civic pressure groups. In the United Kingdom one might expect all of them to engage in public debate about the 'dangers' of the Internet and appropriate forms of control. In Hong Kong, no such debate has been taking place.

Local understanding of the impact of cyber-crime is therefore fairly shallow. Viewpoints are very often limited to brief reports about privacy issues. This is not because Hong Kong has no cyber-crime. Internet virus / intrusion, illegal Internet gambling, hacking / cracking (unauthorised access or access to a computer with criminal or dishonest intent) and the like form the majority of computer-related crimes reported to the police in Hong Kong (see Table 5.1).

The upward trend of cases of online deception is obvious, from two cases in 1997 to 103 in 2003. Although such an increase is no crime wave, the key point is that it has drawn little or no analysis, perhaps because criminological

Table 5.1 Computer-related crimes: reported cases in Hong Kong, 1993–2003

	1993	*1994*	*1995*	*1996*	*1997*	*1998*	*1999*	*2000*	*2001*	*2002*	*2003*
Hacking / cracking	1	5	4	4	7	13	238	275	114	164	403
E-fraud / theft and others	3	6	8	13	8	17	57	49	28 [8]	30 [6]	66 [8]
Online deception	0	0	0	0	2	1	18	29	65	64	103
Criminal damage	0	1	2	4	3	3	4	15	27	16	16
Total	4	12	14	21	20	34	317	368	235	274	588

Sources: MingPao Daily 20 January 2000, p. A6; Hong Kong Police, Technology Crime Division; see Table 11.1–11.3 for further details. Figures in [ ] brackets refer to the number of e-banking thefts.

research in Hong Kong is still in its infancy. There is little indigenous research on computer crime, Internet governance and regulation in Hong Kong. There is also a lack of commonly referenced core literature — until 2003, there was no professional journal devoted specifically to indigenous criminology. There has been a Criminological Society in the territory for some years, but only in 1999 did The University of Hong Kong establish a Centre for Criminology to promote and coordinate indigenous studies of crime and criminal justice. As might be expected, the lack of systematic indigenous research and debate has affected the discussion of cyber-crime in Hong Kong, with knock-on effects for informed policymaking and practice. In this regard, however, Hong Kong has much in common with the rest of the world outside the United Kingdom, United States and Australia, since most countries appear to have been slow to develop such expertise.

The situation in the United Kingdom is quite different. There is an established field of criminology within and outside academia. It has been less difficult for a new field to emerge within UK criminology and for criminologists to shift the focus of their studies to include cyber-crime, although differences remain between them as to its nature and definition. Criminality on the Internet is still a relatively new field. There is, in general, a lack of consensus as to exactly what it entails, though discussion of the topic within and outside academia has increased, particularly in the last two years. One issue is how to view cyber-crime: from a criminological perspective, like Wall[11] and Levi,[12] or from the computer security perspective, like Parker;[13] such debates further the knowledge of criminality on the Internet.

Academics in law as well as science and technology have been involved in debates about regulation of the Internet. Policymakers and lobby groups have raised public awareness of the problems of Internet policing, and the UK media have a much longer tradition of critically discussing the social impact of technology.

Unlike Hong Kong, the strong political tradition of liberty in the United Kingdom has also brought about pressure groups devoted to monitoring the infringement of civil liberties. They have taken a particular interest in attempts to police the Internet. Other groups have proved willing and able to challenge the pronouncements of technological and scientific authorities on the potential impacts of the Internet on everyday life. This strong tradition of civic pressure groups participating in shaping the news and policy (including policing policy) is reflected in the nature of the UK debates on issues such as cyber-liberty and child pornography on the Internet. This critical mass of interest in the subject is lacking in Hong Kong.

Electronic governance in Hong Kong

Hong Kong's long-standing social and cultural norms, as well as its style of governance, have affected discussion about policing the terrestrial world as well as the cyberworld. Hong Kong is not a democracy. Issues such as policing have no democratic inputs. The structure of governance is top-down, the power to govern is always firmly in the hands of the Chief Executive (formerly the Governor). Under this top-down approach, political participation has been, and still is, greatly restricted. Colonial Hong Kong was regarded as a kind of 'administrative state'[14] governed by the local bureaucracy subject only to the control of the Governor. The core members of this local bureaucracy were administrative officers who were encouraged to make policy assessments and assume responsibility from a relatively young age, in preparation for their eventual rise to the top as heads of department and policy branches. They tended to be trained as generalists rather than technocrats and were expected to transfer from one department or policy branch to another.

For 154 years, the Governor of Hong Kong and the administrative officers formed the key framework for such executive-led governance. This system lacked checks and balances among the key institutions of government; the colonial governor had supreme authority and, although there were Executive and Legislative Councils, their function was mainly advisory. The system was one in which executive authorities had ultimate control over all public policies, legislation and public finances. A network of consultative and advisory bodies existed,[15] often consisting of elites from the trade, business, finance and industry sectors (there was basically no grassroots representation), but final policy outcomes often bore little relationship to the input of those advisory bodies.

Under this pro-business government, the three prevailing principles were: maintaining Hong Kong as a free trading port, maintaining stability, and maintaining prosperity.

Although sovereignty has now reverted to the People's Republic of China, Hong Kong largely follows the old colonial model of executive-led, centralised, top-down governance.[16] It is more paternalistic, more Confucian and more business-centred, with tycoons and property developers having the kind of closeness to government not seen in Hong Kong since the 1960s. There is now less accountability than there was before 1997, and the governance was carried out with more caution and deference.[17]

In many ways, Hong Kong Internet governance mirrors its administrative governance. In the beginning, the desire to exercise control over the Internet came from the commercial sector rather than the government. The government primarily adopted a laissez-faire attitude, unless a potential risk was perceived to threaten social order and merited government intervention. This policy on the Internet is in line with the government's overall governing principle of laissez-faire (particularly in the economic sector) and in the maintenance of Hong Kong's free trade port status. In his maiden mini-budget speech on 23 October 2003, Henry Tang, the Financial Secretary, reiterated this laissez-faire policy. He explained that 'the free market has been the bedrock of Hong Kong's success ... the role of the government should be to facilitate the market and its development. Big market, small government is certainly the right way to go.'[18] Gradually, as the Internet has grown, the government has come to see it as a source of prosperity on the one hand, and a potential threat to law and order on the other. As a result, the Hong Kong government has sought to control the Internet via legislative and regulatory measures.

Unlike the United States and the European Union (EU), where governments play a major role in determining Internet infrastructure governance,[19] Hong Kong is largely a follower of global trends, partly because it has never been exercised as a major political power and partly because of its small size and position as a former colony. The United States and the European Union, for example, exercise Internet governance by exerting their influence at board level in the Internet Corporation for Assigned Names and Numbers.[20] The Hong Kong government has not been in a position to adopt such a proactive approach; instead, it has simply incorporated existing international rules on Internet governance and introduced compulsory licensing for Hong Kong ISPs.

In terms of illegal and harmful content on the Internet, there are debates on the need for content regulation but there is very little serious public debate on illegality and harmful content. The nature of the debate also differs from that in the United Kingdom. In Hong Kong, instead of focusing on issues around the social impact of the Internet, debate has mostly centred on commercial issues, such as how the Internet can facilitate and strengthen trade (reflecting Hong Kong's place as a commercial city and its focus on the market). The first Hong Kong government policy document on IT ('Digital 21 Information Technology') in 1998 did state that 'the government is committed to enhancing the community's awareness and knowledge of IT, promoting the wider use of IT in the community and improving public access to online services'.[21]

This implies that, while there is some commitment to widening Internet access to all social groups, the main intention is to facilitate commerce. The Hong Kong government saw its job as no more than promoting the use of IT within the community from a distance. The idea that the government might play a bigger role in the setting of international technical, commercial and legal standards has largely been ignored. Again, in the latest policy consultation paper ('2004 Digital 21 Strategy'),[22] the emphasis is on how the Hong Kong government can be a good middleman or a 'facilitator': 'Our conviction is that the government should be an effective facilitator to enhance the innovative capability of both industry and the community, promote the development of industry and enterprises and, in this process, encourage investment and innovation in information technology.'[23] What is missing is any overall strategy for integrating the Internet and IT. Thus, by default, governance is left to the Internet and IT industries themselves — in other words, self-regulation.

The debate in the United Kingdom has been considerably wider and livelier. The norms of cultural and social discourse among EU member states are relatively fragmented[24] when compared to the more homogeneous nature of Hong Kong. For example, the UK government is strongly inclined to police depictions of certain sexual activities (e.g. child pornography), while other member states, such as the Netherlands, have adopted a less interventionist approach to such Internet use.[25] However, the European Union has (via the European Commission) begun the process of harmonisation of EU cyber-crime legislation, with the Convention on Cyber-crime 2001,[26] agreed and signed by member states on 23 November 2001 in Budapest. (Details of the Convention are given by Peter Csonka in Chapter 15.)

Legislation, another important aspect of electronic governance, is generally also regarded as facilitative rather than restrictive in Hong Kong. There are several key ordinances but most of them deal with cyber-crime by adapting existing laws to the cyber-age, rather than by drafting new legislation specifically designed to police the Internet. The exception is the Electronic Transactions Ordinance (Cap. 553), which deals with electronic commerce. This ordinance is largely regarded as a means of facilitating the Hong Kong Post Office's electronic certificate and electronic surveillance.

The most important ordinance is the Computer Crimes Ordinance introduced in 1993. It is composed of several different ordinances, including the Telecommunication Ordinance (Cap. 106), Crimes Ordinance (Cap. 200) and the Theft Ordinance (Cap. 210). In the late 1990s, other legislation was amended to embrace the advancement of Internet technology including the Copyright Ordinance (Cap. 528), pertaining to illegal copies of Internet material; the Control of Obscene and Indecent Articles Ordinance (Cap. 390) concerning the distribution of pornographic material on the Internet; and the Gambling Ordinance (Cap. 148), which prohibits gambling on the Internet other than under the auspices of the Hong Kong Jockey Club. Lastly, the Personal Data (Privacy) Ordinance (Cap. 468) was introduced in 1996 and became law the same year. This ordinance is not specifically designed for the Internet but it does cover personal data held in a computer system as a record, as well as other types of traditional records such as those on paper.

The Hong Kong government has also established the office of Privacy Commissioner for Personal Data, a statutory body entrusted with the task of protecting the personal data privacy of individuals and ensuring compliance with the Privacy Ordinance. In other words, the Privacy Ordinance has conferred power on the Privacy Commissioner to regulate and enforce the data privacy law, and to provide and issue a code of practice for the private and public sectors on data privacy management. The Hong Kong Privacy Law operates as a semi self-regulatory regime.

The fine balance between business productivity and privacy has gradually become a concern. The former Privacy Commissioner, Stephen Lau, warned: 'While the application of modern technologies in both Government and industries would bring about better efficiency and productivity, it invariably would pose potential dangers in the invasion of privacy … [There is an] increasing trend of employee surveillance by organisations through sophisticated techniques to ensure business interests.'

Arguably, however, a lower value is placed on individual rights and liberties in societies like Hong Kong where democratic governance has been absent and where Confucian paternalism and executive-led government demands information to manage the population. It remains to be seen, therefore, whether the interests of business will receive greater attention than the interests of the individual and individual civil liberties.

The above ordinances form the key components of electronic governance in Hong Kong. They confer on the publicly funded regulatory agencies (including the police) the authority to act, maintain law and order and control crime in cyberspace. However, due to the territory's colonial background, where the colonial police assumed that the main threat to law and order came from the indigenous Chinese population, it may be that the HKP have yet to realise the extent of the 'danger' beyond its borders. Moreover, the past emphasis on stability and prosperity has been reinforced by PR China's insistence that stability must precede economic reform. As a result, policing in post-colonial Hong Kong still takes as its main focus the maintenance of law and order within the territory and along its borders. The policing of cyberspace lies outside these priorities.

Internet Users and User Groups in Hong Kong

Having described the Hong Kong social context and its style of governance, I now discuss the different players or groups that influence policing and control over the cyber-realm in Hong Kong society. Using Wall's methodology,[27] I shall analyse five main groups in an attempt to shed light on where the core power of social control over Hong Kong cyberspace lies. The five main groups are:

1. Internet users
2. Internet user groups (whose influence in Hong Kong is rather weak)
3. Internet service providers
4. State-funded non-public police organisations
5. State-funded police organisation (Hong Kong Police and private policing agencies)

These five groups police cyberspace by maintaining various types and levels of order. Together they form a multi-tiered structure of governance within cyberspace. They use both public and private models of justice. As Wall puts it, 'This model reflects the bifurcation of terrestrial policing. It progresses from maintaining order to the enforcement of law.'[28]

Internet users and user groups

The Internet users and user groups are, theoretically, the largest group of individuals exercising control over cyberspace. As the UK experience shows, they can actively police the Internet. For example, they have set up complaint 'hotlines'. The Cyber Angels claim to preserve and protect 'netiquette'[29] and represent the exemplary citizen. Other examples are the Cyber Vigilantes, who fight against the inequities among insurance companies, and the Adult Site Against Child Pornography, which polices the World Wide Web.

Characteristically, Internet users can draw on a number of user groups with common interests to police websites. Their membership and operation are loose in nature. They are often self-appointed and possess neither a public directive nor a statutory basis.[30] They may not, therefore, be fully accountable for their actions, even though these may be intrusive or, in some cases, bordering on illegality.[31]

How do such groups operate in Hong Kong? Are they an effective force in policing cyber-crime? The nature of civic society in Hong Kong differs markedly from that in the United Kingdom. There is a big difference in cultural and social norms. The United Kingdom is a democratic society where collective civic opinion and citizen participation in public affairs is generally regarded positively by the government. But this is not the case in Hong Kong, where Internet users and user groups have little power or influence and are rarely engaged in policing the Internet. For example, the Hong Kong Linux[32] User Group and Hong Kong Telecommunications Users Group[33] are forums for the dissemination of information and simply share experience; they are not a proactive lobby or pressure group that issues political statements in an attempt to influence the lawmaking process or win public support.

In the United Kingdom, such groups adopt a more proactive approach to policing the Internet and their involvement reflects the democratic maturity or otherwise of UK society. Social interdependence and political participation naturally breed an awareness of the larger social context: one's self-interest cannot be isolated from the interests of society at large. Political rights were won after bitter political conflict and acute social divisions in 19th-century English society.[34] Gradually British society learned that popular participation in government bore political results. People came to pursue their political demands through the political process.

In Hong Kong, by contrast, such groups reflect a rather different political tradition. This is the ethos of the Hong Kong Chinese, who tend to remain aloof and avoid civic or political involvement unless it is a must, and seldom participate in politics and civic affairs.[35] This ethos has been described by commentators such as Lau Sai Kai and Kuan Hsin-Chi.[36] Individual and family interests are valued above societal or collective interests. Social aloofness and political passivity are deeply rooted. The fact that Hong Kong people are excluded from politics by the absence of democracy reinforces such social values. In terms of political participation and civic duties, the Hong Kong Chinese do not believe that an individual or group will have any impact on the decision-making process. Adaptation rather than active intervention thus becomes the guiding principle of their relationship with the government.[37] As a result, individuals tend to think in short-term, piecemeal ways, with attention to things that are directly and immediately experienced, and that affect their individual and familial fortunes.[38] Political reform and local democratisation of a limited kind was introduced with the local district elections in the mid-1980s and the Legislative Council elections in 1995, but this process was halted when Hong Kong was reverted to Mainland China on 1 July 1997.

Internet service providers

The position of ISPs is rather fluid. While they are physically located in one particular jurisdiction, they have a transnational function. For instance, an ISP may register its business address in Quarry Bay on Hong Kong Island or Kowloon Bay in Kowloon but have its Internet server or routing port located somewhere in America or anywhere else in the world. The problem of ISPs policing activities in Hong Kong, however, is not as widespread as in the West; as a result, there is no moral panic about pornography on the Internet. Second, there is no quasi-public body formed with strong central government blessing to receive and process complaints from 'netizens', particularly on child pornography. Although there is an Internet Service Provider Association[39] set up by the industry, it largely provides a forum for discussion, promotes the development of the industry and protects members' interests, and provides and maintains a Code of Practice for ISP members. In other words, it is the industry voice from a business perspective rather than from a civic or public perspective. These ISPs are self-regulated in a way that tends to tread carefully in the policy arena and are user-responsive to police requests for cooperation, for fear of negative publicity. Other considerations include the costing factor — they have been active in limiting the costs of the policing burden — that is, opposing the need to hold archived records for lengthy periods.

Similarly in the United Kingdom, ISPs are mostly self-regulated. There were two events that compelled ISPs to review their policing activities over the server.[40] The first was in the mid-1990s, when there was a moral panic over the perceived threat of widespread pornography on the Internet, especially involving children; this ended up with threats of legal action. Then there was the final settlement of the case *Laurence Godfrey v Demon Internet Ltd.*[41] The case made ISPs see the need to police their servers, and to consider their potential liability. As early as 1996, UK ISPs had already formed an Internet Watch Foundation[42] (IWF) with strong central government blessing to police the Internet and to receive and process complaints from netizens, with particular reference to child pornography. Shortly afterwards the IWF became the quasi-public face of Internet regulation in the United Kingdom. It drew criticism of conflict of interest from many sectors, since it retained the status of a private organisation performing a very public function, at the same time lacking the structure of accountability that normally accompanies public institutions.[43] In the end, such criticism has forced the UK government to review the role and function of IWF, and eventually it was relaunched in 2000.

Private police agencies

With the widespread growth of Internet commerce in the late 1990s in Hong Kong, organisations such as computer consultants and large management consulting firms sought to expand their businesses. They gradually become involved in the investigation of security problems and the policing of cyberspace. The scope of work of these private policing firms mainly falls into four categories:

1. Anti-fraud work, mainly for insurance, including factual and surveillance work
2. Legal work: background and factual work for lawyers in civil and criminal cases
3. Commercial inquiry: private businesses hiring investigators to carry out various tasks, such as debugging, liability investigation, workplace investigations into theft or harassment and pre-employment checks
4. Domestic investigations

The work of these agencies often duplicates or supplements the work of the Hong Kong Police Technology Crime Division, especially in areas related to computer forensics and investigation. Nonetheless, their importance cannot be underestimated in taming cyber-crimes, especially in the trans-border dimension, as explained in Chapter 1 of this book. Their clients come mostly from the private / corporate business sector such as financial institutions and multinational corporations, and the services they offer are contractual. It is not known how extensive their involvement is, or what role they play within the Hong Kong criminal justice system (data is difficult to access). However, private police activity in computer investigative work is considered extensive and likely to grow, in particular on the civil litigation side. This work is mostly of a proactive and preventive kind, with a focus on prevention and the protection of property (particularly in network intrusion and internal fraud cases), whereas the Hong Kong Police focus more on detection[44] and criminal investigation.

As an important financial and commercial centre in the region, Hong Kong's institutions are likely targets for fraud. Hence there is a need for organisations to handle Internet-related fraud cases in a cost-effective manner. Private policing is already playing a substantial role in the territory, in particular in providing surveillance of private property and security guard services at warehouses, shopping malls and housing estates. As a result, the business sector is open to the idea of private policing and its role in servicing industries' security needs.

The relationship between these private police agencies and the Hong Kong Police is in an unusual one. Although, on the one hand, Hong Kong Police managers welcome the idea of not having to expend scarce resources on costly Internet investigations, on the other they are concerned about exchanging criminal intelligence with private agencies (but on some cyber-crime investigations cooperation between the two is unavoidable). The Hong Kong Police also has to underwrite private investigations on behalf of business when such work delivers sufficient evidence or concern to pass into the criminal justice system by the business sector.

The private police agencies are also competing for competent investigators with the Hong Kong Police and other enforcement agencies. This is particularly apparent in the business and commercial sectors. Many private computer investigators are former Hong Kong Police Commercial Crime Bureau police officers. They often have their own informal network of contacts within the Hong Kong Police on which they can draw information and through which new recruits may be solicited for work in the private sector.

State-funded, non-public police organisations

The next level of response to Internet crimes in Hong Kong comes from government agencies. These bodies are neither perceived as 'police' nor given the title 'police'. Nonetheless, such organisations can be found in many countries, such as PR China (excluding Hong Kong) and Singapore. The function of these government agencies is comparable to, and often overlaps with, that of the state-funded police whose job is to control the use of the Internet by forcing residents to register with a government-controlled ISP.

In Hong Kong, there is only one hybrid organisation, the Hong Kong Computer Emergency Response Team Co-ordination Centre (HKCERT/CC), funded by the Hong Kong government and located at the Hong Kong Productivity Council. The objective and function of HKCERT/CC is to provide a centralised 24/7 reporting contact on computer and network security. It also responds to local enterprises and Internet users in case of security, particularly malicious code incidents. It coordinates response and recovery actions for reported incidents to help monitor and disseminate information on security-related issues.[45] The equivalent organisation in the United Kingdom is JANET-CERT run by the JNT Association (trading as UKERNA) formed by the Higher Education Funding Councils for England, Scotland and Wales and the Office of Science and Technology in 1993. It was incorporated as a non-profit company limited by guarantee.[46]

State-funded police

The last and the strongest group of organisations involved in policing cyberspace in Hong Kong is the state-funded public police. The Hong Kong Police is one of the world's largest urban police forces, with one police officer for every 244 citizens.[47] The Police Force Ordinance (Cap. 232, s. 4) states that the Commissioner of Police is subject to the orders and directions of the Chief Executive of the HKSAR. By contrast, in the United Kingdom, most police duties and powers are derived from the common law, and the first duty of the UK police is to the law, not the government.

In addition to the main body of officers in the Hong Kong Police, the Immigration Department, the Independent Commission Against Corruption (ICAC) and the Customs and Excise Department all have a role in policing the Internet from the perspective of their own legislative mandates. They are joined by a further tier of transnational policing organisations, such as Interpol or Europol. However, these international bodies mostly do not exercise an investigative function but act as the contact point for countries requesting assistance from other nations. With regard to computer crime, there are several specialist groups within the police with an interest in the Internet. For example, in Hong Kong, a computer crime unit (now the Technology Crime Division) has been set up to investigate broad issues of Internet-related crime.

However, the Hong Kong Police only become involved in such matters when an Internet crime is reported. Their approach is thus reactive rather than proactive. The criminal justice process will only be invoked when a crime has been reported and determined to be so by the police. The private police agencies have a more flexible approach. They tend to seek compliance by using alternative dispute resolution methods, and invoke the criminal law only when these other alternatives fail.

In the United Kingdom, police are involved in policing the Internet locally as well as nationally. At the local level, computer crime units have been set up by various regional police organisations. Smaller police computer crime units also form strategic alliances with other police forces to provide 'buy-in' services. At the national or trans-regional and international level, the National Criminal Intelligence Service (NCIS) has been established with responsibility for providing intelligence on serious offences (for example, child pornography). Since April 1998, however, the National Crime Squad has largely taken over NCIS's investigative role. In April 2001, the National High Tech Crime Unit was established. Its functions range from the broad perspective of protecting the critical national Internet infrastructure to the policing of specific offences, such as Internet fraud and paedophilia.[48] Thus it was an attempt to better coordinate and centralise policing strategies to combat crime on the Internet.

Electronic Crime Victimisation in Hong Kong

The study of cyber-crime victims in Hong Kong can be problematic due to the lack of accurate information. Available statistics come from the law enforcement authorities and there is little independent scholarly work on the subject to offer alternative explanations of overall crime trends.

In the past two decades, the Hong Kong government has allocated no less than 12% of its annual expenditure to the maintenance of security, which is only exceeded by spending on health and education.[49] There is also a large private security and guarding services sector in Hong Kong, indicating extensive investment by private corporations and individuals in crime prevention and loss reduction.[50] If both private and public investments on policing were taken together, Hong Kong would rank as one of the top spenders on criminal justice, exceeding even more troubled jurisdictions such as Northern Ireland.[51]

Despite this large investment in law and order, there is little work on victimisation. Apart from public satisfaction surveys of the law enforcement agencies, there is a Hong Kong Crime Victimisation Survey carried out by government every few years covering traditional crime victims, repeat victimisation, assistance for crime victims, victim satisfaction and so forth. Unfortunately this survey was last carried out in 1999 in respect of crimes that occurred in 1998 and did not, perhaps understandably, include cyber-crime. In contrast, in the United Kingdom, sophisticated victimisation data is routinely produced by government agencies such as the Home Office and independent university scholars, for instance the annual British Crime Survey, but cyber-crime and its victims were not included in the British Crime Survey. In Hong Kong, although there is some concern about law and order issues at the district level, it is mostly related to youth gangs, vice, theft, incivility and vandalism.[52] At the city-wide level, law and order issues at best occupy a moderate ranking among the concerns of Hong Kong people; other issues, such as housing, employment, immigration, health and education, generally rank higher. As a result, work on victimisation is relatively neglected and work on cyber-crime victimisation is non-existent. There is, of course, always a problem gaining such data from the private sector, since companies strive to protect their reputations and share prices by ensuring that news of such victimisation is kept secret. However, the situation has improved recently with the establishment of HKCERT, which reports the number of computer systems compromised. Furthermore, cyber-crime victimisation estimates derived from a UN Crimes Against Business survey conducted by The University of Hong Kong in July 2003 were reported at the second cyber-crime summit held on November 2003 at the University.[53]

Conclusion

Cyberspace is not a lawless state in Hong Kong nor is it in the United Kingdom. It is far more orderly than many observers would have us believe. Moreover, cyberspace can be regulated by forming a multi-tiered structure of governance based on both public and private models of justice. Such governance can include both publicly funded police agencies (undoubtedly the strongest group for law enforcement) and private policing agencies. Their roles overlap or may even compete, but as Hong Kong practice indicates, informal networks can be maintained between them. At the other end of the scale, Internet users and consumer groups can also play a role in order maintenance, though they are at present the weakest aspect in Hong Kong.

Cyber-justice in Hong Kong differs from that in the United Kingdom, however, in terms of its relative lack of complexity and sophistication. To a large extent, this has to do with Hong Kong's historical background as a colony, as well as its social and cultural norms and its style of governance. Hong Kong is an administrative state, while the United Kingdom has developed a pluralist style of democracy, which is reflected in the difference in online and offline policing strategies. Internet governance in Hong Kong is thus markedly different from that of the United Kingdom.

Internet policing is a mirror-image of policing in the real world. UK police forces have adopted a service-based policing model, which has since the mid-1990s emerged in Hong Kong. The model is much more geared towards the principles of a pluralist society, and is shaped by contributions from the public and private police sectors. More apparent is the civil policing of the Internet, especially by citizens themselves. There has been a recent growth in vigilantism by private citizens and interest groups in the United Kingdom.

Furthermore, the approach to victimisation research and policy in dealing with law and order issues is different between the two places. In Hong Kong, research on victimisation is outdated and is now limited to an assessment of public satisfaction with the police, while key aspects of victimisation such as emergent crimes such as cyber-crime are largely neglected. In the United Kingdom, by contrast, law and order and crime victimisations are highly political issues. Victims vote in the United Kingdom and in Hong Kong, but elected representatives do not form the government in Hong Kong so there is less impetus for research from a wider angle than in the United Kingdom, where voter concern has led to a greater and more immediate understanding of crime victimisation.

The Internet is primarily global in nature, which has resulted in an increasing call for transnational policing and international conventions in maintaining trans-jurisdictional order. However, local policing philosophies and styles must be taken into account. Local styles of governance and local traditions may sometimes inhibit the effect of transnational systems. The case of Hong Kong shows that local culture, values and its style of governance largely shape the local delivery of all policing, including cyber-policing. Wall commented that 'nation-states have tended to underplay the impact of trans-jurisdictionality with regard to policing the Internet … the public police has tended to fix upon "terrestrial crime" … This explains the failure to respond to criminal activities that are conducted through non-territorial spheres such as cyberspace.'[54] I would argue that, while there is a need for transnational and international conventions on, and the policing of, cyberspace, it will take time, in the various jurisdictions, to develop strong local traditions of policing and varying styles of civic participation in social and political governance. The Hong Kong Police could argue that, since the establishment, in 1993, of a small specialist computer crime unit later upgraded to become a division in 2001 (the Technology Crime Division) with more than 60 police officers, they are not behind other police agencies or their international responsibilities.

6

Third Party 'Responsibilisation' Through Telecoms Policing

Keiji Uchimura*

Cyberspace is not only the scene of cyber-crime but also a vehicle for 'traditional' crime.[1] The capabilities of 'telecoms policing', typified by interception and data seizure, have become increasingly vulnerable with the advance of technology and the expansion of telecommunication services. The international roaming function of prepaid mobile telephones, for example, offers ordinary criminals a better tool than fixed landlines. The threat of the 'anonymous re-mailer' (discussed later) to crime control is aggravated by the existence by the cross-jurisdictional nature of some crime. Technologies and telecommunication services are no longer mainly defined domestically in the global age. Rather, the technical configuration of domestic installations and the variation of services are bound by *de facto* standards designed by oligopolistic manufacturers and / or international technical standards. Thus the public police of the state cannot cope on their own with policing needs in cyberspace. The private telecommunications (telecoms) industry, often instrumental to crime facilitation and inhibition, has been persuaded and, at times, compelled to assist in measures that are not automatically in its own short-term economic interests. Focusing on telecoms policing in Japan and elsewhere, I will argue that the state's policing mission requires assistance from the private sector. Throughout this chapter, 'telecoms policing' stands for any policing activities conducted (not necessarily by the public police) in cyberspace for preventing, detecting, investigating and remedying crime. The term specifically includes measures for surveillance of Internet content and telecoms interception, as well as freezing and obtaining traffic data and subscriber data.

The Interception Law in Japan: A New Weapon to Combat Organised Crime

The *Telecommunication Interception for Criminal Investigation Law* (the 'Interception Law') was enacted in 2000 in Japan.[2] The aim of the law is to authorise law enforcement agencies to intercept telecommunications related to organised crime. The history of such investigative methods in Japan is considerably shorter than the long legislative traditions of Western countries.[3] But it does not mean that the country has been so crime-free that such a development was regarded as needless. On the contrary, Japan has been victimised by at least two types of organised crime, which would not be properly controlled without such a strong policing power.

First, organised crime in its traditional form has been a serious problem. In particular, the political, economic and social infiltration of Boryokudan is a nationwide phenomenon (Keisatsucho 1999). Of course, traditional investigative tools have been effective to a certain extent, but it is difficult to control central cores of the organisation without using advanced investigative tools such as telecommunications interception. As a former Director-General of Criminal Police testified,

> Organised crime frequently uses telecommunications since organisation members essentially need to communicate with one another. Even if members were arrested, they would not inform on their ringleaders because severe rules are applied for defence of the organisation. Therefore, present investigative procedures are regrettably not effective enough for arresting masterminds rather than underlings. Few cases are known that impacted them substantially.[4]

Second, a religious organisation also has committed organised crime in Japan. The Aum Shinri Kyo has been a widely noticed cult since it kidnapped and killed, in 1989, the whole family of the lawyer who played a key role in rescuing juveniles influenced by its mind-control activities and lured into the religion. More horrendously, members attacked the underground railway in central Tokyo in March 1995 by emitting poison gas, killing 12 people and injuring more than 6000. They have been suspected of the unsolved case of Kunimatsu who, as the Chief Commissioner General of Keisatsucho (National Police Agency), was shot and seriously injured ten days after the underground attack. They also committed many other crimes including murder, kidnap, unlawful imprisonment, torture and extortion, smuggling and production of physical, chemical and biological weapons (Keisatsucho 1996).

Fortunately, in the course of a vehicle check, police accidentally found files of encrypted instructions from the Aum headquarters, recorded on magneto-optical disks. The investigation would have been unlikely to succeed without such luck, especially since there was no legal framework to intercept their telecommunications. There is evidence that mobile telephones had been used to provide detailed instructions from leaders to units undertaking notorious kidnappings.[5]

Precedents: substituting 'inspection' for 'interception'

There were five precedential cases, all quite exceptional, before legislation was introduced enabling police to intercept telecommunications (Homusho 1998: 29–34). The courts diverted the 'inspection'[6] procedure, issuing warrants that allowed the police to 'inspect' the contents of communications transmitted by certain telephone circuits. These cases were characterised by the system called Tachiainin or 'Presence of the Responsible'. The *Criminal Procedure Code*[7] provides that occupants, keepers, or any other person acting in place thereof at the premises shall be caused to be present during the enforcement of inspection, search or seizure. The purpose of the system is to guarantee procedural appropriateness (Inoue 1997: 77). The court applied the prototypical Tachiainin system that police should ensure their presence at the site of the telephone company personnel concerned (or, failing that, local government personnel). Tachiainin were permitted to monitor telephone conversations in common with investigators. In addition, they were then requested to disconnect temporarily the branched line to prevent monitoring and recording if call contents were not related to the crime (Homusho 1998: 29–34). However, the telephone company staff refused, in all five cases, to become Tachiainin, arguing that monitoring the telephone conversations contradicts the industry's legal responsibility on confidentiality of communications.[8] Consequently, police had to depend on fire-fighters or other local government officials instead of telecommunication experts.

The Tachiainin system and interception law

The Tachiainin system was handed over and developed as a new due process distinctive to telecoms interception. The relevant law stipulates that 'in case interception is to be executed, a person who is responsible for the part of the telecommunication means or any suitable substitute shall be made present on the spot. If such persons are not available, a local government official shall be present.'[9]

Thus the prime persons as eligible Tachiainin are staff of the telecoms service provider involved (Keisatsucho 2000: 60). The presence of Tachiainin at all times is the most important part of the procedure. It may be well explained by the following fact. The prototype of the law, the *Criminal Procedure Code*, allowed the non-attendance of Tachiainin under the exceptional circumstances of the non-availability of such personnel.[10] However, such an exceptional clause was removed from the Bill to place a responsibility on Tachiainin to thoroughly watch the process of interception.[11] Now the Tachiainin of the Interception Law are prohibited to monitor communication contents, and neither the right nor the responsibility of stopping interception is placed on them. In this sense, the new system sets lighter responsibility for Tachiainin than that of the inspection-interception scheme.

As a government delegate of the Yuseisho (Ministry of Posts and Telecommunications) gave testimony,[12] Tachiainin have two important roles. Their first function is to be present during the entire process of the enforcement order (interception) so that the telecoms carrier can maintain its entire service without any side effects to the service of other telecom users. Second, being Tachiainin is an obligation for telecoms service providers, forming a part of the due process of the law. The delegate further set forth that telecoms service providers are fundamentally responsible for carrying out Tachiainin duties to keep the integrity of their own telecommunications business.

The telecoms industry has nevertheless maintained that the burden of constantly seconding personnel over a long period might be too heavy to bear. A newspaper article, criticising the heaviness of the burden, appeared just two days before the Interception Law[13] came into force. It quoted the view of the compliance officers of a fixed-line telephone company that it would be difficult to station Tachiainin if interception is repeatedly enforced over a short time. The article also disclosed a mobile phone company's opinion that it cannot refuse doing Tachiainin because the company has a social responsibility to do so. At least in the period immediately after the law became effective, while the author liaised with them in preparation for the new role, they repeatedly requested police to release them from Tachiainin duties because it would interfere with their business.

Interception capabilities

Another concern about interception investigation was the cost of developments facilitating telecoms interception. Hitherto, unlike the majority of Western countries,[14] Japanese legislation provides neither legal obligation for service providers to install interception systems nor a legal claim for the costs of doing so. To enable the investigative capability given by the Interception Law, lawmakers allowed police to make 'non-compulsory and non-immoderate' requests to the telecoms industry. Since the legal and political circumstances of interception capabilities in Japan are quite different from other countries,[15] it is inevitable that the technical implementation of interception in Japan is limited in extent. Though the cause and effect cannot be fully discussed, it can be reiterated that the technical difficulties combined with operational barriers (especially in securing personnel for Tachiainin) resulted in the limited applicability of the law.[16] Of course the imbalance between telecoms policing needs and capabilities is hardly unique to Japan, as the following will reveal.

Global Concerns: Analogue Technology and the Monopolised Supplier of Service

Traditionally, the technical methods of telecoms policing were fairly simple. As for the primitive form of telephone interception, call content was available as follows. First, a pair of copper telephone cables is branched off near the local switch (see Grabosky & Smith 1998: 21–2; Diffie & Landau 1999: 115–16) and then the branch cables are extended to the interception site. Apart from interception, traffic data (e.g. the length of calls and dialled numbers), were logged in correlation with subscriber data by telephone companies for billing purposes (Lloyd 2000: 179–80) and the most important traffic data (dialled numbers), were also obtainable, without assistance from telephone service providers, by attaching a device called the 'pen-register' to the branch (Diffie & Landau 1999: 117).[17]

Unlike the Internet or mobile phone services, subscribers' static data on fixed line services were easily obtainable for lawful powers because the customers are literally connected. Another factor that facilitated interception in the pioneer days was the monopolisation of telephone services. As Grabosky & Smith (1998: 206) pointed out, 'enlisting the co-operation of a single, large organisation was a relatively routine matter'. Thus the telecoms policing of early days was relatively easy.

Technical development and more anonymous services

Because of advances in the technology and popularity of telecommunication services, the importance of data handled by the industry has grown. Additionally, in contrast with traditional law enforcement style, the technology needed for telecoms policing in modern telecommunication systems becomes far more difficult (see Grabosky & Smith 1998: 206, Diffie & Landau 1999: 97–9). Furthermore, the global popularity of the mobile telephone and the Internet brought about challenging situations. It is almost impossible and arguably inappropriate for public police to install interception capabilities by themselves within these huge networks, whether confidentially or not. There seems to be no other solution than to pre-install capabilities friendly for telecoms policing (Diffie & Landau 1999: 116).

To make matters worse, digital technology is applied in almost all telecoms systems removing identifiable features of human users. In fact, this anonymising nature of telecommunications has given rise to serious concerns about the enhanced risk of high-tech crime (Council of Europe 2001: paragraph 62). In addition to the technology, diversified services have introduced complexity. For example, the traffic data of the modern systems are not usually recorded if the services are flat-rated or free of charge because of the absence of a billing purpose (Council of Europe 2001: paragraph 150). Similarly, the information of Internet protocol addresses allocation (subscriber data) and the history of IP addresses of destination (traffic data) were also immediately deleted by ISPs because they are regarded as valueless in most cases (Council of Europe 2001: paragraph 29). In addition, many free e-mail services are accessible to anybody through the Internet. Such services are not only free of charge but are also practically free from providing information in order to subscribe to the service. The most problematic services to provide anonymity are 'anonymous re-mailers' (Mostyn 2000: 81–2). The problem of anonymity is also found in prepaid mobile phone systems (Denning & Baugh 1997: 128).

International responses

The requirements

Parallel with domestic struggles discussed elsewhere in this chapter, remarkable international efforts have been made since the mid-1990s to regain interception capabilities. The first initiative was under the Police Cooperation

Working Group of the European Union and bore fruits as the Council Resolution in 1995. Unlike EU directives and regulations, any 'resolution' has no direct legal authority but member states are requested to adopt the necessary policy according to the resolution. The structure of the resolution is quite simple. A set of 'requirements' of law enforcement agencies for telecoms policing, often referred to as 'International User Requirements', is acknowledged in the first half of the resolution. Then in the latter half, member states are required to implement the requirement (Council of the European Union 1996). This resolution was epoch-making because it pioneered an international concern about capabilities of telecoms policing.

Standardisation

The international effort was also made by the ITU (International Telecommunication Union) by adopting Resolution 1115, 'International Harmonization of Technical Requirements for Legal Interception of Telecommunications'. The motive for the resolution was 'that the costs of legal interception capability and associated disruptions can be lessened by providing for the capability at the design stage'.[18] Although the ITU has made no progress since 1997, the process of regional standardisation has been actively pursued in Europe. The European Telecommunications Standards Institute (ETSI) has also established many standards relating to lawful interception.[19] The reason for the different outcomes between the two projects is that, whereas the ITU could not coordinate its diverse members' political and economic conditions, the law enforcement needs and industry efforts to respond to them are similar among European countries. Standardisation in the ETSI has produced satisfactory results not only in terms of scale but also in removing trans-border barriers among jurisdictions and markets that originated from different legal requirements (Tsuchiya 2001: 16).

Countermeasures against cyber-crime

Recently the members of the Council of Europe and some additional countries (i.e. Canada, Japan, South Africa and the US) signed the 'Convention on Cyber-crime'. The significance of this treaty for telecoms policing is that it requires states to establish new types of legal measures to enable 'the expeditious preservation of' existing computer data, including traffic data.[20] In complying with the terms of the convention, the Japanese Government is preparing domestic legislation to create new investigative powers to request telecoms service providers to retain traffic data for up to 90 days.[21]

However, the industry has opposed the data retention policy because it costs a great deal of money. The World Information Technology and Services Alliance (WITSA) appealed 'as the global voice of the IT industry' to governments in a statement on the Draft Convention: 'to avoid imposing new requirements [for data preservation] on ISPs that result in significant financial burdens on their operations. Such added costs will ultimately affect the access costs of end users, and may negatively affect the growth of Internet usage' (WITSA 2000).

Case Studies and Telecoms Policing

Legal solution: Internet auction providers' new responsibility

The first case study is about the world's first legal regulation for online auction service providers. The Amendment of the *Second-hand Dealing Law* went into effect in April 2003 in Japan.[22] The amendment requires any online auction provider

- To notify police as a 'service provider of second-hand articles auction mediation' (an Auction Mediator)
- To report to the police if any article on the auction block is suspected of being a stolen item
- To take the appropriate action to halt the auction if the article is obviously recognised as a stolen item
- To create and retain data of mediated auction and the identity information of users.

Further, the amendment established a system that auction mediators and similar overseas providers may be certified, on request, by Japanese police as complying with basic standards of preventive and detection measures against the fencing of stolen goods.

The amending process was tangled. The industry opposed the bill partly because the burden of inspecting the suspiciousness of articles was regarded as too heavy.[23] Moreover, as lawmaker Yoko Tajima noted, 'Police must be admitting the ineffectiveness of their cyber-patrol to lobby this bill ... Presumably, the real intention of the crafty bill might be to divert the responsibility of impotent police onto the industry's shoulder.'[24]

Paralegal solution: 'Know your customer' for prepaid phone services

The next case study, though it is not technical, is about the crime investigation and prevention measures taken by the Japanese telecoms industry. In contrast to the previous case studies, this case may be characterised as being of a paralegal nature, achieved through administrative guidance.

When a prepaid mobile phone was used for a kidnapping case for ransom in 1999, police had difficulty in investigating the case because of the anonymity of the telephone user. In response, the Keisatsucho requested mobile telephone companies and the regulating authority of the telecommunications business (the then Yuseisho) to collect user identification to prevent crime and maintain investigative capabilities.[25]

Encouraged informally by the Yuseisho, industry at first adopted a wait-and-see policy. The grounds of their argument were as follows. The customers' personal identity information in prepaid services is, by definition, not needed for billing purposes. Thus it was considered that the collection and possession of such unnecessary information is prohibited in conformity with the Privacy Guideline for Telecommunications Business recommended by the Yuseisho. In addition, the industry contended that collecting such data was potentially fatal to the service since the convenience of the service is its only raison d'être. The confrontation gradually attracted media and public attention.[26]

An imitative kidnap case using a more sophisticated technique occurred four months after the first case. The Keisatsucho, without delay, made the same request. The reaction of Eita Yashiro, the Minister of Yuseisho, was immediate. He reported in the Diet a few hours later the solution of the kidnap case:

> Prepaid mobile phones were abused in the kidnap case committed in December last year and the case in Kanagawa Prefecture this time. I consider this situation as a serious social problem. Therefore we have just instructed the industry to devise immediate measures against this matter taking privacy concerns into consideration since the service is a sort of disposable-type. In this context, on the ground that a serious social evil has arisen from this service through a variety of crimes, not to speak of drug dealing, we would like to discuss immediately the governmental countermeasure.[27]

Under the guidance of the Yuseisho, the industry then began to collect identity data by checking photo identification at shop fronts on the purchase of handsets.[28] According to a Yuseisho official, this industry measure was made possible by modifying the interpretation of the privacy guidelines. In other words, 'preventing crime' and 'keeping a clue to provide against the time of need' were newly authorised as necessary and the new system was established by immunising interception against the conflicting requirements of privacy.

Theories of state versus non-state crime control

By Max Weber's definition, the 'state' inevitably monopolises legitimate enforcement powers (Weber 1947: 154). However, his classic paradigm was challenged half a century later by Stanley Cohen (1985: 40–1). Cohen noticed that not only the state but also lay volunteers and professionals took overlapping measures to control deviance. The expansion of social control was conveniently justified by the state because benign community and professional services, rather than bloated 'overburdened, inefficient and inhumane' state systems, have the requisite 'natural resources' to exercise the control over deviance (Cohen 1985: 77). According to his elaborate 'net-widening' metaphor, there are many fishers (e.g. parents, neighbours, teachers, social workers, probation officers, prison officers) setting their own nets to catch fish (offenders) in the sea (social and real space). Whereas the 'catch' of the formal net (prison) are politically or fiscally controlled, the coverage of the nets of non-state fishers has widened or the nets have been changed into more finely woven ones to catch more fish (Cohen 1985: 41–2). In addition, 'there is far more room for the weaker form of privatisation [than for that of offender treatment apparatus] where the state contracts out certain services to private enterprise, retaining some measure of control' (Cohen 1985: 64). Here, Cohen's visions of social control are reinforced because the various cases examined above fit into his conception by converting the 'sea' from the real jurisdiction of the state to that of cyberspace. Cyberspace is composed of many private domains with public access, akin to a mass-private property (Cohen 1985: 67) operated by the private telecoms industry.

Cohen's view is reinforced by David Garland's (1996) analysis of the macro crime control strategies of the sovereign state. He began with identifying the limitations of the crime control capability of contemporary states. He discovered three adaptation strategies taken by the sovereign state. One of these is termed the 'responsibilisation' strategy. That is, the state has handed over some crime control roles, which had long been monopolised by government agencies, to non-government organisations and individuals. In this process, risks and costs incurred by crime have been distributed to a 'responsibilised' private sector (Garland 1996: 451).

Grabosky and colleagues (2001) examine the role of the state and non-state sectors in controlling 'electronic theft' crime. Although conventional crime facilitated by telecommunications services is not evaluated, these authors endorse Garland's notion. Due to the limitations of law and law enforcement in cyberspace, the state has 'responsibilised' various parties to prevent cyber-crime largely on the principle of the potential victims' capacity for self-help. Based on this situation, Grabosky and colleagues (2001: 206) predict that technology will be essential in the mission to control electronic theft, and that the state will have a mutually complementary relationship with those institutions in a position to mobilise technological intervention.

A variant of the responsibilisation model for policing and crime prevention is advocated by Peter Manning (2000: 197). Manning regards contemporary policing in new social spaces as the responsibility of both pubic and private police. On the one hand, the new social space, that is, cyberspace, 'is now open to policing as physically defined space' for government agencies (Manning 2000: 193). Meanwhile the space in question is placed under surveillance by industry to protect it from 'hackers'. In his argument, the powerful role of private policing in cyberspace competes with the state's monopolised policing authorities rather than taking the form of a responsibilised function by the state (Manning 2000: 196).

Garland's explanation seems preferable to Manning's. Although Garland, unlike Manning, seemingly pays attention only to intra-territorial matters, phenomena surrounding telecoms policing can be seen as the responsibilising processes in cyberspace. The widening of cyberspace for both legitimate and illegitimate use in the last decade might be comparable to the paradigm shift triggered by the growth of capitalism in the Industrial Revolution era.[29]

The shortcomings of responsibilisation

Garland's criticism of the responsibilisation strategy was that it might result in inequitable distribution of costs and / or benefits. He applied this idea in the real space of society, focusing only on the dimension of the haves versus the have-nots (Garland 1996: 463). Upon reflection, in cyberspace, the dichotomy may be applied to the contrast between conventional telephone services operated by state-owned and / or mega-carriers and small-sized telecoms service providers, for example very small ISPs that have an ethos of self-governance. The former would be arguably more amenable to responsibilisation, for example, in complying with requests to install lawful interception capabilities. From that angle, the responsibilising approach in cyberspace might bring forth disparities in the level of crime control. Those with resources to seek out and engage smaller less compliant ISPs might find it easier to evade detection. This also raises the question of who bears the burden of compliance with the needs of state law enforcement.

Charging the compliance costs to 'those who benefit'

Discussion of the burden-sharing of what is known as 'situational crime prevention', a simple form of responsibilisation for crime control (Garland 1996: 453), has two aspects. First, if the cost of the intervention is 'modest', then the potential victim would likely pay the costs without a major problem. The second approach is to invoice the costs to 'would-be' offenders. That is to say, potential offenders should pay as beneficiaries because they are incapacitated from committing crime. These methods are, at first glance, ethically unproblematic because they conform to the model of 'who pays who benefits' (Duff & Marshall 2000: 23–4).

On reflection, identifying those who benefit from telecoms policing is a complex issue. On the one hand, most targeted crime calling for telecoms policing, for example drug dealing,[30] victimises society in general. In a sense, society has paid the policing costs through taxation and the state ought to compensate industry. Of course, one might argue that industry is the potential victim in an indirect way because its reputation and integrity are at risk.[31] But if this risk is outweighed by compliance costs, shifting the burden to industry may be an inefficient solution.

This logic might justify the diffusion of compliance costs to all subscribers because differentiation between would-be offenders and the good-natured might be impossible and inappropriate. Thus it would be problematic and / or ineffective if the beneficiary-payment principle alone were applied to the telecoms industry. In addition, since crime prevention accounts for only a part of the purpose (or effect) of telecoms policing, a more general accountability is needed.

Boomerang effect on the state

The next method that has already materialised in many jurisdictions[32] is that the financial responsibility of compliance costs is returned to the state by the responsibilised party. Masahito Inoue argues that the compliance costs of the telecoms industry in installing interception capabilities should be compensated by the state if they exceed a reasonable level (Inoue 1997: 212). The central notion of this approach is that the policing ought to be the mission of the state.[33] Either way, since the financial resources of the state are limited, costs would in any event be recovered from the telecom consumer. In this case, the policing regime is reinforced because industry is not only responsibilised but also obligated to comply.[34]

Para-taxation system in Cyberspace: responsibilising cost recovery as well

At least in the traditional policing context, this 'state pays' strategy might be quite appropriate and justified because the citizenry is assumed to be the principal beneficiary of policing. Nevertheless, if the history and dynamism of cyberspace is considered, applying the traditional burden-sharing approach to the responsibilisation of telecoms policing still seems unfair. Rather, the liable party would be industry, as it has ethical responsibility (not an obligation because they are not paid by the state), and the redirection of the costs to subscribers should be justified. Of course, the state, rather than responsibilised industry, continues to hold the primary responsibility for crime control. Consequently, the expenses borne by customers of responsibilised services may be equated with a kind of earmarked tax imposed on them by the industry. Since the author does notice Internet-widening rather than net-widening, these sorts of para-taxation systems can be justified for several reasons.

First, unlike the condition of real-world policing, there was neither criminal opportunity nor a victim in cyberspace. Therefore policing powers were not necessary at all. The balance was lost when the 'new social space'[35] was created. Although at the beginning major telecoms services were state-owned (e.g. the Japanese telephone network[36]) or monopolised for research purposes (e.g. the Internet), unfortunately crime opportunity was facilitated. Through privatisation or commercialisation, some present telecoms service providers are liable as the successors of early players. Second, both the opportunity and victimisation of crime has increased since the early days of the Internet. New entrants to the industry are also responsible for the deterioration of crime control. Third, the criminal customers of telecoms policing are presumably unevenly distributed among telecoms service customers, who pay more for services as well as state tax, than non-customers who pay tax only. Further, within the 'netizen' community, the more the netizens pay for the services, presumably the more criminal opportunities would be provided. The same applies to the distribution of potential victims. Fourth, the trans-border nature of crime facilitated by telecoms services 'is in conflict with the territoriality of national law enforcement authorities' (Council of Europe 2001: paragraph 8). Although the capabilities and experience of state-funded policing has increased, on the one hand such policing practices might threaten the sovereignty of foreign countries (see Sheptycki 2000: 161), and on the other they would be less accountable to domestic taxpayers than domestic policing. Thus, diverting the costs for policing in cyberspace to *netizens* would be justified by the fact that the costs of real-space policing are supported by the state's tax-collection from *citizens* under their jurisdiction.

Feasible Steps Forward

Nevertheless, such a utilitarian solution would not work smoothly. First, although beyond the scope of this chapter, concerns of citizen or *netizen* rights should be settled by establishing appropriate due process systems. In addition, such a cost-redirection policy would arouse the hostility of smaller or new-entrant service providers and benign customers. More substantially, the question of international competitiveness of the domestic industry should be considered. Providing that the responsibilising degrees are unbalanced, customers of domestic services are vulnerable to differentiated redirected costs, degrees of inconvenience, and at least Orwellian fears. By the nature of cyberspace, sensitive customers with sufficient motivation would migrate from nuisance domestic services to 'offshore' providers (APIG 2003: paragraph 159) or elsewhere. In addition, there is no reason for would-be offenders not to hesitate to do so (paragraph 162). Thus, there is the danger of both a 'hollowing out' of the industry and the displacement of crime. In effect, the strategy might ironically cause damage to national interests.

After all, the pursuit of domestic responsibilisation policies without due consideration to these unintended consequences would not be advisable. Rather, the solution should be in facilitating the international harmonisation of (1) the extent and the justification of diverting costs to customers, and (2) the extent of telecoms policing capabilities, that is, the potential degree that human rights are restricted. There may be at least two approaches to harmonise the disparities found in domestic conditions.

First, what is needed is that law enforcement agencies as well as regulatory agencies of the telecoms industry should organise a collective policy on policing needs and regulating telecoms services. The Convention on Cyber-crime is a monumental first step. As the FATF (Financial Action Task Force) have powerfully tackled problems of inter-jurisdictional money laundering, establishing something like the Telecoms Action Task Force ("TATF") for resolving issues of telecoms policing might be worth considering. The agenda of the "TATF" would resemble that of the FATF. The main issue may be how to distribute costs and functions of telecoms policing among jurisdictions. Some existing practical problems in conducting mutual legal assistance might be naturally resolved through these discussions. However, I do not advocate establishing only the "TATF", because such a top-down solution might be less accountable at present than the approach discussed below.

Second, the most recommended approach would be to facilitate the standardisation of *technology* (see Grabosky et al. 2001: 206). Because components of cyberspace are microscopically interconnected only in a technical dimension, and not by market pressure or political dynamism or law, as Lessig (1999: 207) puts it, 'code is law'. Technically, rational system design would be obtained through a sober standardisation process. Thus the friction arising from introducing telecoms policing measures might be smoothed if the measures conform to legitimate technical standards. A part of the standardisation effort, in conjunction with lawful interception capabilities, has already been established by the ETSI. The standardisation process may not necessarily be bound within the purely technical sphere. As ISO 9000 and 14 000 series[37] standardise not only purely technical but managerial matters, the standards of telecoms policing may therefore treat *security* matters in a wider sense. The 'security-related function' may contain functions of surveillance, incapacitating criminals, the removal of harmful contents, the retention of data for the further access of law enforcement, and so on. The functions of an internationally accepted level of due processes should be embedded in policing functions. Above all, the standardisation processes should be operated in an open and democratic way. All stakeholders, for example not only the service providers and manufacturers but also representatives of customers, human rights advocates and law enforcement agencies, should have access to the process. In particular, law enforcement officials have to take the trouble to persuade all stakeholders by explaining the significance of telecoms policing capabilities. At the same time, governments would be well advised to ensure that the costs of controlling cyber-crime do not become an impediment to the creative and productive use of digital technology.

The author neither assumes such a prescription to be Utopia nor advocates that these measures would realise the Orwellian surveillance society.

The absence of police, surveillance, control and responsibilisation *is* the largest happiness of the greatest number provided that there is no crime and no victim. Rather, we, who enjoy the current prosperity and convenience brought about by telecommunication services, should duly be responsibilised to solve the difficult problems arising from these services.

7

Cyber-Security: Country Report on Singapore, 2003

Clement Leong and Chan Keen Wai

The boons and banes of cyberspace are well documented.[1] Singapore, like many modern societies, faces many challenges while manoeuvring to obtain optimal utility from the advent of cyberspace. Issues related to the security of cyberspace are multifaceted and novel, and resolving them requires much interaction and cooperation between organisations, both domestically and internationally.

Singapore, being a small nation with limited resources, has particular constraints that may not be of concern elsewhere. Human resources are deemed precious and the resolve to groom each individual's talent to its fullest has proved to be pivotal to the way of life that Singaporeans now enjoy. In the course of maximising the potential of its talents, Singapore found itself to be an early and fervent adopter of infocomm technologies. Now, with one of the highest penetration rates of infocomm technology use among nations, Singapore finds itself having a large stake in the overall well-being and safety of cyberspace.

Legislation has been enacted to protect the users of cyberspace. However, cyber-security issues are felt in so many aspects of our lives that a single-pronged approach could not be effective. A combination of legislation by government, self-regulation by industry and continuous education of consumers is Singapore's approach to the challenges posed by this new age.

The government would not be able to overcome many of the challenges without rallying both private and corporate citizens to support its efforts. Many initiatives taken in tackling cyber-security issues are aimed at improving confidence in the local electronic commerce scene and hence promoting the use of e-commerce. Other initiatives are aimed at enlarging the pool of Singapore's quality infocomm security expertise to feed corporate demands and sustain local research and development efforts. Consortia are formed by industry and supported by the government to provide the focus for self-regulation and the platforms for reflective discussions between industry players and the government. Along with the institutions set up to acquaint citizens with the benefits of cyberspace, campaigns are conducted to inculcate safe habits online.

This report provides further details on the governmental and industrial organisations that are instrumental to the implementation of policies and initiatives related to cyber-security in Singapore. A brief overview of the relevant legislations and administrative measures are included as well. A compilation of references to these organisations on the Web is also included at the end of the report to facilitate further investigation of the subjects discussed.

Singapore Statutory Organisations on Cyberspace

The Infocomm Development Authority (IDA) is charged by the government to develop, promote and regulate info-communications in Singapore. Among IDA's main responsibilities are fostering a competitive world-class IT industry in Singapore, preparing residents for living and working in the new economy, spearheading the delivery of citizen-centred e-government services, building and operating the government's IT infrastructure. Recognising infocomm security as a key area, IDA announced in September 2003 that it would set aside S$21 million to help promote the growth of the infocomm security industry. On the front of technology leadership, IDA released the 'Infocomm Security Technologies an E-Commerce Roadmap' in November 2002 as part of its five-year technology vision for the nation.

IDA's Infocomm Security Division (iSec) plays an active role in establishing and facilitating robust and secure government and national infocomm infrastructures in Singapore. The iSec oversees the establishment of infocomm security policies, standards and guidelines for the government and provides infocomm security consultancy and support. It also provides incident-handling services, reviews infocomm security technologies and collaborates with industry in infocomm security research and development. The iSec is also very much involved in raising awareness of infocomm security issues within both the private and public sectors through seminars and exhibitions.

Recognising the necessity for inter-agency collaboration on cyber-security, the government set up a National Infocomm Security Committee (NISC), with membership drawn from relevant agencies within the Singapore government, to spearhead the development of national infocomm security policies.

The NISC recently endorsed a three-year Infocomm Security Masterplan designed to identify and implement strategic projects relevant for the people, and private and public sectors. The masterplan represents Singapore's commitment to continually enhancing its infocomm security capabilities in the course of retaining the Republic's economic and competitive edge.

Singapore's e-Commerce Policy

Much of the emphasis in Singapore's e-commerce policy is placed on the security of cyberspace, the heightening of awareness of e-commerce's potential and risks, and the engendering of suitable solutions. The e-commerce policy aims to establish a conducive regulatory environment by removing barriers and clarifying marketplace rules. A framework is designed to instil trust and confidence in e-commerce by addressing the following three areas:

- *A secure environment.* Encourage the adoption of Public Key Infrastructure (PKI) and the use of risk assessment tools and profiling services
- *User confidence.* Promote trust marks (authenticity or quality control labelling) and the protection of consumer privacy
- *Education.* Raise the general public's awareness of the dangers and risks in cyberspace, and to inculcate safe computing practices

With an eye towards striking a balance between encouraging business innovation and maintaining social safeguards, the government regularly reviews the framework to keep it relevant and in line with international developments. It also works closely with industry to complement its efforts and directions.

Infocomm Laws

Electronic Transactions Act

In Singapore, the *Electronic Transactions Act* (ETA) establishes the supporting legal infrastructure for the development of PKI (Public Key Infrastructure).

It was enacted in 1998 to provide a legal basis for electronic signatures and electronic records, and to give predictability and certainty to electronic contracts. It is modelled after the Illinois Electronic Commerce Security Act and the UNCITRAL Model Law on Electronic Commerce, which sets the framework for electronic commerce laws in many countries. UNCITRAL, or the United Nations Commission on International Trade Law, has a charter to 'further the progressive harmonisation and unification of the law of international trade'. UNCITRAL does its work through six working groups, which include a Working Group on E-commerce.

The ETA addresses the following issues:

- *Commercial code for electronic commerce transactions.* This creates a predictable legal environment for electronic commerce and deals with legal aspects of electronic contracts, use of electronic signatures and electronic records and authentication and non-repudiation concerns. It is noteworthy that electronic signatures have the same legal binding effect as that of written signatures.
- *Use of electronic applications and licences for the public sector.* This allows government departments to accept electronic applications and to issue electronic licences and permits without amending their respective Acts.
- *Liability of service providers.* This exempts network service providers from criminal or civil liability for content that they merely provide access to.
- *Provision for a PKI.* This provides for the appointment of a Controller of Certification Authorities (CCA) to enable regulations to be made for the licensing of Certification Authorities (CA). The Infocomm Development Authority is currently appointed the CCA of Singapore. The Act provides for certain minimum standards for all certification authorities, whether or not they are licensed, as well as higher standards for licensed authorities. Cross-certification and cross-recognition is also strongly encouraged, but is not mandatory.

Electronic Transactions (Certification Authority) Regulations

In 1999, the *Electronic Transactions (CA) Regulations* were made to establish a voluntary licensing scheme for CAs. Public CAs are strongly encouraged to obtain licences. Netrust is the current operating licensed public CA in Singapore and is used by the Singapore government for online applications.

The Singapore government is currently reviewing possible amendments to the ETA modelled on legislative developments internationally, including a new draft UNCITRAL Convention on Electronic Contracting, and other legislative amendments to promote the use and development of electronic transactions and commerce.

Computer Misuse Act

The *Computer Misuse Act* (CMA) was first enacted in 1993 and amended in 1998. It is aimed at protecting computers, computer programs and information stored in computers from unauthorised access, modification, use or interception. The CMA also applies to any person, irrespective of his physical location, who hacks into computers located in Singapore. It also applies to any person in Singapore who hacks into computers outside Singapore.

The 1998 amendments ensure that newer forms of cyber-crime (such as Trojan horses, password trafficking or denial of service attacks) are addressed. It provides enhanced penalties for computer crime proportionate to the potential and actual harm caused. The amendment also gives police the power to gain lawful access to computer material including the decryption of encrypted materials.

The *Computer Misuse (Amendment) Act 2003* introduced a new section, 15A, to allow necessary measures to be taken, with the authorisation of the Minister, to prevent or counter any threat to a computer or computer service or any class of computers or computer services. Such measures may be taken by an authorised person or organisation if the Minister certifies that he is satisfied that such measures are necessary to prevent or counter any threat to national security, essential services, defence or foreign relations of Singapore.

Evidence Act

The *Evidence Act* was amended in 1996 to permit the use of electronic records as evidence in courts. The provisions are modern and adapted to the network and Internet environment. The Act also allows the use of litigation support systems and the use of video-conferencing in Singapore courts.

Recently in September 2003 the Technology Law Think Tank — Technology Law Development Group of the Singapore Academy of Law issued a consultative paper on the review of the computer output provisions in the *Evidence Act* entitled 'Computer Output as Evidence'. If government eventually accepts the recommendations, the computer output provisions in the *Evidence*

Act may be improved and updated to take into account recent changes in technology.

Administrative Measures

IDA recognises the important role played by encryption in promoting confidence in e-commerce in Singapore and has lifted import controls on cryptographic products since January 2000. IDA believes this will further promote confidence among companies to conduct e-commerce in Singapore as well as support Singapore's goal to become an international e-commerce hub. Additionally, IDA encourages businesses to implement key recovery measures to minimise disruptions to business operations.

IDA also released guidelines in January 2000 to safeguard the interests of subscribers of Internet Access Service Providers (IASP) when the IASPs perform preventive security scanning exercises. IDA advocates a self-regulating approach by the IASP industry to ensure that the accountability of the IASPs, and the transparency of the exercises, are not compromised.

IDA is also reviewing measures against spam, beginning with e-mail spamming. In studying what can be done to address the problem, IDA has engaged the ISPs in the review process and is considering a number of additional measures, including legislative measures, against e-mail spam.

In addition, the Monetary Authority of Singapore (MAS) issued the 'Internet Banking Technology Risk Management Guidelines' in July 2001, and updated them in July and September 2002. The guidelines were developed in consultation with the financial sector and the technology industry, and are designed to direct financial institutions to:

- Establish a sound and robust technology risk management process
- Strengthen system availability, security and recovery capability
- Deploy strong cryptography to protect customers' data and transactions

MAS encourages financial institutions and industry associations to take an active part in educating customers on the benefits and risks of online financial services and products offered via the Internet or other computer networks. Public confidence in online financial systems will be enhanced through a process of disclosure of the high standards of risk management and security practices prevailing in the industry.

The National Internet Advisory Committee issued a voluntary 'Model Data Protection Code' for the private sector in February 2001. The Code, which is modelled on 1980 OECD 'Guidelines on the Protection of Privacy and Transborder Flows of Personal Data', the 1995 EU Directive, and the 1996 'Canadian Standards Association's Model Code for the Protection of Personal Information', serves to establish minimum acceptable standards for electronic data protection.

Public incident response capabilities and disaster recovery

The Singapore Computer Emergency Response Team (SingCERT) was established to facilitate the detection, resolution and prevention of security-related incidents on the Internet. SingCERT also issues advisories and alerts when incidents or events so warrant, and maintains a website and a hotline to facilitate the reporting and dissemination of advisories.

SingCERT is also a founding member of the Asia Pacific Computer Emergency Response Teams (APCERT) Forum. APCERT consists of members from the national Incident Response Teams (IRTs) of countries such as Australia, Japan, Korea as well as Singapore and aims to promote collaboration with other international IRTs and security groupings such as the Forum of Incident Response and Security Teams (FIRST). Furthermore, APCERT provides assistance for other regional countries that would like to establish their own IRTs.

At the 3rd Telecommunications and Information Technology Ministers Meeting held in September 2003, ASEAN countries, of which Singapore is a member, agreed to take concrete steps to create a more secure cyberspace and ICT by developing and operationalising national Computer Emergency Response Teams by 2005. All member countries were due, by 2004, to have in place a common framework for sharing infocomm security threats and vulnerability assessment information. Infocomm security expertise and information is to be shared among member countries to help develop relevant policies and exchange real-time information on infocomm security issues.

Singapore's strategic and natural disaster-free location makes it an ideal place to site disaster recovery facilities. Initiatives were taken to enhance this capability by developing the pertinent value chain in Singapore including global and local leaders in business continuity consultancy, infocomm technology solutions, data centres and work-desk recovery services, and infrastructure and connectivity solutions. Specifically, IDA has identified training programmes to develop relevant expertise and subsidise their costs, defined processes to expedite passages of foreign personnel in the event of disaster recovery, and facilitated the development of industry standard in this field.

Technology Crime Investigation Capabilities

The Criminal Investigation Department (CID) is the premier investigation agency in Singapore vested with the staff authority for all criminal investigation matters within the Singapore police. Apart from investigating all major and specialised crime cases, CID houses a Technology Crime Division. As the authority on technology crimes, the division comprises investigation specialists, forensic specialists as well as builders of a technology crime capability for the entire police force. Its scope of operation goes beyond computer crime and includes traditional crimes committed with the use of technology such as encrypted mobile devices, Internet and even the wireless platform. To ensure that the nation is ready for such crimes of the future, the approach adopted by the division was also to build capabilities through research, alliance building and education.

Tasks of the Technology Crime Division include the following:

- Carry out investigation and forensic analysis on all technology crimes reported
- Prevent and deter unlawful acts involving computer and information technologies that threaten or target the security of electronic infrastructures in Singapore through public education and awareness programmes
- Raise the competency and proficiency of SPF in dealing with technology crime, which includes both computer-related crime and cyber-crime
- Lead other law enforcement entities of SPF on issues related to technology crime
- Shape the national investigation capacity for technology crimes through alliances with the local partners
- Ensure operational readiness of SPF in handling technology crime

Table 7.1 Computer-related offences, 1997–2002

Offence	*Number of cases*					
	1997	*1998*	*1999*	*2000*	*2001*	*2002*
Hacking	3	5	13	9	15	8
Access to commit a further offence (computer fraud)	4	2	3	1	4	35
Unauthorised use of computer service	20	101 (6)*	159 (86)	157 (101)	52 (12)	41 (4)
Other offences under CMA	12	8	10	24	66	48
Total	39	116	185	191	137	132

Note: **Brackets denote cases involving Global Roaming Services*

As the use of infocomm technology becomes more pervasive in society, an increasing trend in the perpetration of technology-related crimes can be expected and is further validated by local statistics.

To cater to technological needs, local universities are tapped to provide research capabilities and researchers to gain more field exposure in the process. For example, the Singapore Police and Nanyang Technological University are collaborating to tackle the increasingly prominent role of technology in crimes, particularly in the area of forensics.

The National Emergency System and the National Critical Infrastructures Assurance

New security threats that emerged in the post-11 September era are real and require closer cooperation between the military and Homefront agencies. Singapore has been giving priority to the enhancement of existing homeland security so that the capacity to handle a conventional security threat is not diminished as efforts are multiplied to deal with new non-conventional threats and terrorism. The National Emergency System is an all-comprehensive system encompassing civil security, civil defence, the provision of essential services, and the smooth operation of the Republic's economy during an emergency.

An immediate follow-up to 11 September taken by the Homefront agencies was a quick review of the vulnerabilities and strengths of Singapore's national critical infrastructures, which include the financial, telecommunications, information, utilities, transport and public health sectors. The review reinforced the point that longer-term preparedness for the homeland would require the involvement not just of the government but the private sectors and the Singaporean community at large.

Public Awareness and Professional Competency

IDA envisages an infocomm-savvy Singaporean society and has initiated several initiatives in this direction. In particular, IDA implemented the three-year e-Lifestyle and Marketing programme to demystify infocomm technology and enable Singaporeans to use it to enhance their quality of life and standard of living in the information society. A month-long national campaign, e-Celebrations Singapore, is held each March to get everyone connected online; it showcases a series of events planned by various strategic partners to educate consumers on infocomm technology.

On the infocomm security front, IDA organises public awareness campaigns aimed at the public and private sectors as well as the general public to inculcate safe computing practices. The 'Trust and Security Month' was held in July 2003. It features fun and interesting activities designed to show consumers and businesses how to protect themselves on the Internet. The Security and Trust Month is the first of four additional thematic months under the e-Celebrations 2003 banner and now part of IDA's annual campaign to promote an e-lifestyle. The e-Celebrations website also hosts a variety of entertaining and informative awareness materials on infocomm security topics.

Adhering to its mission of increasing the nation's competency in infocomm security, SingCERT regularly conducts workshops, seminars and courses on more technical topics, which are freely available to the public. These events are publicised on SingCERT's website and through its mailing lists.

The National Infocomm Competency Centre (NICC) is an industry-led, government-supported organisation that assists individuals and organisations to maintain a high level of infocomm technology competency. NICC has initiatives in the following areas:

- Providing government funding to assist individuals and organisations
- Working at the strategic level to bring in, or to commission, the development of high-value infocomm technology courses or certification schemes that are required for the nation's competitiveness
- Helping to identify and accredit high-quality certification schemes to allow more informed decisions to be made by those who wish to take up certification
- Providing advice and assistance to individuals and organisations on infocomm technology competency matters

NICC has identified infocomm security technology as a critical skill and has assisted organisations such as SANS, ISC, ISACA and their respective certification programmes to have increasing visibility and better affordability in Singapore. This provides more avenues for quality training and means that employers can ascertain the proficiency of infocomm security professionals.

Professional Organisations

The Information Technology Standards Committee is an industry-led effort made up of volunteer members from the industry, supported by SPRING

Singapore, Singapore's national standards authority, and IDA. It is a neutral and open platform for interested industry and government parties to come together to agree on technical standards. Its Security and Privacy Standards Technical Committee has published *the IT Security Standards Framework (SS493)* Part I in 2001 and subsequently the *Public Key Infrastructure Security Standards (SS501)* Part 1 in 2003.

The *IT Security Standards Framework (SS493)*, a multipart standard, specifies an IT security standards framework that provides a comprehensive approach to developing IT security standards and helps to achieve a rigorous application of IT security standards for an organisation. This will enable organisations to implement appropriate IT security measures to meet their business needs. As changes in IT and other business environments are rapid, relevant documents in the SS493 will be reviewed and revised, and other parts will be added whenever necessary. The Security and Privacy Standards Technical Committee will be responsible for adopting or developing the relevant standards for the different components of the framework.

The *PKI Standards Framework (SS501)* provides a comprehensive overview of the technology, its use and limitations. It enables companies implementing PKIs to be better prepared to take the appropriate measures that will meet their business and IT security needs. The document also gives an overview of the *PKI Standards Framework* with the aim of facilitating the development and adoption of Public Key Infrastructure Standards in Singapore.

The National Trust Council (NTC) is an IDA-supported but industry-led council to build confidence in the e-commerce scene in Singapore. The NTC's purposes are primarily the following:

- Help businesses and consumers increase trust and confidence in e-commerce
- Develop and promote the 'National Trust Mark Programme' (the TrustSg programme is an approved certification scheme to accredit organisations whose members are bound by an online Code of Practice to promote good business practices, including e-commerce)
- Develop a Risk Management Framework to reduce fraud in e-commerce transactions as well as to promote good business practices
- Develop and promote thought leadership and best practices for a trusted e-commerce environment
- Identify and make recommendations for policies and relevant areas to promote trust and reduce fraud in e-commerce transactions
- Enhance the awareness of consumers and businesses in fraud in e-commerce transactions through seminars, case studies and research.

Existing and potential trust mark providers such as trade associations and chambers of commerce and businesses are encouraged to accredit themselves under the TrustSg Programme. If their Code of Practice meets the standards set by NTC, they will be appointed as authorised code owners and be given the authority to award the TrustSg seal to worthy online merchants within their industry. There are presently two authorised code owners for the B2C category: the Consumers Association of Singapore, and CommerceTrust Ltd.

Online merchants have to comply with the Code of Practice set by their respective authorised code owner to obtain the TrustSg seal. The TrustSg programme is an important initiative that contributes towards the development of Singapore as a trusted e-commerce hub. Accredited online merchants are recognised as trusted and secure players by consumers locally and globally. Consumers, in turn, feel safe to deal with a TrustSg accredited merchant, thus gaining confidence in online transactions.

In its bid to bring convenient and reliable e-services to citizens, the Singapore government has joined the TrustSg programme. The Ministry of Finance's Managing for Excellence Directorate is the authorised code owner for the government. The Ministry ensures that the government's Code of Practice complies with the TrustSg core principles and awards the TrustSg seal to respective public sector agencies.

The Public Key Infrastructure Forum Singapore was initiated by IDA as the key platform for industry and government collaboration to spur PKI adoption in the local e-commerce environment. The PKI Forum Singapore participates in key international forums on e-commerce security. Four working groups are to be formed to focus on specific areas such as business, interoperability, awareness and implementation. The forum is involved in the Asia PKI Forum that was formed to promote use of PKI in Singapore, Japan, Korea, Malaysia, Taiwan, Hong Kong and China.

The KSJ (Korea, Singapore, and Japan) Interoperability Working Group of the Asia PKI Forum was conceived in July 2001 as a step towards achieving objectives of PKI interoperability across the region. APKI KSJ-IWG conducted the Interoperability Project to explore how nationally certified Certification Authorities can interoperate with each other. The goal of the project is to develop a test-bed framework and implement an inter-working PKI framework that demonstrates the possibility of an integrated heterogeneous PKI.

The Singapore Information Technology Federation (SITF) is a trade association of, principally, companies in the infocomm industry, which include computer software and services, hardware manufacturers and suppliers, systems integrators, software developers, Internet and web-based content and service providers, access service providers and services bureaus, providers of IT education and training products, computer components, and telecommunications equipment. SITF is the national organisation representing the infocomm industry and acts as the advisory, consultative and coordinating body for the industry. It recently launched its Security Chapter to give recognition to companies and focus efforts in this specialised field.

Objectives of the Security Chapter are to:

- Build the visibility and reputation of Singapore as a security capital
- Fulfil Singapore's strategic objectives of building security competencies and growing an important piece of the global pie in the coming years
- Accelerate growth of the infocomm security industry through support for activities of the Security Chapter

Research and Development

The National University of Singapore and Nanyang Technological University operate research centres that perform research in infocomm security areas. Other research institutes in Singapore with R&D capabilities in this area include DSO National Laboratories and the former Laboratories for Information Technology.

DSO National Laboratories conducts research and development in science and technology for Singapore's defence. It comprises 13 centres of excellence, one of which is the Centre for Information Systems Security that focuses on R&D in information security for Singapore's defence.

The Laboratories for IT is now the Institute of Infocomm Research (I^2R) upon its merger with the Institute for Communications Research since November 2002. The I^2R retains its focus on infocomm security and has particular interests in the fields of cryptography, information and network security.

The Defence Science and Technology Agency is the national authority for defence science and technology, providing leading-edge solutions for the military defence and security of Singapore. It initiates and facilitates collaboration between local R&D facilities and overseas counterparts.

Infocomm Security Developers in Singapore

Numerous local Singaporean companies offer infocomm security consultancy, services and products. While many are spin-offs from research institutes, others have situated their development efforts in Singapore. The following are some of the developers located in Singapore:

CE-InfoSys is one of the world's leading providers of advanced network and data security systems. Founded in 1981 in Germany, CE-InfoSys successfully expanded its international activities around the world and now covers three major continents: Asia, Europe and North America. The company relocated its headquarters from Bodenheim (near Frankfurt) to Singapore. See www.ce-infosys.com.

D'Crypt believes that Personalised Security is the wave of the future. In a highly connected world brought about by Internet and advanced wireless telecommunications technology, sensitive information and / or transactions that are stored on magnetic media, or are transmitted over an open communications channel, have become highly valued assets that need to be protected. See www.d-crypt.com.

DataMark Technologies provides digital watermarking technologies targeted at B2B and B2C e-commerce markets. The steganography technologies allow digital data to be imperceptibly embedded in printed documents as well as in digital visual contents. See www.datamark-tech.com.

DigiSAFE develops, markets and supports a range of information security products and services. Solutions cover e-commerce, network security, Internet security, security appliances and encryptors. These products help companies safeguard valuable information through advanced security measures and are widely used by government agencies, military and paramilitary organisations, banks and financial institutions as well as enterprises. See www.digisafe.com.sg.

Encentuate was created to help companies move from weak logins to secure and manageable digital systems in an incremental manner. Its goal is to ensure customers of the most effective possible journey to strong digital identity. Encentuate delivers architecture for transitioning companies to strong digital identity and leapfrogs traditional single sign-on solutions that are cumbersome, expensive and prone to security breaches. See www.encentuate.com.

Hello Technology's innovation is the concept of Real-Time Customizable Security. Individuals can help themselves to configure their security options to meet their needs. Institutions can customise the security of their services to enable better protection for their customers as well as to mitigate their own business risks. This revolutionises how security can be offered to the mass consumer market once and for all. Consumers have the choice of security that matches their needs. Institutions gain trust from consumers in provisioning their products and services via cost-effective security measures. See www.hello-technology.com.

i-Sprint Innovations is a leading provider of enterprise application security solutions. Its products make it easy for financial institutions, security-sensitive organisations and large corporations to centralise security administration, authorisation, authentication and the audit services of their business applications. i-Sprint's suite of security solutions is designed to meet the stringent requirements of any security sensitive environment, thus enabling clients to enjoy end-to-end security and secure access to mission-critical applications. See www.i-sprint.com.

PrivyLink provides high-assurance secure wireless and e-commerce solutions, and consultancy services on Internet business strategy and applications deployment. Its security e-commerce solutions cover areas such as Internet banking, mobile banking, cross-country e-commerce payment processing hubs, banking network infrastructure, and online government services delivery. See www.privylink.com.

REDiSAFE develops data protection software that provides data backup for enterprises. It is designed as a simple administration-free appliance that offers high security, total data privacy, and off-site backup replication for rapid disaster recovery. The solution is also very scalable, working in environments from single PCs to office networks. See www.redisafe.com.

SecureAge provides seamless application and data security solutions for governments and corporations in the Asia Pacific region. Its flagship product helps companies to safeguard their proprietary corporate information by fully securing their e-mail, digital documents, files transfer, remote access, as well as online and wireless transactions. See www.secureage.com.

Sentry Technologies provides solutions to segregate dual uses of the personal computer in a foolproof manner. The typical uses of computers involve inter-mixing of sensitive information and IT systems with a risky environment such as the Internet. Sentry Technologies allows a safe way to use computers via a hardware solution. See www.sentrytech.com.sg.

Ufinity is a leader in providing secure identity management and mobile-related products and solutions. With successful deployments in leading regional telecommunication operators, government and media organisations, Ufinity has extensive experience to meet complex deployment needs. Its suite of security products increases the security of digital assets and increase convenience with Single Sign-On capabilities. See www.ufinity.com.

Conclusion

The scarcity of human resources poses a significant barrier to Singapore's endeavour to address cyber-security issues. Colleges and universities worldwide do not readily churn out expertise in this area; the training of a single proficient professional takes much field experience and peculiar aptitude, and the individual's trustworthiness becomes a weightier factor in his or her eventual employment. None of these problems sit well with the immediate and wide-ranging issues that demand our attention. Nonetheless, the Singapore government has embarked on the aforementioned initiatives to reap strategic returns and maximise the utility of available resources.

Much is at stake and much remains to be done. The Singapore government believes that by realising synergies among the stakeholders, domestic or international, it fulfils the promise of prosperity and vibrancy that cyberspace offers.

8

Cyber-Crime in the 21st Century: Windows on Australian Law

Simon Bronitt and Miriam Gani*

In the Second Reading speech of the Cyber-crime Bill 2001 (Cth), the Federal Attorney-General claimed that the legislation 'aims to place Australia at the forefront of international efforts to address the issue of cyber-crime'.[1] In the wake of the terrorist attacks in the United States on 11 September 2001, the Bill has been represented as a measure to combat the growing threat of cyber-terrorism.[2] In truth, the legislation was the product of a national law reform process commenced a decade earlier, and which has produced a Model Criminal Code. The code, drafted by an inter-governmental committee called the Model Criminal Code Officers Committee (MCCOC), was intended to serve as a comprehensive model for adoption in all Australian jurisdictions. The *Cyber-crime Act 2001* (Cth) enacted by Federal Parliament was based on MCCOC recommendations contained in a report published in January 2001 dealing with damage and computer offences.[3] As the table of legislation below reveals, the process of harmonisation has just begun. New South Wales amended its computer crime provisions in line with the Model Criminal Code in 2001[4] and the Australian Capital Territory did likewise in 2002.[5] Victoria followed suit in mid-2003.[6]

Given the moves towards codification and uniformity in Australia,[7] and the potential broad reach of federal jurisdiction over cyber-crime (discussed below), this chapter focuses discussion on the Model Criminal Code, the federal *Cyber-crime Act* and the New South Wales adaptations of those provisions. Cyber-crime legislation in other jurisdictions is detailed in the tables of legislation below. As this chapter reveals, the federal model represents a watershed in Australian legislative responses, not only embracing a new rationale for the offences, but also significantly expanding rules governing jurisdiction and powers of investigation. On face value, these reforms appear to temper past legislative excesses, but the spectre of overcriminalisation continues to lurk in the fine print.

The Nature and Incidence of Cyber-Crime

The term 'cyber-crime', a techno-neologism of the past decade, has now filtered into international treaties, domestic statutes and the wider legal consciousness. But what is it? In the Australian context, cyber-crime has been defined as 'any unauthorised activity, which involves or uses computers, digital technology, the Internet, communications systems or networks'.[8] These forms of illegality encompass a wide range of activities, which are either directed at or performed through the medium of a computer. Such broad definitions encompass two distinct categories of criminality: first, traditional crimes (such as theft or fraud) where the connection to computer technology is relatively peripheral to the offence; and second, new forms of behaviour only made possible by the technology itself (such as infection of databases by computer viruses and denial of service attacks). In relation to the second category, these behaviours may involve the unlawful accessing, distribution or exploitation of *information* — whether that information is commercially sensitive, copyrighted or confidential, or whether it constitutes offensive or obscene material. Historically, the protection of information has largely fallen outside the province of the criminal law, and has been more frequently addressed by intellectual property, privacy, commercial, and even tort laws.[9]

The Model Criminal Code has adopted a more focused approach to the definition and scope of cyber-crime, addressing through computer-specific offences *only* those activities, which cannot be dealt with as offences under the general criminal law. As the MCCOC Report acknowledged, where computers are used as the tool for committing conventional crimes like fraud, deficiencies and gaps in existing offences can be remedied simply by extending or amending existing definitions.[10] Consequently, the *Cyber-crime Act 2001* (Cth) legislates primarily in relation to the second category of computer-related crime discussed above. While the stated objective of the *Cyber-crime Act* is 'protecting the security, reliability and integrity of computer data and electronic communications'[11] along with remedying deficiencies in the existing law, as we will explore below, the Federal Act and its New South Wales counterpart may give undue protection to the data itself.

There is little doubt that computer misuse is a widespread and increasingly frequent phenomenon in Australia. In 2002, a broad cross-section of Australian organisations from the private and public sectors were surveyed in relation to recent computer security incidents.[12] The types of incidents reported by respondents ranged widely in terms of seriousness and type and included misuse of Internet access or e-mail by employees (80% of respondents); virus, worm or Trojan infection (76%); theft of laptops (74%); denial of service attacks (43%); unauthorised privileged access (39%); breach of proprietary or confidential information (24%); misuse of internal computer resources (23%); system penetration by an outsider (20%); financial fraud (16%); theft or sabotage of data or networks (15%); telecommunications fraud (10%); eavesdropping (1%); and wiretapping (1%).[13]

The findings of the survey reveal the extent and nature of computer crime and misuse in the commercial context in Australia. The key findings include:

- 67% of respondents suffered a computer security incident in 2002 despite significant investment in security technologies, with 35% of respondents experiencing six or more such incidents.[14]
- 89% of respondents reporting a computer security incident were attacked from an external source, whereas fewer than 65% experienced internal attacks.[15] This appears to be a reversal of the situation reported in the 1999 survey,[16] and earlier studies, which found that most computer misuse related to the unauthorised access to computers by internal persons rather than by external 'hackers'.[17]
- Only 31% of organisations reported incidents to law enforcement authorities. Over 60% of respondents reported that they did not take any legal action whatsoever, citing lack of confidence in the authorities' ability to apprehend perpetrators and fear of negative publicity as major reasons for the failure to report.[18] Most significantly, respondents who did report incidents were four times more likely to seek recourse from the criminal law than to pursue civil remedies — a reverse of the trend in the United States.[19]

These data provide the empirical context in which to analyse deficiencies in the law and to evaluate the likely impact of recent Australian reforms. In our view, this raises the following critical issues:

- The criminalisation threshold
- The dangers of overcriminalisation
- The enforcement deficit

The criminalisation threshold

There remains a lack of consensus over the forms of computer misuse that should attract a criminal sanction, as opposed to a civil remedy such as those attaching to intellectual property and commercial laws. Indeed, some of the 'security incidents' reported above do not properly fall within the province of the criminal law. Many forms of e-mail or Internet misuse by employees, for example, would raise industrial relations or management issues, rather than necessarily warranting criminalisation. On the other hand, where that use of e-mail or Internet is intended to harass or intimidate a fellow employee, that conduct may amount to stalking or 'cyber-stalking', for which criminal sanctions are both available and appropriate.[20] The point at which computer misuse becomes computer crime, therefore, is a question that needs to be carefully addressed by both policymakers and lawmakers. A key question has been whether, and under what conditions, unauthorised access to data should be criminalised.

The dangers of overcriminalisation

A related issue is the potential for overcriminalisation through either the creation of broadly defined offences or the over-extension of jurisdiction. The recognition by law reformers that much computer misuse may be prosecuted under the ordinary criminal law, with minor amendments,[21] has largely addressed the first concern about overbroad definitions. Indeed, the new offences in the *Cyber-crime Act 2001* (Cth) seem more focused than their predecessors. While the substantive offences are more limited in scope, their geographical reach has been expanded significantly to deal with the increasing reports, noted above, of external attacks. The multi-jurisdictional dimension of the Internet has supported the enactment of special extraterritorial jurisdiction for these offences, exceptionally attaching liability to Australian citizens who commit computer offences overseas that have no real or significant links to their home jurisdiction. It is the globalisation of cyber-crime, rather than draconian offence definitions, which constitutes a new dimension of overcriminalisation.

Enforcement deficit

Another question raised by the data is the extent to which the reluctance to report computer misuse is related to the perceived inadequacy of existing offences and investigative powers, or to the low priority attached to cyber-crime investigation within law enforcement agencies themselves.

The Changing Rationale for Computer Offences

In Australia, criminal law is not primarily a federal responsibility. Each of nine jurisdictions in Australia — the Commonwealth, six States and two Territories — have the power to legislate in this area. While States and Territories enjoy plenary legislative powers, federal criminal jurisdiction is limited by the competence of the Commonwealth Parliament to enact offences under a head of power in the Constitution. Accordingly, the Commonwealth has power to make laws to protect its own computers and data, as well as the power under s. 51(v) of the Constitution, to make laws with respect to 'postal, telegraphic, telephonic and other like services'.

Every jurisdiction in Australia has enacted computer offences. Within this decentralised system of criminal law, divergence between jurisdictions is inevitable: see tables of legislation. However, as discussed above, the Model Criminal Code is a powerful force for criminal law uniformity.

A further impetus towards a national approach is the dominance of the Internet and its role in federalising criminal jurisdiction: the new offences in the *Cyber-crime Act 2001* (Cth) apply to activities involving Commonwealth data, computers or use of a 'telecommunications service'.[22] With access to networks and Internet depending on such services, Alex Steel has concluded that 'the Commonwealth has taken over a large proportion of all "cyber-crime" in Australia'.[23]

Creative adaptation: old crimes for new criminality

Like computer anti-virus software, laws addressing computer crime need regular updating. Over time, there have been distinct shifts in legal approach ranging from adapting old crimes to enacting computer-specific offences. In the absence of specific computer offences in the 1980s, there was little choice but to attempt to use the existing criminal law (most notably property offences) to deal with computer misuse. By the late 1980s, it was becoming apparent that the criminal law was having difficulty keeping up with modern technology.[24] This was largely because the criminal law found it difficult to incorporate computer data within its traditional concept of 'property'. The reported cases exposed the difficulties of applying theft to computer hackers who engaged in unauthorised copying of confidential information from a computer database. The courts held that information (even if confidential) was not property capable of being stolen and, since the hackers did not intend to prevent retention of the information by the owner of the database, there could be no intention to permanently deprive.[25] For these reasons, Gordon Hughes suggested in an article written in 1990 that hacking did not constitute theft under Australian criminal law.[26]

Even where the hacker went beyond mere access or copying, and caused damage to data or computer systems, it was not clear that the behaviour constituted criminal damage, an offence, which traditionally is limited to damage to tangible property.[27] While there were no reported prosecutions in Australia, cases in England and Canada[28] suggested that this kind of behaviour could constitute damage to property. In *Re Turner* (1984) 13 CCC (3d) 430 at 434, Justice Gray of the High Court of Ontario focused not on a restrictive definition of 'property', nor on the distinctions between tangible and intangible property, but rather on the 'gist of the offence' and whether there had been 'interference with the enjoyment of the property'. On that basis, defendants who had gained access to a business competitor's computer tapes and had tampered with the program so that operators were unable to access the data without a new access code were found to have caused malicious damage to property.

Such strained interpretation of traditional offences demonstrated to many commentators the inadequacy of applying existing laws to computer misuse, and the desirability of a distinct statutory regime of computer offences.[29] That said, some commentators still maintain that special offences are largely redundant, and that minor definitional amendment to existing theft, deception and damage offences could achieve the same results.[30]

First generation laws: Part VIA, *Crimes Act 1914* (Cth)

The first generation of legislative responses had begun as early as 1983 in the Northern Territory.[31] By the late 1980s, the desirability of a coordinated national strategy for computer crime was recognised by the Standing Committee of Attorneys-General. The former Chief Justice, Sir Harry Gibbs, was appointed to chair a review of computer crime for the Commonwealth.[32] The model legislation developed by the Gibbs Committee was adopted in the Commonwealth, New South Wales, Tasmania and the Australian Capital Territory. The major concern in the Committee's Report was the protection of the confidentiality and integrity of data or programs stored in Commonwealth computers. Commonwealth legislation implemented the recommendations of the Gibbs Committee by inserting into the *Crimes Act 1914* (Cth) a new Part VIA — Offences relating to Computers.

In line with the other jurisdictions, there was no effort to redefine 'property' but rather the focus became the creation of specific offences criminalising unauthorised access (and related activity) to a Commonwealth computer system or to any system through a telecommunications carrier. Section 76B created three categories of intentional and unauthorised access to Commonwealth data with a graduation of penalties depending on differing circumstances of aggravation. Section 76D created offences of unauthorised access to data through the use of Australian facilities or facilities provided by telecommunications carriers (e.g. Telstra). Sections 76C and 76E created offences where data is intentionally and without authority destroyed, erased or altered, or inserted, or if the lawful use of the computer is interfered with, interrupted or obstructed. These offences were punishable by a maximum of ten years' imprisonment.

Section 76E (c) was aimed, in particular, at hacking activities such as 'denial of service' attacks. Under that subsection, any person who, using a facility provided by a telecommunications carrier, impeded or prevented access to, or impaired the usefulness or effectiveness of, data stored in a computer was guilty of an offence punishable by a maximum of ten years' imprisonment.

Only New South Wales, Tasmania and the Australian Capital Territory followed the federal model in specifically addressing the problem of damage to electronically stored data. The provisions mirrored s. 76C of the *Crimes Act 1914* (Cth) by prohibiting the destruction, erasure, alteration or insertion of data in a computer or the unauthorised interference, interruption or obstruction of the lawful use of a computer.[33] No other jurisdiction in Australia included a comparable offence to s. 76E(c) to deal with denial of service attacks. Tasmania did, however, extend the protection from unauthorised interference, interruption or obstruction to the lawful use of a system of computers or the data stored in that computer or system of computers.

Other jurisdictions, while addressing the issue of unauthorised access (see Table 8.1) took a minimalist approach to the creation of computer-specific offences. Victoria, for example, enacted a widely drafted, strict liability offence of computer trespass. Section 9A of the *Summary Offences Act 1966* (Vic), as amended by the *Crimes (Computers) Act 1988* (Vic), provides: 'A person must not gain access to, or enter, a computer system or part of a computer system without lawful authority.' While unauthorised access was prohibited, these jurisdictions did not proscribe the modification, alteration or deletion of data.

A Queensland report concluded that such provisions were unnecessary because the common law, as discussed above, had been able to adapt existing criminal damage offences to cover data damage.[34] It may be presumed that the other jurisdictions were equally content to rely on adaptation of existing crimes to computer misuse.[35]

In sum, the first generation of legal responses to cyber-crime in Australia display, depending on the jurisdiction, characteristics of under-reaction, appropriateness and overzealousness. In relation to the latter, the decision of the Federal Parliament to prohibit mere unauthorised access — without anything more — posed a significant risk of overcriminalisation. By making unauthorised access to information held in computerised form a serious offence, the legislature embarked on a path that the common law had avoided. As was observed in the Canadian Supreme Court: 'The criminalisation of certain types of conduct should not be done lightly. If the unauthorized appropriation of confidential information becomes a criminal offence, there would be far reaching consequences that the courts are not in a position to contemplate.'[36]

These defects in the federal legislation were exacerbated for those jurisdictions, which modelled their computer laws on the Gibbs Report. This is because the criminal activity was no longer restricted to unauthorised access to data held on government computers (usually on a restricted access system), but rather was extended to encompass unauthorised access to *any* computer data held *anywhere*.[37] The effect of these provisions was that data held in computerised form enjoyed the protection of the criminal law when, if the same information were recorded in paper form, it would not. The question became: why should secret or private information held in computer programs be treated differently from secrets held in locked rooms or filing cabinets?

Furthermore, those jurisdictions which modelled their provisions on s. 76C of the Federal *Crimes Act 1914* (Cth) not only prohibited the modification of data but also interference with or interruption or obstruction of the lawful use of a computer (i.e. the physical object). The literal scope of such provisions was so wide as to extend to conduct which may involve any function at all of the computer or its programs.

While suggesting that protection of Commonwealth facilities and computers by such provisions may be justified, the MCCOC Report acknowledged that such slavish adoption of the federal offences by other jurisdictions and in relation to computers in general amounted to the creation of 'blunderbuss' provisions: 'One might just as well argue for offences of impeding the lawful use of a television set or record player.'[38]

Second generation laws: model criminal code and *Cyber-crime Act 2001* (Cth)

The *Cyber-crime Act 2001* (Cth) marks the beginning of second generation laws in Australia. The new Act exhibits a more appropriate and proportionate response to cyber-crime than the laws enacted in the 1980s and 1990s, some of which continue to operate in several jurisdictions in Australia (see Table 8.1). Furthermore, these second generation laws demonstrate a shift in focus towards protecting the *integrity* of data systems, rather than viewing the data itself as a *specie* of property capable of being damaged or appropriated without consent. This new generation of cyber-crime laws aims to protect the commercial value of the integrity of the systems that process and store that information, rather than the information itself. In this sense, these laws could be viewed as examples of what Alldridge terms 'crimes against the market' — that is, behaviour which prevents a market functioning according to its professed objectives of competition and the freedom of autonomous individuals to enter into contracts according to their respective perceptions of their own self-interest.[39]

Clearly, then, the MCCOC report acknowledged the problems of overcriminalisation inherent in the first generation laws enacted in Australia: the sections clarified that the offences required proof of fault, namely intention, recklessness or knowledge (see Table 8.2). The report recognised the inappropriateness of singling out confidential information in electronic form for protection by the criminal law and endorsed the principle of 'online-offline consistency' — the notion that regulation of unlawful conduct should as a rule be consistent in relation to conduct in cyberspace and conduct in the physical world.[40] Specifically, in relation to confidential information, 'The committee could discern no principle or basis for a distinction between secrets held in locked rooms, bureaus or filing cabinets and secret or private information stored in computer programs.'[41]

It further suggested that any move by the criminal law to extend its ambit to the protection of privacy and data secrecy should be a legislative one, of general and not particular application, so that all confidential information is treated in the same way regardless of whether it is in paper or computerised form. Accordingly, rather than centring on the protection of privacy or secret information, the MCCOC Report asserted, the computer offences proposed for the Code focused on ensuring the integrity of computer systems.

The *Cyber-crime Act 2001* (Cth) enacts seven computer offences into the Federal Criminal Code (see Table 8.2).[42] These offences draw heavily on the *Computer Misuse Act 1990* (UK), and drafts of the Council of Europe Convention on Cyber-Crime (see Csonka in Chapter 15).[43]

Table 8.1 Computer crime offences by jurisdiction: non-Model Criminal Code offences

Prohibited Conduct		*TAS Criminal Code Act*	*SA Summary Offences Act*	*QLD Criminal Code Act*	*WA Criminal Code*	*NT Criminal Code*
Unauthorised access (UA)		s257D	s44	s408D(1)	s440A	s222
	Physical Element (PE)	UA to a computer, system of computers or any part of a system of computers	Unauthorised operation of a restricted-access computer system (CS)	Use of a restricted computer without the consent of the controller[2]	UA to info on / operation of a restricted-access CS or a part or application of a CS	Unlawfully abstracting confidential information from a computer
	Fault Element (FE)	Intention				Intent to cause loss, to gain benefit or to publish
	Penalty (Pen)	$2000 or 2 years[1]	$2500	2 years	$4000 or 1 year	3 years
Data modification		s257C	⊗	⊗	⊗	See the Code table
	PE	Damaging data its or obstructing use				
	FE	Intention				
	Pen	$2000 or 2 years				
		s257E				
	PE	Introducing into a CS false information as data				
	FE	Dishonesty				
	Pen	$2000 or 2 years				
Fraud, Theft or Deception		s257B	⊗	⊗	⊗	s 276E
	PE	Using a computer (including by manipulating data or obstructing its use)				Unlawful use of access time charged to another person
	FE	Intent to defraud				
	Pen	$2000 or 2 years				3 years
Aggravated access		⊗	s44	s408D(2) and (3)	⊗	s276B
	PE		Unauthorised operation of a restricted-access computer system	See footnote 2		Unlawful access or use of data unlawfully accessed
	FE		Intention to benefit from or cause detriment to another			Intention to cause loss or harm or to gain a benefit
	Pen		$2500 or 6 months			10 years

SYMBOL KEY: ⊗ = No equivalent provision. [1] s 43A, *Police Offences Act 1935* (SA).[2] This section contains a range of aggravated offences. Section 408D(2) imposes a five-year imprisonment penalty where a person 'causes or intends to cause detriment or damage, or gains or intends to gain a benefit'. Section 408D(3) imposes a ten-year imprisonment penalty where a person 'causes a detriment or damage or obtains a benefit for any person to the value of more than $5 000, or intends to commit an indictable offence'.

Table 8.2 Computer crime offences by jurisdiction: Model Criminal Code offences

Prohibited Conduct		*MCC*	*Cth Criminal Code Act 1995*	*NSW Crimes Act 1900*	*ACT Criminal Code 2002*
Unauthorised access (UA) or unauthorised modification (UM) of restricted data		Summary offence	s478.1	s308H	s120
	PE	UA to or UM of restricted data held in a computer	UA to or UM of restricted data held in a computer*	UA to or UM of restricted data held in a computer	UA to or UM of restricted data held in a computer
	FE	Intent to cause access or modification and knowledge that this is unauthorised	Intent to cause access or modification and knowledge that this is unauthorised	Intent to cause access or modification and knowledge that this is unauthorised	Intent to cause access or modification and knowledge that this is unauthorised
	Pen	2 years	2 years	2 years (summary offence)	2 years and / or $20 000
Unauthorised modification (UM) of data with intent to cause impairment		s4.2.5	s477.2	s308D	s116
	PE	UM of data	UM of data*	UM of data	UM of data
	FE	Knowledge that unauthorised and intent to impair data or access to it / recklessness as to impairment	Knowledge that unauthorised and recklessness as to impairment	Knowledge that unauthorised and intent to impair data or access to it / recklessness as to impairment	Knowledge that unauthorised and intent to impair data or access to it / recklessness as to impairment
	Pen	10 years	10 years	10 years	10 years and / or $10 000
Aggravated offences		s4.2.4	s477.1	s308C	s115
	PE	UA to or UM of data or unauthorised impairment (UI) of electronic communication	UA to or UM of data or UI of electronic communication by means of a telecommunications service	UA to or UM or data or UI of electronic communication	UA to or UM of data or UI of electronic communication
	FE	Knowledge that unauthorised and intent to commit or facilitate a serious indictable offence	Knowledge that unauthorised and intent to commit or facilitate a serious offence	Knowledge that unauthorised and intent to commit or facilitate a serious indictable offence	Knowledge that unauthorised and intent to commit or facilitate a serious offence
	Pen	Maximum applicable to serious offence	Not exceeding serious offence penalty	Maximum applicable to serious indictable offence	Maximum applicable to serious offence

Table 8.2 *(continued)*

Unauthorised Impairment (UI)		s4.2.6	s477.3	s308E	s117
	PE	UI o1f electronic communication	UI of electronic communication*	UI of electronic communication	UI of electronic communication
	FE	Knowledge that unauthorised and intent to impair / recklessness as to impairment	Knowledge that impairment is unauthorised	Knowledge that unauthorised and intent to impair / recklessness as to impairment	Knowledge that unauthorised and intent to impair / recklessness as to impairment
	Pen	10 years	10 years	10 years	10 years and / or $10 000
Unauthorised Impairment (UI) of data held on disks, credit cards or other device used to store data by electronic means		Summary offence	s478.2	s308I	s121
	PE	UI of data held in computer disk, credit card or other electronic data storage device	UI of data held on a computer disk etc owned or leased by the Cth	UI of data held in computer disk, credit card or other electronic data storage device	UI of data held in computer disk, credit card or other electronic data storage device
	FE	Knowledge that unauthorised and intent to impair	Knowledge that unauthorised and intent to impair	Knowledge that unauthorised and intent to impair	Knowledge that unauthorised and intent to impair
	Pen	2 years	2 years	2 years (summary offence)	2 years and / or $20 000
Ancillary offences		s4.2.7	s478.3	s308F	s118
	PE	Possession or control of data	Possession or control of data	Possession or control of data	Possession or control of data
	FE	Intent to commit (or facilitate) a computer offence	Intent to commit (or facilitate) an offence against Division 477	Intent to commit (or facilitate) a serious computer offence	Intent to commit (or enable) a serious computer offence
	Pen	3 years	3 years	3 years	3 years and / or $30 000
		s4.2.8	s478.4	s308G	s119
	PE	Producing, supplying or obtaining data	Producing, supplying or obtaining data	Producing, supplying or obtaining data	Producing, supplying or obtaining data
	FE	Intent to commit (or facilitate) a computer offence	Intent to commit (or facilitate) an offence against Division 477	Intent to commit (or facilitate) a serious computer offence	Intent to commit (or enable) a serious computer offence
	Pen	3 years	3 years	3 years	3 years and / or $30 000

* There must be a connection with a Commonwealth computer, a computer where data is held on behalf of the Commonwealth or the access, modification or impairment (whichever applies) must be via a telecommunications service.

Table 8.2 *(Continued)*

Prohibited Conduct		*NT Criminal Code*	*VICCrimes Act 1958*
Unauthorised access (UA) or unauthorised modification (UM) of restricted data			s247G
	PE		UA to or UM of restricted data held in a computer
	FE		Intent to cause access or modification and knowledge that this is unauthorised
	Pen		2 years
Unauthorised modification (UM) of data with intent to cause impairment		s276C	s247C
	PE	Unlawful modification of data	UM of data
	FE	Intent to impede access to or adversely affect reliability, security or operation of data.	Knowledge that unauthorised and intent to impair data or access to it / recklessness as to impairment
	Pen	10 years	10 years
Aggravated offences			s247B
	PE		UA to or UM of data or UI of electronic communication
	FE		Knowledge that unauthorised and intent to commit or facilitate a serious offence
	Pen		Maximum applicable to serious offence
Unauthorised Impairment (UI)		s276D	s247D
	PE	Unlawful impairment of electronic communication	UI of electronic communication
	FE	Intent to impair	Knowledge that impairment is unauthorised and intent to impair / recklessness as to impairment
	Pen	10 years	10 years
Unauthorised Impairment (UI) of data held on disks, credit cards or other device used to store data by electronic means			s247H
	PE		UI of data held on a computer disk, credit card or other electronic data storage device
	FE		Knowledge that unauthorised and intent to impair
	Pen		2 years
Ancillary offences			s247E
	PE		Possession or control of data
	FE		Intent to commit (or facilitate) a serious computer offence
	Pen		3 years
			s247F
	PE		Producing, supplying or obtaining data
	FE		Intent to commit (or facilitate) a serious computer offence
	Pen		3 years

The MCCOC report noted that any protection of confidential information flowing from these provisions is incidental to the protection of the integrity of computer systems. That said, the new laws continue to offer some measure of protection to data alone, provided that the data has been protected by an access control system (e.g. a password). Conceived as a minor summary offence, s. 478.1 and the New South Wales equivalent make mere access to restricted data an offence, conferring considerable legal protection on the information thereby accessed. There appear to be two distinct tiers of computer offence: serious computer offences focus on protecting system integrity, while the minor summary offence protects access to restricted data. Notwithstanding legislative attention to serious computer crime, the bulk of enforcement, like drug law enforcement, may be directed towards these minor, less serious forms of cyber-criminality.

Cross-Border Enforcement: Jurisdiction in Cyberspace

Cybercrime knows no borders, yet the criminal law remains fundamentally territorial in nature. This paradoxical tension between the geographically bounded nature of criminal law and the trans-border quality of cyber-criminality is a recurrent theme in the literature. The traditional resolution of this paradox has been to recommend a radical reformulation of the rules governing jurisdiction. At the outset, we should disclose our scepticism towards the globalisation of cyber-crime and the pressure to embrace extraterritorial offences as the solution. We will return to this theme later.

In Australia, the process of reshaping the rules governing jurisdiction has occurred through a combination of judicial development of the common law and, more recently, legislative reform. A fundamental assumption of the criminal law is that 'all crime is local'.[44] This idea of territoriality is embodied in the presumption that statutes creating offences do not have extraterritorial effect. Of course, the presumption is rebuttable and the modern legislative trend is firmly in favour of expanding the extraterritorial reach of offences.[45]

The principle of territoriality — the bedrock of criminal jurisdiction — remains elusive, revealed only in cases where an accused claims that the court has no power to hear the charges. Early cases dealing with jurisdiction have tended to involve single-element offences — common crimes, such as murder, albeit committed in bizarre factual settings. For example, in a shooting homicide which occurred across the Murray River (the border between New South Wales and Victoria), the High Court in *Ward* (1980) 142 CLR 308 held that jurisdiction was conferred on the place where the *consequences* of the accused's conduct occurred (the terminatory theory), rather than the place where the *conduct causing death* initiated (the initiatory theory). The terminatory theory has been regarded as the basis for criminal jurisdiction under the common law in the Australian Capital Territory, New South Wales, South Australia and Victoria.

As a general test of jurisdiction, the terminatory theory has significant limitations. First, it is ill-suited to offences with multiple physical elements that may be committed at different times and different locations — the test in *Ward* was modelled on an offence (homicide) that had 'one core element which dictates where it may be tried'.[46] This problem is particularly acute in relation to cyber-crime where, for example, a hacker based in one jurisdiction may hack into a server in another, with a view to cause damage to data in a third. Second, the approach in *Ward* is also modelled around offences committed by human beings rather than legal entities such as corporations. While a human being cannot be in more than one place at a time, multinational corporations, acting through their legal officers and employees, may be simultaneously engaged in unlawful activity across numerous jurisdictions.[47]

The failure to include extraterritorial provisions in earlier State and Territory computer trespass offences was regarded as a significant drawback to 'effective administration of justice in a borderless high-technology environment'.[48] Reflecting this concern, some legislatures moved in the 1980s to adopt a wider test of jurisdiction based on territorial or geographical 'nexus' to supplement the common law.[49] In some jurisdictions, the legislature responded by creating an ad hoc exception in favour of extraterritoriality for computer offences.[50]

Perhaps influenced by these early signs of legislative dissatisfaction with the principle of territoriality, the High Court reconsidered its approach to jurisdiction in *Lipohar v The Queen* (1999) 168 ALR 8. The majority held that, in relation to conspiracy to defraud, the test ought to be whether there is a 'real connection', 'sufficient connection' or 'real link' between the offence and the jurisdiction seeking to try it.[51] Such flexibility reflects the increasing judicial acknowledgment that the decision to grant or decline jurisdiction involves careful consideration of policy matters (such as the location of necessary resources and evidence for a successful prosecution). In cases of crimes crossing international borders, questions of state policy and the requirements of comity between nations will also be relevant.[52] Although flexibility in determining jurisdiction was welcomed, there was also concern that the new test would confer upon police and prosecutors too much discretion in deciding where to institute proceedings, introducing unacceptable levels of uncertainty into the administration of criminal justice.[53]

Moreover, as reflected in Justice Kirby's dissent,[54] fundamental changes to the rules of jurisdiction should be left to the legislature rather than the courts.

The law governing jurisdiction was reviewed in the late 1990s by the MCCOC. Highly critical of the uncertainty in the common law, the committee adopted a principled rather than ad hoc approach to the rules for determining jurisdiction. It concluded that the legislature should address jurisdictional considerations prior to the enactment of an offence, rather than leave it to judges to resolve post hoc in the context of litigation.

The MCCOC scheme for jurisdiction, which was inserted into the Commonwealth *Criminal Code* in 1999, establishes standard geographic jurisdiction as the default, supplemented by four extended geographic bases for jurisdiction (Categories A–D) of varying breadth. Categories A–D do not require the crime to be geographically connected to the Territory (see Appendix to chapter). Jurisdiction extends overseas because of the citizenship or resident status of the accused and / or nature of the offence, not because of any geographic or territorial connection with Australia. Allaying fears of an over-reaching federal criminal jurisdiction, the drafters of the provision suggested: 'Naturally, it is intended that extended forms of jurisdiction will only be applied where there is justification for this, having regard to considerations of international law, comity and practice.'[55]

The Cyber-crime Bill 2001 (Cth) contained some of the first offences to benefit from this new approach. Category A jurisdiction was selected for the offences contained in the Bill: s. 476.3, *Criminal Code* (Cth), see Appendix. According to the Attorney-General, the use of Category A was justified because 'computer crime is often perpetrated remotely from where it has effect'.[56] In summary, the effect of this subsection was that federal computer offences extended to situations where:

1. The *conduct* constituting the offence occurs partly in Australia or on board an Australian ship or aircraft; or
2. The *result of the conduct* constituting the offence occurs partly in Australia or on board an Australian ship or aircraft; or
3. The offender is an *Australian citizen or company*.

The last ground is the most significant in terms of extraterritoriality, identifying the alleged offender's 'national status' as the basis for conferring jurisdiction. While consistent with the principle of nationality under international law, the extension of criminal jurisdiction beyond geographic territory to nationality is more common in legal systems based on the Roman / civil law rather than English common law.[57] The extraordinary breadth of jurisdiction under '3' above is revealed in the Explanatory Memorandum which notes:

'An Australian citizen who travels to a country where hacking is not an offence and, while there, uses a laptop to hack into a computer in a third country would also be caught by the proposed jurisdiction.' Australians travelling abroad now need to remember to take a copy of the *Cyber-crime Act 2001* (Cth) as well as their passports!

Recent commentary on these jurisdictional reforms suggested that 'the process of normalisation of extraterritoriality in the criminal law will be fostered and legitimated by the large (and increasing) number of international treaties dealing with transnational and global crime'.[58] Significantly, when the federal Cyber-crime Bill was introduced, the then draft of the Council of Europe Convention on Cyber-crime[59] was cited in the Explanatory Memorandum as providing a further justification for extraterritorial effect. What the memorandum failed to acknowledge was that the convention created an imperfect obligation, allowing States Parties to 'opt out' of creating offences with extraterritorial effect (Art. 22(2)).

The obvious danger with the new approach to jurisdiction is over-inclusiveness. It is regrettable that there are no guiding principles in the Criminal Code or elsewhere to assist with, or limit, the selection of a particular jurisdictional category. Although the Attorney-General promised that a conservative approach to extraterritoriality would be adopted, it may be difficult for the government or legislature to resist pressures to fight all forms of crime at the international level.

The federal code provision above did not, in the end, provide the template for a national model on jurisdiction. The extended approach would have encouraged the over-reaching of State and Territory criminal jurisdiction; had it been adopted, the political pressure to wage war on cyber-crime at the global as well as the local level would have been equally hard to resist.

While the Commonwealth adopted initial recommendations of the MCCOC, the State and Territories did not follow suit. Indeed, this reticence for adopting a 'category approach' is apparent in the MCCOC final report dealing with jurisdiction, released in early 2001.[60] Responding to concerns raised by state judges and legal academics, a narrower approach was proposed for dealing with State and Territory jurisdiction. Rather than adopt the Federal Criminal Code Categories A–D, the MCOCC final report recommends that a geographical nexus test be adopted for States and Territories (Clauses 2.7.1–2.7.3). The nexus between the State or Territory and the defendant may transcend geographic borders to those offences which, though committed wholly outside the State or Territory, have an effect therein. The place in which an offence has an effect is defined as including any place whose 'peace, welfare or good government' is threatened by the offence (see Clause 2.7.3).

This approach is a reversion to the test of jurisdiction favoured by the courts in Australia prior to changes made by the High Court in *Lipohar*.[61] It has been embraced, with some modifications, by several States and Territories.[62] The ebb and flow of jurisdictional reform in Australia reflects the wider tensions arising from the globalisation of crime, namely the recurring conflict between the local and federal, and the national and international legal orders.

Returning to our earlier note of cyber-scepticism, it is important not to overstate the jurisdictional difficulties created by cyber-crime. The problems of cross-border criminality are neither new nor unique to cyber-crime. What is novel in the federal jurisdiction is the significant shift beyond territoriality to nationality in defining the limits of jurisdiction, a move we believe warrants further critical attention. Bearing in mind the peripatetic tendencies of Australians, the Australian Federal Police will undoubtedly shudder at the new cyber-mandate for policing its citizens abroad. Practical and financial limitations, as well as competing local law and order concerns, will curb the tendency to extraterritoriality in all but the most serious of cases.

The gaps that allow cyber-criminals to hack and attack across borders with impunity are due more often to the lack of modern computer-specific offences than to the want of jurisdiction — indeed, we believe that the better strategy would be to encourage a regional harmonisation of laws and effective extradition arrangements, rather than to extend the geographic reach of the criminal law. Promoting extraterritoriality as the solution — under the mantra 'cyber-crime knows no borders' — may prove to be an impotent symbolic gesture that will only enliven jurisdictional disputes between nations and further discourage international collaboration in this field.

In some senses, proponents of the global approach to cyber-crime have been seduced by the 'cyberspace fallacy' — namely, that cyber-crime occurs outside physical geographic space and therefore beyond the frontiers of law and legal institutions.[63] This sustains the view that distinct transnational legal responses to cyber-crime are required.[64] However, as Chris Reed recently noted, computers and legal actors (whether individual or corporate) 'all have a real-world existence and are located in one or more physical world legal jurisdictions'.[65] In the context of cyber-crime, what hampers prosecution is not lack of jurisdiction or even appropriate and uniform laws, but rather lack of evidence (an issue discussed below). That said, it is unlikely that the present impulse to over-criminalise and over-extend computer offences can be halted post-11 September, an event that has led to the enactment of broad extraterritorial offences in many jurisdictions.

The extraterritorial application of computer offences will undoubtedly prove controversial, particularly in cases where links to the prosecuting jurisdiction are remote or tenuous. Recognising the practical limitations of extraterritoriality, we believe that it is preferable to approach transnational cyber-crime by fostering the role of private actors. An exclusive focus on state actors, whether national or supra-national policing agencies, ignores the considerable law enforcement capacity of private multinational corporations. Much cyber-crime uses infrastructure maintained by corporate entities that have strong commercial and financial interests to minimise and deter unlawful computer activity. They are also better placed to gather evidence of unlawful activity using computers, increasingly providing expertise and resources to fund police investigations. As discussion at a regional summit on cyber-crime in 2001 revealed, detection and investigation of cross-border fraud and copyright piracy is increasingly being coordinated by the private stakeholders, such as the major credit card companies and the Motion Picture Association of America.[66]

The role of these corporate interests in crime prevention and law enforcement has been largely neglected in the current literature. In relation to cyber-crime prevention, corporations may use various self-help strategies to frustrate and neutralise those perpetrating computer attacks. As the MCCOC noted, although 'strike-back' strategies (ranging from collecting information to disabling the intruder's system) may themselves violate various computer offences, some protective counterattacks may constitute the defence of property within the scope of the new self-defence provisions of the Model Criminal Code.[67] In relation to law enforcement, corporations can play a vital role in providing technical expertise, preparing briefs of evidence, supporting state prosecutions and participating in proactive policing operations. But unlike policing agencies, the power of multinational corporations to engage in investigation of cyber-crime is not restricted when they reach a geo-political border, nor subject to the same constitutional limitations as state officials in respecting due process rights during investigation. For example, the legal remedies against entrapment — namely the exclusion of evidence or stay of proceedings — seem to be directed to instances of *state*-created crime, that is, crime caused or instigated by police or informers acting under police direction.

There are only a handful of cases involving non-police entrapment. In one such case in Singapore, *SM Summit Holdings v PP*,[68] Chief Justice Yong Pung How did recognise that there was a judicial discretion to exclude evidence obtained by a private informer who, acting as agent provocateur, incited the commission of several copyright offences. The recognition of such a remedy in Singapore was more remarkable since the jurisdiction generally refuses to recognise remedies for entrapment beyond mitigation of sentence.[69]

Chief Justice Yong Pung How emphasised that this discretion was limited to cases where the illegal conduct of the informer itself constituted an essential ingredient of the offence charged — in these cases, he regarded the illegality and the threat to the Rule of Law that it involves as assuming a particularly malignant aspect. We consider the evidential rules relating to covert investigation below.

As Grabosky noted in Chapter 2, developing systems of accountability for private investigation is crucial: it involves a sensible assessment of the benefits, as well as disadvantages, in promoting further private policing of cyber-crime.

Cyber-crime Enforcement: Enhancing Police Powers of Investigation

A number of significant changes have been made to the powers available to law enforcement agencies to investigate computer offences. This section focuses on two areas: the search and seizure of computer evidence and the legal issues raised by using undercover methods to investigate cyber-crime. It discusses recent amendments to federal law governing criminal procedure, although it should be noted that many jurisdictions in Australia have also reformed their rules governing the admissibility of computer-based evidence in civil and criminal proceedings.[70]

Rather than enact offence-specific powers, federal parliament widened the scope of existing warrant powers to permit the search for and seizure of computerised material. With increasing use of computers and the Internet in work and home life, seeking warrants to search computer systems will become an increasingly routine aspect of criminal investigation.

The *Cyber-crime Act 2001* (Cth) provided an opportunity to update the search powers related to computer evidence. Although inserted into the *Crimes Act 1914* (Cth) in 1994, the search and seizure powers had failed to keep pace with technological advances, particularly the growth of encryption technologies. As the explanatory memorandum accompanying the Bill observed: 'The large amounts of data which can be stored on computer drives and disks and the complex security measures, such as encryption and passwords, which can be used to protect that information present particular problems for investigators.'[71]

Another perceived deficiency was that existing warrants were tied to particular physical locations. Within a networked environment, data is not necessarily located in one defined place but may be dispersed across a number of computers located elsewhere; this is commonly so where data is placed on an offsite storage system or centralised server. The dispersal of data across physical space hampers investigation, obliging police to obtain multiple warrants. To address this shortcoming, the *Cyber-crime Act* clarifies that police executing the warrant may search for data across different physical locations, not just at the search premises.[72] The provision dispenses with any need to notify or seek consent of third parties before searching and seizing any off-site data accessible from computers located on the search premises.

The federal *Cyber-crime Act* also inserted a new provision empowering a law enforcement officer to apply to a magistrate for an assistance order. This order directs a person with knowledge of a computer on which it is reasonably suspected there is evidential material to provide information or assistance to allow police to access or copy data, or convert it to documentary form. Thus computer operators, whether or not suspected of any criminal activity, can be compelled to reveal passwords to a system or provide the key to encrypted, otherwise confidential data. Failure to cooperate has been made an offence punishable by six months' imprisonment.[73] Also, the Act allows computer equipment to be removed from the premises to be searched elsewhere if this is faster, less costly or necessary to access relevant expertise. The new amendments also expand the power to copy material: previously, the authorities were only empowered to copy material believed to be evidential material. This meant that large volumes of data had to be examined on site, which could be time-consuming and costly.[74] The Act now clarifies that officers executing the warrant have the power to copy *all* of the data on the computer if it is reasonably suspected that the computer or data storage device contains some evidential material.[75]

Compared with ordinary search warrants, these powers are significantly wider in several respects. Ordinary search warrants of private premises do not allow the seizure of material unrelated to the investigation — for reasons of convenience and practicality, warrants targeting data allow the police to copy and analyse large quantities of data without any obligation to mitigate any negative impacts on the privacy interests of suspects or innocent third parties. While privacy is not absolute, under international human rights law, it is well established that intrusion into the lives and affairs of citizens for the purpose of crime detection must be necessary, reasonable and proportionate.[76] This power may not meet these standards.

Another novel and worrying feature of these new powers is the obligation placed on system operators (even when they may be suspects) to assist police gaining access to data. From a law enforcement perspective, imposing a duty on a person to assist with an investigation seems reasonable, an incremental extension of the existing legal duty on persons to refrain from hindering the execution of a search warrant.[77] This view, however, fails to give any weight to the countervailing interests in protecting the fundamental human rights of persons under criminal investigation. The Act does not address the potential for self-incrimination in cases where the person ordered by a magistrate to provide information or assistance to the police is also a suspect. The Act and Explanatory Memorandum provides no guidance on the relationship between these competing interests, simply noting that the creation of a statutory compulsion to assist police has been used in a range of Commonwealth regulatory legislation and is contained in the Council of Europe Convention on Cyber-crime. The courts will undoubtedly be called upon to decide whether evidence obtained as a result of statutory compulsion should be excluded on the grounds of unfairness or impropriety,[78] and whether there is an implied defence based on 'lawful excuse' for those persons who refuse to furnish information to police on the grounds that it might incriminate them. The prospect of suspected persons being compelled to reveal information under pain of prosecution exposes the underlying values on which the privilege against self-incrimination was designed to protect: the importance of ensuring fairness and respect for human dignity during criminal investigation.[79]

Statutory powers to facilitate covert investigation have also been applied to the detection of cyber-crime. The powers to intercept telecommunications, based on a federal statute, were originally confined to serious drug offences. In 1997, these powers to intercept were extended to investigation of computer offences, though annual reports tabled before Federal Parliament (1998–2001) reveal that only 23 warrants targeting computer offences were issued over that three year period — this compares with the 3163 warrants related to narcotic and trafficking offences.[80] These data suggest that computer crime, like white-collar crime generally, continues to be a subordinate priority for law enforcement agencies. It also implies that the police continue to rely on traditional investigative tools such as search warrants, as opposed to electronic surveillance, to gather evidence of computer offences. It may be that the cooperation of employers, system managers and ISPs in voluntarily reporting suspect activity to police has obviated the need for expensive surveillance operations.

Some restraints on covert investigation are applied through the ordinary rules of evidence and procedure. The dubious legality and propriety of undercover operations where police and informers themselves commit offences (commonly through the 'controlled deliveries' of drugs) were exposed to judicial scrutiny in *Ridgeway* (1995) 184 CLR 19. In this case, the majority of the High Court held that evidence of an offence procured by police illegality should be excluded, particularly where the illegality was a central element of the offence charged. As a result of this decision, federal legislation was enacted in 1996 that allowed police to obtain a certificate providing *prospective* immunity for serious narcotic offences committed in the course of approved operations. The legislation was originally limited to narcotic offences but was expanded by the *Measures to Combat Serious and Organised Crime Act 2001* (Cth) to include a long list of serious Commonwealth offences, including 'misuse of a computer or electronic communications'. These expanded powers permit police to commit various cyber-crimes, such as manufacturing and marketing viruses or hacking tools with a view to procuring the commission of computer offences by others. The extent to which this legislation condones entrapment or is desirable from a legal or policy perspective is a matter of continuing controversy.[81]

Conclusion

In the late 1980s, the legal construction of new categories of crime, such as hacking, responded to a 'moral panic'[82] about antisocial and disruptive behaviour involving computers. Legislatures responded by typically criminalising unauthorised access or trespass, coupling widely drawn offences with inadequate investigative powers and penalties. Not surprisingly, given the problems of definitional vagueness and lack of evidence discussed above, computer offences have not been vigorously prosecuted in Australia.

In the latest round of reforms, the rationale for computer offences has shifted from protection of information as a specie of property, to protecting the integrity of computer systems, their significance to national infrastructure and significant commercial value. The *Cyber-crime Act 2001* (Cth) is intended to serve as a national model and constitutes a significant watershed in legal responses to computer crime. Unlike earlier reforms, the Act bears the transnational influences of the Council of Europe Convention on Cyber-crime, which is emerging as a powerful force of harmonisation outside Europe — the text of the convention has been influential in shaping the policy and scope of the new legislation, as well as supporting an expanded jurisdictional reach for these offences.

With the emergence of a national approach, Australia seems well placed to respond to emerging cyber-crime threats: new offences protecting the integrity of computer systems are now supported by an expanded extraterritorial jurisdiction, recognising the multi-jurisdictional dimensions of cyber-crime within Australia and overseas. Evidence-gathering has also been facilitated by new expanded search warrant powers and powers to conduct covert surveillance. That said, it must be recalled that this upgrade has not occurred everywhere and, as the table of legislation reveals, several jurisdictions retain offences drafted in the late 1980s, with particular gaps in offences dealing with data modification.

These recent developments, from a law enforcement perspective, seem highly desirable. From a critical perspective, however, our concern is that these reforms reinforce the fallacy that cyber-crime is something *sui generis*, an offence whose definitional, jurisdictional, evidential and procedural rules are 'extraordinary'. This claim to uniqueness has the potential to serve as a cloak for ill-considered and draconian legal responses. Law reform over the past two decades has been a pastiche of complacency, appropriate reaction, and overzealous statutory responses.

The current enforcement deficit is not due to lack of legal powers. Although the police have always avidly enlisted technology in their fight against crime,[83] they have been slower to focus on computer offences as a law enforcement priority. A significant change to the priorities within policing and the politics of law and order would be required to shift focus from drugs and street crime, towards cyber-crime and white-collar criminals. That said, it is important to recognise the constraints on public policing, most notably financial ones. A more productive strategy may be to harness the resources of private corporate interests in a partnership to fight cyber-crime. As noted above, multinational corporations have powers to prevent and detect crime that transcend national borders.

Our final comment should be reserved for the looming threat of cyber-terrorism. The key terrorism provisions inserted into the Federal Criminal Code by the *Security Legislation Amendment (Terrorism) Act 2002* (Cth) prohibit a wide range of activities connected with 'terrorist acts'.[84] To constitute a terrorist act, the action must cause specified consequences or outcomes, such as causing physical harm, death or endangering life and so on. As well as these personal harms, the list of terrorist acts includes action that seriously interferes with, seriously disrupts, or destroys, an electronic system including an information system, a telecommunications system; or a system used for the delivery of essential government services.[85] These provisions have a broad extraterritorial effect, having been designated as Category D offences by s. 102.9 of the Code (discussed above).

While it would be wrong to conclude that the new cyber-crime laws in Australia are a direct response to terrorism, the events of 11 September have provided a powerful impetus for creating a new national framework for multi-jurisdictional crime in Australia. In April 2002, the prime minister and State and Territory leaders signed the Commonwealth, State and Territories Agreement on Terrorism and Transnational Crime (2002). While focusing primarily on measures to combat terrorism and organised crime, the agreement also contains arrangements for dealing with multi-jurisdictional crime. This includes a commitment by all Australian governments to modernise the criminal law in three priority areas — model forensic procedures, drug offences and computer offences.[86] It seems that the events of 11 September may have had one unintended consequence: to promote national consensus, hitherto impossible, on the future direction of cyber-crime laws in Australia.

Appendix

Summary of the jurisdiction rules under the Federal Criminal Code

Criminal Code Act 1995 (Cth) – Part 2.7 – geographical jurisdiction

Standard geographic jurisdiction (Division 14, Section 14.1)
The default test applies where the offence provision does not address the issue jurisdiction. This standard is similar to the common law principle of territoriality, that is, applying where the 'conduct' or a 'result' specified by the offence occurs wholly or partly in Australia.

Extended geographic jurisdiction (Division 15, Sections 15.1–15.4)

- CATEGORY A — covers Australian citizens or body corporates anywhere in the world, subject to a foreign law defence.
- CATEGORY B — covers Australian citizens, body corporates and residents anywhere in the world, subject to a foreign law defence.
- CATEGORY C — covers anyone anywhere regardless of citizenship or residence, subject to a foreign law defence.
- CATEGORY D — covers anyone anywhere regardless of citizenship or residence, no foreign law defence.

Extract from the Criminal Code Act 1995 (Cth)

15.1 Extended geographical jurisdiction—category A

(1) If a law of the Commonwealth provides that this section applies to a particular offence, a person does not commit the offence unless:
  (a) the conduct constituting the alleged offence occurs:
    (i) wholly or partly in Australia; or
    (ii) wholly or partly on board an Australian aircraft or an Australian ship; or
  (b) the conduct constituting the alleged offence occurs wholly outside Australia and a result of the conduct occurs:
    (i) wholly or partly in Australia; or
    (ii) wholly or partly on board an Australian aircraft or an Australian ship; or
  (c) the conduct constituting the alleged offence occurs wholly outside Australia and:
    (i) at the time of the alleged offence, the person is an Australian citizen; or
    (ii) at the time of the alleged offence, the person is a body corporate incorporated by or under a law of the Commonwealth or of a State or Territory; or

(d) all of the following conditions are satisfied:
  (i) the alleged offence is an ancillary offence;
  (ii) the conduct constituting the alleged offence occurs wholly outside Australia;
  (iii) the conduct constituting the primary offence to which the ancillary offence relates, or a result of that conduct, occurs, or is intended by the person to occur, wholly or partly in Australia or wholly or partly on board an Australian aircraft or an Australian ship.

9

Cyber-Crime: Current Status and Countermeasures in Japan

Masao Tatsuzaki

The development of the information and telecommunications industries is affecting the growth of many aspects of Japan's society and economy. It is driving research and development, as well as new business strategies and is increasing employment in information and telecommunications-related businesses. Conversely, developments in the industries have been accompanied by an increase in cyber-crime. Both government and private sectors understand that enhancing information security is essential, and police departments have been devising measures against cyber-crime.

This chapter outlines the situation on the IT revolution and cyber-crime in Japan, it introduces information security measures taken by the Japanese government and police, and reviews trends in cooperation with international efforts to combat cyber-crime.

The IT Revolution in Japan

In 2001, the Japanese government enacted the *Basic Law on the Formation of an Advanced Information and Telecommunications Network Society* (the Basic IT Law)[1], helping to ensure that everyone in Japan's 'knowledge-emergent society' can use IT and fully enjoy its benefits. The law is the premise of the IT Strategy Headquarters, led by the Prime Minister. The headquarters drew up the e-Japan Priority Policy Programme,[2] which clarifies all measures the government intends to rapidly implement, with emphasis on building an advanced information and telecommunications network.

With help and facilitation from the government and private sectors, the number of Internet users in Japan has been increasing (see Figure 9.1). At the end of 2001, users amounted to about 56 million, about 44% of the population.[3,4]

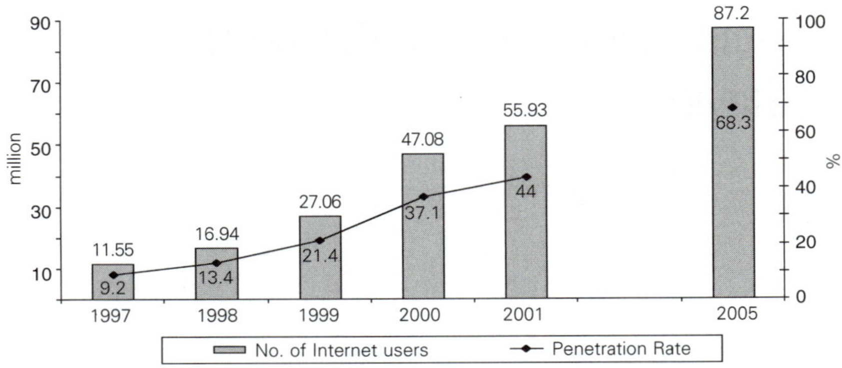

Figure 9.1 Trends in Internet Penetration in Japan

Cyber-crime, however, is one of the major challenges facing the IT revolution. The National Police Agency divides cyber-crime, or high-tech crime, into three categories:[5] crime against computers and data, Internet crime, and unauthorised computer access (violation of the *Unauthorised Computer Access Law*).[6] Crime against computers and data includes computer fraud,[7] the illegal production of electro-magnetic records,[8] obstruction of business by destroying computers,[9] destruction of public documents[10] and destruction of private documents.[11] These crimes were added to the Criminal Law in 1987 to deal with computer crime. Crime against computers and data also includes illegal production of electro-magnetic records for payment cards such as credit cards and bank cards,[12] which was added in 2001.

Internet crime, taken as an offence that takes place while the offender is using the Internet or in which the Internet is an essential factor, includes various kinds of crime such as fraud, defamation, intimidation, infringement of copyright, child prostitution, child pornography, distribution of obscene objects, narcotics-related crime, and makes up about 90% of all cyber-crime. Child prostitution also accounts for a major part of Internet crime. Child exploitation through the Internet, such as child prostitution, child pornography and violation of the juvenile protection ordinance, is a huge problem in Japan. Internet fraud, particularly concerning auctions conducted through the Internet, is the third largest concern (see Table 9.1 and Figure 9.2).

Table 9.1 Analysis of Cyber-Crime

	2002 Jan–Jun	*2001 Jan–Jun*	*2001*	*% change*
Crime against computer / data	**18**	**33**	**63**	**-15**
Computer fraud	12	28	48	-16
Illegal production / destruction of electro-magnetic data	5	2	11	3
Obstruction of business by destroying computer	1	3	4	2
Internet crime	**443**	**319**	**712**	**124**
Child prostitution	114	46	117	68
Child pornography	64	55	128	9
Fraud	59	53	103	6
Distribution of obscene object	55	49	103	6
Violation of juvenile protection ordinance	25	2	10	23
Intimidation	18	28	40	-10
Infringement of copyright	16	10	28	6
Defamation	13	18	42	-5
Others	79	58	141	21
Unauthorised computer access	**27**	**13**	**35**	**14**
Total	**488**	**365**	**810**	**123**

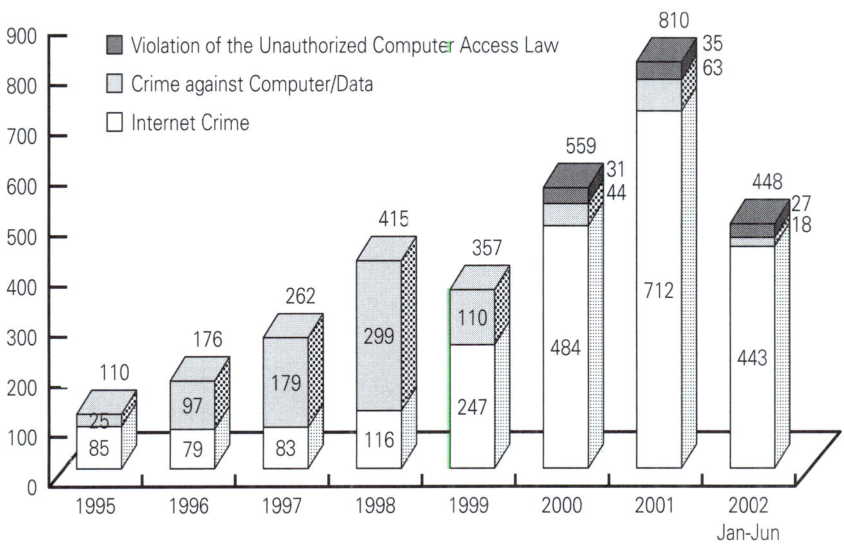

Figure 9.2 Arrest trends for Cyber-Crime

Countermeasures by the Government[13]

The Basic IT Law is intended to secure advanced information and telecommunications networks.[14] In addition, the 'e-Japan Priority Policy Programme' lists several measures concerning 'Ensuring of Security and Reliability over Advanced Information and Telecommunications Networks'.

Since September 1999, the Deputy Chief Cabinet Secretary has regularly convened IT Security meetings attended by director-generals of relevant ministries and agencies. One result of the meetings was the 'Action Plan on Building Infrastructure to Counter Hackers and Other Cyber-threats',[15] which was released in January 2000. Based on this plan, the Cabinet Secretariat established 'Guidelines for IT Security'[16] in July 2000 and the 'Special Action Plan on Countermeasures to Cyber-terrorism of Critical Infrastructure'[17] in December 2000.

In February 2000, a branch for IT Security was established at the Cabinet Secretariat for National Security and Crisis Management. As mentioned above, in January 2001 the IT Basic Law went into effect and the IT Strategy Headquarters, which is the centre of the IT security structure, was established (see Figure 9.3). The IT Security Promotion Committee and the IT Security Expert Committee are included in the IT Strategy Headquarters. The IT Security Promotion Committee consists of ministry and agency directors-general responsible for IT security. The IT Security Expert Committee consists of private sector IT security experts.

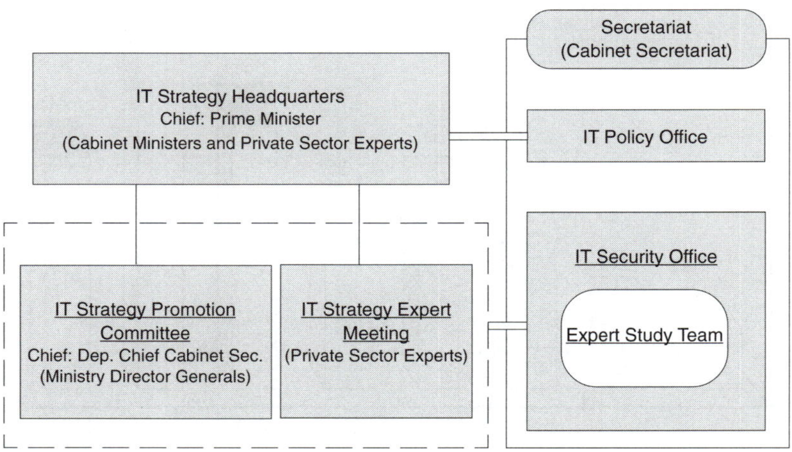

Figure 9.3 The IT security chain of command

In October 2001, a national policy 'How Government and the Private Sector Can Work Together to Fight Cyber-terrorism'[18] was established based on the Special Action Plan on Countermeasures to Cyber-terrorism of Critical Infrastructure. To realise secure e-government, which was scheduled to be achieved by 2003, the 'Action Plan for Ensuring IT Security of Electronic Government'[19] was established and, based on this action plan, the National Incident Response Team (NIRT) was set up within the Cabinet Secretariat (see Figure 9.4).

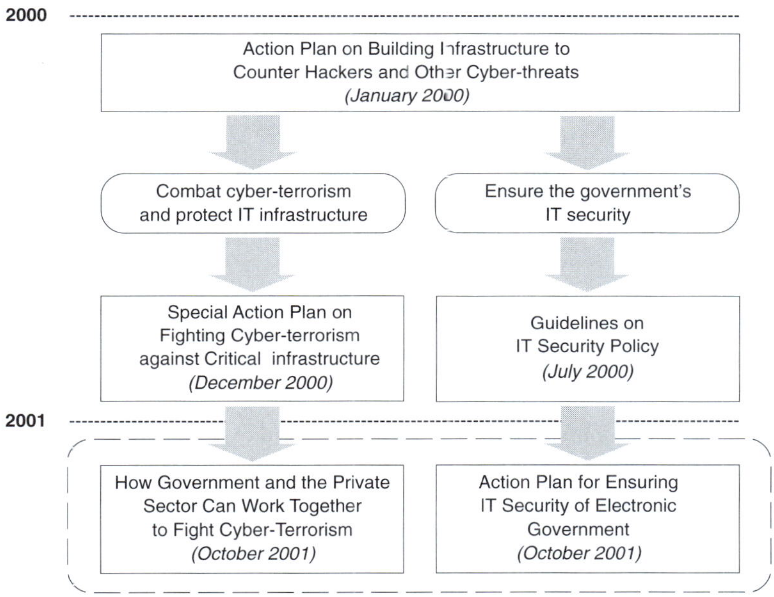

Figure 9.4 Major government policies

Countermeasures by the Police

Framework

Japan has 47 local (Prefectural) police headquarters, seven regional police bureaus, and the National Police Agency (NPA). The NPA does not have its own jurisdiction and does not carry out its own investigations; its function is to coordinate and advise local police departments which carry out their own investigations.

To deal with cyber-crime, each local police department has a task force against high-tech crime, and hires agents with high-tech skills to train their staff in up-to-date information technology. The NPA, as mentioned, coordinates local police investigations, advises local police and provides technical assistance. For this assistance, it has established the High-Tech Crime Technology Division and High-Tech Crime Technological Support Centre.

Because the investigation of cyber-crime can be difficult and complex, prevention is considered important. Promoting public awareness on IT security plays an essential part in prevention and, to achieve this goal, local police have Information Security Advisors who carry out duties of public relations, education, consultation and assistance on cyber-crime and IT security.

Cooperation between law enforcement agencies and the private sector is also essential to IT security. Each local police department has an ISP Liaison Council, which consists of police and private entities such as ISPs. Through this council, information on cyber-crime and IT security is exchanged. The NPA also has an advisory panel of well-informed individuals to discuss how law enforcement agencies and industries can promote the cooperation necessary to deal with cyber-crime.

Unauthorised Computer Access Law[20]

The *Unauthorised Computer Access Law*[21] was enacted in 2000. The law penalises unauthorised computer access in which another's identification code relating to access control (including passwords) is stolen, and security hole attacks. Punishment for unauthorised computer access is imprisonment for not more than one year or a fine of not more than 500 000 yen.[22] Punishment for a person who gives out another person's identification code to another person is a fine of not more than 300 000 yen.[23]

In addition to punishing unauthorised computer access, the law stipulates additional protective measures that are required to be undertaken by IT professionals and law enforcement agencies. The access administrator of a network computer is required to manage identification codes and verify the effectiveness of the network's access control function.[24] Local police are required to provide advice and guidance when the access administrator of a network computer that has been violated requires such assistance.[25] The purpose of the assistance is to prevent a recurrence of unauthorised access (see Figure 9.5).

In 2001, 35 charges were laid under this law. During the first half of 2002, 27 further cases resulted in charges being made.[26]

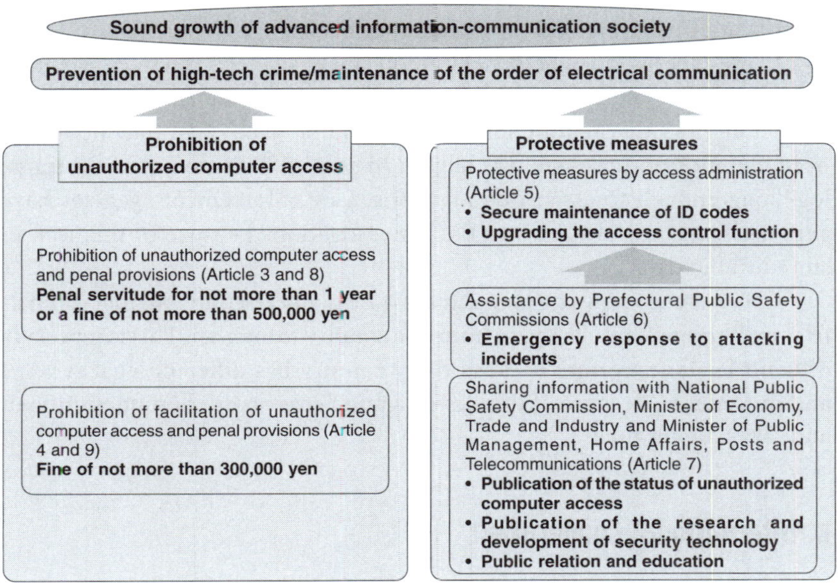

Figure 9.5 Unauthorised Computer Access Law

Countermeasures against cyber-terrorism

Although no such incidents have been recognised in Japan, the threat of cyberterrorism has been increasing, especially since the 11 September terrorist attacks in the United States in 2001. To deal with cyberterrorism, the NPA has established the Cyber Force, a special unit to deal with technological aspects of counter-cyberterrorism. Within the Cyber Force is the NPA's Cyberterrorism Technology Office, a command and information centre, whose mission is to foil cyberterrorism, prevent the spread of damage and investigate acts of cyberterrorism.

Obstacles to investigating cyber-crime

Cyber-crime has several formidable characteristics such as anonymity, no traceability and virtually no boundary. These characteristics make cyber-crime difficult to investigate. The physical world has many identifying features such as face, voice and signature but in cyberspace an identification number is often the only identifying feature, making it much more difficult to identify criminals. Cyber-criminals, for example, can steal another person's identification, and pretend to be the other person.

In the cyberworld, whether law enforcement agencies can trace criminals or not depends on traffic data or traffic logs. In Japan, there are no data protection laws that require ISPs to retain traffic data when they no longer need them for purposes such as billing. In general, ISPs do not retain traffic logs long enough to assist investigations. Law enforcement agencies have experienced many obstacles to their investigations because of this lack of stored traffic data.

Cyber-crime knows no boundary. It is easy, indeed common, for criminals to commit crimes in cyberspace from one country to another. This is especially difficult for investigators because every country has different legal systems and procedures. Because of this, investigating cross-border crime is difficult and takes a long time.

International Cooperation

Investigating crimes in other countries requires international cooperation, which is essential and draws much attention at international conferences and meetings. Tracing networked communication, cooperation between law enforcement agencies and the private sectors, and a 24/7 contact point network have been extensively discussed in the G8 countries. The Council of Europe drafted the Convention on Cyber-crime in late 2001. More than 30 countries, including Japan, signed it and indicated they will ratify it. In other international organisations such as the United Nations and APEC, cyber-crime has become an urgent issue.

In 2001, the General Assembly of the United Nations adopted a resolution, 'Combating the Criminal Misuse of Information Technologies' (55/63).[27] Recently, especially after the 11 September attacks in the United States, APEC has been dealing with cyber-crime. Its 'APEC Leader's Statement on Fighting Terrorism and Promoting Growth'[28] puts emphasis on cyber-security.

Japanese initiatives

Japan in particular, among Asian nations, has shown leadership in its development of countermeasures to deal with cyber-crime. The NPA has held seminars and conferences such as the Seminar on International Law Enforcement Cooperation and the Asian Conference on Cyber-crime

Investigations and Forensics. The NPA has established the 'Cyber-crime Technology Information Network System,' which connects ten Asian countries and areas.[29] This network provides a database, a bulletin board system and an e-mail service.

Japan has made major efforts, both domestically and internationally, to confront cyber-crime. The Basic IT Law and the *Unauthorised Computer Access Law* provide a firm legislative foundation. The NPA plays a key role in coordinating and advising local police departments. Extensive liaison with the private sector reflects the recognition in Japan that the control of cyber-crime and cyberterrorism is not solely the responsibility of governments.

Japan is also active in the world arena through its roles in the G8 and APEC, as a signatory to the Council of Europe Convention on Cyber-crime and as a regional leader in training and information exchange.

Appendix

Unauthorised Computer Access Law (Law No. 128 of 1999) (provisional translation)

(Purpose)

Article 1. The purpose of this Law is, by prohibiting acts of unauthorised computer access as well as by stipulating penal provisions for such acts and assistance measures to be taken by the Metropolitan or Prefectural Public Safety Commissions for preventing a recurrence of such acts, to prevent computer-related crimes that are committed through telecommunication lines and to maintain the telecommunications-related order that is realised by access control functions, and thereby to contribute to the sound development of the advanced information and telecommunications society.

(Definitions)

Article 2. In this law, 'access administrator' means a person who administers the operations of a computer (hereafter referred to as 'specific computer'), which is connected to a telecommunication line, with regard to its use (limited to such use as is conducted through the telecommunication line concerned; hereafter referred to as 'specific use').

2. In this Law, 'identification code' means a code that is granted to a person (hereafter referred to as 'authorised user') who has been authorised by the access administrator governing a specific use of a specific computer to conduct the specific use, or to the access administrator (hereafter in this paragraph, authorised user and access administrator are referred to as 'authorised user', etc.) to enable the access administrator to identify the authorised user, etc., distinguishing the latter from another authorised user, etc.; and that falls under any of the following items or that is a combination of a code which falls under any of the following items and any other code:

(1) A code whose content the access administrator concerned is required not to make known to a third party wantonly;
(2) A code that is compiled in such ways as are defined by the access administrator concerned using an image of the body, in whole or in part, of the authorised user, etc., concerned, or his or her voice;
(3) A code that is compiled in such ways as are defined by the access administrator concerned using the signature of the authorised user, etc., concerned.

3. In this Law, 'access control function' means a function that is added, by the access administrator governing a specific use, to a specific computer or to another specific computer which is connected to that specific computer through a telecommunication line in order to automatically control the specific use concerned of that specific computer, and that removes all or part of restrictions on that specific use after

confirming that a code installed into a specific computer having that function by a person who is going to conduct that specific use is the identification code (to include a code which is a combination of a code compiled in such ways as are defined by the access administrator concerned using an identification code and part of that identification code; the same shall apply in Article 3, paragraph 2, items (1) and (2)) for that specific use.

(Prohibition of acts of unauthorised computer access)

Article 3. No person shall conduct an act of unauthorised computer access.

2. The act of unauthorised computer access mentioned in the preceding paragraph means an act that falls under one of the following items:

(1) An act of making available a specific use which is restricted by an access control function by putting into operation a specific computer having that access control function through installing into that specific computer, via a telecommunication line, another person's identification code for that access control function (to exclude such acts conducted by the access administrator who has added the access control function concerned, or conducted with the approval of the access administrator concerned or of the authorised user for that identification code);

(2) An act of making available a restricted specific use by making in operation a specific computer having that access control function through installing into it, via a telecommunication line, any information (excluding an identification code) or command that can evade the restrictions placed by that access control function on that specific use (to exclude such acts conducted by the access administrator who has added the access control function concerned, or conducted with the approval of the access administrator concerned; the same shall apply in the following item);

(3) An act of making available a restricted specific use by making in operation a specific computer, whose specific use is restricted by an access control function installed into another specific computer which is connected, via a telecommunication line, to that specific computer, by installing into it, via a telecommunication line, any information or command that can evade the restrictions concerned.

(Prohibition of acts of facilitating unauthorised computer access)

Article 4. No person shall provide another person's identification code relating to an access control function to a person other than the access administrator for that access control function or the authorised user for that identification code, in indicating that it is the identification code for which the specific computer's specific use, or at the request of a person who has such knowledge, excepting the case where such acts are conducted by that access administrator, or with the approval of that access administrator or of that authorised user.

(Protective measures by access administrators)

Article 5. The access administrator who has added an access control function to a specific computer shall endeavour to properly manage identification codes relating to that access control function and codes used to confirm such identification codes through that access control function, and shall always verify the effectiveness of that access control function, and, when he deems it necessary, shall endeavour to promptly take necessary measures to protect that specific computer from acts of unauthorised computer access, including the upgrading of the access control function concerned.
(Assistance, etc., by Metropolitan and Prefectural Public Safety Commissions)

Article 6. The Metropolitan or Prefectural Public Safety Commission (each of the Area Public Safety Commissions in case of the Areas (that means the Areas mentioned in Article 51, paragraph 1, main part, of the Police Law (Law No. 162 of 1954); the same shall apply hereafter in this paragraph) except the Area which comprises the place of the Hokkaido Prefectural Police Headquarters: the same shall apply hereafter in this Article), in case an act of unauthorised computer access is recognised to have been conducted and if, for the purpose of preventing a recurrence of similar acts, assistance is requested by the access administrator of the specific computer involved in that act of unauthorised computer access, attaching to such request any documents or articles regarding referential matters, such as the situations of operation and management of that specific computer at the time of that act of unauthorised access, shall provide, when it deems such request reasonable, that access administrator with assistance, including provision of relevant materials, advice and guidance, so that necessary emergency measures can be properly taken in accordance with the modus operandi of that act of unauthorised access or its cause to protect that specific computer from acts of unauthorised access.

2. The Metropolitan or Prefectural Public Safety Commission may entrust to a person to be stipulated by National Public Safety Commission Regulation with all or part of the work of implementing a case analysis (which means making a technical study and analysis on the modus operandi of the act of unauthorised computer access relating to that request and the cause of such act; the same shall apply in the following paragraph) which is necessary for the providing of the assistance mentioned in the preceding paragraph.

3. A person who has engaged in the work of implementing a case analysis entrusted by the Metropolitan or Prefectural Public Safety Commission in accordance with the preceding paragraph shall not reveal secrets he or she has learned with regard to such implementation.

4. The necessary matters, other than those stipulated in the preceding three paragraphs, relating to the assistance mentioned in the first paragraph shall be stipulated by National Public Safety Commission Regulation.

Article 7. The National Public Safety Commission, the Minister of International Trade and Industry and the Minister of Posts and Telecommunications shall publicise, at least once a year, the situation of occurrence of acts of unauthorised computer access

as well as the situation of research and development of the access control function-related technology in order to help protect specific computers having access control functions from acts of unauthorised computer access.
2. In addition to the preceding paragraph, the State shall endeavour to assure the enlightenment and diffusion of knowledge regarding the protection of specific computers having access control functions from acts of unauthorised computer access.

(Penal provisions)

Article 8. A person who falls under one of the following items shall be punished with penal servitude for not more than one year or a fine of not more than 500 000 yen:
(1) A person who has infringed the provision of Article 3, paragraph 1;
(2) A person who has infringed the provision of Article 6, paragraph 3.

Article 9. A person who has infringed the provision of Article 4 shall be punished with a fine of not more than 300 000 yen.

SUPPLEMENTARY PROVISION
This Law shall come into force when a period of six months has elapsed counting from the date of its promulgation; provided that the provisions of Article 6 and of Article 8, item (2) shall come into force on the date to be stipulated by Cabinet Order within the scope not exceeding one year counting from the date of its promulgation.

10

Cyber-Crime in India: The Legal Approach

Pavan Duggal

India is a land of ancient heritage, a country that signifies unity and diversity. It has been declared a 'sovereign, socialist, secular, democratic, republic' by the Preamble to the Constitution of India. India achieved independence from the British on 15 August 1947 and thereafter, through a series of consecutive Five Year Plans, aimed to progress in economic development with a focus in specific areas. More recently the Indian economy began to operate in the context of a more open and market-driven approach, stimulated in part by developments in information technology.

The state-owned Videsh Sanchar Nigam Ltd first introduced the Internet commercially on 15 August 1995. Beginnings of the Internet in India were small and the pace of growth slow. It took time for Internet use to catch on, but the trend is changing. The following data (in Figures 10.1 and 10.2) show the growth of the Internet in India in terms of actual figures.[1]

The late 1990s saw a spurt in the number of cyber-cafés opening in India, and tremendous growth occurring between 2000 and 2002, bringing an increase in the number of people accessing the Internet. With increasingly cheap Internet access available through cyber-cafés, the number of Internet users in India has grown remarkably, as the growth projections by Nasscom show (http://www.nasscom.org/).

The Nasscom Internet survey on Internet Usage Trends, conducted in 68 cities and towns in India in January 2001 (accounting for more than 92% of total Internet users in the country), came up with some interesting findings:

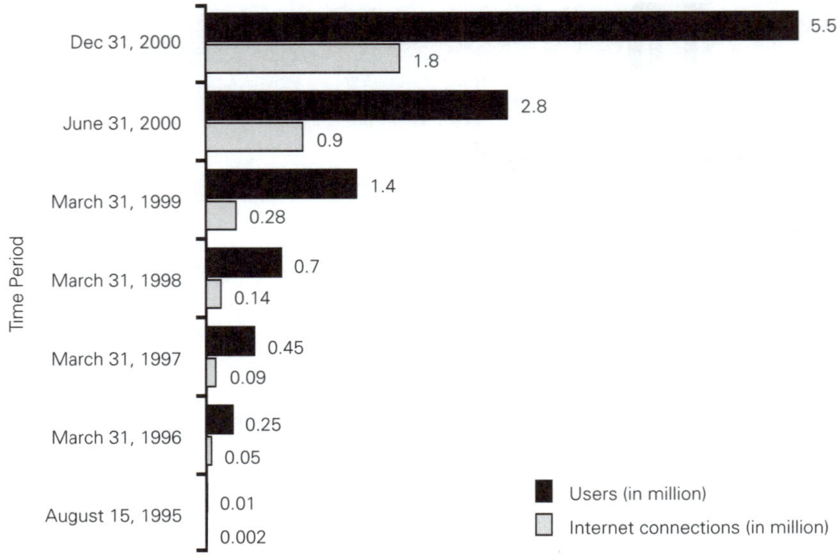

Figure 10.1 Internet growth in India

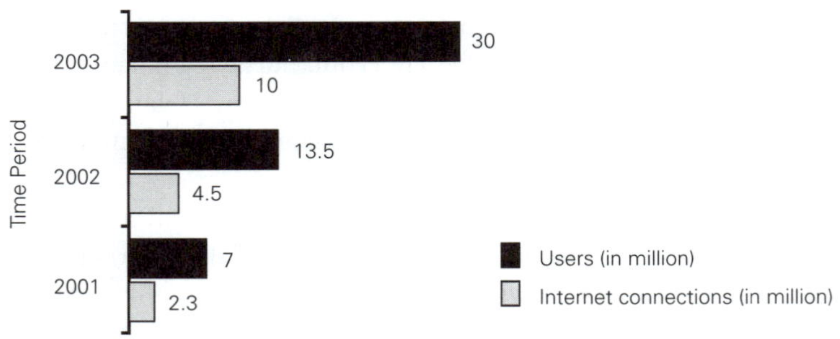

Figure 10.2 Projected growth of the Internet in India

- More than 200 cities and towns in India have Internet connections
- As of December 2000, there was a PC base of 5 million machines; of these, more than 3.7 million machines had the capacity for Internet use
- More than 120 private ISPs were to be fully operational by 31 June 2001 (out of a projected 500 licences to be given by that date)
- At least 12 private international gateways for Internet were expected in the same period. Seven private international gateways were already operational by December 2000

- More than 81% of PCs sold during 1999–2000 were acquired because of the need to access the Internet
- More than 86% of the top 100 companies that responded to the survey had endorsed the Internet and e-commerce as being an integral part of their corporate strategic framework for next year
- 91% of India's corporate websites are located overseas
- India's capital cities today account for 79% of Internet connections across the country[2]

The slow growth in the number of Internet users over the first couple of years, which restricted the development of the Internet in India, was due to a lack of awareness as well as the exorbitant cost of access. The dramatic growth in the number of users since 1997 is illustrated by the numbers in Table 10.1.[3]

Table 10.1 Internet penetration, March 1997 to March 2005

	1997	*1998*	*1999*	*2000*	*2001*	*2002*	*2003*	*2004*	*2005*
Population (in millions)	961	977	993	1010	1027	1089	1156	1226	1301
PC penetration per '000 population	1.63	2.17	2.83	3.72	4.94	6.41	7.81	9.63	11.92
Internet subscribers (in thousands)	25	150	350	650	1130	1763	3661	4403	6674
Internet users (in millions)	–	–	–	–	6.7	10.7	29.0	31.7	52.8

The growth and ready adoption of the Internet in India has meant a significant economic advancement, given a strong IT and software industry. On the other hand, Indians are beginning to use the Internet for unauthorised access and other categories of cyber-crime. According to one estimate, between February 2000 and December 2002, Indian government and corporate websites were hacked and defaced about 780 times.[4] A large number of cyber-crimes has been reported in the media, and it is pertinent to note that the Indian press appears to have a great liking for reporting cyber-crimes; the early cases of Internet crimes in India were reported extensively. The early days of cyber-crime reporting also jolted the conscience of lawmakers, who felt a need to legally regulate this new area of offending.

The *Indian Penal Code 1860* is a very comprehensive piece of penal legislation but, of course, it could hardly have covered an activity not even remotely visualised in the 19th century. The various challenges posed by criminal exploitation of cyberspace therefore needed new legislation. The *Indian Penal Code* was amended by an indigenous cyber-law, the *Information Technology Act 2000* ('the IT Act'), which was passed by both houses of Parliament on 17 May 2000, received the assent of the president on 9 June 2000 and was finally implemented on 17 October 2000.[5] The amendments contained in the IT Act, however, are purely related to making certain categories of offences of the Indian Penal Code applicable to electronic records, and this neglects a variety of other offences.

Chapter XI of the Act deals with cyber-crimes, detailing certain specified kinds of behaviours, which have been designated as cyber-crimes. These behaviours have been declared as penal offences, which are made punishable by imprisonment and fines (the fines declared are in the Indian denominations, one lakh rupees being Rs 100 000). We now examine relevant provisions of Chapter XI of the IT Act.

Section 65 of the IT Act deals with the offence of causing damage to computer source code. Any person who knowingly or intentionally conceals, destroys or alters or intentionally or knowingly causes another to conceal, destroy or alter any computer source code used for a computer, computer program, computer system or computer network, when the computer source code is required to be kept or maintained by law for the time being in force, is guilty of an offence under this provision. This offence is made punishable with imprisonment for up to three years, or with a fine, which may extend up to two lakh rupees, or with both. The Act defines 'computer source code' as the listing of programs, computer commands, and design and layout and program analysis of computer resources in any form.

Hacking has been made a penal offence under s. 66. The offence of hacking involves the following ingredients:

- There should be an intent of the accused to cause wrongful loss or damage to the public or any person
- There should be knowledge of or attributable to the accused that he is likely to cause wrongful loss or damage to the public or any person
- The accused must destroy, delete or alter any information residing in a computer resource
- The accused must diminish the value or utility of any information residing in a computer resource
- The accused must affect any information residing in a computer resource injuriously by any means

If these conditions are satisfied, then that constitutes the offence of hacking within the meaning of s. 66.

Section 67 deals with the offence of publishing obscene electronic information. Thus, under this provision, whoever publishes or transmits or causes to be published in electronic form any material which is lascivious or appeals to prurient interest, or if its effect is to deprave and corrupt persons who read, see or hear it, will be punished on first conviction with imprisonment for a term which may extend to five years, and with a fine which may extend to one lakh rupees and, in the event of a second or subsequent conviction, with imprisonment for a term which may extend to ten years and also with a fine which may extend to two lakh rupees.

Section 68 deals with the offence of failing to comply with the orders of the Controller of Certifying Authorities. Section 68 empowers the controller to give directions and may order the Certifying Authority, or any employee of such authority, to take measures or cease carrying on such activities specified in the order as necessary to ensure compliance with the provisions of the Act, rules or any regulations made under it. The section further states that any person who fails to comply with the order passed under subsection (1) of s. 68 shall be made liable for a term of not more than three years of imprisonment or a fine not exceeding two lakh rupees or both.

Section 69 deals with the offence of failure to assist any government agency in extending facilities of decryption, when called upon by that agency to do so. Section 69 authorises the controller to direct a subscriber to extend facilities to decrypt information. If the controller is satisfied that it is necessary or expedient to do so in the interest of the sovereignty or integrity of India, the security of the state, friendly relations with foreign states or public order or for preventing incitement to the commission of any cognisable offence, he or she may direct any government agency to intercept any information transmitted through any computer resource. It further states that the subscriber or any person in charge of the computer resource will, when called upon by any agency which has been so directed under this section, be obliged to extend all facilities and technical assistance to decrypt the information. Further, the section states that, if the subscriber or any person fails to assist the agency referred to under this section, he will be punished by imprisonment for a term up to seven years.

Section 70 deals with the offence of accessing or attempting to secure access to a protected system. It defines a protected system and gives the terms under which a system can be defined as a protected system. It states that the appropriate government may, by notification in the official gazette, declare any computer, computer system or computer network to be a protected system. Further, the government may by an order in writing authorise persons to access protected systems. Any person who secures access or attempts to secure access to a protected system in contravention of the provisions of s. 70 will be punished by imprisonment for a term that may extend to ten years and will also be liable to a fine.

Section 71 deals with the offence of misrepresentation or suppression of any material fact from the Controller or Certifying Authority when obtaining any licence or Digital Signature Certificate. It specifies a penalty for misrepresentation and states that whoever makes any misrepresentation to, or suppresses any material fact from, the Controller or the Certifying Authority when applying for any licence or Digital Signature Certificate, will be punished by imprisonment for a term of up to two years, or by a fine of up to one lakh rupees, or both.

Section 72 deals with the offence of breach of confidentiality and privacy. It specifies that, unless otherwise provided in the Act or any other law, any person who, in pursuance of any of the powers conferred under the Act or the rules or regulations made under it, has gained access to any electronic record, book, register, correspondence, information, document or other material and, without the consent of the person concerned, discloses such material to any other person will be punished by imprisonment for a term of up to two years, or by a fine of up to one lakh rupees, or by both.

Section 73 deals with the offence of publication of a Digital Signature Certificate that is false in certain particulars. The section provides that no person shall publish a Digital Signature Certificate or otherwise make it available to any other person with the knowledge that the Certifying Authority listed in the certificate has not issued it; or that the subscriber listed in the certificate has not accepted it; or that the certificate has been revoked or suspended, unless such publication is for the purpose of verifying a digital signature created prior to such suspension or revocation. It also specifies the penalty for contravention and states that any person who contravenes the provisions of subsection (1) shall be punished by imprisonment for a term that may extend to two years, or fined up to one lakh rupees, or by both.

Section 74 deals with the offence of publication of a Digital Signature Certificate for fraudulent or unlawful purposes. It lays down that if a person knowingly creates, publishes or otherwise makes available a Digital Signature Certificate for any fraudulent or unlawful purpose he will be punished by imprisonment for a term that may extend to two years, or by a fine that may extend to one lakh rupees, or by both.

Section 75 deals with the applicability of the IT Act for an offence or contravention committed outside India. This section also applies to any offence or contravention committed outside India by any person irrespective of nationality. Further, it states that for the purposes of subsection (1) the

Act also applies to an offence or contravention committed outside India by any person if the offence involves a computer, computer system or computer network located in India.

Section 76 provides for the power of confiscation and specifies the conditions under which computers, computer systems, floppy and compact disks, tape drives or any other accessories can be confiscated. It further states that these articles can be confiscated provided that, where it is established that the person in whose possession the articles are found is not responsible for the contravention of the provisions of the Act, the court may make an alternative order.

Section 77 elaborates on the issue of non-interference of penalties with other punishment. It provides that no penalty imposed or confiscation made under the Act will prevent the imposition of any other punishment to which the offender is liable under any other law.

Section 78 deals with the power to investigate offences under the IT Act. The section provides that notwithstanding anything contained in the *Code of Criminal Procedure 1973* (CrPC) of India, a police officer not below the rank of deputy superintendent of police is to investigate any offence under this Act.

Chapter XI appears to be sketchy and selective in its approach. While it has made hacking, damage to computer source code, publishing obscene electronic information and offences relating to digital signatures into penal offences, it has distinct and inherent weaknesses as it does not cover a variety of cyber-crimes that have already emerged in India and that are incapable of being brought within the ambit of the Indian Penal Code.

The IT Act is based on the UNCITRAL Model Law on e-commerce and is not a law on cyber-crimes. However, a distinct chapter has been added in the Act to address certain specific kinds of cyber-crime. While this approach has been helpful in some cases, it has also contributed to the non-coverage of various categories of cyber-law under the *Indian Penal Code*. It appears that the specific categories of cyber-law stipulated in Chapter XI of the IT Act have been inserted to ensure the further robust growth of e-commerce and to act as a deterrent for criminal elements. Viewed holistically, Chapter XI is indicative of the government's intention to have in place appropriate enabling legal and regulatory framework relating to e-commerce, and to make material breaches penal offences.

Thus, for example, offences against the person such as cyber-stalking, cyber-defamation and cyber-nuisance have not been covered under the IT Act. India has witnessed such cases, but there exists no legal remedy. This has led to the situation where cyber-criminals are often emboldened to continue committing their cyber-crimes and criminal activities on the Internet, knowing well that the law is not yet competent enough to reach them. This is why people's confidence in the regime for regulating and preventing cyber-crimes in India is not as high as it should be.

Another important aspect of cyber-crime jurisprudence in India is that the law on hacking in India is not specific enough. Section 66 of the IT Act has defined the offence of hacking so widely that a large number of activities that are not hacking would also be legally covered by it.

A classic example of the problem of definitions is a debate that began in India about the scope of the criminalisation of the misuse of computers. The debate revolves around whether a web-host service provider, who has a username and password for his webspace, can make changes on the website of another person who has not yet paid for the webspace on which his website is hosted. This issue revolved around the matter of Amit Pasari and Kapil Juneja. We now look at the facts of this peculiar case.

In India's possibly first case of hacking under s. 66 of the IT Act, the Cyber-crime Cell of Delhi Police registered a case against Amit Pasari and Kapil Juneja. This case was registered under s. 66 of the IT Act along with s. 406 of the *Indian Penal Code*.[6] This case involved a web-hosting business run by Amit Pasari and Kapil Juneja under the name of Softweb. Softweb was the subject of a complaint by one Mr Manmohan Gupta who stated that he had operated his website, www.go2nextjob.com, on the web-hosting service of Softweb. Mr Gupta's complaint was that his site had been 'hacked' into by Mr Amit Pasari of Softweb. It was also reported that there was a payment dispute between Softweb, the owners of the web-hosting server, and Mr Gupta, the site-owner. Consequently, Softweb allegedly blocked the site and put up a notice that read 'This site is closed due to non payment of bills' along with their address, e-mail ID and telephone number. The complainant further alleged that Mr Pasari had displayed an animated advertisement on the website www.go2nextjob.com showing Softweb's complete address, web and e-mail address. The complainant further insisted that this caused a major loss affecting the reputation of the company. The accused (Mr Pasari) stated in court at the time of bail that Mr Gupta had not paid the money for the webspace on which the website was hosted; despite repeated attempts to get him to pay, Mr Gupta failed to pay the amount for webspace and hence there was no hacking in the eyes of law. After six days in Tihar Jail, both Amit Pasari and Kapil Juneja were granted bail by the court.

The case raised the issue of whether a web-hosting company can block access to a website due to non-payment of their web-hosting dues by the subscriber. In that scenario, the important question is whether s. 66 of the IT Act can apply if the web-hosting company blocks or removes the site of any defaulting client who has failed to pay its due fees. Opinions are divided on this matter. Arguably, such an act could legally come within the ambit of the offence of hacking, but no case law has yet evolved in India on this matter. It will be interesting to see how the law develops.

It is important to note that a couple of phrases in s. 66 of the IT Act have suddenly expanded the scope and ambit of the offence of hacking to an extent that could not have been the intention of lawmakers. The phrase 'diminishing of value and utility of electronic information' has made this provision leapfrog into areas not intended or visualised. Further, the phrase 'or affecting it injuriously by any means' in the context of electronic information is wide enough to cover a large number of other acts which do not amount to hacking. Yet these acts are punishable as hacking under s. 66 of the Act.

Another problem is the applicability and the scope of s. 66, given that no restrictions or parameters on the applicability of s. 66 have been prescribed under the Act. Thus s. 66 is beginning to attain notoriety because it is being applied to any offence for which there is no specific legal provision, either under the *Indian Penal Code* or the IT Act. This exercise, though adventurous in the beginning, can have disastrous consequences, thereby impairing and hampering the confidence of users and 'netizens' and the general population of India in the control of cyber-crime in the country. At various conferences and meetings with different stakeholders, I have repeatedly pointed out the urgent need to amend s. 66 of the Act so as to limit its ambit and build into it mechanisms to prevent its misuse and abuse.

India has convicted its first cyber-criminal, thereby reiterating its commitment to preserving the rule of law.[7] The court of Shri Gulshan Kumar, Metropolitan Magistrate, New Delhi, convicted Arif Azim in a case of online cheating. However, Shri Kumar took a lenient view of the accused and sentenced him to probation with a personal and surety bond of one year. However, Arif Azim was convicted under the provisions of the *Indian Penal Code 1860*. The case arose on the complaint of M/s Sony India Private Limited. Sony filed a complaint for a case of cheating with the Central Bureau of Investigation (CBI). The accused allegedly used a stolen credit card number to order for himself a Sony colour television and a cordless headphone. On discovering the crime, the matter was reported by Sony to the CBI. The CBI promptly investigated the matter and, after identifying the accused, arrested him. The matter came up for hearing before the court of Shri Gulshan Kumar, MM, Patiala House, New Delhi, and the accused was convicted. This incident shows that the police have started investigating cyber-crimes under existing laws.

Another major issue that comes up concerning cyber-crime in India is how to address the transnational nature of cyber-crime and its effective detection, investigation and prosecution. Section 1(2) provides that the IT Act extends to the whole of India and, except as otherwise provided in the Act, it applies also to any offence or contravention committed outside India by any person. Further, s. 75 provides that the provisions of the Act apply also to any offence or contravention committed outside India by any person irrespective of his nationality. And, for the purposes of s. 75(1), the IT Act applies to an offence involving a computer, computer system or computer network located in India.

Practically speaking, a number of investigations of offences committed outside India reach a dead end. India has not yet become a signatory of the Council of Europe's Convention on Cyber-crime, which could help India harmonise its laws so as to deal effectively with the various challenges of cyber-crimes and to cooperate with other nations. At the time of writing, India has not yet made any effort in this direction. India is, however, a member of the G8 24/7 Network for High Tech crime, which was established by the G8 countries as a practical point of contact network and assistance in investigation and prosecution of cross-border cyber-crimes.

Another issue is the exclusive applicability of the IT Act. There is a school of thought in India, which argues that in all crimes where a computer is used, only the IT Act should be invoked and not the *Indian Penal Code*. This argument can be dealt with by arguing that the IT Act does not deal comprehensively with all kinds of cyber-crime and has only listed certain broad categories of such crime. If a cyber-crime occurs that is not specifically covered under the IT Act, it does not mean that police and society can merely look on as helpless spectators. Arguably, the provisions of the 1860 Penal Code need to be duly invoked, given the non-comprehensive coverage of cyber-crimes under the IT Act.

This coverage suffers from other problems. The Act does not cover various crimes such as cyber-stalking, cyber-harassment, cyber-defamation or cyber-terrorism; neither does it deal with the risk of abuse arising in certain chat rooms, or the misappropriation and misuse of credit card numbers. A large number of such cyber-crimes also cannot be effectively dealt with under the *Indian Penal Code* given the absence of any specific provision.

The IT Act is also silent about the availability of bail in respect to the various offences detailed under Chapter XI. There is nothing in the new Act that details which offence is 'bailable' and which is not. In addition, the Act is also silent about which court is competent to take cognisance of the offences specified in the Act. Consequently, our approach has to be governed by Part II of Schedule I of the *Criminal Procedure Code* (CrPC).

Since the IT Act is not legislation relating primarily to cyber-crime, it is completely silent on the issue of the compound effects of various offences prescribed in it. Due to the operation of s. 320 CrPC, offences under the IT Act are non-compoundable, which is a major drawback. There should have been provisions that enable any consequential minor offences to have been declared expressly compoundable under the Act.

In addition, the Act does not display a uniform approach in prescribing punishment. The various provisions of Chapter XI show an imbalance between the degree of culpability and the prescribed punishment. In many instances the law appears to be unjust and not in tune with other established principles of criminal jurisprudence. The Act therefore fails to have effective checks and balances in its sentencing provisions relating to cyber-crimes.

It is interesting to note that the IT Act is silent on the issue of the time limitation for taking cognisance of any offence. As such, one has no option but to fall back on s. 468 of CrPC. Under s. 468(1) CrPC, no court can take cognisance of any offence of the category specified under 468(2) after the expiry of the period of limitation to bring forth charges prescribed under s. 468(2). Most of the offences detailed under Chapter XI of the Act fall in the same category specified under s. 468(2) CrPC. Yet s. 81 of the IT Act states that its provisions will take effect notwithstanding anything inconsistent with it contained in any other law in force at that time. Since the provisions relating to statutory limitations for taking cognisance under s. 468 CrPC are not inconsistent with the provisions of the IT Act, the same applies for the purposes of calculating the relevant limitation on the time elapsed between an alleged offence and subsequent legal action by any party.

Another important problem is that, although the law has given the power to investigate cyber-crimes to a police officer of the rank of deputy superintendent, effectively investigative capability has not changed. There is a huge gap between the provisions of the law and the reality, especially the capacity to investigate cyber-crime even at the ranks specified.

The reality is that a tremendous effort is required for training and orienting the law enforcement agencies including deputy superintendents of police, on various aspects of the detection, investigation and the prosecution of cyber-crimes. A large number of police officers and others in various agencies are not well equipped with the latest cyber-forensic tools, methods and procedures, with the practical result that the detection, investigation and prosecution of cyber-crimes takes a back seat. There is a tremendous need for government training and awareness-raising programmes in this area.

Cyber-forensics is a field constantly changing and growing, but law enforcement agencies as a whole have not kept abreast of latest developments. There is also a great need to make the judiciary aware of the various aspects of cyber-crime and its prosecution. The provisions of Indian cyber-law relating to cyber-crimes and their import need to be thoroughly explained.

India has a further need for dedicated investigators specialising in cyber-crime. A limited beginning in this direction has already been made with the establishment of the Cyber-crime Police Station in Bangalore in the South Indian State of Karnataka. The station investigates all cyber-crimes that emerge in Karnataka and all cyber-crimes arising or reported to anyone in Karnataka are transferred for investigation and prosecution to the Bangalore station. India is now also planning to enter an era of online justice; we may in the future see distinct cyber-crime courts in India.

Another approach that India has adopted is to make certain categories of activities, which have criminal connotations but are subject to civil not penal liability. Thus a number of activities that are cyber-crimes in other parts of the world have not been so declared by the Indian legislature because it would be far more effective to impose civil liability on such acts rather than to saddle them with penal responsibility.

Thus, for example, the IT Act provides for damages by way of compensation to the tune of rupees one crore (Rs 10 million). These damages can be awarded by the adjudicating officers if, in their opinion, one or more of the various conditions stipulated in s. 43 of the IT Act are satisfied. The section details that if any person without permission of the owner or any other person who is in charge of a computer, computer system or computer network commits any of the acts detailed in the section he is liable to pay damages by way of compensation not exceeding one crore rupees to the person so affected. Offenders are liable if they commit any of the following acts:

- Access or secure access to such computer, computer system or computer network
- Download, copy or extract any data, computer data base or information from such computer, computer system or computer network including information or data held or stored in any removable storage medium
- Introduce or cause to be introduced any computer contaminant or computer virus into any computer, computer system or computer network
- Damage or cause to be damaged any computer, computer system or computer network, data, computer data base or any other programs residing in such computer, computer system or computer network
- Disrupt or cause the disruption of any computer, computer system or computer network

- Deny or cause the denial of access to any person authorised to access any computer, computer system or computer network by any means
- Provide any assistance to any person to facilitate access to a computer, computer system or computer network in contravention of the provisions of this Act, rules or regulations made thereunder
- Charge the services availed of by a person to the account of another person by tampering with or manipulating any computer, computer system, or computer network

Under the same section, the Act further defines a 'computer contaminant' to mean any set of computer instructions that are designed to modify, destroy, record, transmit any data or program residing within a computer, system or computer network; or by any means to usurp the normal operation of the computer, computer system, or computer network. It also defines 'computer data base' to mean a representation of information, knowledge, facts, concepts or instructions in text, image, audio, video that are being prepared or have been prepared in a formalised manner or have been produced by a computer, computer system or computer network and are intended for use in a computer, computer system or computer network. It defines a 'computer virus' as any computer instruction, information, data or program that destroys, damages, degrades or adversely affects the performance of a computer resource or attaches itself to another computer resource and operates when a program, data or instruction is executed or some other event takes place in the computer resource. Further the term 'damage' means to destroy, alter, delete, add, modify or rearrange any computer resource by any means.

A perusal of s. 43 makes it clear that there is a considerable overlap between the provisions of s. 43 and s. 66. A large number of actions that would come under the legal offence of hacking under s. 66 can also be effectively covered under s. 43. Thus the legislature has, in these cases, provided for twin remedies, one not only for damages by way of compensation up to the tune of Rs 10 million but also one of penal provisions including imprisonment for three years or a fine of up to Rs 2 million or both.

For the categories of acts that are not specifically covered by Chapter XI of the Act, s. 43 provides a further means of including a non-listed conduct. By virtue of this provision, companies, individuals, semi-government organisations and government can seek damages of up to Rs 10 million. The only caveat in s. 43 is that the person who caused the damage or breach must be clearly identifiable and his identity clearly established. It is pertinent to note that an act of releasing a computer virus in anyone else's computer system or network is an act that is clearly covered as a stipulated ground for the grant of damages by way of compensation up to Rs 10 million. But the practical task of clearly identifying the perpetrator is a daunting one.

However, there have been some positive features in this direction. The first conviction under the IT Act has shown that in a number of cases, if applied ingeniously, the existing criminal provisions under the *Indian Penal Code* can be used to cover some of the newly emerging crimes. The government is embarking on training programmes and some institutes have been set up to disseminate information about cyber-forensics. The National Police Academy in Hyderabad is doing a considerable amount of training on cyber-crime. As time goes on, it is expected that the government may allocate specific funds for the detection, investigation and prosecution of cyber-crimes.

Examining developments in India in the global context, it is apparent that India has had the vision to enact specific provisions on cyber-crime. It is hoped that India will soon evolve a distinct code on cyber-crime that will supplement the *Indian Penal Code* and the IT Act and be the forerunner of a comprehensive jurisprudence on the issue of cyber-crime. The government has already indicated its intentions to develop countermeasures in this way.

As cyber-crime is constantly evolving, there is a need for the regular enhancement of methods, techniques, procedures and mindsets. India should adopt a pragmatic approach to ensure the successful and effective detection, investigation and prosecution of cyber-crimes. A strong political will is necessary to ensure that cyber-crime laws are put in place and effectively implemented by law enforcement agencies. Further, it is the responsibility of the judiciary to ensure that the existing provisions of law relating to cyber-crimes are effectively and pragmatically interpreted in such a manner as to serve the interests of justice.

At the time of writing, the Indian government was considering a move to make amendments to its current cyber-laws. The major thrust of amendments point to the fact that the IT Act needs to provide for the investigation of cyber-crimes not on the basis of the rank of the police officer but on the basis of an officer's merit and competency. However, while Indian cyber-law provides extra-territorial jurisdiction for law enforcement agencies, the *Indian Penal Code* is still limited by its applicability only to the territorial boundaries of India. It is believed that such amendments to the criminal laws will help law enforcement agencies achieve more effective detection, investigation and prosecution of cyber-crimes in India.

11

Computer Crimes: What Everyone Should Know About Them

K H Pun, Venus L S Cheung, Lucas C K Hui, K P Chow, W W Tsang, H W Chan, C F Chong

With advances in computer and network technology, especially the Internet, and an increase in electronic commerce, society has become more aware of the dangers of white-collar crimes committed via computers and networks. Computer scientists have deployed various security technologies to protect computer systems from being hacked into or used for illegal purposes, or to guard against information being stolen (Stallings 2000). But to date, most security technologies have focused only on the protection of computer resources from hacking or from other forms of misuse, and have ignored the issue of evidence collection. In this chapter, we briefly introduce what hacking is about and how evidence can be collected for use in courts.

What Is Cyber-Crime and Computer Crime?

Cyber-crime is a general term used to describe crimes related to the abuse and misuse of computers and networks, including the Internet. Within cyber-crime is the special category of computer crime, which refers to the use of computers as a main tool of crime commission. In a broad sense, computer crime is 'damaging someone's interests by means of a computer'. It encompasses unauthorised access to, reading, writing (or altering), deleting (or copying) data in a machine, or getting into another person's machine (Icove 1997).

Icove (1997) classified computer crimes according to four classical breaches of security: physical security, personnel security, security of communications and data, and operations security. Physical security is about the protection of tangible assets such as computers and cables. Personnel security is about prohibiting illegal access, either purposely or accidentally, into the computers or systems of an organisation. Security of communications and data is about securing data from end-users and the software that manipulates the data. Operations security is about taking care of the operations for detecting and preventing intrusions from outsiders.

What are 'hackers' and 'crackers'?

The word 'hacker' originally referred to talented computer programers who used their knowledge to breach the security of other computers and networks. 'Crackers' are more specific than hackers in that they break into systems by pinpointing their vulnerabilities with specialised tools and techniques. Casey (2000) quoted an analysis of how crackers operate when they do not have access to, or inside knowledge of, a system:

1. Reconnaissance to collect information about potential targets
2. Probe and attack: crackers probe for system weaknesses and deploy their tools
3. Toehold. After that, they exploit the security weakness and gain access into the targeted system
4. Advancement: crackers advance from unprivileged accounts to privileged accounts
5. Stealth: crackers secure their operations from detection and install 'backdoors' to cover their actions
6. A listening post is established to monitor activity on the compromised system
7. Takeover: once the above is achieved, most crackers successfully gain control of a system and may expand their control from a single host to other hosts on a network

Hacking scenario

No software is perfectly secure. There may be security loopholes inside the software that make the computer vulnerable to attack. For example, when a user clicks (or sometimes even highlights) a data file (say, an image file) in a browser, a hidden application program is invoked. This action, often allowed or ignored by the browser, contributes to a security loophole. The hidden application program may be a malicious code that automatically copies itself in the machine and duplicates and forwards itself to other users listed in the victim's address book. Or it will scrutinise the victim's computer for password files and thus gain control of the computer.

Another powerful attack by a hacker is a technique called 'buffer overflow attack'. In this, an attack program feeds some designated invalid parameters into the memory of the victim's computer which then modifies memory locations associated with the (binary) executable codes of the original programs installed in the victim's computer. This changes the execution sequences of the original programs. The carefully designed attack program enables the hacker to extract information from the victim's computer (without undergoing the normal execution sequences which would reveal themselves), insert or delete information or programs in the victim's computer (harming the victim's interests). An illustration is shown in Figure 11.1. After a machine has been hacked into, one or more of the following can occur:

1. Information in the victim's computer can be stolen
2. Files can be modified
3. Under control of the hacker, a machine may be used to attack other computers in a network

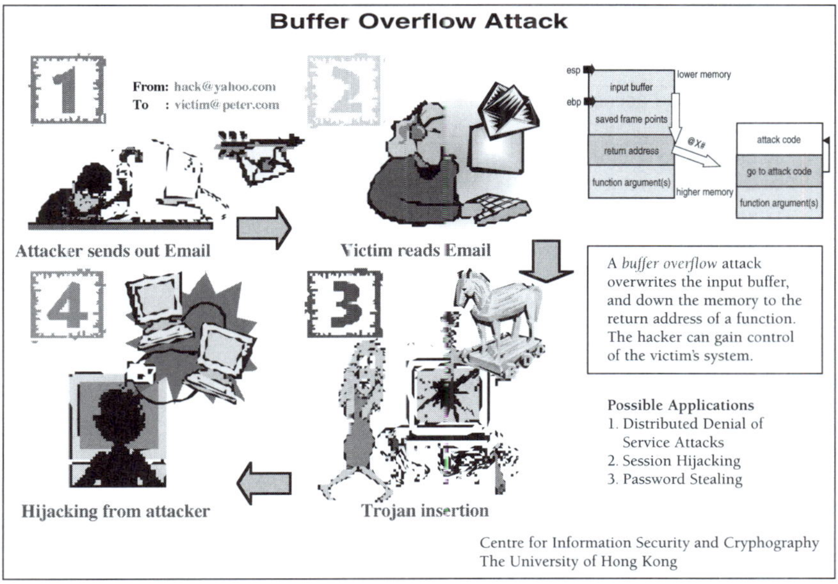

Figure 11.1 A hacking example using the Buffer Overflow technique

Computer Crimes in Hong Kong

With advances in technology and the popularity of network services, the number of computer crimes in Hong Kong has grown quickly in recent years, as statistics below illustrate.

Table 11.1 Technology crimes recorded in Hong Kong, 2000–03

Title of offence	*2000*	*2001*	*2002*	*2003 (Aug)*
Unauthorised access to computer by telecommunication	275	33	26	40
Access to computer with criminal or dishonest intent	–	81	138	248
Criminal damage	15	27	16	13
Obtaining property by deception	29	32	45	62
Obtaining services by deception	–	33	19	11
Thefts (e-banking related)	–	8	6	4
Other miscellaneous thefts	–	8	15	–
Others*	49	13	7	23
Total	368	235	272	401

Source: Technology Crime Division, Commercial Crime Bureau, Hong Kong Police
Note: *Others include traditional offences such as criminal intimidation, using a false instrument etc.

Table 11.2 Computer crime cases in Hong Kong, January to June 2003

Title of Offence	*Jan*	*Feb*	*Mar*	*Apr*	*May*	*Jun*	*Total*
1. Unauthorised access to computers by telecommunication	4	8	7	6	4	5	34
2. Access to computer with criminal or dishonest intent	12	33	35	36	33	36	185
3. Criminal damage	0	5	0	3	0	1	9
4. Obtaining property by deception (online shopping)	3	3	7	10	8	6	37
5. Obtaining services by deception (computer related)	1	1	1	1	1	2	7
6. Theft (e-banking related)	0	3	0	0	1	0	4
7. Other miscellaneous theft (computer related)	1	3	4	0	1	1	10
8. Others	0	3	3	3	3	1	13
Total	21	59	57	59	51	52	299
Accumulated total	21	80	137	196	247	299	299

Table 11.3 Monthly computer crime cases in Hong Kong, 2002

Title of offence	*Jan*	*Feb*	*Mar*	*Apr*	*May*	*Jun*	*Jul*	*Aug*	*Sep*	*Oct*	*Nov*	*Dec*	*Total*
1. Unauthorised access to computer by telecommunication	4	2	3	0	4	1	6	1	3	2	0	0	26
2. Access to computer with criminal or dishonest intent	13	7	14	12	11	6	16	10	10	17	14	8	138
3. Criminal damage	0	4	2	2	2	0	1	1	1	0	1	2	16
4. Obtaining property by deception (on-line shopping)	2	4	3	9	6	1	5	5	3	1	4	2	45
5. Obtaining services by deception (computer related)	5	0	2	1	1	3	3	1	1	0	1	1	19
6. Theft (e-banking related)	1	0	1	0	0	1	0	0	0	0	3	0	6
7. Other miscellaneous theft (computer related)	0	1	1	2	1	1	3	2	1	0	0	3	15
8. Others	0	1	0	0	0	1	0	0	1	1	1	2	7
Total	25	19	26	26	25	14	34	20	20	21	24	18	272
Accumulated total	25	44	70	96	121	135	169	189	209	230	254	272	272

Source: Hong Kong Police

Although the Hong Kong Police have endeavoured to respond to computer crime, the number of offences is increasing, as seen in the figures. The setting up of comprehensive approaches to prevent computer crimes and to collect sufficient evidence when crimes do take place is, therefore, of great importance.

How can computer crimes be prevented?

To prevent computer crimes, Icove (1997) identified three distinct tools:
1. Firewalls
2. Auditing
3. Risk assessment

Firewalls are security gateways between the Internet and a local host. Auditing is carried out by means of logs that keep track of operations of a computer. Risk assessment is a detailed plan, which anticipates risks, and balances them against the costs of bringing security and privacy to a system (Icove 1997). Other technologies include:
- E-mail server security
- Virus scanners
- Communication port scanning protection
- Operating system bugs and patches
- Software bugs and patches
- Password security
- User education and / or training.

E-mail server security is about scanning e-mails and blocking those suspected of containing viruses or malicious codes. Virus scanners are about preventing and alerting users to virus intrusions and scrutinising their computers for viruses. Communication port scanning is about safeguarding the essential active ports (e.g. port 80 for HTTP requests, port 21 for FTP requests) — unnecessary ports are not used for secret communication. Operating systems and software bugs and patches mean correcting or removing the security loopholes (bugs) of the operating systems and software with updated codes (patches) or newer versions of software. Password security is about protecting passwords within a system, if they are stored in a local machine. User education and training is nothing to do with technology but refers to human behaviour. No matter how strong the security implementation, a hacker can easily gain access to a computer system if a user is careless.

Educating users in the ethics of computer systems and security concerns when using computers is, therefore, very important. Ways in which computers may be protected by using digital signatures and encryption are shown in Figures 11.2 and 11.3.

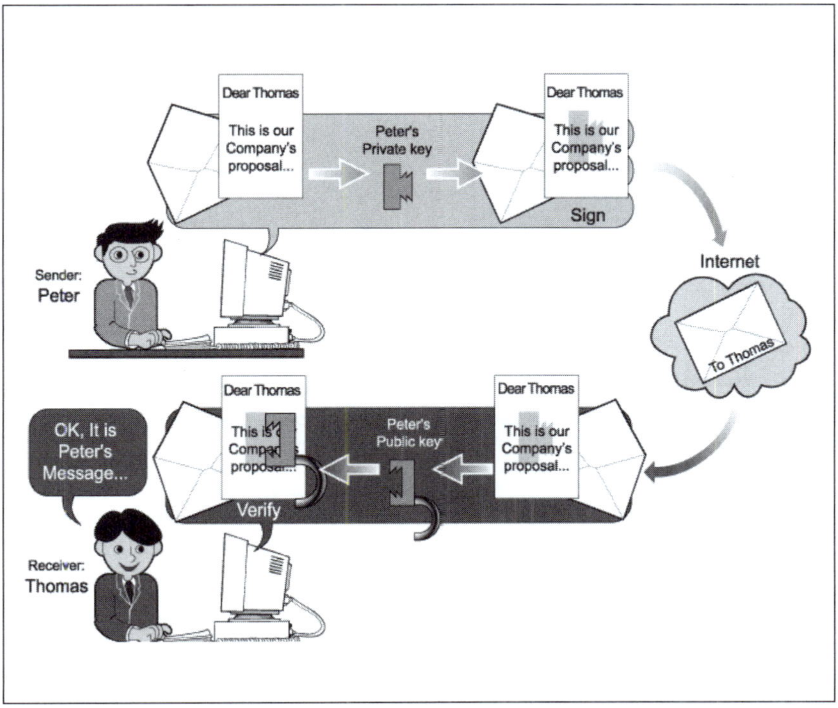

Figure 11.2 Use of digital signatures

What can we do when computer crime takes place?

When a computer crime has been committed, we can trace the source of the attack and collect sufficient digital evidence to trace and, if possible, to identify the hacker. This is especially important if the evidence is to be used in a court of law. Evidence must be collected and presented in a way that is admissible to the court (McKemmish 1999). For example, in the process of cloning a hard disk, the correctness of the cloned copy has to be ensured. Various security technologies used for the collection of evidence include: operating

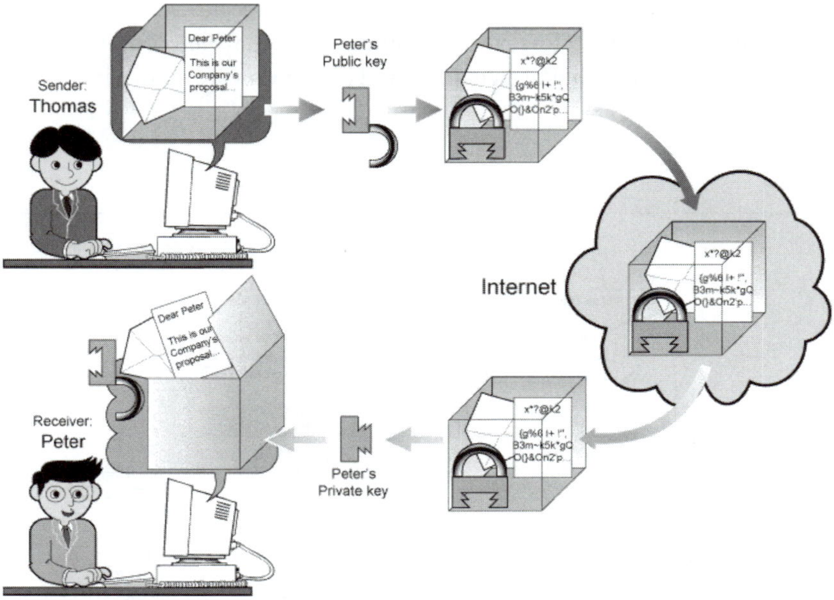

Figure 11.3 Use of data encryption to protect confidentiality

system log inspections, software log inspections, copying (cloning) for file systems, and file integrity checking (e.g. a hard disk). Operating systems and software log inspections are about inspecting log files of the operating systems and software to get clues from the activities that took place. A log file contains information on when and where (location of file) a certain action took place. The copying or cloning of file systems is important for investigation purposes, as the seized hard disk cannot be used directly by prosecutors. A copy of it should be made and examiners should only work on the copy. This is to preserve the integrity of the original hard disk as court evidence. File integrity checking ensures that files are not altered after seizure.

Digital Evidence Search Kit (DESK)

Various software tools can be used to collect evidence after a computer has been hacked into. Also, if criminal evidence is purposely stored on a computer, tools can be used to dig it out. One such tool is the Digital Evidence Search Kit (DESK), developed by the Centre for Information Security and Cryptography at The University of Hong Kong, in collaboration with the Hong

Kong Police. DESK is a forensic tool that supports two major functions: a File System Integrity Checker, and a Digital Evidence Search Function.

The File System Integrity Checker ensures the validity and reliability of the electronic evidence. It allows users to check if their files have been modified and enables them to examine their files using hash values.[1] In DESK, each file in a file system has two hash values that are computed by using two different hash functions, MD5 and SHA-1. These hash values will be stored in the database. If a file is suspected of being modified by someone, users can use the file's new hash values to verify against the original hash values stored in a database.

Three steps are involved in using the File System Integrity Checker:

Step 1: Create a hash value database for disk drive(s) / directory.

Step 2: Use the database file.

Step 3: Scan the file system from disk drive(s), a directory, a certain group of files in directory / disk drive(s), or a single file.

In addition to the File System Integrity Checker function, DESK also provides a text pattern searching function, which supports bilingual (English and / or Chinese) and multi-code (Big-5[2], GB2312[3] and Unicode UTF16) searching. Unlike other search functions, DESK searches contents of the files instead of searching for their filenames.

There are three types of search operations: physical, logical, and deleted file searches. Physical search facilitates the searching of a suspect's files hidden in the used or unused sectors of a file system (independent of what type of file systems the suspect is using). Logical search facilitates the searching of files that reside across sectors that cannot be traced by a physical search. When files are 'deleted', they are not destroyed in the hard disk. The deleted file remains in the file system until overwritten by new files. The deleted file search facilitates searching for deleted file patterns that remain in the file system.

DESK has two potential uses. When it is suspected that a computer has been hacked into, it can be used to check whether any files have been modified. It can also be used to build a database for standard commercial software, and to check whether some of the software's standard files (e.g. Freecell.exe) have been modified to store illegal information.

Without tools such as DESK, the investigation of computer crimes is slow and expensive. Moreover, all steps in the computer crime evidence collection have to be performed properly to ensure that the evidence is acceptable in a court of law.

Conclusion

In Hong Kong, the number of computer crimes has increased in recent years. Consequently, there is a growing need to respond appropriately as the crimes directly hinder the development and advancement of electronic commerce in Hong Kong. This chapter gives a brief introduction to computer crime and to hackers and their motives. A forensic tool, DESK, was introduced to demonstrate how forensic software can be used to assist the investigation of computer crimes and to provide lawful evidence for courts of law. To conclude, effective control of computer crime requires both technological and management expertise.

12

Cyber-Crime Legislation in the Asia-Pacific Region

Gregor Urbas*

Increasingly, 'cyber-crime' is becoming recognised as a serious problem requiring the attention of governments, law enforcement agencies and the justice systems of countries in the Asia-Pacific region. Jurisdictions that already have highly developed computing and digital communications infrastructures have, over the last decade or so, been forced to confront the expansion of criminality into the cyberworld and to evaluate the adequacy of existing legal systems to deal with this phenomenon. Other countries developing their information technology systems from a less advanced base are similarly forced to evaluate the adequacy of their legal systems to ensure the transnational investment and cooperation required for such development.

Substantive criminal law, supplemented by commercial and intellectual property protection law may, in part, already prohibit a range of misconduct directed towards or involving computers or associated information technology. However, the experience of many jurisdictions is that gaps and inadequacies in traditional offence provisions necessitate the consideration of more specific laws targeting cyber-crime. The emergence in mid-2000 of the infamous 'Love Bug' computer virus serves to illustrate both the threat of cyber-crime and the difficulty of an effective legal response in the absence of adequate legislation. This piece of malicious code (actually a virus / worm combination) appeared in Hong Kong on 11 May 2000 and rapidly spread throughout the world's computer networks:[1]

> In offices of the German newspaper Abendblatt in Hamburg, system administrators watched in horror as the virus gobbled up 2000 digital photographs in their picture archive. In Belgium ATMs were disabled, leaving citizens cashless. In Paris cosmetics maker L'Oréal shut down its e-mail servers, as did businesses throughout Europe. As much as 70% of computers in Germany, the Netherlands and Sweden were laid low. The companies affected made up a Who's Who of industry and finance, including Ford, Siemens, Silicon Graphics and Fidelity Investments. Even Microsoft ... was so badly battered that it finally severed outside e-mail links at its Redmond, Washington, headquarters.
>
> Governments, too, felt the pain. In London, Parliament shut down its servers before the Love Bug's assault ...
>
> On Capitol Hill, crippled e-mail systems forced an atypical silence in the halls of Congress ...
>
> The bug infected 80% of all federal agencies, including both the defense and state departments, leaving them temporarily out of e-mail contact with their far-flung outposts ... The virus corrupted no fewer than four classified, internal Defense Department e-mail systems ...

The Love Bug virus is estimated to have caused some US$7 billion in damage to computer systems and global commerce. Experts quickly identified the Philippines as the likely source of the code, and an investigation by the Philippines National Bureau of Investigation assisted by US FBI agents produced a suspect, a former computer science student.[2] Warrants for a search of premises and computer equipment were executed, and enough evidence emerged for the suspect to be charged. However, the prosecution ran into difficulties in selecting appropriate offences under Philippine law, as there was no existing offence of disseminating harmful computer viruses. The closest available offences involved theft and credit card fraud, but these were dismissed in subsequent legal proceedings as inapplicable and unfounded.[3] Moreover, the 'double criminality' requirement for extradition was not satisfied, meaning that the suspect could not be prosecuted in jurisdictions (such as the United States) which did have applicable computer crime laws.

Within six weeks, the Philippines legislature enacted new laws relating to electronic commerce. From 15 June 2000, a penalty of six months' to three years' imprisonment applied to 'hacking', 'cracking' and computer virus offences, with fines ranging to a maximum commensurate with the damage incurred.[4]

As this example shows, legislatures need to assess the adequacy of their laws before cyber-crime occurs, rather than after the event. While it cannot be known with certainty whether a prosecution would have succeeded in the Love Bug case had the new Philippines law been in place, as this would depend on the actual intention and circumstances of the particular suspect, it is clear that the case focused attention on a legislative gap. Like many other jurisdictions, the Philippines had no laws directly applicable to acts of computer misconduct like hacking and virus dissemination. The incident prompted not only the Philippines legislature but many others in the region to reconsider the adequacy of their cyber-crime laws. A range of new offences and penalties can now be identified and compared.

The following investigation looks at the main existing legislative offence provisions applicable to cyber-crime in the Asia-Pacific region, focusing on the following jurisdictions (in alphabetical order): Australia, China, Hong Kong, India, Japan, Korea (South), Malaysia, New Zealand, Philippines, Singapore, Taiwan and Thailand. The aim is to identify those jurisdictions with more comprehensive laws, and to suggest how they might provide a model for other jurisdictions. The approach taken includes consideration of the differing legal, social and political contexts of these laws, and emphasises aspects of effective policing and enforcement that go beyond criminal or penal sanctions.

It should be stressed that criminal or penal sanctions can only be one element of the overall response to cyber-crime in each country, and such sanctions are not necessarily the most efficient or desirable form of response. Other ways of preventing or minimising the harm of cyber-crime include technological measures, other regulatory controls, and civil proceedings. There are also informal measures, most clearly seen in the steps taken by owners of intellectual property to protect their commercial interests, such as intensive cooperation with public authorities and educational campaigns directed at the public. Sometimes such measures can be more effective than actual or threatened criminal prosecution. In the last resort, however, most jurisdictions have recognised the need for some form of punitive measures, particularly where the level of criminality or harm caused or threatened are especially serious.

The Importance of Adequate Legislation to Address Cyber-Crime

What is cyber-crime?

There is no single universally accepted general definition of 'cyber-crime' in criminological analysis, and little national legislation explicitly employing the term.[5] Grabosky & Smith identify the following categories of 'telecommunications-related' crime emerging in the digital age:[6]

- Illegal interception of telecommunications
- Electronic vandalism and terrorism
- Stealing communications services
- Telecommunications piracy
- Pornography and other offensive content
- Telemarketing fraud
- Electronic funds transfer crime
- Electronic money laundering.

These categories can be seen to comprise two overlapping domains. The first is illegal activities directed at or perpetrated through the use of *computers*. This can involve theft of computers, wilful damage to computers or computer systems, unlawful access to or interference with the operations of computers, transmitting offensive or illegal content using computers, and committing fraud or other offences through the use of computers. This area of criminality is naturally most amenable to regulation through laws specifically directed at computer use and misuse.[7]

A wider but related area is the protection of *information*, which in the digital age increasingly means the protection of computer data and networks. Protection of information has been a concern of legal systems from well before the introduction of modern technologies of mass communication, but is clearly brought into sharp focus by the development of global computer-based information networks such as the World Wide Web and the Internet.[8] Principal legal measures related to the protection of information from unlawful use, distribution or exploitation include telecommunications laws, intellectual property laws, privacy laws, laws relating to secrecy and national security, and laws relating to unfair commercial advantage.[9]

Adequacy of national legislation

Whether the existing legal system in any country can adequately address cyber-crime depends on the precise scope and interaction of its criminal, commercial, intellectual property and computer-related laws. As a general rule, the development of each of the later categories has been necessitated in part by the perceived inadequacy of legal remedies provided by other categories. The reliance on specific intellectual property laws to protect valuable information, for example, is partly attributable in jurisdictions based on the English legal system to the common law doctrine that information is not property capable of being stolen. In addition, there may be no intent to deprive the owner of the information permanently, another requirement of the traditional offence of theft. Thus information piracy is not usually amenable to prosecution under the criminal law relating to theft or dishonest acquisition.[10]

In many countries there are also difficulties in prosecuting under criminal law acts which may be performed outside the jurisdiction but which result in harm within it, such as the posting of offensive or obscene content on the Internet.[11] Clearly, there are also significant differences in the legal, social and political contexts within which these laws have been formulated and are enforced. Though geographically proximate, the countries of the Asia-Pacific region have very different historical backgrounds, which inevitably influence their respective legal systems. Most retain some elements of indigenous laws and customs, overlaid by laws imposed during periods of colonisation (including the English, French, German, Dutch, Spanish and Portuguese legal systems), and some have also modelled their laws in accordance with broader political philosophies such as communism.[12]

Moreover, political considerations are often involved in the way in which laws are promulgated and enforced. One difference arises in the balance between public and private enforcement of legal rights. For example, in the domain of intellectual property protection, private litigation is still difficult within existing legal structures in China, while in Australia this is the usual way of resolving intellectual property disputes, with police and public prosecution involvement being less frequent.[13]

Minimum requirements for substantive cyber-crime offences

As long ago as 1989, the Select Committee of Experts on Computer-Related Crime of the Council of Europe produced a 'minimum list' of computer crimes to be prohibited and prosecuted by international consensus:[14]

> *Computer fraud*: The input, alteration, erasure or suppression of computer data or computer programs, or other interference with the course of data processing, that influences the result of data processing thereby causing economic or possessory loss of property for another person with the intent of procuring an unlawful economic gain for himself or for another person;
>
> *Computer forgery*: The input, alteration, erasure or suppression of computer data or computer programs, or other interference with the course of data processing, in a manner or under such conditions, as prescribed by national

law, that it would constitute the offence of forgery if it had been committed with respect to a traditional object of such an offence;

Damage to computer data or computer programs: The erasure, damaging, deterioration or suppression of computer data or computer programs without right;

Computer sabotage: The input, alteration, erasure or suppression of computer data or computer programs, or other interference with computer systems, with the intent to hinder the functioning of a computer or a telecommunication system;

Unauthorised access: The access without right to a computer system or network by infringing security measures;

Unauthorised interception: The interception, made without right and by technical means, of communications to, from and within a computer system or network;

Unauthorised reproduction of a protected computer program: The reproduction, distribution or communication to the public without right of a computer program, which is protected by law;

Unauthorised reproduction of a topography: The reproduction without right of a topography protected by law, of a semi-conductor product, or the commercial exploitation or the importation for that purpose, done without right, of a topography or of a semi-conductor product manufactured by using the topography.

The Select Committee also provided an 'optional list' on which it would be harder to reach international consensus:[15]

Alteration of computer data or computer programs: The alteration of computer data or computer programs without right;

Computer espionage: The acquisition by improper means or the disclosure, transfer or use of a trade or commercial secret without right or any other legal justification, with intent either to cause economic loss to the person entitled to the secret or to obtain an unlawful economic advantage for oneself or a third person;

Unauthorised use of a computer: The use of a computer system or network without right, that either: (a) is made with the acceptance of a significant risk of loss being caused to the person entitled to use the system or harm to the system or its functioning, or (b) is made with the intent to cause loss to the person entitled to use the system or harm to the system or its functioning, or (c) causes loss to the person entitled to use the system or harm to the system or its functioning;

> *Unauthorised use of a protected computer program*: The use without right of a computer program which is protected by law and which has been reproduced without right, with the intent, either to procure an unlawful economic gain for himself or for another person or to cause harm to the holder of the right.

Many elements of these 'minimum' and 'optional' lists have by now found their way into national computer crime legislation, along with significant improvements in criminal investigative powers and procedures necessitated by the challenges of prosecuting cyber-crime.[16] A significant impetus in this regard is the development of the Council of Europe's Convention on Cyber-crime, which provides a model for many European legislatures as well as several non-European ones. However, there are still jurisdictions, including some within the Asia-Pacific region, lacking legislation that incorporates all of the minimum requirements. Nonetheless, many legislatures have recognised the need for adequate laws to address cyber-crime and have begun the process of legislative reform.

Legislative reform

A recent McConnell International report on cyber-crime laws in 52 countries assessed the following Asia-Pacific countries as having updated their laws in relation to the prosecution of cyber-crime: Australia, China, Japan, Malaysia and the Philippines; New Zealand and Vietnam were assessed as being in the process of developing such laws.[17]

However, the report noted that such crimes are not treated uniformly across countries, or even in some instances within countries (such as Australia, which has both federal and state laws in relation to computer access), and that penalty levels vary widely. A comparison of computer-related offence provisions and penalty levels is made in the next part of this chapter.

The emergence of international cooperation

There have been several significant contributors towards a more systematic international understanding of the legal aspects of cyber-crime.

The OECD made an early contribution in a 1986 report entitled *Computer-related Crime: Analysis of Legal Policy*, which recommended that member states pay particular attention to the coverage under their national penal laws of specific knowingly committed acts:

- The input, alteration, erasure and / or suppression of computer data and / or computer programs made willfully with the intent to commit an illegal transfer of funds or of another thing of value
- The input, alteration, erasure and / or suppression of computer data and / or computer programs made wilfully with the intent to commit a forgery
- The input, alteration, erasure and / or suppression of computer data and / or computer programs, or other interference with computer systems, made wilfully with the intent to hinder the functioning of a computer and / or of a telecommunication system
- The infringement of the exclusive right of the owner of a protected computer program with the intent to exploit commercially the program and put it on the market
- The access to, or the interception of, a computer and/or telecommunication system made knowingly and without the authorisation of the person responsible for the system, either by infringement of security measures or for other dishonest or harmful intentions.

The OECD continues to contribute to international computer security policy, recently updating its *Guidelines for the Security of Information Systems and Networks*.[18]

The United Nations has been monitoring developments in computer-related crime for over a decade, starting with the 8th Crime Congress in Havana in 1990. This was followed in 1994 by the publication of a *Manual on the Prevention and Control of Computer-Related Crime*, and the Vienna Declaration on Crime and Justice: Meeting the Challenges of the 21st Century adopted by the Tenth United Nations Congress on the Prevention of Crime and the Treatment of Offenders in April 2000.[19] A United Nations symposium on 'The Challenge of Borderless Cyber-crime' was also held in conjunction with the Palermo signing conference of the Convention Against Transnational Organised Crime in December 2000.[20]

In 1997, the Group of Eight (G8) countries agreed on a set of ten Principles to Combat Hi-Tech Crime, dealing with issues such as cross-border investigation and mutual assistance.[21]

The Council of Europe's Convention on Cyber-crime is undoubtedly the most significant international instrument to date dealing with cyber-crime.[22] Opened for signature on 23 November 2001 in Budapest, the Convention came into force in July 2004.[23] A draft protocol relating to the criminalisation of acts of a racist or xenophobic nature committed through computer systems was also unanimously approved by the European Committee on Crime Problems at its plenary meeting in June 2002.[24]

The Convention on Cyber-crime provides a comprehensive structure for both substantive and procedural cyber-crime laws. Chapter II identifies a range of offences, which should be incorporated into the substantive criminal law of participating jurisdictions:

- Offences against the confidentiality, integrity and availability of computer data and systems (illegal access and interception, data interference and system interference, and misuse of devices)
- Computer-related offences (forgery and fraud)
- Content-related offences (child pornography)
- Offences related to infringements of copyright and related rights.

The convention also deals with ancillary liability and sanctions (attempt and aiding or abetting) as well as corporate liability. Chapter II goes on to canvass procedural matters such as collection and preservation of evidence, production orders, search and seizure, data interception and jurisdictional issues. Chapter III deals with mechanisms for international cooperation, including extradition and mutual assistance.

Given that the Convention on Cyber-crime has been adopted, not only within Europe but also by influential non-European countries like the United States and Japan, it provides the most obvious model for harmonisation of national cyber-crime laws internationally, within the Asia-Pacific region as elsewhere.

Regional Computer-Related Crime, Offences and Penalties

A US Government inter-agency working group on the President's International Crime Control Strategy noted: [25]

> As worldwide dependence on technology increases, high-tech crime is becoming an increasingly attractive source of revenue for organised crime groups, as well as an attractive option for them to make commercial and financial transactions that support their criminal activities. With little of the risks and penalties associated with more traditional criminal activity, high-tech crime allows criminals to operate in the relative security of computer networks, often beyond the reach of law enforcement where the crime was committed.

While the risks and penalties attached to cyber-crime may still be less than those associated with traditional crimes, it was noted above that many legislatures have already amended or are in the process of updating their cyber-crime laws.[26] This section presents a comparative analysis of the main computer and computer-related offence provisions in force in the Asia-Pacific region, together with applicable maximum penalties.

However, it should be added that comparison of criminal laws across Asia-Pacific jurisdictions must be treated with some caution due to the difficulty of obtaining legislation in reliable translation and the inherently idiosyncratic ways in which legislative provisions are drafted, promulgated, interpreted and enforced in differing legal systems. In addition, there is great variability in the degree to which penalties approaching the maximum available in legislation are imposed, and the range of sentencing options available to courts beyond those stated in the relevant offence provisions. With these reservations in mind, we can contrast the different national approaches.

Australia

Computer offence provisions have been part of Australian Commonwealth, State and Territory criminal law since the mid-1980s. The Commonwealth's first computer offences were enacted in 1989, in the form of a new Part VIA (ss. 76A–76F) of the *Crimes Act 1914* (Cth), which criminalised unlawful access to, or impairment of, Commonwealth computers and data, and carried penalties of up to ten years' imprisonment.[27] A Commonwealth computer is defined as 'a computer owned, leased or operated by a Commonwealth entity'.[28] The restriction to offences against Commonwealth computers and data was due to constitutional limits on Commonwealth legislative jurisdiction, which does not extend to general criminal matters. Thus the initial Commonwealth computer offences were limited in their application to the protection of national interests such as the taxation and social security systems. Numerous prosecutions have succeeded under these provisions, mostly against employees or former employees of relevant federal departments. Since then, the Commonwealth has extended its computer crime jurisdiction by relying on its constitutional power with respect to communications services.[29] New offences added under the *Cyber-crime Act 2001* (Cth) cover unauthorised computer access, modification of data, or impairment of electronic communications where this is effected by means of a 'telecommunications service', defined to mean 'a service for carrying communications by means of guided or unguided electromagnetic energy or both' (s. 476.1). Importantly, this covers the use of the Internet to commit offences, both under Commonwealth and state / territory law (Table 12.1).

Table 12.1 Computer crime offence provisions, Australia

Australia (Cth)	*Criminal Code Act 1995* (Cth) as amended by the *Criminal Code Amendment (Theft, Fraud, Bribery and Related Offences) Act 2000* and the *Cyber-crime Act 2001* (Cth):
	Unauthorised access, modification or impairment with intent to commit a serious offence (s. 477.1) Penalty: as for the serious offence (punishable by life imprisonment or a period of five or more years)
	Unauthorised modification of data to cause impairment (s. 477.2) 10 yrs max.
	Unauthorised impairment of electronic communication (s. 477.3) 10 yrs max.
	Unauthorised access to, or modification of, restricted data (s. 478.1) 2 yrs max.
	Unauthorised impairment of data held on a computer disk etc. (s478.2) 2 yrs max.
	Possession or control of data with intent to commit a computer offence (s. 478.3) 3 yrs max.
	Producing, supplying or obtaining data with intent to commit a computer offence (s. 478.4) 3 yrs max.
Australia (States and Territories)	New South Wales: *Crimes Act 1900*, ss. 308–308I (added by *Crimes Amendment (Computer Offences) Act 2001*)
	Queensland: *Criminal Code Act 1899*, s. 408D (added by *Criminal Law Amendment Act 1997*)
	South Australia: *Summary Offences Act 1953*, s. 44 (added by Summary Offences Act Amendment Act 1989 and amended by *Summary Offences (Offensive and Other Weapons) Amendment Act 1998*)
	Tasmania: *Criminal Code Act 1924*, ss. 257A–257F (added by Act No. 13 of 1990)
	Victoria: *Crimes Act 1958*, ss. 247A–247I (added by *Crimes (Property Damage and Computer Offences) Act 2003*)
	Western Australia: *Criminal Code*, s. 440A (added by Act No. 101 of 1990)
	Australian Capital Territory: *Criminal Code 2002*, ss. 112–121 (replacing provisions under the *Crimes Act 1900*)
	Northern Territory: *Criminal Code*, s222 and ss. 276–276F (added by *Criminal Code Amendment Act 2001*).

Sources: http://www.austlii.edu.au (Australasian Legal Information Institute);
http://scaleplus.law.gov.au (Commonwealth Attorney-General's Department)

One of the first states to create a specific computer offence was Victoria, which in 1988 enacted a new s. 9A (Computer Trespass) of the *Summary Offences Act 1966* (Vic). The latter provision stated simply that 'a person must not gain access to, or enter, a computer system or part of a computer system without lawful authority to do so'.[30] Other state / territory offences have sometimes been framed in terms of unauthorised use of a computer to commit other crimes, such as fraud or criminal damage.

Unlike the Commonwealth offences, state and territory laws are not restricted to particular computers or data, but serve to protect all computers and data within their respective jurisdictions. Unfortunately, however, there has been a lack of consistency across jurisdictions, so that computer crime laws in Australia have been difficult to enforce in any national or cross-jurisdictional sense. Increasingly, the states and territories are revising their computer crime laws in line with the Commonwealth model.[31] These reforms will hopefully achieve greater national consistency.

Further legislative reforms have been announced by the federal government relating to use of the Internet for offensive or menacing purposes.[32] Anti-spam legislation was also recently passed by the federal parliament, though it contains substantial civil rather than criminal penalties.[33]

China

The People's Republic of China has enacted several legal measures to deal with computer-related crime (Table 12.2). As with other areas of regulation, however, it should be noted that legislative and administrative measures are equally important in PR China. It has been observed that 'a sharp distinction between law and policy does not exist in PR China. Stated government policy can have exactly the same effect as formally enacted legislation'.[34]

Recent attention has also been directed towards control of Internet content and access.[35] On 28 December 2000, the 19th Session of the Standing Committee of the National People's Congress reportedly passed a resolution on maintaining the security of computer networks, making it a criminal offence to transmit the following over the Internet:

- Slander and rumours or harmful information
- State, intelligence or military secrets
- Incitement of ethnic hatred or discrimination
- Information in support of cults
- Advertising of fake or substandard products or services

- Material damaging business reputation
- Material infringing intellectual property
- False information on securities or futures trading
- Pornography
- Insulting or defaming material.[36]

Table 12.2 Computer crime offence provisions, China

Regulations on Protecting the Safety of Computer Information (Order No. 147 of the State Council of the People's Republic of China, 18 February 1994) Warnings may be given, fines imposed and illegal income confiscated in cases of deliberate input of a computer virus or selling special safety protection products without permission.
Revised Provisional Regulations Governing the Management of Chinese Computer Information Networks Connected to International Networks (promulgated in February 1996 and revised in May 1997) Computer information networks conducting direct international networking required to use international access channels provided by the national public telecommunications networks of the Ministry of Posts and Telecommunications (Art. 6); New Internet networks must have the approval of the State Council (Art. 7); Internet access networks must conduct international networking through Internet networks (Art.8). Public security organs shall order those who violate these to stop networking, issue them a warning, and impose a fine of no more than 15 000 RMB; earnings from illegal activities shall be confiscated where applicable. (Art.14) Computer Information Network and Internet Security, Protection and Management Regulations *(promulgated 30 December 1997)* Prohibition of use of Internet to: - Harm national security, disclose state secrets, conduct illegal activity etc. (Art. 4), punishable by relevant State regulations (Art. 19) - Transmit information inciting illegality or overthrow of the Government etc. (Art. 5), punishable by warnings, confiscation of illegal income, and fines of not more than 5000 RMB for individuals or 15 000 RMB for Internet service providing units (Art. 20) Prohibition of activities harming the security of computer information networks including: - Unapproved use of computer networks or resources, change of network functions, adding/deleting/altering stored data etc. - Creation or transmission of computer viruses, punishable as for Art. 5.
Internet Security Law *State Secrecy Protection Regulations For Computer Information Systems on the Internet* (January 2000)

Sources: http://www.qis.net/chinalaw/lawtran1.htm (China Law Web);
http://www.chinaonline.com (China Online);
http://www.bakerinfo.com/apec/chinaapec.htm (Baker McKenzie)

Hong Kong SAR

Despite its reversion to China in 1997, the Special Administrative Region of Hong Kong retains its jurisdictional identity. The main computer offence is s. 161 of the *Crimes Ordinance* (Cap. 200), which prohibits access to a computer with 'criminal or dishonest intent', punishable on conviction by imprisonment for five years. This very widely drafted provision does not require that the access be unauthorised (Table 12.3).

Table 12.3 Computer crime offence provisions, Hong Kong

Crimes Ordinance (Cap. 200) Extends definition of 'criminal damage to property' to include 'misuse of a computer' i.e. unauthorised function, altering, erasing or adding any program or data; 10 yrs max. or life imprisonment if property intentionally destroyed so as to endanger life (ss. 59, 60, 63) Access to computer with criminal or dishonest intent 5 yrs max. (s. 161)
Theft Ordinance (Cap. 210) 14 yrs max. for burglary defined to include unlawful interference with computer (s. 11)
Telecommunication Ordinance (Cap. 106) Unauthorised access to computer by telecommunications Fine of HK$20 000 (s. 27A)

Sources: http://www.justice.gov.hk/home.htm (Bilingual Laws Information System);
http://www.hklii.org/hk/legis/ord (HKLII);
http://www.worldlii.org/hk/legis/ord (WorldLII)

India

India made a considerable advance in its legislative coverage of computer technology with the enactment of the *Information Technology Act* in 2000. This statute provides a comprehensive new regulatory system for digital signatures and e-commerce, as well as amending the Penal Code and the Evidence Act to provide for the prosecution of computer offences. Offences include unauthorised access and damage, tampering with computer source documents, hacking, and publication of obscene material in electronic form (Table 12.4). The latter offence carries severe penalties including imprisonment up to five years for a first conviction and ten years for a subsequent conviction.

Table 12.4 Computer crime offence provisions, India

Information Technology Act 2000 (No. 21 of 2000) [see also *Electronic Commerce Act 1998* and *Electronic Commerce Support Act 1998* incorporating computer-related amendments to the *Indian Penal Code*]
Unauthorised access, damage etc. (s. 43) Damages not exceeding one crore rupees
Tampering with computer source documents (s. 65) 3 yrs max. and / or fine to two lakh = 200 000 rupees
Hacking with computer system (s. 66) 3 yrs max. and / or fine to two lakh rupees
Publishing obscene information in electronic form (s. 67) 5 yrs max. and fine to one lakh rupees; 10 yrs max. and fine to two lakh rupees for second or subsequent conviction
Unauthorised access to protected computer system (s. 70) 10 yrs max. and unspecified fine

Sources: http://www.mit.gov.in/it-bill.htm (Ministry of Information Technology) and http://commin.nic.in/doc/ecact.htm (Ministry of Commerce)

The inclusion of hacking and similar provisions in e-commerce legislation has been described as unusual, but justified on the grounds that 'the electronic environment needs to be made secure from intrusion to promote trustworthiness and public confidence in the medium'.[37]

Japan

Japan's computer crime laws are to be found in the Penal Code, as well as a more recent offence specifically prohibiting unauthorised access (Table 12.5). The latter criminalises acts enabling unauthorised access to computer functions which are restricted by an 'access control function' such as an identification code. Laws relating to e-commerce and prohibiting the distribution of child pornography have also been finalised in the last few years.

Republic of Korea

Korea has also modernised its criminal laws to include computer offences (Table 12.6). Particularly severe penalties attach to the impairment or alteration of data held by public authorities, with substantial penalties also for the impairment of privately held information or data.

Table 12.5 Computer crime offence provisions, Japan

Unauthorised Computer Access Law (No. 128 of 1999) Unauthorised computer access (Art. 3,8) 1 year max. or fine to ¥500 000 Facilitating unauthorised access (Art. 4,9) Fine to ¥300 000
Computer Crime Act *(under the Japanese Penal Code)* *Intentional and fraudulent misuse of electronic records* *5 years or fine not more than ¥50 000 (ss. 161–2).* *Intentional interference with electronic business transactions* *5 years or fine not more than ¥100,000 (s. 246–2).*

Sources: http://www.npa.go.jp/hightech/fusei_ac2/ucalaw.html (National Police Agency of Japan) and http://www.isc.meiji.ac.jp/~sumwel_h/Codes/comp-crim.htm (unauthorised translation by Takato Natsui)

Table 12.6 Computer crime offence provisions, Republic of Korea

Criminal Code (No. 5057 of 1995) Invalidity of Public Documents, etc. and Destruction of Public Goods (Art. 141) 7 yrs max. or fine to 10 million won Falsification or Alteration of Public Electromagnetic Records (Art. 227–2) 10 yrs max. Falsification or Alteration of Private Electromagnetic Records (Art. 232–2) 5 yrs max. or fine to 10 million won Interference with Business (Art. 314) 5 yrs max. or fine to 15 million won Fraud by Use of Computer, etc. (Art. 347–2) 10 yrs max. or fine to 20 million won Destruction and Damage, etc. of Property (Art. 366) 3 yrs max. or fine to 7 million won
Promotion of Utilisation of Information and Communications Network Act (No. 5986 of 1999) and *Computer Program Protection Act* (No. 3920 of 1986) Impairing data etc. (Art. 28) 5 yrs max. or fine to 50 million won Impairing protective measures (Art. 29) 3 yrs max. or fine to 30 million won Unauthorised disclosure (Art. 30) 1 yr max. or fine to 10 million won Breach of other regulations (Art. 30) Fine to 5 million won

Sources: http://icic.sppo.go.kr/english_d_1.htm and http://icic.sppo.go.kr/english_d_2.htm (Internet Crime Investigation Centre); http://www.cybik.com/tn/home.cgi (Cyberlaw Institute of Korea)

Malaysia

A package of 'cyberlaws' was introduced in Malaysia in 1997, covering computer crimes, copyright, telemedicine and digital signatures.[38] These were promoted by the Malaysian Government's Multimedia Super Corridor as a basis for the country's entry into electronic commerce, and Malaysia has maintained a leadership role in the response to computer-related crime such as Internet fraud in the region.[39] The main computer offences are to be found in the *Computer Crimes Act 1997*, with penalties up to ten years' imprisonment applying to unauthorised access and modification (Table 12.7).

Table 12.7 Computer crime offence provisions, Malaysia

Computer Crimes Act 1997 [see also *Digital Signatures Act 1997* and *Communications and Multimedia Act 1998*]
Unauthorised access (ss. 3,4) 5 yrs max. and / or fine to RM 50 000; 10 yrs max. and / or fine to RM 150 000 if with intention to commit offence
Unauthorised modification (s. 5) 7 yrs max. and / or fine to RM 100 000; 10 yrs max. and / or fine to RM 150 000 if with intention of causing injury
Unauthorised disclosure of access code (s. 6) 3 yrs max. and / or fine to RM 25 000

Sources: http://www.ktkm.gov.my/organisation/acts/crimeact/3.html (Communications and Multimedia Malaysia);
http://www.bakerinfo.com/apec/malayapec_main.htm#Crime (Baker McKenzie);
http://www.mdc.com.my/msc.comm/html/cyberights01.html (Malaysian Government);
http://www.nitc.org.my/resources/cyberlaw.shtml (National Information Technology Council);
http://www.mycert.mimos.my (MyCert)

New Zealand

New Zealand lacked adequate computer crime laws until an amendment to the Crimes Act was introduced into Parliament in 1999. Even then, the proposed legislation was subject to considerable scrutiny and debate and finally came into force early in 2002. Its main provisions include offences of accessing a computer system for a dishonest purpose, and damaging or interfering with a computer system (Table 12.8).

Table 12.8 Computer crime offence provisions, New Zealand

Crimes Amendment Act (No.6) 1999 (No. 322–2 of 2001, in force from 1 February 2002)
Accessing computer system for dishonest purpose (s. 250) - Obtain benefit or cause loss 7 yrs max. (s. 250(1)) - With intent to obtain benefit or cause loss 5 yrs max. (s. 250(2))
Damaging or interfering with computer system (s. 251) - Knowing that danger to life likely to result 10 yrs max. (s. 251(1)) - In other cases 7 yrs max. (s. 251(2))
Making, selling, or distributing or possessing software for committing crime (s. 252) 2 yrs max.
253 Accessing computer system without authorisation (s. 253) 2 yrs max.

Sources: http://rangi.knowledge-basket.co.nz (New Zealand Research Archive); http://www.sli.net.nz/crimebill/bill (Internet NZ)

Philippines

As noted earlier, the Philippines legislature reacted rapidly to the Love Bug incident by enacting a new law on electronic commerce, with potentially large penalties (commensurate to the damage caused) for 'hacking or cracking'. The same applies to electronic piracy (Table 12.9).

Table 12. 9 Computer crime offence provisions, Philippines

Electronic Commerce Act 2000 (in force from 15 June 2000)
Hacking or cracking (s. 33 (a)) Mandatory imprisonment from 6 months to 3 years and minimum fine of P100 000 with a maximum commensurate to the damage incurred
Piracy (s. 33 (b)) Penalty as for s. 33(a)
Violations of *Consumer Act* or *Republic Act* No. 7394 (s. 33 (c)) Penalties as provided in those Acts
Other violations of provisions of *Electronic Commerce Act 1999* (s. 33 (d)) 6 yrs max. or maximum fine of P1 million

Source: http://www.icon.com.ph/dti/ecom.htm (Department of Technology and Information)

Singapore

Singapore's *Computer Misuse Act* (Cap. 50A) has offences based on provisions in the United Kingdom's similarly named legislation, dealing with unauthorised access, access with intent to commit or facilitate a crime, unauthorised modification, and unauthorised use, interception, obstruction or disclosure.[40] There is an increasing scale of penalties for subsequent convictions, enhanced if damage is caused or special protected computers are involved (Table 12.10).

Table 12.10 Computer crime offence provisions, Singapore

Computer Misuse Act (Cap. 50A)
Unauthorised access to computer material (s. 3) 2 yrs max. and / or fine to S$5000 for first offence 3 yrs max. and / or fine to S$10 000 for second or later offence 7 yrs max. and / or fine to S$50 000 if damage caused
Access with intent to commit offence or facilitate commission (s. 4) 10 yrs max. and / or fine to S$50 000
Unauthorised modification of computer material (s. 5) 3 yrs max. and / or fine to S$10 000 5 yrs max. and / or fine to S$20 000 for second or later offence 7 yrs max. and / or fine to S$50 000 if damage caused
Unauthorised use or interception of computer service (s. 6) 3 yrs max. and / or fine to S$10 000; 5 yrs max. and / or fine to S$20 000 for second or later offence; 7 yrs max. and / or fine to S$50 000 if damage caused
Unauthorised obstruction of use of computer (s. 7) 3 yrs max. and / or fine to S$10 000 5 yrs max. and / or fine to S$20 000 for second or later offence 7 yrs max. and / or fine to S$50 000 if damage caused
Unauthorised disclosure of access code (s. 8) yrs max. and / or fine to S$10 000; 5 yrs max. and / or fine to S$20 000 for second or later offence
Enhanced punishment for offences involving protected computers (defence, law enforcement etc.) (s. 9) 20 yrs max. and / or fine to S$100 000

Sources: http://www.lawnet.com.sg/freeaccess/CMA-Details.htm (Law Net); http://www.bakerinfo.com/apec/singapec.htm (Baker McKenzie)

Taiwan

Taiwan's computer crime law incorporates provisions allowing injured persons to apply for statutory damages (Table 12.11).

Table 12.11 Computer crime offence provisions, Taiwan

Computer Processing Personal Information Protection Law (proclaimed August 1995)
Illegal output, distortion, change or deletion 3 yrs max. and / or fine to NT$50 000
Information leak for profit 2 yrs and / or NT$40 000
Private institutions liable to fine of NT$100 000 for breach; injured persons can apply for damages up to NT$20 million

Sources: http://www.qis.net/chinalaw/lawtran1.htm (China Law Web); http://www.chinaonline.com (China Online)

Thailand

Thailand is in the process of enacting new information technology laws, the first of these commencing in 1998, including laws relating to computer crime (Table 12.12).

Table 12.12 Computer crime offence provisions, Thailand

The *Computer Crime / Computer-related Crime Law* will prohibit unauthorised access, interception of data, use of a computer; computer-related espionage, forgery, fraud, and sabotage; reproduction of a protected computer program; and online child pornography

Sources: http://www.bakerinfo.com/apec/thaiapec.htm (Baker & McKenzie); http://www.tillekeandgibbins.com/FAQs/e-commerce.htm (Tilleke & Gibbons)

Overview of computer-related offences

Of the jurisdictions under consideration, Australia, Hong Kong, Malaysia, New Zealand and Singapore arguably have the most fine-grained discrimination of computer offences, while jurisdictions such as China, Taiwan and the Philippines tend towards more general offence descriptions.[41]

Only some of the Asia-Pacific jurisdictions incorporate specific fraud and forgery offences into their main computer crime legislation.[42] However, fraud and forgery can usually be prosecuted under the commercial and criminal laws of most jurisdictions whether committed using a computer or by more traditional paper-based means. Similarly, few computer crime laws in the region have specific child pornography and similar offensive-content measures.[43] However, such publication may be punishable under existing obscenity or content-classification laws. Finally, offences relating to copyright are to be found in intellectual property legislation rather than computer crime legislation in most jurisdictions.[44]

There is also considerable variety in the extent of associated procedural provisions.

Ancillary liability

Some Asia-Pacific computer crime laws contain specific provisions relating to attempt, aiding and abetting, conspiracy and corporate liability. For example, Malaysia's computer crime law provides that abetments and attempts are punishable as offences.[45] Ancillary liability may arise also from applicable criminal, commercial or corporations law.[46]

Special enforcement units

Recognising the highly specialised knowledge and skills required for investigation and evidence-gathering in relation to cyber-crime, some countries have moved towards setting up specialised computer crime units within their law enforcement agencies. Examples include:

- The Computer Security Unit established within the Hong Kong Police Crime Prevention Bureau[47]
- The High-Tech crime Technical Expert Center established to act as a 'cyber police force' by the National Police Agency of Japan[48]
- The Korean National Police Agency's Cyber Terrorism Response Center and recently announced General Investigation Center of Computer Crimes under the Prosecutor-General's Office[49]
- The Cyber Crime Investigation Cell within the Central Bureau of Investigation in India, with the power to investigate offences under the *Information Technology Act 2000* as well as other high-tech crimes.[50]

Organised crime / money laundering

Computer crime and intellectual property piracy may constitute 'predicate offences' under some jurisdictions' legislation directed towards organised crime and money laundering. This approach is based on the United States' *Racketeer-Influenced and Corrupt Organisations* statute enacted in 1970, which has been a model for some legislative developments in the Asia-Pacific region, such as the Philippines.

Forfeiture / restitution

Apart from the imposition of terms of imprisonment and fines, courts are empowered under some computer crime legislation to order forfeiture of equipment used and / or assets acquired, or to require restitution to victims. In Taiwan there is a statutory maximum for damages that can be awarded to injured persons under the *Computer Processing Personal Information Protection Law*. In the Philippines, maximum penalties imposed for hacking or cracking under the *Electronic Commerce Act* are commensurate with the damage incurred.[51]

Undercover surveillance / search and seizure

Standard search and seizure powers for the investigation of criminal offences may not extend to the investigation of computer data or the interception and covert surveillance of electronic transmissions such as e-mail. Some computer crimes legislation expands the range of investigatory powers available to law enforcement agencies, for example by making it an offence for a person with knowledge of a computer system to refuse to divulge passwords or provide information about encryption.[52]

International agreements and mutual assistance

Many countries have arrangements in place for mutual assistance in criminal matters, which allow for cross-border investigation and extradition of offenders.[53] A comprehensive framework for the development of such agreements is to be found in Chapter III of the Council of Europe's Convention on Cyber-crime.

Regional Intellectual Property Piracy, Offences and Penalties

There is considerable overlap between computer crime laws and intellectual property laws. For example, computer hardware may constitute a patentable invention, a registered design, or be protected under legislation relating to circuit layouts. Computer software may likewise be protected under copyright law, and similarly with data and information transmitted or stored on files. Conversely, it has been observed that 'the explosion of digitisation and the Internet has further enabled IPR (intellectual property rights) violators to easily copy and illegally distribute trade secrets, trade marks and logos'.[54] Thus it is important to consider applicable intellectual property protection regimes alongside more specific computer crime laws in the analysis of legislative responses to cyber-crime. The overlap of legal and other enforcement measures, such as anti-circumvention technologies and industry anti-piracy campaigns, is also an important feature of intellectual property protection in the Asia-Pacific region.[55]

Software piracy

The Business Software Alliance identifies the Asia-Pacific region as an area of particular concern, with an average piracy rate in 2002 of 55% representing annual dollar losses of nearly US$5.5 billion (Table 12.13).

Another example of the interaction between computer misuse and intellectual property crime is the growth in music piracy associated with the digital copying of audio files. The International Federation of Phonographic Industries has reported that:

> Music piracy poses a greater threat to the international music industry than at any other time in its history. Traffic in pirate recordings is not only proliferating worldwide — it is rapidly diversifying into new technologies and formats. Commercial pirate recordings today range from the traditional cassette to the manufactured CD, and from the CD-R disc replicated in a garage or laboratory to the audio file distributed on the Internet. Adding to the threat of commercial piracy is the spread of CD burning, made possible by advances in digital copying technologies. The impact of this diversification goes far wider than the music industry — piracy stunts the growth of the information-based economy; erodes innovation and cultural creativity and increasingly impacts on the international reputations of countries that fail to protect intellectual property rights.[56]

As remarks like this indicate, intellectual property piracy is a significant problem overall in the Asia-Pacific region. Part of the response has been in the form of legislative amendments.

Table 12.13 Software piracy rates and US dollar losses in the Asia-Pacific region

Asia-Pacific	*Piracy rates* *Retail software revenue lost to piracy (in 1000s)*						
	1996	*1997*	*1998*	*1999*	*2000*	*2001*	*2002*
Australia	32% $128 267	32% $129 414	33% $192 237	32% $150 390	33% $132 533	27% $91 011	32% $138 479
China	96% $703 839	96% $1 449 454	95% $1 193 386	91% $645 480	94% $1 124 395	92% $1 662 404	92% $2 407 719
Hong Kong	64% $129 109	67% $122 169	59% $88 627	56% $110 190	57% $86 195	53% $164 040	56% $82 308
India	79% $255 344	69% $184 664	65% $197 333	61% $214 557	63% $239 629	70% $365 318	70% $342 530
Indonesia	97% $197 313	93% $193 275	92% $58 756	85% $42 106	89% $69 991	88% $79 463	89% $138 306
Japan	41% $1 190 323	32% $752 598	31% $596 910	31% $975 396	37% $1 666 331	37% $1 721 050	35% $1 473 194
Korea	70% $515 547	67% $582 320	64% $197 516	50% $197 269	56% $302 938	48% $186 574	50% $425 416
Malaysia	80% $121 488	70% $82 552	73% $79 268	71% $84 154	66% $95 567	70% $94 544	68% $99 522
New Zealand	35% $29 271	34% $20 284	32% $21 758	31% $19 656	28% $12 373	26% $11 445	24% $6 415
Pakistan	92% $23 144	88% $20 395	86% $22 667	83% $18 913	83% $31 379	83% $11 429	80% $13 755
Philippines	92% $70 735	83% $49 151	77% $31 138	70% $33 163	61% $27 091	63% $24 655	68% $37 780
Singapore	59% $56 553	56% $56 599	52% $58 262	51% $61 758	50% $44 299	51% $41 802	48% $31 927
Taiwan	66% $116 980	63% $136 850	59% $141 274	54% $122 946	53% $154 754	53% $136 735	43% $113 283
Thailand	80% $137 063	84% $94 404	82% $48 613	81% $82 183	79% $53 082	77% $41 123	77% $81 900
Vietnam	99% $15 216	98% $10 132	97% $10 328	98% $13 106	97% $34 938	94% $32 246	95% $49 195
Other Asia / Pacific	86% $49 113	83% $31 974	74% $16 739	71% $20 262	75% $7 566	70% $62 616	69% $40 144
TOTAL	55% $3 739 304	52% $3 916 236	49% $2 954 812	47% $2 791 531	51% $4 083 061	54% $4 726 454	55% $5 481 891

The regional response

Estimated copyright piracy levels and associated trade losses figures are compiled annually by the International Intellectual Property Alliance (IIPA) for release in a 'Special 301' Report.[57] This information is then used by United States Trade Representative (USTR) as a basis for trade policy directed to the protection of intellectual property. In a recent report, the IIPA commented in detail on the Asia-Pacific region:

> Throughout the region, legislative reform will be running at full tilt this year, and careful attention must be paid to the impact of any deficiencies in these new laws — and in their enforcement — to ensure they meet the obligatory standards in the TRIPS Agreement and also lift protection to that provided in the WIPO 'Internet' Treaties which have now become the new world minimum standard of copyright protection. IIPA also urges USTR to maintain close vigilance over legislative developments and enforcement activity in other key territories in the region, notably Japan, Australia and Hong Kong, which do not appear on the Special 301 lists. In addition, IIPA continues to support the inclusion of the highest standards of protection and enforcement in the Singapore FTA IPR chapter.[58]

Clearly, the enforcement of intellectual property rights must occur within the context of legislative protection. The following discussion presents a comparative analysis of intellectual property offence provisions in the jurisdictions under consideration.

Australia

Intellectual property protection in Australia falls under Commonwealth legislative jurisdiction.[59] There are significant penalties for commercial infringement of copyright and trade marks, though none for other categories of intellectual property (Table 12.14). Prosecutions are relatively infrequent with sentences imposed well below the maximum penalties available.[60]

Table 12.14 Intellectual property offence provisions, Australia

Commonwealth only: Australian States and Territories have no intellectual property legislation
Patents Act 1990 No criminal penalties for infringement
Trade Marks Act 1995 2 yrs max. and / or fines to AUD$55 000 (ss. 145–149)
Designs Act 1906 (New *Designs Act 2003* to come into force in 2004) No criminal penalties for infringement
Copyright Act 1968 as amended by Copyright Amendment (Digital Agenda) Act 2000 (in force from March 2001) 5 yrs max and/or fines to AUD$60 500 (s. 132); fine increases to AUD$93 500 for infringement by conversion from analog to digital copy (s. 132(6AA))
Circuit Layouts Act 1989 No criminal penalties for infringement

Sources: http://scaleplus.law.gov.au (Attorney-General's Department); http://www.ipaustralia.gov.au (IP Australia)

PR China

PR China has, for much of the recent past, had a substantial problem with copyright piracy and trade mark counterfeiting, with very high levels of infringing products on domestic markets and exported to other countries in the region and beyond. However, PR China's recent entry into the World Trade Organization has been accompanied by a renewed effort to curb these illicit activities. The response of public authorities has concentrated on criminal enforcement measures. In PR China, criminal infringement proceedings for copyright infringement are the norm, while civil litigation is of secondary importance.[61] Penalties apply to all forms of infringement (Table 12.15).

Table 12.15 Intellectual property offence provisions, PR China

Patent Law (adopted in March 1994 and amended in Sept 1992) Unspecified criminal liability for serious infringement (Art. 63–66)
Trademark Law (adopted in Aug 1982 and amended in 1993, 2001) Unspecified criminal liability for serious infringement (Art. 38–40) *Supplementary Provisions under* Criminal Law (see below)
Designs and utility models are included as patentable invention-creations under the *Patent Law*
Copyright Law and *Regulations for Implementation* (adopted May 1991) Penalty of 3–7 yrs and fines for serious infringements (Art. 46, 51) Supplementary Provisions under *Criminal Law* (see below)
Regulations for the Protection of Computer Software (promulgated 4 June 1991) Range of executive punishments (Art. 30) Note: Computer hardware design may be patentable under the *Patent Law*
Criminal Law of the People's Republic of China (Adopted by the Second Session of the Fifth National People's Congress on 1 July 1979 and amended by the Fifth Session of the Eighth National People's Congress on 14 March 1997)[62] Additional penal provisions under Section 7. Infringement of Intellectual Property Rights: Penalties from 3 to 7 years with fine for criminal trademark infringement (Art. 213–215); Max. 3 year penalty and / or fine for criminal patent infringement (Art. 216); Penalties from 3 to 7 years with fine for criminal copyright infringement (Art. 217–218); Penalties from 3 to 7 years with fine for criminal trade secrets infringement (Art. 219).

Sources: http://www.qis.net/chinalaw/lawtran1.htm (China Law Web);
http://www.chinaonline.com (China Online);
http://www.cpo.cn.net (China Patent Office);
http://www.unesco.org/culture/copy/copyright/china/fr_sommaire.html (UNESCO)

Hong Kong

Hong Kong's intellectual property laws are still largely based on UK legislation, but there have been recent reforms, particularly in regard to copyright and trade marks. In addition, Hong Kong has made concerted efforts in recent years to curb piracy and counterfeiting.[63] As in Australia, Hong Kong's intellectual property legislation imposes criminal penalties for infringement only in relation to these two categories (Table 12.16).

Table 12.16 Intellectual property offence provisions, Hong Kong

Patents Ordinance (Cap. 514)
2 yrs max. for falsification of register etc.; no criminal penalties for infringement (s. 141)
Trade Marks Ordinance (Cap. 43)
7 yrs max. and fine of HK$50 000 for falsification of register (s. 86)
Note: The new *Trade Marks Ordinance* (Cap. 559) imposes fines for falsely representing that a sign is a registered trade mark (s. 94)
Registered Designs Ordinance (Cap. 522)
2 yrs max. for falsification of register etc.; no criminal penalties for infringement (s. 85)
Copyright Ordinance (Cap. 528)
8 yrs max. and fine of HK$500 000 (ss. 118–120)[64]
Prevention of Copyright Piracy Ordinance (Cap. 544)
Optical disk piracy: 2 yrs max. and fine of HK$500 000 on first conviction, or 4 yrs max. and HK$1 million thereafter (ss. 3–4, 21–22)
Lay-out Design (Topography) of Integrated Circuits Ordinance (Cap. 445)
No criminal penalties for infringement

Sources: http://www.justice.gov.hk/home.htm (BLIS – Bilingual Laws Information System);
http://www.hklii.org/hk/legis/ord (HKLII);
http://www.worldlii.org/hk/legis/ord (WorldLII);
http://info.gov.hk/ipd/eng/index.htm (Intellectual Property Department)

India

Although India enacted a modern information technology law in 2000, its intellectual property legislation remains somewhat less updated, though the Copyright Act has been amended to include copyright program protection (Table 12.17). High levels of computer software piracy persist according to estimates of the IIPA and government sources.

Table 12.17 Intellectual property offence provisions, India

Patents Act 1970 Patents (Amendment) Act 1999
Trade and Merchandise Marks Act 1999 6 months to 3 yrs max. and fine from Rs 50 000 to Rs 2 million (ss. 76–95)
Designs Act 1911 (subject to revision under *Designs Bill 2000*)
Copyright Act 1957 (as amended by *Copyright Act 1994* No. 38 of 1994) [includes computer software] 6 months to 3 yrs max. and fine from Rs 50 000 to Rs 2 million (ss. 63, 63A) infringing computer programs 3 yrs max. and fine to Rs 2 million (s. 63B)

Source: http://www.unesco.org/culture/copy/copyright/india/fr_sommaire.html (UNESCO)

Japan

Japan developed much of its intellectual property system at the time it began to emerge as an advanced industrial manufacturer. Some of its intellectual property and commercial laws were influenced by European, particularly German, legislation — and it has in turn provided a model for several other Asian countries. Japanese law includes criminal provisions in relation to all categories of intellectual property (Table 12.18).

Table 12.18 Intellectual property offence provisions, Japan

Patent Law of 1959 5 yrs max. with labour or fine to ¥5 million (ss. 196-204)
Trademark Law of 1957 5 yrs max. with labour or fine to ¥5 million (ss. 78–85)
Design Law and *Utility Model Law* of 1959 3 yrs max. with labour or fine to ¥3 million (ss. 69–77; ss. 56–64)
Copyright Act of 1970 3 yrs max. with labour or fine to ¥3 million (Art. 113, 119) Circumvention devices: 1 yr max. or fine to ¥1 million (Art. 120bis)
Circuit Layout of Semi-conductor Integrated Circuit Act of 1985 3 yrs max. or fine to ¥1 million (Art. 51–56)

Sources: http://www.jpo.go.jp (Japan Patent Office);
http://www.unesco.org/culture/copy/copyright/japan/fr_sommaire.html (UNESCO)

Republic of Korea

Like Japan, Korea has criminal penalties for intellectual property infringement in all categories (Table 12.19).

Table 12.19 Intellectual property offence provisions, Republic of Korea

Patent Law (No. 950 of 1961) Infringement: 7 yrs max. or fine to 100 million won; 300 million won for a corporation (Art. 225–232)
Trademark Law (No. 71 of 1949) Infringement: 7 yrs max. or fine to 100 million won; 300 million won for a corporation (Art. 93–98)
Design Law (No. 951 of 1961) and *Utility Model Law* (No.952 of 1961) Infringement: 7 yrs max. or fine to 100 million won; 300 million won for a corporation (Art. 82–89; Art. 18)
Copyright Act (No. 3816 of 1986) and *Computer Program Protection Act* (No.3920 of 1986) Infringement: 3 yrs max. or fine to 3 million won (Art. 98–101; Art. 46(1))
Semi-conductor Integrated Circuits Lay-Out Design Act (No. 4526 of 1992) Infringement: 3 yrs max. and/or 50 million won (Art. 45–49)

Source: http://www.kipo.go.kr (Korean Intellectual Property Office)

Malaysia

Malaysian intellectual property offences are mainly restricted to copyright (Table 12.20). Infringement levels are reportedly high but declining, according to IIPA estimates.

Table 12.20 Intellectual property offence provisions, Malaysia

Patents Act 1983 No criminal penalties for infringement
Trade Marks Act 1976 No criminal penalties for infringement
Industrial Designs Act 1999 No criminal penalties for infringement
Copyright Act 1987 and *Copyright (Amendment) Acts 1990*, 1996, 1997, 2000 5 yrs max. and fine to 10 000 ringgit per infringing copy; 10 yrs max for second or later offence (s. 41)
Layout-Designs of Integrated Circuits Act 2000 No criminal penalties for infringement
Note also *Optical Discs Bill 2000* including criminal penalties.

Source: http://www.kpdnhq.gov.my/homepage/english/mainlp.html (IP Infonet Malaysia)

New Zealand

As in Australia, intellectual property infringement offences apply only in relation to copyright and trade marks (Table 12.21). New trade marks legislation adopting models taken from various jurisdictions (including Singapore) was enacted in 2002, including increased criminal penalties.

Table 12.21 Intellectual property offence provisions, New Zealand

Patents Act 1953 No criminal penalties for infringement
Trade Marks Act 2002 5 yrs max. or fines to NZ$150 000 (ss. 120–125)
Designs Act 1953 No criminal penalties for infringement
Copyright Act 1994 3 months max. or fine of NZ$5000 per infringing copy to a max. of NZ$50 000 (ss. 131, 198)
Layout Designs Act 1994 No criminal penalties for infringement

Source: http://www.knowledge-basket.co.nz/gpacts/actlists.html (New Zealand Research Archive)

Philippines

The Philippines has a range of infringement offences with increasing penalties for second and third offences, rising to a maximum of nine years' imprisonment (Table 12.22). This is in addition to the piracy offence under the *Electronic Commerce Act*.

Table 12.22 Intellectual property offence provisions, Philippines

Intellectual Property Code of the Philippines (Republic Act No. 8293) includes Part II: *Patents*, Part III: *Trademarks, Service Marks and Trade Names*, Part IV: *Copyright* – including computer programs (in force from 1 January 1998)
First infringement offence: 1 to 3 yrs and fine from P50 000 to P150 000; Second offence: 3 to 6 yrs and fine from P150 000 to P500 000; Third offence: 6 to 9 yrs and fine from P500 000 to P1 500 000 and in all cases, subsidiary imprisonment in case of insolvency (s. 217.1)

Sources: http://ipophil.gov.ph/laws.asp?id=1 (Intellectual Property Office, Philippines);
http://www.chanrobles.com (Chan Robles)

Singapore

Criminal offences in Singapore apply to trade marks and copyright infringement (Table 12.23).

Table 12.23 Intellectual property offence provisions, Singapore

Patents Act (Cap. 221) No criminal penalties for infringement
Trade Marks Act (Cap. 332) Counterfeiting offences (ss. 46–49) 5 years max. and / or S$100 000 fine
Registered Designs Act (Cap. 266) No criminal penalties for infringement
Copyright Act (Cap. 63) Infringement (s. 136) 5 yrs max. and / or S$10 000 per infringing copy to a max. of S$100 000
Layout-Designs of Integrated Circuits Act (Cap. 159A) No criminal penalties for infringement

Source: http://www.lawnet.com.sg (LawNet Singapore)

Taiwan

As in Japan and Korea, Taiwan's intellectual property legislation has criminal infringement offences in all categories (Table 12.24).

Table 12.24 Intellectual property offence provisions, Taiwan

Patent Law Infringement - Invention patents:(fine to NT$600 000); - Utility model patents: 2 yrs max. and / or fine to NT$150 000
Trademark Law Penalty for fraudulent infringement 3 yrs max. and / or fine to NT$200 000 (Art. 62)
Patent Law Infringement: New design patents: 1 yr max. and / or fine to NT$60 000
Copyright Law (includes computer software) Infringement: 7 yrs max. and fine to NT$450 000
Integrated Circuit Layout-Design Protection Law Constructive damages to NT$5 million, but no criminal punishment

Sources: http://www.qis.net/chinalaw/lawtran1.htm (China Law Web); http://www.chinaonline.com (China Online)

Thailand

Intellectual property laws have been substantially revised in Thailand, with greater emphasis in recent years on deterring infringement.[65] The legislation includes a range of criminal penalties (Table 12.25). Interestingly, Thailand is one of very few jurisdictions to have a specialised Intellectual Property Court, which was established in 1997 with both civil and criminal jurisdiction.[66]

Table 12.25 Intellectual property offence provisions, Thailand

Patent Act B.E.2522 (1979), amended B.E.2535 (1992), B.E.2542 (1999) 3 yrs max. or fine to 400 000 baht (ss. 81–88)
Trademarks Act B.E.2534 (1991), amended B.E.2543 (2000) 4 yrs max. or fine to 400 000 baht (ss. 107–116)
Copyright Act, B.E.2537 (1994) (includes computer software) *Protection of Lay-out Designs of Integrated Circuits Act* B.E.2543 (2000) Direct infringement: fine from 20 000 baht to 200 000 baht; max. 4 yrs and / or fine from 100 000 baht to 800 000 baht if offence committed for commercial purpose (ss. 27–30, 52, 69) Indirect infringement: fine from 10 000 to 100 000 baht; max. 2 yrs and / or fine from 50 000 to 400 000 baht if offence committed for commercial purpose (ss. 31,70) Penalty doubled for further offence committed within 5 yrs of discharge of first offence penalty (s. 73)

Sources: http://ipthailand.org (IP Thailand); http://www.s-l-asia.com (S&I International); http://members.tripod.com/asialaw/database.html (Thailand Law Forum)

Overview of intellectual property offences

The general capacity of countries in the Asia-Pacific region to protect intellectual property through criminal enforcement measures appears adequate, as indicated in the availability and range of penalties for infringement in various categories. Piracy and counterfeiting levels, nevertheless, remain high in much of the region, despite concerted efforts to attack the problem.

Offence classification

The classification of intellectual property laws into those dealing with patents, trade marks, designs, copyright and (in some jurisdictions) computer circuit layouts is fairly standard. However, the legislation of some jurisdictions combines a number of these categories (e.g. China, Taiwan, the Philippines), while others have specific laws for additional categories such as utility models (Japan, Korea). Moreover, not all intellectual property statutes make infringement an offence (in Australia, for example, only the *Trade Marks Act* and *Copyright Act* have such offence provisions).

Computer software

Unauthorised duplication of computer software (except to make a back-up copy for personal use) is now explicitly included as infringement under most copyright laws. The amendments introduced to effect this range from merely including computer software in the definition of copyrightable material or literary works (e.g. Taiwan, Thailand, Vietnam), to entirely new legislation (e.g. the *Computer Program Protection Act* of Korea). Given the commercial interests involved in computer software distribution, it is not surprising that leading corporations have taken dominant roles in enforcement strategies, both through civil litigation and through assisting public authorities in criminal enforcement.[67]

Corporate campaigns against Internet piracy and criminal counterfeiting

Over the last few years, the Microsoft Corporation has undertaken a campaign against software piracy and counterfeiting in numerous countries including many in the Asia-Pacific region.[68] In cooperation with law enforcement agencies, the company has succeeded in taking down over thousands of Internet sites offering counterfeit software. Raids have been conducted in China (including Hong Kong and Macau), Malaysia, the Philippines, Singapore, Taiwan and Thailand leading to numerous arrests and seizures of counterfeit software, CDs, optical disks and production equipment. Similar action has also been initiated by representatives of the film and music industries, leading to the dismantling of numerous piracy operations in the region.

Optical disk piracy

Some Asia-Pacific jurisdictions have laws explicitly relating to optical disk piracy. For example, Hong Kong's *Prevention of Copyright Piracy Ordinance* prohibits the manufacture of optical disks without a valid licence, punishable by a fine of HK$500 000 and imprisonment for two years on a first conviction, and HK$1 million or four years on a subsequent conviction (Cap. 544, s. 21). Penalties for optical disk piracy have also been included in Malaysia's *Optical Disks Bill 2000*.

Circumvention of technological protection measures

Offence provisions in relation to the circumvention of technological protection measures such as encryption devices, user identification and electronic rights management information regimes are in early stages of introduction in the Asia-Pacific region. Amendments in Australia's *Copyright Act 1968*, ss. 132(5A)–(5J), relating to circumvention, came into force on 4 March 2001. Penalties for manufacture, sale or commercial promotion of such devices range up to five years' imprisonment and fines of AUD$60 500 (five times this amount for a corporation). Similar provisions have also been enacted in Hong Kong, Japan, Korea and Malaysia. The Malaysian *Copyright (Amendment) Act 1997* (in force from 1 April 1999) provides for fines up to 250 000 ringgit and / or imprisonment for up to three years for a first offence, or 500 000 ringgit and / or five years for subsequent offences.

International intellectual property agreements

International agreements for the protection of industrial and intellectual property date back over 100 years. Many countries within the Asia-Pacific region are signatories to intellectual property agreements administered by WIPO, UNESCO and the WTO.[69] Some of these instruments, such as the TRIPs agreement, require countries to take appropriate measures against copyright piracy and trade mark counterfeiting. Intellectual property protection has become an increasingly important component of trade negotiations, both bilateral and multilateral (under the auspices of the WTO). The most significant recent development in this regard is China's accession to the WTO in 2002.[70]

Conclusion

Cyber-crime legislation in the Asia-Pacific region is still in the early stages of development and exhibits wide variation in terms of legislative approach, overlap with general criminal, commercial and intellectual property law, and differentiation between offences and penalty levels. This variation is not surprising given the vastly different historical, social and political contexts within which these laws have evolved, and the differing levels of technological development within the region.

However, it is now conventional wisdom that cyber-crime knows no national borders and, as a result, defences against the threats increasingly posed to computer and information infrastructures can only be as strong as the weaker links in the chain. It is therefore important for each jurisdiction to continually assess the adequacy of its cyber-crime laws and, where deficiencies can be identified, to reform those laws appropriately. While there is no single model to be emulated in this process, guidance can be gained from legislation in force in jurisdictions with longer experience of the threat and prosecution of cyber-crime, and also from concerted international efforts such as the Council of Europe's Convention on Cyber-crime. By offering a regional overview of computer and intellectual property offences and penalties, it is hoped that this chapter will contribute to greater cohesion and effectiveness of legislative responses to cyber-crime in the Asia-Pacific region.

13

Law Enforcement in Cyberspace: The Hong Kong Approach

Michael Jackson

On 1 April 2003, at the height of the SARS crisis in Hong Kong, a 14-year-old Form III schoolboy prepared a bogus news report stating that Hong Kong had been declared an infected port, that its stock market index (the Hang Seng Index) had collapsed, and that the Chief Executive, Tung Chee-hwa, had resigned. He placed this 'news report' on his website and, significantly, added the logo of a popular Chinese-language Hong Kong newspaper, copied from the latter's website. Whatever his intent — note the date was 1 April — this 'news report' was picked up and distributed widely in Hong Kong by e-mail and phone calls, sparking panic buying at supermarkets and a brief plunge in the Hang Seng Index. The Hong Kong government was forced to issue a denial; it also sent out millions of text messages to mobile phone users denying the rumours.[1]

Initially arrested for allegedly gaining access to a computer with criminal or dishonest intent,[2] carrying a possible sentence of five years' imprisonment, the boy was subsequently charged with the distinctly non-cyber summary offence of 'knowingly furnishing any information which is false concerning any [infectious] disease or death', contrary to Regulation 7 of the Prevention of the Spread of Infectious Diseases Regulations,[3] which carries a maximum penalty of a fine of HK$2500.

Why was this conduct not prosecuted as a computer crime, given its significant cyber elements: the use of the Internet and the World Wide Web? The answer, surprising perhaps, given Hong Kong's technologically savvy, highly 'wired' community, was simply that, in the absence of a provable criminal or dishonest intent, no existing 'computer crime' under Hong Kong law readily covered this conduct. The reason for this largely lies in the fact that Hong Kong's current body of cyber-crimes were enacted in 1993 and reflect a view of computer criminality current at that time, rather than in today's Internet-driven information society.

More specifically, responding to growing international and domestic concerns about the spreading computer crime problem, and in particular hacking, and drawing on the United Kingdom's *Computer Misuse Act 1990*, Hong Kong enacted its first piece of legislation expressly directed at computer-related crime, the Computer Crimes Ordinance (Ordinance No. 23 of 1993), in 1993.[4] This Ordinance, despite its name, was neither a comprehensive response to the computer crime problem nor was it intended to provide Hong Kong with a stand-alone, computer-specific legislative framework. Rather, it attempted to deal with Hong Kong's most immediate needs by filling clear legislative gaps. To that end, two new computer-specific offences — dealing with unauthorised access to a computer by telecommunication, and access to a computer with criminal or dishonest intent — were enacted, although they were added to existing criminal legislation rather than located in a separate ordinance. In addition, several existing offences were amended to ensure their application to the virtual, and not just the physical, world. Even then, there was only grudging acceptance of the legislation by many interested technology groups, which were quick to criticise it as 'patchwork', 'late', put together without consultation with interested parties, and based on a poor understanding of the technology involved.[5] Specific complaints included the failure to define the term 'computer' as used in these new offences, and that the new offences were so broadly stated that sending an unsolicited fax would seemingly amount to an offence.

This does not mean that Hong Kong has ignored the technological advances since 1993, or failed to address the new criminal opportunities and methodologies created by the Internet age and information society and the development of cyberspace, but there has been relatively little in the way of further cyber-crime legislation. Legislation against the making and dissemination of child pornography — including online and electronic child pornography — has been enacted,[6] as has legislation dealing with the 'wiretapping' of computer networks (though this legislation[7] has yet to come into effect). A draft order aimed at expanding criminal jurisdiction over computer crimes is also presently before the legislature.[8] But most of the existing legislation remains rooted in concepts and 'crimes' formulated in the early 1990s, before the use of the Internet exploded and gave rise to today's information society.

Instead of a proactive legislative programme, the Hong Kong government has given priority to strengthening its law enforcement resources and capabilities in dealing with computer crime and gaining the cooperation of the private sector in the fight against computer crime, while simultaneously promoting public education about the Internet and computer crime. For example, since 1993 Hong Kong has seen the establishment of specialist computer crime and crime prevention units within the Hong Kong Police (including a Computer Crime Section set up in 1993, and a Technology Crime Division set up in 2001), the Independent Commission Against Corruption, the Customs and Excise Department (which has set up an Anti-Internet Piracy Team), and the Prosecutions Division at the Department of Justice. Computer forensics has received attention with the formation in 1998 of a Computer Forensic Examination Working Group (involving The Hong Kong University of Science and Technology, the Police and the ICAC) and the establishment of professional computer forensic training programmes. The protection of Hong Kong's computer infrastructure gained added impetus with the establishment in early 2001 of a government-funded Computer Emergency Response Team (HKCERT).[9] Steps have also been taken to improve the evidence-gathering abilities of Hong Kong's law enforcement agencies both in Hong Kong and overseas, and likewise to facilitate evidence-gathering for overseas agencies, both through increased cooperation and coordination, and by putting in place mutual assistance arrangements.

Furthermore, in early 2000, responding to renewed concerns about reported increases in computer-related crime, the HKSAR Government convened an Inter-departmental Working Group to review the effect of changes introduced by the 1993 Computer Crime Ordinance, and to consider future developments.

In its Report (Inter-departmental Working Group on Computer Related Crime, September 2000 ['Report']), the Working Group expressed confidence that the thrust of the legislative changes effected by the Computer Crimes Ordinance in 1993 (particularly the two new offences of unauthorised access to computer by telecommunication (s. 27A, Telecommunications Ordinance) and access to computer with criminal and dishonest intent (s. 161, Crimes Ordinance)) remains on the right lines (para. 2.5), that the changes have enabled the successful prosecution of most instances of reported computer crime, and that the changes should be retained.

At the same time, the Working Group recognised that new initiatives have become necessary. Accordingly, it made a series of recommendations covering a broad range of cyber-crime issues, including further amendments to Hong Kong's existing substantive and procedural law.[10] Mindful of the criticisms levelled at it in 1993, the Administration undertook consultation with interested parties over several months[11] before bringing the Report and its recommendations (in some instances with amendments in the light of comments during public consultation) before the Chief Executive in Council (Exco) in July 2001. Exco broadly approved most of the recommendations and adopted a Tentative Implementation Plan setting out short, medium and long-term actions to be taken to implement the Working Group's Report.[12] A dedicated inter-departmental Task Force on Computer Related Crime has been established to follow up on this Implementation Plan.

Recently, delivering the keynote speech at an IEE Symposium, 'Internet law in Hong Kong', the Secretary of Justice, Elsie Leung, reiterated the Administration's view that 'the Computer Crimes Ordinance remains broadly adequate to deal with illicit acts such as hacking, the spreading of computer viruses and criminal damage of computer data'.[13]

The government, she affirmed, nonetheless remained committed, in accordance with the tentative implementation plan formulated in July 2001, to a threefold strategy for enhancing Hong Kong's cyber-crime readiness: '(1) strengthen the existing regulatory regime; (2) increase the involvement of the community in the prevention and detection of computer-related crimes; and (3) improve co-ordination and institutional arrangements to prevent cyber attacks and promote cyber security.'[14] In formulating its strategy, the Administration has also taken into account contemporaneous international developments, such as the Council of Europe's Convention on Cyber-crime. This has already occasioned the enactment of legislation dealing with child pornography, but it will also likely lead to further proposals for change.

The Present Legislative Framework

To facilitate comparison with other jurisdictions, Hong Kong's present legislative regime will be outlined using the framework and categories adopted by the Council of Europe in its Convention on Cyber-crime.

At the outset, it is worth reiterating that Hong Kong still lacks a clear definition of 'computer' that can be applied in all statutory contexts. Where 'computer' has been defined, it has been done narrowly, along the lines of 'a device for storing, processing or retrieving information' (see, for example, s. 22A, Evidence Ordinance (Cap. 8), s. 26A, Inland Revenue Ordinance (Cap. 112), and s. 19, Business Registration Ordinance (Cap. 310)). In 2000, the much broader expression 'information system' was adopted in the Electronic Transactions Ordinance (Cap. 553), and defined as a system which:

(a) Processes information
(b) Records information
(c) Can be used to cause information to be recorded, stored or otherwise processed in other information systems (wherever situated)
(d) Can be used to retrieve information, whether the information is recorded or stored in the system itself or in other information systems (wherever situated).[15]

In its 2000 Report on computer-related crime, the Working Group recommended that the expression 'information system' should be adopted instead of 'computer' in existing and future legislation.[16] Like most of the recommendations for legislative action, this has yet to be implemented.

Computer and Data Offences

(Offences against the confidentiality, integrity and availability of computer data and systems)

Illegal access (Art. 2) / Illegal interception (Art. 3)

These activities are presently covered principally by s. 27A of the Telecommunications Ordinance (Cap. 106) and s. 161 of the Crimes Ordinance (Cap. 200); both provisions were added in 1993 (s. 27A was further amended by s. 28, Ord. No. 36 of 2000). Additional provisions have also been enacted in the Interception of Communications Ordinance (Cap. 532) but are not yet in operation (and may be amended after further review in the light of overseas developments, notably the United Kingdom's Regulation of Investigatory Powers Act 2000).

One preliminary point to be emphasised is that since July 1997, new legislation must comply with Art. 30 of the Basic Law, which states:

> The freedom and privacy of communication of Hong Kong residents shall be protected by law. No department or individual may, on any grounds, infringe upon the freedom and privacy of communication of residents except that the relevant authorities may inspect communication in accordance with legal procedures to meet the needs of public security or of investigation into criminal offences.

This requires the government to balance the needs of law enforcement with the rights of its citizens to protection of their privacy, not always an easy balancing act.

Telecommunications Ordinance (Cap. 106)

Section 27A(1)

This section deals with unauthorised access to a computer *by telecommunication*, that is, hacking. It provides: 'Any person who, by telecommunications, knowingly causes a computer to perform any function to obtain unauthorised access to any program or data held in a computer commits an offence and is liable on conviction to a fine of HK$20,000.'

'Telecommunications' is defined in the Ordinance (s. 2) as 'any transmission, emission or reception of communication by means of guided or unguided electromagnetic energy or both, other than any transmission or emission intended to be received or perceived directly by the human eye'.

Section 27A(1) requires proof that the person who caused a computer to perform any function enabling unauthorised access did so 'knowingly'; however, under subsection (2)(a), his intent need not be directed at (i) any particular program or data, (ii) a program or data of a particular kind, or (iii) a program or data held in a particular computer (s. 27A(2)(a)).

Section 27A(2)(b) further declares that access is unauthorised if the hacker is not entitled to control access of the kind in question to the program or data held in the computer, and (i) has not been authorised to obtain access of the kind in question to the program or data held in the computer by any person who is so entitled, (ii) does not believe that he has been so authorised, and (iii) does not believe that authorisation would have been given if application had been made to the appropriate authority (s. 27A(2)(b)). Proceedings for an offence under this section must be commenced within three years of the commission of the offence or six months of its discovery by the prosecutor, whichever period expires first (s. 27A(4)).

In 2000, the Inter-departmental Working Group on Computer Related Crime described the HK$20 000 penalty under s. 27A as 'a woefully inadequate deterrent', given the 'very significant damage that hacking may bring about' (Report, para. 2.7); it duly recommended the addition of a custodial term, but this has yet to be implemented. In addition, the Working Group recommended that unauthorised access to a computer by any means, and not just by telecommunication, should be made unlawful (see *Report*, Recommendation 12, and para. 6.19). Similarly, this has yet to be implemented.

Other offences

Several additional sections of the Telecommunications Ordinance deal with offences involving the interception, alteration and such like of 'messages'; a 'message' being 'any communication sent or received by telecommunications or given to a telecommunications officer to be sent by telecommunications or to be delivered' (s. 2).

Section 24 makes it an offence for a 'telecommunications officer' ('any person employed in connection with a telecommunications service', s. 2), or any other person having 'official duties in connection with a telecommunications service', to (a) wilfully destroy, secrete or alter a message, (b) knowingly forge or utter a message, (c) wilfully intercept, detain or delay, or wilfully abstain from transmitting a message, or (d) copy a message or disclose a message or its purport to any person other than its addressee.

Section 25 makes it an offence for a person who is not a telecommunications officer, or who has official duties in connection with a telecommunications service, or who has been entrusted by a telecommunications officer to deliver a message, to wilfully secrete, detain or delay a message intended for delivery to some other person, or to refuse or neglect to deliver up a message in his possession when required by a telecommunications officer to do so.

Section 27 makes it an offence for any person to damage, remove or interfere with a 'communications installation' 'with intent' (a) to prevent or obstruct the transmission or delivery of a message, or (b) to intercept or discover the contents of a message.

Finally, s. 28 criminalises the transmission by telecommunications of a false distress message, knowing or believing the message to be false and intending its transmission to deceive.

Breaches of ss. 24, 25, 27 or 28 are all punishable upon summary conviction with a fine of HK$20 000 (at level 3 in the case of s. 28) and imprisonment for up to two years.

Section 161, Crimes Ordinance (Cap. 200)

Section 161 (similarly enacted in 1993) deals with accessing a computer with criminal or dishonest intent. Subsection 161(1) creates a more serious offence, and is punishable on conviction on indictment to imprisonment for five years. It reads:

> (1) Any person who obtains access to a computer –
>
> (a) with intent to commit an offence

(b) with a dishonest intent to deceive
(c) with a view to dishonest gain for himself or another
(d) with a dishonest intent to cause loss to another whether on the same occasion as he obtains such access or on any future occasion,

commits an offence … .[17]

Section 161 has been considered by the courts on several occasions. In *Hung Hak Sing* ((1995) Cr App No. 642 of 1995), Hung was charged under s. 161(1)(c) with obtaining access to the Immigration Department's computer system. The prosecution alleged that he acted at the request of a friend of his, a senior customs officer (who was party to a separate criminal conspiracy), to discover whether certain people were on the customs watch list. The prosecution alleged but failed to prove that Hung expected to be paid for his acts; seemingly Hung acted out of friendship and without knowledge of the separate conspiracy. Hung's conviction was quashed by the Court of Appeal, on the ground that, even if 'gain' included the mere fact of obtaining information, the prosecution had failed to prove that Hung acted 'with a view to *dishonest* gain' (per Mortimer JA).

In *HKSAR v Tong Ka Kin* ((1996) Mag App No. 1031 of 1995), Duffy J adopted a broad view of 'with a dishonest intent to cause loss' under (d), holding that it was enough for the prosecution to establish that the defendant's conduct, in giving out details of customer's accounts at the telecom company where he was a customer services officer, involved potential loss to subscribers or the company, rather than any actual loss to a particular subscriber.

In *HKSAR v Tsun Shi Lun* ([1999] 2 HKC 547), a hospital technical assistant was prosecuted for accessing the hospital's computer, printing-out an x-ray report relating to the Secretary of Justice, and later anonymously faxing copies of it to two newspapers, allegedly to correct what he considered was a misimpression given to the public by the government as to the state of the secretary's health. Tsun was charged under s. 161(1)(c). He argued that his conduct did not fall within (c) since it was done neither with a view to gain for himself, nor dishonestly. Both arguments were rejected in the Court of First Instance. Chan CJHC held that the legislative objective in enacting s. 161(1)(c) was to criminalise the fact of access to a computer in itself, provided it was dishonest; accordingly, it was not restricted to acts that could be proved to be preparatory to the commission of a crime or fraud. Following *Hung Hak Sing*, above, Chan CJHC held that 'gain' included obtaining information not available prior to access, including transient information such as that read on a computer screen.[18] As regards 'dishonesty', the court applied the *Ghosh* test, concluding that the only reasonable inference to be drawn from the facts was that Tsun knew and must have realised it was dishonest conduct to access the computer, print out a copy of the report, and leak it to the press. At trial, Tsun was sentenced to six months' imprisonment; on appeal, this was set aside and a community service order of 100 hours was substituted.[19]

In *Li Man Wai v Secretary for Justice* ((2003) FACC No. 6 of 2003), Li, an Assistant Assessor of the Inland Revenue Department (IRD), was similarly charged with obtaining access to a computer, namely the IRD's computer, with a view to dishonest gain for himself, contrary to s. 161(1)(c). The prosecution established that Li had used his IRD user identity and password to access the IRD's computer records to obtain the identity card number and address of one of his IRD colleagues, without the latter's authorisation. Li had then used this information to apply for membership of the World Wide Fund for Nature Hong Kong on behalf of the complainant, although Li gave his own name and credit card number in the application form by way of payment of the membership fee. There was no evidence of any other gain by Li. At trial, the magistrate acquitted Li on the ground that, although he had committed a serious breach of IRD rules, no dishonest intent of gain had been proved. On appeal, Beeson J, in the Court of First Instance[20] concluded that the magistrate had erred in concluding that Li had not thereby acted dishonestly, and directed that the case be returned to the magistrate to enter a conviction and impose sentence (the magistrate subsequently fined Li HK$1000). On further appeal to the Court of Final Appeal, Chan PJ, delivering the judgment of the court, concluded that on the particular facts, it was properly open to the magistrate to conclude that Li had not acted with the necessary dishonesty; Li's conviction was accordingly quashed.

In *HKSAR v Tam Hei Lun* ([2000] 3 HKC 744), the Court of Appeal noted that there are many considerations to be taken into account in sentencing under s. 161, including: the loss and damage which was caused to the victim; the gravity of the offence to the victim; the purpose of the access; and whether there was any gain, financial or otherwise, to the person perpetrating the access. Without laying down guidelines, the court observed that, save for most unusual circumstances, a non-custodial sentence would be inappropriate for offences against s. 161.[21]

Jurisdiction

The Working Group recommended that the two principal offences created by the Computer Crimes Ordinance in 1993, namely unauthorised access, contrary to s. 27A, Telecommunications Ordinance, and access with dishonest or unlawful intent, contrary to s. 161, Crimes Ordinance, along with the offence of criminal damage as it applies to the misuse of a computer, contrary to s. 60, Crimes Ordinance, should be added to the list of offences set out in the Criminal Jurisdiction Ordinance (Cap. 461)[22] which may be prosecuted in Hong Kong even though not committed entirely within Hong Kong (see Recommendation 3, and paras 4.15 and 4.17). A draft order to this effect has been prepared and laid before the Legislative Council,[23] but remains under consideration by a subcommittee set up in early 2003.

Interception of Communications Ordinance (Cap. 532) ('ICO')

This ordinance, which is not yet in effect, will (assuming it is eventually activated) prima facie prohibit the interception of e-mail communications, that is, wiretapping, while also providing a framework for authorising interception.

Section 3(1) provides that 'a person who intentionally intercepts a [tele]communication in the course of its transmission ... by means of [a telecommunication system] prima facie commits an offence, punishable by a fine and imprisonment for up to two years. 'Interception' is defined as 'the aural or other acquisition of the contents of any ... telecommunication through the use of any electro-magnetic, acoustic, mechanical or other device' (s. 2, ICO).

However, s. 3(1) also recognises exceptions whereby interception would not be unlawful. In particular, no offence would be committed if the interception is pursuant to a court order given under s. 4 of the ordinance (s. 3(2)(a), ICO), if the person making the interception 'has reasonable grounds for believing that the person to whom, or by whom the communication is made, has consented to the interception' (s. 3(2)(b), ICO), or if the communication is intercepted in accordance with the Post Office Ordinance (Cap. 98) or the Telecommunications Ordinance (s. 3(3)(a)(b), ICO). Subsection 3(4), ICO further provides that it will be a defence for an accused to prove that the interception was conducted in good faith for the purpose of revealing a serious threat to public order or to the health and safety of the public.

A court order under s. 4 may be made by a judge of the High Court upon ex parte (s. 5(2), ICO) application by a senior officer in the police, customs, immigration or correctional services department, or ICAC (s. 5(1), ICO), only if it is necessary (a) to prevent or detect a 'serious crime' (s. 4(2)(a), ICO) ('serious crime' is defined as any offence punishable by a maximum period of imprisonment of not less than seven years; s. 2, ICO); or (b) in the interests of security in Hong Kong (s. 4(2)(b), ICO) (these two grounds reflect Art. 30, Basic Law, above). In deciding whether it is 'necessary' to make an order, the judge must find that (a) reasonable grounds exist for believing that an offence is being committed, has been committed or is about to be committed, (b) where application is made under subsection 4(2)(a), there are reasonable grounds to believe that information concerning the 'serious crime' will be obtained by the interception, (c) all other methods of investigation have been tried and have failed, or are unlikely to succeed, and (d) there is good reason to believe the interception will result in a conviction (s. 4(3), ICO).

A court order is valid for up to 90 days (s. 6(4), ICO), although it may be renewed by a judge for a further period of 90 days (s. 6(6), ICO).

Exceptionally, interception may take place without a court order if there is a serious threat of death or bodily harm and it is impracticable to apply for a court order, provided written permission of the relevant Commissioner (of Police, Customs, Correctional Services, or ICAC), or Director (of Immigration) is obtained (s. 5(3), ICO). Such interception will become unlawful unless an application for a court order is duly made within 48 hours after the interception begins. If the court then refuses permission, any intercepted material must be destroyed immediately (s. 5(6), ICO).

Intercepted material must be sealed and kept away from public access (s. 7(1), ICO). If criminal charges are laid against the person against whom the interception order was made, a judge may order the release of the intercepted material to the prosecutor if required as evidence in the prosecution (s. 7(2), ICO). The prosecutor must notify the accused of his intention to tender intercepted material at least ten days before trial and furnish him with copies of all relevant court orders (s. 7(3), ICO). If no charges are laid within 90 days, the court must notify the investigating officer and the person against whom the interception order was made of its intention to destroy the intercepted material (s. 7(5), ICO; the latter must also be given additional details of the type of communication intercepted, time and date of interception, and reasons for interception, s. 7(7)(b), ICO), and the material must thereafter be destroyed (s. 7(7), ICO), unless a court orders otherwise upon application in writing (s. 7(6), ICO).

The intentional disclosure of intercepted material, known or believed to have been unlawfully obtained, is an offence, punishable on summary conviction with a fine and up to two years' imprisonment (s. 7(9), ICO).

Other gaps

The Working Group also recommended that the following two gaps in the present law should be criminalised: first, receiving, retaining and handling / trafficking of computer data known to have been obtained through unauthorised access to the computer (Report, Recommendation 13, para. 6.19); and second, selling, distributing and making available computer passwords or access codes for wrongful gain, for an unlawful purpose or to cause wrongful loss to another (Report, Recommendation 14, para. 6.19).

Data Interference (Art. 4) / System Interference (Art. 5) / Misuse of Devices (Art. 6)

Crimes Ordinance (Cap. 200) ('CO')

Sections 59–62 of the Crimes Ordinance, dealing with criminal damage, were amended in 1993 to cover non-tangible 'damage' to computers and computer systems (tangible damage, for example by smashing a computer screen, was already covered). Specifically, the definition of 'property' in s. 59 was amended to include 'any program, or data, held in a computer or in a computer storage medium, whether or not the program or data is property of a tangible nature' (s. 59(1)(b), CO). This definition applies to and affects the following offences: criminal damage (s. 60(1)), aggravated criminal damage (s. 60(2)), arson (s. 60(3)), threatening to destroy or damage property (s. 61), and possessing anything with intent to destroy or damage property (s. 62). However, the terms 'computer', 'program' and 'data' are not defined. These offences are not restricted to acts done 'intentionally', as specified in the Convention on Cybercrime; instead, they may be committed 'recklessly'.

Additionally, 'destroying or damaging property', which lies at the heart of the offence of criminal damage, was expressly declared to include 'the misuse of a computer' (s. 59(1A), CO). This expression was, in turn, defined in s. 59(1A):

> In this subsection, 'misuse of a computer' means –
>
> (a) To cause a computer to function other than as it has been established to function by or on behalf of its owner, notwithstanding that the misuse may not impair the operation of the computer or a program held in the computer or the reliability of data held in the computer
>
> (b) To alter or erase any program or data held in a computer or in a computer storage medium

(c) To add any program or data to the contents of a computer or of a computer storage medium, and any act that contributes towards causing the misuse of a kind referred to in paragraph (a), (b) or (c) shall be regarded as causing it.

The punishment for these offences is provided for in s. 63, CO, which establishes a maximum penalty of life imprisonment for arson (s. 60(3)) and aggravated criminal damage (s. 60(2)), and ten years' imprisonment for the other offences.

In *HKSAR v Chan Chi Kong* ([1997] 3 HKC 702), it was argued on behalf of the defendant that regard should be had to the maximum penalty available under s. 161(1), namely five years' imprisonment, when sentencing under s. 60(1). This was rejected by the Court of Appeal, holding that it was right to have regard to the legislative intention laid down as regards penalty under s. 60(1), as indicated by the stipulated maximum term of imprisonment. At trial, Chan was sentenced to concurrent terms of two years and eight months' imprisonment on each of three counts to which he pleaded guilty. On appeal, this was reduced slightly to concurrent terms of one year and nine months.

In *HKSAR v Ko Kam Fai* ([2001] HKCA 199), the defendant pleaded guilty to two charges of criminal intimidation, contrary to s. 24, CO, and also eight charges of criminal damage, contrary to s. 60(1), CO. The defendant had hacked into the e-mail accounts of his two female victims at The University of Hong Kong, where they were all undergraduates sharing the same dormitory. Ko variously altered data, transferred some of the data stored in one of the accounts to his own account, and interfered with the operation of the victim's computer mouse. He also overloaded their e-mail accounts with e-mails sent by him, including highly obscene articles and pictures and other sexually explicit material. One e-mail sent by Ko read, 'Don't you believe that I will go to your hall to rape you'; this formed the basis of the two counts of criminal intimidation. Ko was sentenced to concurrent terms of 12 months' imprisonment on each count of criminal intimidation, and four months' imprisonment on each of the criminal damage charges. Ko appealed unsuccessfully against the sentence on the criminal intimidation charges, arguing that it was wrong in this regard for the trial judge to have regard to the observations in *Tam Hei Lun*, above, regarding s. 161(1), that offences of access should normally be dealt with by a term of imprisonment. While accepting that *Tam* concerned s. 161, the Court of Appeal was of the view that there was a great deal to commend the deterrent approach of the trial judge in this case. 'The acts of criminal intimidation', commented Stuart-Moore VP (at 4), 'by accessing [the victims' computers], was a serious invasion of their privacy and the consequences of such acts were likely to be not only extremely upsetting but also very alarming to both of them.' The lower sentences for the criminal damage charges, he commented, 'was a reflection … of the short-term nature of the damage done to the computers'; while possibly too short, this reflected the fact that the gravamen of the offences lay in the criminal intimidation charges.

Section 11, Theft Ordinance (Cap. 210) ('TO')

Amendments to the law of criminal damage are also reflected in the offence of burglary, contrary to s. 11 of the Theft Ordinance. Section 11 was amended so that burglary includes, *inter alia*, unlawful entry with intent to unlawfully cause a computer to function other than as it has been established or to alter, erase or add any computer program or data.

Section 11(1)(a) makes it an offence to 'enter any building or part of a building as a trespasser and with intent to commit any such offence as is mentioned in subsection (2)'. The offences mentioned in subsection (2) include: '(c) doing unlawful damage to the building or anything therein'.

Subsection (3A), expressly added in 1993 (see Computer Crime Ordinance above, s. 6), incorporates the amended offence of criminal damage:

> (3A) The reference in subsection (2)(c) to doing unlawful damage to anything in a building includes –
> (a) Unlawfully causing a computer in the building to function other than as it has been established by or on behalf of its owner to function, notwithstanding that the unlawful action may not impair the operation of the computer or a program held in the computer or the reliability of data held in the computer
> (b) Unlawfully altering or erasing any program, or data, held in a computer in the building or in a computer storage medium in the building (c) Unlawfully adding any program or data to the contents of a *computer in the building or a computer storage medium in the building*

The penalty for burglary is up to 14 years' imprisonment (s. 11(4), TO).

Computer-Related Offences

Computer-related Forgery (Art. 7) / Computer-related Fraud (Art. 8)

Forgery

Hong Kong's present provisions dealing with forgery are found in ss. 68 to 79 of the Crimes Ordinance. Section 71 provides that a person commits the offence of forgery by 'making a false instrument, with the intention that he or another shall use it to induce somebody to accept it as genuine, and by reason of so accepting it to do or not to do some act to his own or any other person's prejudice'.[24] This provision largely reproduces s. 1 of the *Forgery and Counterfeiting Act 1981* in the UK, which was considered by the House of Lords in *R v Gold, R v Schifreen* ([1988] AC 1063), and found to be wanting in relation to computer crime. Specifically, it was held that the unauthorised use of a password and number to access a computer could not be successfully prosecuted as 'forgery'. Entering the access codes by keyboard did not amount to 'making a false instrument', since the definition of 'instrument' (s. 8(1), FC Act 1981; s. 68(1), CO) requires proof that the defendant made a 'device' 'on or in which information is recorded or stored'; this, it was held, required 'the preservation of the 'information' for an appreciable time with the object of subsequent retrieval and recovery'. It was held that the momentary existence of the password and number upon entry did not satisfy this test. In the United Kingdom, this decision led to the enactment of the *Computer Misuse Act 1990* to deal with unauthorised access; in Hong Kong, it similarly led to the enactment and amendment of the sections discussed above, (i.e. s. 27A, Telecommunications Ordinance, s.161, CO; and also amendments to ss. 59, 60, CO, and s.11, TO).

Where the forgery involves the use of a physical device (i.e. the 'instrument' is '(d) [a] disc, *card*, tape, *microchip*, sound track or other device on or in which information is recorded or stored by mechanical, electronic, *optical* or other means', s. 68(1); the terms highlighted did not appear in the original UK offence), then a prosecution under s. 71 remains possible.

The penalty for forgery is 14 years' imprisonment, considerably higher than that provided for unauthorised access under s. 161 (five years).

Fraud

Computer-related fraud is dealt with in several different statutory provisions. First, s. 85 of the Crimes Ordinance, which makes it an offence for any person, with intent to defraud, to, *inter alia*, (a) make any false entry or alter any word or figure in any of books of account, or (b) in any manner falsify any of the accounts … in any [such] books. This section was extended in 1993 (see Computer Crimes Ordinance, s. 4) by expressly stating that 'books' of account includes books kept by electronic, optical or other means (s. 85(2): '"books" include any disk, card, tape, microchip, sound track or other device on or in which information is recorded or stored by mechanical, electronic, optical or other means'; this is the same amendment that was made to 'instrument', for the purposes of forgery, in s. 71, above). The penalty for this offence extends to life imprisonment.

Second, the offence of false accounting, contrary to s. 19 of the Theft Ordinance, expressly includes computer-related activities. This section was similarly amended in 1993, in this instance by stipulating that 'record' includes 'a record kept by means of a computer' — though there is no definition of 'computer' in the Theft Ordinance (see Computer Crimes Ordinance, s. 7).

Additionally, a general offence of fraud, inserted in 1999 (see Theft (Amendment) Ordinance, Ord. No. 45 of 1999, s. 3) as s. 16A of the Theft Ordinance, exists under Hong Kong law.[25] Since this offence does not expressly refer to the use or misuse of computers to carry out the fraud, can it be used in such cases? On the one hand, there is nothing in the definition of the offence that would exclude computer-related fraud. On the other hand, the offence requires proof that the defendant, with intent to defraud, 'by any deceit' induced another person to act to the latter's financial prejudice or in a manner resulting in benefit to someone else (including the defendant). Even though the deceit does not have to be the sole or main inducement, the necessity of proving 'deceit'[26] may operate as a limitation on the use of s. 16A in relation to computer-related fraud, since it has traditionally been understood as requiring a 'human' victim — a machine cannot be deceived.

In its Report in 2000, the Working Group considered the question whether this problem (human victim) should be specifically addressed. It concluded (Report, Recommendation 17) that, while existing legislation is adequate to deal with 'deceptions' of computers (Report, para. 7.9), consideration should be given to rectifying the present gap whereby the 'deception' of a machine other than a computer is not an offence (Report, para. 7.10).

Section 161 of the Crimes Ordinance, mentioned above, also deals with computer-related fraud; specifically, s. 161 makes it an offence not only to access a computer (a) with intent to commit an offence, but also (b) with a dishonest intent to deceive, or (c) with a view to dishonest gain, or (d) with a dishonest intent to cause loss to another, whether this intent is to be effected on the same occasion as he obtains access or on a future occasion.

Computer records

Electronic Transactions Ordinance ('ETO')

In 2000, with a view to facilitating the use of electronic transactions for commercial and other purpose, Hong Kong enacted the Electronic Transactions Ordinance (Cap. 553).[27] This Ordinance *inter alia* provides for the use of electronic records (s. 5) and digital signatures (s. 6), and expressly states in s. 17 that contracts may be made by means of electronic records. Part XI (ss. 46–48) provides for secrecy in carrying out various functions permitted or prescribed under the Ordinance, and creates several offences relating to disclosure and the provision of false information.

Specifically, s. 46 stipulates that persons having access to 'any record, book, register, correspondence, information, document or other material in the course of performing a function under or for the purposes of this Ordinance' shall not 'disclose or permit or suffer to be disclosed' such record, book, etc., to any other person (s. 46(1), ETO). 'Record' means 'information that is … stored in an electronic or other medium and is retrievable in a perceivable form' (s. 2(1), ETO). 'Electronic record' means a 'record generated in digital form by an information system, which can be (a) transmitted within an information system or from one information system to another; and (b) stored in an information system or other medium' (s. 2(1), ETO). 'Information system' means a system which '(a) processes information; (b) records information; (c) can be used to cause information to be recorded, stored or otherwise processed in other information systems (wherever situated); and (d) can be used to retrieve information, whether the information is recorded or stored in the system itself or in other information systems (wherever situated)' (s. 2(1), ETO); and 'information' includes 'data, text, images, sound codes, computer programs, software and databases' (s. 2(1), ETO).

Contravention of s. 46(1) is an offence, punishable by a level 6 fine and, where the offence is committed by an individual, six months' imprisonment (s. 46(3), ETO). Several exceptions are provided for in s. 46(2), including disclosure (a) which is necessary for performing or assisting in the performance of a function under or for the purposes of the ETO, (b) for the purpose of any criminal proceedings in Hong Kong, (c) for the purpose of complying with a requirement made under a rule of law[28] with a view to instituting criminal proceedings in Hong Kong, and (d) under the direction or order of a magistrate or court.

Section 47, ETO, makes it an offence to knowingly or recklessly make, orally or in writing, sign or furnish any declaration, return, certificate or other document or information required under the Ordinance which is 'untrue, inaccurate or misleading'; this offence is likewise punishable by a level 6 fine and, in the case of an individual, six months' imprisonment.

Finally, s. 48, ETO, makes it an offence for a person falsely to claim that someone is a 'recognised certification authority',[29] also punishable by a level 6 fine and, in the case of an individual, six months' imprisonment.

Other computer records

There are also numerous other statutory provisions, which deal with unlawfully accessing, altering, damaging, and such like, of records, including those kept by electronic means.

An example is provided by the Births and Deaths Registration Ordinance (Cap. 174). Section 5A requires the Registrar to compile a computer record of the particulars to be registered under the Ordinance. Section 22(4) prohibits searches of this computer record except by a registrar and officers specially authorised by the Births and Deaths Registrar. Section 25, as amended in 1997,[30] deems it to be a 'breach' of the provisions of the Ordinance for anyone having custody of, or access to, the computer record to (i) alter any data in the computer record or allow such data to be altered, other than for the purpose of carrying out duties under the Ordinance; (ii) carelessly lose or damage any data in the computer record or allow such data to be lost or damaged; or (iii) otherwise tamper with the database in the computer record so that the data contained in it or any part of such data becomes incapable of being retrieved or reproduced in legible form. Pursuant to s. 28, a person who commits a breach of the Ordinance is liable on summary conviction to a fine at level 1 or to imprisonment for six months.

Content-Related Offences

Child pornography (Art. 9)

One of the more unpalatable byproducts of the growth of the Internet has been its use as a means of disseminating child pornography, leading to an outcry both domestically and internationally for immediate preventive action. This concern is reflected, for example, in Art. 9 of the Convention on Cybercrime, which expressly deals with child pornography, and requires parties to enact domestic legislation criminalising a range of activities involving or relating to child pornography on the Internet.[31]

After several false starts, Hong Kong in 2003 followed this lead by enacting the Prevention of Child Pornography Ordinance (Cap. 579) ('PCPO'). This legislation, which came into effect on 19 December 2003, is not dedicated to the problem of child pornography on the Internet, but it establishes a wide statutory framework for the investigation and prosecution of child pornography in all forms, including online child pornography and even what has been called 'virtual child pornography' or 'pseudo-photographs'; that is, images created on a computer involving computer manipulation.

The Ordinance has created several offences, including 'printing, making, producing, reproducing, copying, importing or exporting' child pornography (s. 3(1)), 'publishing' child pornography (s. 3(2)), 'possessing' child pornography (s. 3(3)), and 'publishing or causing to be published any advertisement that conveys or is likely to be understood as conveying the message that any person has published, publishes or intends to publish any child pornography' (s. 3(4)). Penalties for the offences against ss. 3(1), 3(2) and 3(4) extend to eight years' imprisonment and a fine of up to HK$2 million; whereas the possession offence in s. 3(3) carries a maximum penalty of five years' imprisonment and a HK$1 million fine.[32]

'Child' means a person under the age of 16 (s. 2(1), PCPO), and 'child pornography' is defined in the section as including:

> (a) A photograph, film, computer-generated image or other visual depiction that is a pornographic depiction of a person who is or appears to be a child, whether it is made or generated by electronic or any other means, whether or not it is a depiction of a real person and whether or not it has been modified; or
>
> (b) Anything that incorporates a photograph, film, image or depiction referred to in paragraph (a), and includes data stored in a form that is capable of conversion into a photograph, film, image or depiction referred to in paragraph (a) and anything containing such data.

'Pornographic depiction' means '(a) a visual depiction that depicts a person as being engaged in explicit sexual conduct, whether or not the person is in fact engaged in such conduct; or (b) a visual depiction that depicts, in a sexual manner or context, the genitals or anal region of a person or the breast of a female person' (s. 2(1), PCPO), (excluding a depiction of any such part of the body if it is for a genuine family purpose).

Section 4, PCPO contains several defences. Under s. 4(1), it is a defence 'for the defendant to establish' that the depiction has artistic merit (s. 4(1)(a)). Section 4(2) confers a defence on a defendant who can establish that he committed the act giving rise to prosecution 'for a genuine educational, scientific or medical purpose' (s. 4(2)(a); if the act 'otherwise served the public good' (s. 4(2)(b)); if he had not himself seen the child pornography and did not know, nor have any reasonable cause to suspect, it to be child pornography (s. 4(2)(c)); or if he took all reasonable steps to ascertain the age of the person, took all reasonable steps (where able to influence how a person is depicted) to ensure that the person depicted was not depicted as a child, and believed on reasonable grounds that the person was not a child at the time of the depiction and was not depicted as a child (s. 4(2)(d)). Section 4(3) deals specifically with possession under s. 3(3), PCPO, and provides a similar range of defences, with the addition of a defence that the defendant had not asked for any child pornography and, after it came into his possession, endeavoured to destroy it within a reasonable time (s. 4(3)(d), PCPO). This latter defence would go some way towards protecting a person who, for example, inadvertently opened images falling within the broad definition of 'child pornography' while surfing the Web, or received such images by way of junk e-mail.

The application of offences such as these to computer images has been considered in England. 'Making', for example, has been held to include downloading images to disk (whether or not the image is also printed) (*Bowden* [2000] 2 W.L.R. 1083, CA), opening an e-mail attachment (provided mens rea is established) (*Smith, Jayson* 7 March 2002, CA), and voluntarily downloading an indecent image from a web-page onto a computer screen (again, subject to proof of mens rea) (*Smith, Jayson*). Further, it has been held that the mere storage of images in a computer's temporary cache may amount to 'possession' of child pornography (*Smith, Jayson*).

The Ordinance also contains provisions facilitating the investigation of these offences, including search and seizure powers, forfeiture powers, and related matters (ss. 5 to 13, PCPO).

Racism and xenophobia

The use of computer systems and networks to spread material of a racist or xenophobic nature, which are the subject of an Additional Protocol to the Convention on Cyber-crime, signed in January 2003, are not presently dealt with under Hong Kong legislation.

Online gambling

Steps have also been taken to add online gambling and bookmaking to Hong Kong's existing gambling regulations. Gambling in Hong Kong is essentially criminal, pursuant to the Gambling Ordinance (Cap. 148) ('GO'), except for social gambling, horseracing under the auspices of the Hong Kong Jockey Club and, more recently, soccer betting. In 2002, the Gambling Ordinance was amended[33] by extending the definition of 'bookmaking' (s. 2) to include bookmaking by 'online medium (including the service commonly known as the Internet)', thereby including online bookmaking in the category of activities that are prima facie criminal (s. 3(1); s. 7(1), GO). In addition, the Ordinance was expressly amended to make it clear that online bookmaking is an offence whether carried out ('engaged in') in Hong Kong or outside Hong Kong (s. 7(1A), with penalties of up to seven years' imprisonment and a fine of up to HK$5 million; thus overseas bookmakers commit an offence under Hong Kong law if they take bets from someone in Hong Kong by any means, including via the Internet. Furthermore, the bettor himself commits an offence by making a bet with a bookmaker 'whether the bet is received within or outside Hong Kong' (s. 8, GO), with maximum penalties on first conviction of three months' imprisonment and a fine of HK$10 000. Finally, a new part, Part IIIA (ss. 16A–16F, GO), was added, to make it an offence to operate premises or places for promoting or facilitating bookmaking, to promote or facilitate bookmaking, to offer tips, and such like, unless the bet can only be placed or is placed by a person outside Hong Kong.

Copyright-Related Offences

Copyright related offences are found in two ordinances, the Copyright Ordinance (Cap. 528), and, specifically in relation to optical discs, the Prevention of Copyright Privacy Ordinance (Cap. 544).

Copyright Ordinance

A measure of criminal protection against the infringement of copyright and related activities is presently provided by the Copyright Ordinance (Cap. 528), especially in s. 118. First, s. 118(1) provides that a person commits an offence if, without the licence of the copyright owner, he makes, imports, exports, possesses, sells or lets for hire, offers or exposes for sale or hire, exhibits in public, or distributes infringing copies[34] of a copyright work.[35]

Second, s. 118(4) makes it an offence to make, import, export, possess, sell or let for hire, or offer or expose for sale or hire, articles specifically designed or adapted for making copies of copyright works. It is a defence for a person charged with either of these offences to prove he did not know and had no reason to believe that the copy in question was an infringing copy, in the case of a charge under s. 118(1) (s. 118(3)), or that the article was used or was intended to be used to make infringing copies for sale or hire or other trade or business use, in the case of a charge under s. 118(4) (s. 118(5)).

Third, s. 118(8) makes it an offence to possess an article knowing or having reason to believe that it is used or is intended to be used to make infringing copies of any copyright work for subsequent sale or hire or other trade or business use. An offence against s. 118(1) is punishable with a fine at level 5 in respect of each infringing copy and four years' imprisonment (s. 119(1), Copyright Ordinance), whereas an offender convicted under s. 118(4) or (8) is liable to a fine of HK$500 000 and eight years' imprisonment.

Section 120(1)(2)(3) of the Ordinance adds further protection by making it an offence to carry out similar acts outside Hong Kong; s. 120(4) extends liability further to persons who in Hong Kong or elsewhere, aid, abet, counsel or procure the commission by another of an offence under subsection 120(1), (2) or (3). These offences are punishable on conviction on indictment with a fine of HK$500 000 and eight years' imprisonment (s. 120(6)).

The prosecution of these offences must be commenced within three years from the date of commission of the offence or one year from the date of discovery of the offence by the prosecutor, whichever is the earlier (s. 120A, Copyright Ordinance).

The Ordinance supplements these offences with various investigative and enforcement powers (ss. 122 to 132), including search and seizure powers (s. 122) and the protection of informers in criminal proceedings (s. 127), as well as providing for the forfeiture and disposal of seized articles (ss. 131 to 132).

Prevention of Copyright Piracy Ordinance

The Prevention of Copyright Piracy Ordinance (Cap. 544) gives additional copyright protection to optical disks by prohibiting the manufacture of optical disks in Hong Kong without a licence issued under the Ordinance (s. 3(1)). Manufacturing optical disks without a licence amounts to an offence, punishable on a first conviction, by a fine of HK$500 000 and two years' imprisonment, and thereafter by a fine of HK$1 million and four years' imprisonment (s. 21(1)). Additionally, s. 4(1) prohibits the manufacture of optical disks in any place in Hong Kong other than a licensed premises, punishable on a first conviction, by a level 6 fine and two years' imprisonment, and thereafter by a fine of HK$200 000 and four years' imprisonment (s. 21(2)). Section 21(3) additionally makes it an offence for a licensee to manufacture optical disks in contravention of any conditions endorsed on his licence, punishable on a first conviction, by a level 2 fine and six months' imprisonment, and thereafter by a level 4 fine and one year's imprisonment.

Ancillary Liability and Sanctions

Hong Kong criminal law presently incorporates statutory provisions dealing with most of the issues of ancillary liability and sanctions set out in the Convention on Cyber-crime, although such provisions tend to be general and not specific to computer-related crime.

In particular, aiding and abetting (Art. 11(1), Convention) is addressed in s. 89 of the Criminal Procedure Ordinance (Cap. 221),[36] and attempt (Art. 11(2), Convention) is criminalised in ss. 159G to 159L of the Crimes Ordinance (Cap. 200). Corporate liability (Art. 12, Convention) broadly remains a matter of common law.

Conclusion

Hong Kong's method of dealing with criminal activity in cyberspace has followed a reasonably common path. In the first place, Hong Kong has set about putting in place appropriate legislative prohibitions, but this process is far from comprehensive, and Hong Kong's substantive cyber-crime legislation remains largely a patchwork of traditional crimes, roughly amended to capture more readily their commission in cyberspace, and several computer crime-related offences specifically introduced to deal more immediately with the cyber-crime concerns of the public and law enforcement agencies in the early 1990s. Attempts are being made to introduce further legislation, designed to enhance the present law and to ensure greater law enforcement responsiveness, but caution has been the hallmark of the legislators and progress has been only moderate. Where cyber-crime has occurred, prosecutions have generally been able to be brought, certainly in the most obvious cases, but there remains a temptation for judges to over-interpret existing legislation to accommodate the demands and needs of law enforcement in today's technology-driven information age.

The Administration has also appreciated that the fight against cyber-crime is one that the government cannot wage by itself, especially as the Internet and the information society have taken hold and previous notions about 'computer-related crime' have given way to concepts based on today's highly interconnected 'information systems', involving devices and activities significantly different from those confronting law enforcement agencies in the early 1990s. One simple example of this is encryption. As encryption tools have become both increasingly sophisticated and more readily available to the public, so they have also been employed by cyber-criminals to avoid detection and to impede evidence-gathering, thereby presenting new difficulties for law enforcement agencies. The question of how best to respond to the problems posed by encryption was considered by the Working Group on Computer Related Crime, which recommended that legislation should be introduced to enable law enforcement agencies to be provided with decrypted text or with the necessary decryption tools to decode computer records.[37]

As has been commonly recognised elsewhere, controlling computer and online activity in the cyber-age increasingly requires a cooperative effort between the government and law enforcement agencies, on the one hand, and the private sector on the other, along with extensive public education as to the dangers and risks of the cyberage and also as to appropriate standards of online and computer behaviour. Many of the recommendations in the Working Group's Report in 2000 are directed at the question of how best to seek this cooperation and establish a firm foundation for the future. Thus Chapter VIII is on obtaining 'Assistance from ISPs', with a central recommendation being that communication between law enforcement agencies and ISPs should be enhanced by (i) 'establishing a forum of exchange for both sides to discuss matters of mutual concern at the macro level at regular intervals' and (ii) 'setting up a contact point system for ISPs and law enforcement agencies for dealing with computer crime investigation requests' (Report, Recommendation 30, para. 8.33). Of particular importance are the questions of how best to ensure ISPs retain log records of transactions to facilitate computer crime investigation, given the inevitable cost associated with such activities (Report, Recommendations 21–25, paras 8.22–8.27), and the establishment of take-down procedures in relation to offensive material (Report, Recommendation 27, para. 8.30).

Similarly, attention was expressly directed at 'the Private Sector's Role' (Chapter XI), with a clear commitment on the part of the government to 'continue to involve the private sector in the formulation of policies on computer crime and seek its input on a more regular basis' (Report, Recommendation 43, paras 11.10 and 11.11). Considerable attention was also given to the question of public education.[38]

Assessed in overall terms, much has been achieved in Hong Kong, at both the regulatory and the administrative levels. But equally, many of the recommendations of the Working Group in its Report have still to be implemented. If Hong Kong is to keep abreast of cyber-crime, then more inevitably needs to be done, especially as technological progress, along with its potential for misuse, like time, will not wait around for effective government action.

14

International Cooperation in Combating Cyber-Crime in Asia: Existing Mechanisms and New Approaches

Jeffrey G Bullwinkel*

The explosive growth in information technology during the last decade has precipitated unprecedented economic and social changes. Our virtually unlimited electronic access to information and telecommunication services has profoundly and irrevocably changed the way we live and the way we think. So too have technological advances dramatically altered the manner in which criminals carry out their activities. Information technologies not only have created an additional platform for launching traditional crimes but also have paved the way for new and pernicious forms of criminality, including cyberterrorism — a threat made all the more real by the tragic events of 11 September 2001. One of the most disturbing aspects of these developments is that cyber-criminals are not confined by national boundaries but rather, with a few keystrokes or the simple click of a mouse, can perpetrate acts with devastating *global* implications — and can eliminate crucial evidence with the same degree of ease. Crimes committed today rarely touch only a single jurisdiction and, indeed, even relatively unsophisticated forms of cyber-crime commonly resonate on multiple continents.

As a result, the need for reliable and efficient mechanisms for international cooperation in law enforcement matters has never been more urgent. And indeed, the international community has taken a number of significant steps to facilitate cross-border cooperation in criminal matters, including in the investigation and prosecution of cyber-crime. This chapter considers some of the cooperation regimes currently in force in Asia and elsewhere and suggests a number of steps that might be taken to improve the capacity of government officials in the Asian region to collaborate in the battle against cyber-crime.

Cyber-crime is broadly understood to encompass a wide range of activities including both the core cyber-offences that threaten computer data and systems and the use of computer systems and information technologies to carry out offences against interests that traditionally have been protected under the criminal law. The Council of Europe's (COE) Convention on Cyber-crime ETS No. 185 (the 'Cyber-crime Convention')[1] obligates signatories to criminalise the following specific offences, when committed intentionally and without right:

- *Core offences:* Title 1 addresses offences against the confidentiality, integrity and availability of computer data such as: (1) illegal access of a computer system; (2) interception of non-public transmissions of computer data to, from, or within a computer system; (3) interference with computer data; (4) interference with computer systems, such as computer sabotage; and (5) the misuse of computer-related devices (e.g. 'hacker tools'), including the production, sale, procurement for use, import or distribution of such devices.
- *Computer-related offences:* Title 2 covers the traditional offences of fraud and forgery when carried out through a computer system. With respect to forgery, the intent of this provision is to protect computer data in the same manner as tangible documents, where such data may be acted upon or used for legal purposes. With regard to fraud, the COE drafters recognised that the technological revolution has brought with it extraordinary opportunities for committing economic crimes. Credit card companies, other banking-related institutions, and their customers are particularly at risk, as cyber-criminals have increasingly targeted and manipulated moneys represented or administered in computer systems.
- *Content-related offences:* Title 3 seeks to control the use of computer systems as a vehicle for the sexual exploitation of children.[2]
- *Offences related to copyright infringement:* Among the most common offences carried out via the Internet are infringements of intellectual property rights. Technological innovations have given cyber-criminals extremely powerful tools to reproduce and disseminate, on a mass scale, protected works. The Internet also provides offenders with an enormous and global marketplace in which to buy and sell pirated merchandise, including pirated music, films, and software. Accordingly, Title 4 requires each signatory to criminalise copyright infringement (as defined in relevant intellectual property and trade-related agreements) when carried out on a commercial scale by means of a computer system.
- *Ancillary liability and sanctions:* Title 5 obliges signatories to criminalise

> the attempt to commit certain offences on which the convention imposes a criminalisation obligation, as well as aiding and abetting the commission of offences. Title 5 also provides for the liability of legal persons.

The list of offences specified in the Convention on Cyber-crime is by no means exhaustive but rather a minimum standard for criminalisation. As such, it helpfully illustrates where there is already consensus within a significant portion of the international community as to legislative priorities in this area.

Unique Challenges to International Cooperation

The cyber-crime phenomenon, while creating an unprecedented need for concerted action from government and industry, has at the same time created unprecedented challenges to effective international cooperation. A few of the major issues commonly encountered in the investigation, prosecution and prevention of cyber-crime are enumerated below.

One frequent problem is jurisdictional in nature. It is not always clear where computer-related offences take place for purposes of the assertion of criminal jurisdiction. Indeed, the offence may produce victims in numerous countries or territories, as in cases involving virus attacks, copyright violations, and other offences carried out globally through the Internet. This in turn may result in cross-border conflicts regarding which jurisdiction(s) should properly prosecute the offender and how such prosecutions can be carried out to avoid inconvenience to witnesses, duplication of effort, and unnecessary competition among law enforcement officials.

Additionally, the inherently international nature of information networks allows criminals to operate across borders far more easily than law enforcement authorities can. This raises several difficult investigative issues affecting sovereignty interests and cross-border cooperation.

First, what are the limits within which law enforcement officials should operate when conducting a lawful domestic search of a suspect's computer system? In the case of a computer connected to an external network, the police might have access to (and the capacity to seize) data known to be located in another jurisdiction, or it might be difficult or impossible to determine where the searched data geographically resides. Even where it is clear the data resides outside the jurisdiction of the searching state, under what circumstances should that state seek authorisation from the searched state before seizing the data?

Second, where it is necessary to seek authorisation or assistance from the searched state, highly volatile computer data will often be lost forever unless international legal assistance can be provided immediately. Traditional mechanisms for mutual legal assistance and information-sharing are often too slow and cumbersome to be relied on for the preservation of crucial evidence such as traffic data. Moreover, the availability of needed legal assistance may depend on dual criminality or whether the state from which assistance is requested has under its domestic law provided for searches and seizures in an electronic environment; this highlights the importance of global harmonisation of substantive and procedural criminal law.

Third, even where needed evidence can be seized, there is the challenge of authenticating it in a manner that will satisfy the evidentiary requirements of the requesting state.

Another more general problem is that many law enforcement agencies are understaffed, under-resourced and insufficiently trained to deal effectively with increasingly sophisticated forms of cyber-crime. There is an urgent need to equip law enforcement officials in all jurisdictions with the right tools and training, including instruction on forensic standards for retrieving and authenticating electronic data for use in criminal proceedings — a challenge that many countries, particularly those with economies in transition, will be unable to meet without considerable technical assistance from other states.

Finally, close cooperation between the public and private sectors is vital if we are to get to grips with cyber-crime. Not only can industry representatives play a crucial role in helping to locate and identify cyber-criminals, but they can also assist in identifying enforcement priorities, developing technical solutions to existing and future problems, and supporting training initiatives.

Existing Mechanisms for International Cooperation

Governments have long recognised the need for international cooperation in law enforcement matters, and a broad array of agreements and arrangements — both bilateral and multilateral — have grown up around the shared goal of preventing criminals from exploiting international boundaries to avoid punishment. For purposes of this discussion, the term 'international cooperation' should be understood to encompass both informal police-to-police cooperation as well as assistance provided pursuant to formal agreements or arrangements, such as treaties and conventions relating to mutual legal assistance treaties on criminal matters (MLATs), extradition, and other forms of cross-border assistance such as training, technical assistance, and capacity-building.

Cross-border cooperation of any type supposes that the parties share a common objective, which would be more easily attained by a joint approach. As the following discussion illustrates, in some cases the interests of two parties are sufficiently aligned or intertwined to justify a formal bilateral agreement. In other cases there is a need for broader international cooperation, perhaps in relation to a particularly severe crime problem with regional or global implications. In those instances, a group of like-minded countries — brought together variously by geographic proximity, cultural ties, or similarities in legal, economic or political systems — might elect to join forces under a formally defined structure.

Quite clearly, the increasingly global battle against cyber-crime can be won only if governments take effective measures — bilaterally, regionally, and globally — to strengthen cooperation at all levels and among all relevant agencies and industries.

Bilateral information-sharing among law enforcement agencies[3]

The police channel has long been recognised as an efficient means for law enforcement officials to obtain certain types of investigative assistance directly from their counterparts in foreign countries, without having to rely on more time-consuming procedures associated with formal legal assistance. As one way of facilitating the rapid exchange of information among police officials, many countries have posted liaison officers (representing particular domestic law enforcement agencies) in their diplomatic missions in key jurisdictions.

Among other types of data, police officials commonly exchange information concerning: the identity and location of persons suspected of criminal conduct, as well as criminal records; the movement of proceeds and instrumentalities of crime; trends and patterns of criminal activity; and means and methods used by criminal groups. Additionally, law enforcement officials routinely provide their foreign counterparts with many other types of cross-border assistance, for example arranging voluntary interviews or depositions of individuals who may have information relevant to an investigation, and assisting in the examination of articles of evidence.

Principles of sovereignty sometimes impede informal (and even formal) law enforcement cooperation. To be sure, nations cannot be expected to compromise sovereignty interests in the name of cross-border cooperation in criminal matters. Moreover, where requests for international assistance so clearly implicate the requested country's interest in protecting its citizenry and territorial integrity (e.g. requests for the execution of a search and seizure, or for the arrest of a fugitive), there is a need for the more formal procedures and safeguards built into treaty relationships.

But many countries jealously guard their sovereignty interests in a manner that frustrates the commonly shared goal of fighting crime. As just one example, a surprising number of jurisdictions, as an official matter, still object to their nationals being questioned directly by foreign government representatives in connection with a criminal investigation, even where circumstances make clear that the witness is not suspected of criminal activity and would voluntarily submit to an interview or deposition.

Given the inexorable internationalisation of crime, well exemplified by cyber-crime in particular, there is a pressing need for more flexible cooperation; wherever possible, governments should relax the application of sovereignty-based rules that may impede cross-border assistance.

Bilateral mutual legal assistance and extradition

More and more, cyber-crime investigations and prosecutions depend on the availability of effective and efficient MLA and extradition regimes, which may be embodied in reciprocal domestic legislation, bilateral treaties, or multilateral conventions. Indeed, as effective as the law enforcement channel can be under many circumstances, certain types of assistance (e.g. in cases requiring judicial process in order to compel testimony or the production of documents, or where the requesting state seeks the execution of a search warrant in the territory of the requested state) are available only through formal mechanisms. Formal procedures may also be required to ensure that the requested evidence be authenticated and provided in a manner that will satisfy the evidentiary requirements of the requesting state.

Domestic legislation

Many countries have domestic statutes relating to legal assistance and extradition. And indeed, reciprocal domestic legislation sometimes makes extensive cross-border cooperation possible even in the absence of a formal treaty relationship.[4] Accordingly, such provisions can be of critical importance to the vast majority of countries, which do not have the benefit of a seamless web of MLA, extradition treaties and other cooperation agreements with their key law enforcement partners.

It is no surprise, however, that domestic legislation, while providing a useful framework for certain types of cooperation, will never be an adequate substitute for well-developed bilateral (or even multilateral) agreements on cooperation. One limitation to such provisions is that the requested state typically has discretion in deciding whether to grant or deny assistance, whereas parties to bilateral treaties are legally obliged to honour incoming requests, subject of course to the overall confines of the agreement. And even in cases involving a favourable exercise of discretion on the part of the state from which assistance is requested, statutory cooperation regimes generally cannot be relied on in cases involving urgency. For example, in the absence of a treaty establishing a direct relationship between central authorities, requests for legal assistance must often be transmitted through the cumbersome and time-consuming diplomatic channel.[5] Experience has clearly shown that this method of cooperation is insufficient to meet the challenges posed by 21st-century crime.

Bilateral treaties

Bilateral agreements such as MLATs and extradition treaties are among the most reliable and efficient mechanisms for international cooperation in criminal matters. Because governments will not embark on bilateral negotiations without real confidence in the legal system of future treaty partners, bilateral treaties ordinarily set forth clear, binding obligations and limited grounds on which to deny assistance. (By contrast, multilateral agreements are frequently marred by soft, hortatory language that can be a basis for refusing cooperation in a manner inconsistent with the spirit of the instrument.)

Extradition treaties fall into two general categories: so-called 'list' treaties and more modern 'dual criminality' treaties. In the case of list treaties, the contracting parties are bound to extradite only with respect to those offences specified in the agreement and for which extradition is requested. This is a potentially significant limitation, particularly in cases involving newer forms of crime (including many manifestations of cyber-crime) that could not have been foreseen by the original drafters. The clear trend in modern treaty practice is to provide for extradition for offences punishable under the laws of both contracting parties by deprivation of liberty for a period of more than one year.[6]

Of course, dual criminality extradition treaties are as broad as the criminal laws of the state from which extradition is requested. And indeed, extradition for cyber-offences may sometimes prove difficult, since some jurisdictions have not yet criminalised such conduct. In such cases — as well as in cyber-crime cases involving list treaties — the requested state should follow the practice (commonly accepted in international law) of interpreting the treaty broadly, in favour of extradition.[7]

Bilateral mutual legal assistance treaties are an increasingly popular mechanism for ensuring more rapid and reliable cooperation than is available as a matter of domestic statute. The advantages of a bilateral treaty are many, but among the most significant is that such treaties to a substantial degree eliminate the requested state's ability to refuse assistance as a matter of discretion.[8] Subject to limited exceptions and the overall scope of the agreement, bilateral treaties ordinarily oblige the signatories to provide a wide measure of assistance — and, importantly, the requested assistance must often be provided even in the absence of dual criminality. A typical provision specifying the range of available assistance reads as follows:

> 1. The Contracting Parties shall provide mutual assistance, in accordance with the provisions of this Treaty, in connection with the prevention, investigation, and prosecution of criminal offences, and in proceedings related to criminal matters.
> 2. Assistance shall include:
>   (a) Taking the testimony or statements of persons
>   (b) Providing documents, records, and items of evidence
>   (c) Serving documents
>   (d) Locating or identifying persons or items
>   (e) Transferring persons in custody for testimony or other purposes
>   (f) Executing requests for searches and seizures
>   (g) Assisting in proceedings related to forfeiture of assets, restitution, and collection of fines
>   (h) Any other form of assistance not prohibited by the laws of the Requested States
> 3. Assistance shall be provided without regard to whether the conduct, which is the subject of the investigation, prosecution, or proceeding in the Requesting State would constitute an offence under the laws of the Requested State.[9]

Another significant advantage is that bilateral treaties typically oblige each signatory to designate a 'central authority', which serves as a direct point of contact (most often within each signatory's ministry of justice) for receiving and transmitting requests for assistance. The importance of this requirement cannot be overstated, as an active and muscular central authority will ensure the proper implementation of the treaty and, in particular, that requests will be treated with the appropriate degree of urgency.

As effective as bilateral agreements can be, however, the pace of computer crime and the evanescence of evidence transmitted by or stored in telecommunication and information systems have created the need for more rapid assistance than may be available even under the strongest and most up-to-date treaty.

Bilateral treaties in Asia: As necessary, jurisdictions in the region should endeavour to negotiate bilateral agreements with close partners (within and without Asia) and to accelerate the pace of those negotiations.[10] In addition, existing treaties should be reviewed and, if necessary, updated to ensure coverage for modern forms of criminality. Because resource limitations may prevent some jurisdictions from developing a comprehensive network of bilateral agreements, efforts should be made to utilise or construct frameworks for regional and global cooperation.

Multilateral approaches to cooperation

As noted, cyber-crime and other sophisticated forms of criminality continue to transcend national boundaries, threatening national, regional and global economic security. One positive byproduct of this darker side of globalisation is that multilateralism is on the rise. Government leaders — recognising the insufficiency of unilateral action to fight global crime — are increasingly committed to pursuing a common approach to shared problems.

Discussed below are various multilateral organisations dedicated at least in part to cross-border cooperation in criminal matters. In some cases, the work of these groups is directly relevant to computer-related crime; for example, during the last several years the Council of Europe, the G8 and, increasingly, the APEC group and the United Nations, have been especially active in this area. In other cases, inter-governmental organisations are discussed because they supply useful frameworks for (or models of) cooperation in criminal matters more generally.

Serious consideration should be given to whether some of the solutions proposed or structures created by these groups can be implemented as part of a pan-Asian approach to cyber-crime.

The Council of Europe, founded in 1949, represents the first association of European nations and today comprises 45 countries, including the 15 members of the European Union (a distinctly separate entity), as well as 21 countries from Central and Eastern Europe. Headquartered in Strasbourg, France, the COE was formed as a vehicle for political integration in Europe, and its aims include agreements and common actions in economic, social, cultural, legal and administrative matters. As one of the two principal supranational organisations in Europe (the other being the European Union), the COE is responsible for creating and implementing a wide variety of measures aimed at international crime and has adopted a number of widely used conventions on interstate cooperation in penal matters (e.g. COE Convention on the Transfer of Sentenced Persons; European Convention on Extradition; European Convention on the Suppression of Terrorism; European Convention on Mutual Assistance in Criminal Matters; COE Convention on Laundering, Search, Seizure and Confiscation of the Proceeds from Crime).

In November 1996, in recognition of the fact that rapid developments in the field of information technology had led to the criminal misuse of computer systems and telecommunications networks, the COE's European Committee on Crime Problems established a committee of experts to address cyber-crime. The following April, a separate committee (the Committee of Experts on Crime in Cyber-Space, or 'PC-CY') was created with the mandate to elaborate a comprehensive international instrument on cyber-crime. The PC-CY completed its work late in 2001.

The three principal aims of the Cyber-crime Convention are to harmonise the domestic criminal laws of signatories in the area of cyber-crime; to ensure that signatories have adequate capacity to conduct effective domestic investigations of cyber-crime; and to facilitate effective cross-border investigation of such offences.

Chapter III of the Cyber-crime Convention contains extensive provisions designed to ensure that signatories assist one another to the widest possible extent in the investigation and prosecution of high-tech crime. Article 24 specifies extradition procedures for offences within the scope of the instrument. Articles 25–35 include extensive provisions concerning mutual legal assistance, many of which reflect generally accepted principles in this area but some of which are specifically tailored to meet the unique obstacles to effective international cooperation in the cyber-crime arena. For instance, Articles 29–31 address the expedited preservation and disclosure of stored computer data; Article 33 provides for assistance with respect to the real-time collection of traffic data; and Article 35 obliges signatories to designate a point of contact, available on a 24/7 basis, to ensure the provision of immediate assistance in international cyber-crime investigations.

At this stage, the Cyber-crime Convention is open to signature by COE member states and a few non-member states that participated in the elaboration of the instrument.[11] However, in the future, based on the unanimous consent of the contracting states party to the convention, the COE's Committee of Ministers may invite other non-COE countries to accede to the Convention.[12] Given the pressing need for a broader multilateral structure for cross-border cooperation in the computer crime area, every effort should be made to open up the convention for accession by a wide number of signatories as soon as is practicable.

G8 Senior Experts Group on Transnational Organised Crime: Initially convened for the purpose of coordinating economic policy, the Group of Seven (comprising Canada, Germany, France, Italy, Japan, the United Kingdom and the United States) has for years dedicated considerable resources to addressing social and law enforcement issues as well as holding frequent summits and developing initiatives to combat international crime. As a result of Russia's participation in such activities, the G7 has evolved (at least for some purposes, including law enforcement cooperation) into the G8. And the G8's energetic response to the challenges of 21st-century crime, high-tech crime in particular, provides a useful model with relevance to the broader international community.

At the Halifax Summit in 1995, G8 heads of state established a cross-disciplinary group of senior government experts (sometimes referred to as the 'Lyon Group') to address methods of combating transnational organised crime. The structure and composition of the Lyon Group offer distinct advantages missing from some multilateral cooperation mechanisms.

First, the group's membership includes senior officials with specialised expertise and representatives of police agencies, justice ministries, and foreign ministries. The effect of this horizontal structure (visible in other highly successful multilateral organisations, such as the Financial Action Task Force, discussed below) is to ensure representation of a broad cross-section of perspectives, all of which are critical to the development of a sound and comprehensive approach to a particular crime problem.

Second, the group coordinates closely with (and effectively answers to) minister-level officials, as well as reporting directly to heads of state (with G8 leaders providing guidance through communiqués issued at annual G8 summits). This helps to ensure buy-in for the group's activities at the highest levels of government, and thus that the group has the capacity to develop policies and practices that will be implemented. Additionally, the Lyon Group has recognised the importance of involving representatives of the private sector in discussions on issues of mutual concern.

In April 1996, under the French presidency of the G8, the Lyon Group devised 40 recommendations (the 'Forty Recommendations') aimed specifically at increasing the efficiency of collective government action against transnational organised crime.[13] The Forty Recommendations cover a broad range of issues and emphasised in particular the need to eliminate bottlenecks in international cooperation regimes and the importance of a coordinated approach in tackling high-tech crime.

With respect to traditional forms of cross-border assistance (such as informal police cooperation, mutual legal assistance, and extradition), the Forty Recommendations urge that governments take the following steps, among others:

- Identify central points of contact that can facilitate cooperation among operational agencies, including by making full use of the Interpol National Central Bureau and by posting law enforcement liaison officers in other countries (see Recommendation 20);
- Develop written agreements or treaties to promote MLA and exercise flexibility in executing requests for assistance (e.g. by rendering assistance even in the absence of dual criminality) (see Recommendations 2, 3), and establish a central authority to provide speedy coordination of incoming and outgoing requests for legal assistance (see Recommendation 5);
- Develop effective extradition regimes, such as by modernising existing agreements to include a 'dual criminality' standard; simplifying procedural and evidentiary requirements for rendition; extraditing nationals or, where that is impermissible under the law of the requested state, conducting an effective domestic prosecution of the fugitive in lieu of extradition (see Recommendation 10);
- Prepare, and distribute to other states, materials describing channels of communication for MLA and extradition and the process for obtaining such assistance (see Recommendation 6);
- In cases involving offences which take place in more than one country and over which more than one state has jurisdiction, coordinate prosecutions in a manner that will achieve efficiency (see Recommendation 7);
- Promote other techniques for mutual education that will expedite cross-border cooperation (e.g. secondments and exchanges of personnel between relevant justice officials, training, joint seminars, etc.) (see Recommendation 13).

Recommendation 16 established the groundwork for subsequent Lyon Group activity in the area of cyber-crime:

> States should review their laws in order to ensure that abuses of modern technology that are deserving of criminal sanctions are criminalised and that problems with respect to jurisdiction, enforcement powers, investigation, training, crime prevention and international cooperation in respect of such abuses are effectively addressed. Liaison between law enforcement and prosecution personnel of different states should be

improved, including the sharing of experience in addressing these problems. States should promote study in this area and negotiate arrangements and agreements to address the problem of technological crime and investigation.

In early 1997, the Lyon Group established five subgroups, including one devoted to high-tech crime (Subgroup V or the 'High-Tech Crime Subgroup'), and tasked the subgroups to devise practical methods to meaningfully implement the specific but broadly worded Forty Recommendations. Further to that goal, the Lyon Group meets in plenary (i.e. with all subgroups and other members in attendance) three times each year. Subgroup V has been among the most active of the subgroups and frequently holds additional meetings throughout the year to carry forward its work.

As noted, justice and interior ministers have been active participants in the G8 dialogue on law enforcement cooperation and in December 1997 convened a ministerial meeting to agree on a specific plan of action to achieve two interrelated goals embodied in the Forty Recommendations: (1) strengthened capacity in the investigation and prosecution of high-tech crime; and (2) more effective regimes for cross-border cooperation in criminal matters. In their communiqué, the ministers emphasised the serious threat to public safety posed by the criminal misuse of information systems, recognising as well that 'the nature of modern communications networks makes it impossible for any country acting alone to address this emerging high-tech crime problem' and that a 'common approach addressing the unique, borderless nature of global networks is needed'.[14] The ministers further stressed that 'the need for enhanced cooperation in extradition and mutual assistance is particularly acute with respect to high-tech crime and other areas of emerging significance', committing to 'remove impediments in existing cooperation regimes by such means as approaching issues of dual criminality with flexibility' and ensuring that cyber-crime offences have sufficient criminal penalties to make them extraditable.[15]

In furtherance of these goals, G8 ministers endorsed a statement of principles and an ambitious action plan calling on relevant G8 officials, among other things, to:

- Designate a point-of-contact, available on a 24/7 basis, to provide a rapid and effective response to transnational cyber-crime cases
- Ensure that law enforcement agencies have adequate personnel and training to address high-tech crime
- Ensure that domestic legislation criminalises such offences
- Ensure that relevant evidence, including traffic data, can be preserved and obtained expeditiously

- Coordinate with industry to ensure that new technologies are developed in a way that will facilitate law enforcement action against cyber-criminals.[16]

G8 ministers gathered again in Moscow in late 1999, in part to further joint action against cyber-crime. At the Moscow meeting, ministers acknowledged progress made in implementing prior directives (e.g. the establishment and effective use of a 24/7 network of officials, now expanded beyond the G8, and the completion of a comprehensive review of national laws relating to cyber-crime).[17] Further, recognising the ease with which cyber-criminals can operate across borders and store (and quickly destroy) incriminating data all over the world, ministers endorsed a number of principles on trans-border access to stored computer data and called for a comprehensive response to Internet fraud and more extensive coordination with industry.[18]

As recognised by the G8 and addressed more fully below, an effective response to cyber-crime requires unprecedented cooperation between government officials and industry representatives. And G8 officials have taken important steps in this direction, including by hosting government / industry conferences to discuss common concerns and possible solutions.[19]

United Nations involvement in crime prevention and control

Included among the vast number of subject matters addressed by United Nations institutions are law enforcement and crime control. Indeed, early in its history the UN expressed a willingness to assume a leadership role in criminal justice matters and in 1948 established a secretariat unit (originally known as the Social Defence Section) to address these issues.

As addressed below, the UN is an increasingly effective forum in which states can seek to enhance international law enforcement cooperation, including in the area of computer-related crime. The UN is a mechanism for, among other things: the elaboration of international legal instruments dealing with cross-border cooperation; the issuance of resolutions and declarations with the potential to drive government policy and inter-governmental initiatives on emerging crime problems; international meetings aimed at promoting cooperation; and the development of useful training materials and programmes designed to aid law enforcement officials in carrying out their work.

Today, most UN crime-related activities are centered in Vienna, home to the Office of Drug Control and Crime Prevention and its subsidiary body, the

Centre for International Crime Prevention (CICP). In carrying out its work, the CICP takes direction from the Commission on Crime Prevention and Criminal Justice (the 'Crime Commission') — an intergovernmental organisation comprised of 40 member states elected by the Economic and Social Council (ECOSOC) for specified terms — which now acts as the central policy-making organ for the UN in criminal matters and meets annually in Vienna.[20] (Non-government organisations can apply for observer status.) The UN's criminal justice programme also includes the UN Congresses (held every five years) and what is referred to as the Crime Prevention and Criminal Justice Program Network of Institutes, which includes a number of regional and interregional bodies, including the Tokyo-based Asia and Far East Institute for the Prevention of Crime and the Treatment of Offenders UNAFEI, discussed below.

As noted, the Crime Commission meets annually for the purpose of developing policy initiatives for the coming year and guiding the work of the CICP — in effect, determining how the UN's fairly limited crime budget will be allocated. Stated simply, the Crime Commission's method of work is to generate consensus around draft resolutions, which, once approved, are recommended to the General Assembly or ECOSOC for adoption. Resolutions might call for a new global convention (such as the Convention Against Transnational Organised Crime, discussed below), or might call upon the CICP to carry out training initiatives or develop reference materials in a particular area for use by member states.

Due to the worldwide implications of cyber-crime, consideration should be given to using the Crime Commission to enhance global cooperation in this area. As just a few examples, the commission can allocate resources for regional and sub-regional meetings or training programs, or can call upon the CICP to prepare informational materials or even model legislation for member states.[21]

The periodic crime congress has been largely supplanted by annual Crime Commission meetings, which are generally more substantive and efficient. Nonetheless, crime congresses provide another opportunity for high-level policymakers to convene and discuss means of collaborating in the battle against international crime. And indeed the Tenth Congress, held in Vienna in April 2000, included a workshop on crimes related to the computer network.[22] Following a one-day discussion, workshop participants reached the following conclusions: (1) governments should take steps to criminalise computer-related crime and develop adequate procedures for the investigation of such offences; (2) government and industry should collaborate in combating computer crime; (3) there is a need for improved international cooperation in this area; and (4) the UN should increase efforts to provide states with necessary technical assistance.[23] Further, the political declaration generated at the Congress and since endorsed by the Crime Commission and the General Assembly invites the Crime Commission to develop action-oriented recommendations on enhancing global capacity to prevent, investigate and prosecute high-tech crime.[24]

The Convention Against Transnational Organised Crime (the 'TOC Convention'), negotiated in Vienna and finalised in late 2000, is one of the most promising recent multilateral initiatives with real potential to enhance cooperation in the cyber-crime area.[25] Unlike the COE Convention, the TOC Convention was not specifically designed to address cyber-crime per se. However, the instrument, which includes comprehensive provisions on international cooperation, is broad enough to encompass many of the most common manifestations of high-tech crime.

The scope of the TOC Convention includes particular offences signatories are obliged to criminalise (Articles 5, 6, 8 and 23)[26] as well as 'serious crime' (as defined in the Convention), 'where the offence is transnational in nature and involves an organised criminal group'.[27] Importantly, the definitions of 'serious crime' and 'organised criminal group' reflect an understanding on the part of the drafters that organised criminal activity is no longer confined to a relatively narrow range of offences traditionally associated with highly structured organisations such as the Cosa Nostra.

Specifically, 'serious crime' is defined in Article 2(b) to include conduct punishable by imprisonment for a period of at least four years (or a more serious penalty). And the term 'organised criminal group' refers to 'a structured group of three or more persons, existing for a period of time and acting in concert with the aim of committing one or more serious crimes or offences established in accordance with the convention to obtain, directly or indirectly, a financial or other material benefit'.[28]

To ensure that this definition would not be susceptible to an overly narrow construction — and therefore that the convention as a whole would offer States Parties the widest possible measure of assistance — the drafters clarified that the phrase 'structured group' refers to a group that is not 'randomly formed for the immediate commission of an offence' (e.g. a street demonstration that spontaneously erupts into a riot), but the group need *not* have 'formally defined roles for its members, continuity of its membership or a developed structure'.[29] Likewise, the requirement that the offence be 'transnational in nature' is constructed with a high degree of flexibility. For purposes of the convention, an offence is 'transnational' if it is: (a) committed in more than one state; (b) committed in a single state but planned, prepared, directed or controlled in another state; (c) committed in one state but involved an organised group whose activities cross national boundaries; or (d) committed in a single state but has 'substantial effects' in another state.[30]

In light of the discussion above, it is clear that many of the most common forms of cyber-crime seen today would qualify as 'serious crime' because such offences so commonly affect more than a single jurisdiction, involve at least to some degree three or more actors, and are committed with the aim of achieving some financial or other material benefit.

That the TOC Convention is broad enough in scope to encompass cyber-crime is significant because, while one central objective of the instrument is to require signatories to criminalise certain types of conduct not specifically related to cyber-crime, the instrument is fundamentally a vehicle for cross-border cooperation of all types, including informal law enforcement cooperation, mutual legal assistance and extradition, asset confiscation and the sharing of forfeited proceeds of crime, and the provision of training and technical assistance.

Article 27 deals principally with police-to-police cooperation and merely reflects the types of assistance routinely provided among police officials in the absence of a formal agreement. Nonetheless, the article is significant insofar as it indicates broad international consensus on the need for close coordination and information-sharing among law enforcement authorities around the world. As a means of achieving this goal, States Parties are encouraged to promote the exchange of personnel and other experts, including liaison officers.

Additionally, signatories are required to 'make full use of agreements or arrangements, including international or regional organisations, to enhance the cooperation between their law enforcement agencies'.[31] As set forth below, every effort should be made to enhance regional cooperation under the auspices of APEC, ASEAN or other inter-governmental bodies in Asia.

With respect to formal MLA, Article 18 contains provisions nearly as lengthy and detailed as would be found in a comprehensive bilateral MLAT. States Parties may seek assistance in connection with: taking evidence or statements from persons; executing searches and seizures; obtaining business and / or government records; and identifying and tracing the proceeds of crime.[32] A requested state party has the discretion to decline assistance on the ground of the absence of dual criminality — a potentially significant limitation in the cyber-crime context, as many countries do not have fully developed legislation in this area.[33]

The TOC Convention also provides for extradition with respect to the offences covered by the instrument.[34] Even where a state party makes extradition conditional on the existence of a bilateral treaty, Article 16 represents a major step forward because its effect is to incorporate into existing bilateral treaty relationships the numerous offences 'covered by' the convention.[35] Thus where two States Parties had been relying on an outdated and overly narrow extradition agreement (such as a list-based treaty providing for extradition only in relation to a specified list of offences), the TOC Convention will substantially expand the range of extraditable offences as between those two countries.

Another important aspect of the TOC Convention is the provision of training and technical assistance, the need for which is especially acute in the context of cyber-crime. Pursuant to Article 29, each signatory is expected to have in place adequate training programmes to assist its own justice and law enforcement officials in addressing offences involving organised criminal groups. Moreover, States Parties are obliged to assist one another in planning and implementing research and training programmes covering numerous areas, including 'methods used in combating transnational organised crime committed through the use of computers, telecommunications networks or other forms of modern technology'.[36] Recognising the resource implications of implementing these provisions and the TOC Convention as a whole, the drafters also included a separate article outlining the need to provide developing countries with technical assistance and other forms of material support.[37]

UNAFEI

UNAFEI is a regional institute of the UN and was established in 1962 by agreement between the UN and the government of Japan for the purpose of promoting the development of sound criminal justice systems and mutual cooperation among countries in the entire Asia-Pacific region.[38] One of the UN's most active and effective regional institutes, UNAFEI has sponsored numerous seminars and training sessions for regional justice and law enforcement officials on a wide array of topics — including, in 1998, a seminar on effective countermeasures against computer crime. In light of the scope of its mission and its impressive track record, UNAFEI is ideally situated to make continuing contributions, through further seminars and the sharing of information and best practices, to the efforts of governments in the region to collaborate against cyber-crime.

ASEAN

Under the auspices of ASEAN, government officials at the ministerial and head of state level in Southeast Asia have recently accelerated their efforts to join together in combating crime in the region. Due to its limited membership (consisting of Brunei Darussalam, Cambodia, Indonesia, Laos, Malaysia, Myanmar, the Philippines, Singapore, Thailand, and Vietnam), ASEAN may not offer a forum for the development of a pan-Asian approach to cyber-crime, but the group's considerable progress in creating clear regional modalities for effective law enforcement cooperation provides a useful model with the potential for wider application. As early as 1986, ASEAN ministers of justice and attorneys general expressed a strong commitment to partnership in law enforcement, issuing a communiqué articulating a commonly held desire to 'facilitate the realisation of cooperation in the legal field on matters of mutual interest', which was initially to include the exchange of legal materials, judicial cooperation, and legal education and research.[39]

In late 1997, ASEAN interior and home affairs ministers gathered in Manila for the First ASEAN Conference on Transnational Crime and promulgated a political declaration outlining a variety of creative and aggressive measures aimed at enhancing regional coordination and cooperation in criminal matters. Fully implemented and adequately resourced, the proposals set forth in this document would represent an enormous advance in regional and sub-regional law enforcement cooperation, both institutionally and operationally. Among other things, ASEAN ministers agreed to:

- Convene a biannual ministerial meeting to coordinate the activities of relevant bodies such as the ASEAN chiefs of national police (ASEANAPOL)
- Hold discussions with a view to signing MLATs, other bilateral treaties and memoranda of understanding among ASEAN member countries
- Consider the establishment of an ASEAN centre on transnational crime with the task of coordinating regional efforts against international crime through intelligence-sharing, harmonisation of policies and operational coordination
- Convene a high-level ad hoc experts group tasked with developing an action plan for tackling transnational crime and an institutional framework for regional cooperation in this area
- Encourage member states to facilitate cooperation among law enforcement authorities through the posting of foreign liaison officers.[40]

At the Second ASEAN Ministerial Meeting on Transnational Crime (held in Myanmar in 1999), ASEAN ministers issued a far-reaching follow-up communiqué outlining a broad and ambitious plan of action (developed by the ad hoc experts group) to further a collective effort against the many forms of organised criminality afflicting the region. As explained by the ministers, the plan of action would

> establish a cohesive regional strategy to prevent, control and neutralise transnational crime; foster regional cooperation at the investigative, prosecutorial, and judicial level … enhance coordination among ASEAN bodies dealing with transnational crime; strengthen regional capacities and capabilities to deal with the sophisticated [*sic*] nature of transnational crime; and develop sub-regional and regional treaties on cooperation in criminal justice, including mutual legal assistance and extradition. The programme of activities would encompass information exchange, cooperation in legal and law enforcement matters, institutional capacity building, training and extra-regional cooperation.[41]

The institutional framework for implementation of the plan includes as its highest policymaking body the ministerial meetings on transnational crime. During these biannual meetings, ASEAN ministers will review and help coordinate the activities of ASEAN bodies engaged in combating international crime, and will develop strategies and programmes to facilitate international cooperation. A group of senior government officials (referred to as the Senior Officials Meeting on Transnational Crime or SOMTC) has been tasked to assist in the execution of ministerial initiatives and directives.[42]

At the 1999 meeting, ministers also agreed to establish an ASEAN centre for combating transnational crime. The centre, among other things, serves as a repository of information on relevant national legislation and regulations; promotes data-sharing among member states on individual criminals, methodologies, arrests and convictions; and analyses trends and patterns in transnational crime and recommends appropriate regional strategies.[43]

The theme of greater cooperation carried over to the Third ASEAN Ministerial Meeting on Transnational Crime, at which ASEAN ministers reiterated their commitment to collaborate further in the battle against computer-related crime. Significantly, the communiqué called for a stronger partnership between ASEAN and other partners and agencies, including Interpol and the United Nations.[44]

As the preceding discussion indicates, in some important respects the architecture of ASEAN anti-crime institutions (particularly the SOMTC) closely resembles that of the G8's Lyon Group and related entities, indicating the broader international relevance of such frameworks for collective government action. Particularly significant is that ASEAN's law enforcement experts group reports directly to ministers and thus, like the G8's Lyon Group, has the capacity to develop policies with support at the highest levels.

The European Union and Europol

The 1957 Treaty of Rome paved the way for the European Economic Community, which in turn evolved into the European Union (EU), established under the Treaty of Maastricht in 1992. Today, the EU has 25 member states (with 10 new members joining in May 2004). It includes supranational institutions that address international crime by adopting joint positions, directives and other instruments addressing a wide variety of criminal activities. Among the most prominent examples of EU coordination in law enforcement matters are the following:

- Adoption of a common position on negotiations relating to the COE Cyber-crime Convention[45]
- Elaboration of an EU convention on mutual assistance in criminal matters[46]
- Elaboration of an EU convention on extradition[47]
- Establishment of a 'European Judicial Network,' consisting of liaison magistrates and representatives of central authorities of member states responsible for international judicial cooperation, and tasked with facilitating cross-border cooperation.[48]

Included within the EU is the European Police Office or Europol, a law enforcement organisation dedicated to increasing the efficiency of cooperation among the police agencies of EU member states, with an emphasis on targeting organised crime.[49] Based in Brussels, Europol is accountable to the EU's Council of Ministers for Justice and Home Affairs. The organisation comprises of European Liaison Officers (who represent national law enforcement agencies across the EU, including police, customs, and immigration officials), and Europol staff officers and analysts. Like Interpol, Europol's primary function is to support the operational activities of national law enforcement officials.[50] Towards that end, its representatives facilitate the exchange of information, provide analyses of criminal intelligence, generate strategic reports on trends and patterns of criminal activity, and provide technical expertise for ongoing investigations within the EU. In addition, the indications are that Europol will eventually assume a greater investigative and operational role.[51]

The OECD

Established in 1960 by 20 countries and based in Paris, the OECD is dedicated to, among other things, promoting economic and social welfare throughout the OECD area by helping member states to coordinate their efforts to aid less developed nations.[52] Today, the OECD has 30 members (including among jurisdictions in the Asian region, Australia, Japan, the Republic of Korea, and New Zealand).

Member states meet and exchange information in committees, including specialised committees devoted to particular areas and smaller working groups. Committees take direction from the council, which is an overarching committee that meets regularly at the level of ambassador (with one representative for each member state). The council also meets annually at the ministerial level to set policy and guide the group's overall work plan for the year. The activities of the approximately 200 committees are supported by a sizeable secretariat.

Despite its initial focus on economic matters, the OECD has established a presence in law enforcement as well. For example, the OECD established a Bribery Working Group, whose efforts ultimately led to the adoption of a convention against commercial bribery. The group has in recent years also begun to increase its activity in the areas of cyber-crime and online security. The OECD has been active in the area of encryption technology, evaluating the balance between law enforcement and privacy concerns and the means by which member states can coordinate encryption policy, and in 1997 the OECD issued a series of guidelines addressing these issues. More recently, in the wake of the terrorist attacks of 11 September 2001, OECD governments developed a series of guidelines designed to counter cyber-terrorism, computer viruses, hacking and related threats.[53] Although the recommendations do not have the force of law, they nonetheless reflect consensus among a number of key jurisdictions on important issues affecting the security of the online environment.

One notable feature of the OECD is that significant efforts are now being made to develop multidisciplinary approaches to problems, drawing on expertise in various fields of policy analysis.

Money laundering task forces

One extremely effective model for inter-governmental law enforcement coordination is the Financial Action Task Force.[54] There are several reasons for the group's success: it is composed of like-minded jurisdictions similarly committed to taking meaningful action against a common crime problem (money laundering); representatives include government officials from all agencies with a major role in addressing the problem; the group draws on the experience and expertise of non-member governments and the private sector, and progress is measured through a process of mutual evaluation. As indicated below, these structures and procedures have been widely adopted by governments at the regional level and might also be applied effectively in the context of efforts to address cyber-crime.

FATF was established at the G7 Paris Summit in 1989.[55] It is a policymaking body with the stated goal of building political will for the implementation of legislative and regulatory reforms needed to combat money laundering. In 1990, the FATF issued a series of 40 recommendations addressing ways in which to combat and deter money laundering. The recommendations are grouped into three broad categories (criminal law, banking law and international cooperation) and serve as the basis for the group's activities.

Each year, FATF holds three plenary meetings to discuss policy direction and initiatives based on the 40 recommendations. Government representatives at FATF meetings typically include senior officials from various agencies with responsibility in the money laundering area (e.g. justice, finance and law enforcement experts). This strong horizontal component ensures that the group's work reflects a breadth of perspectives.

As noted, FATF has also developed mechanisms to export policy ideas and initiatives and to draw on the expertise of other organisations and non-member governments, as well as the private sector. For example, the group hosts an annual 'typologies' meeting to address money laundering techniques; this forum brings FATF experts together with other relevant international organisations and representatives from jurisdictions outside FATF, and thus is an extremely effective mechanism for gauging the overall money laundering problem, detecting emerging global trends, and developing possible solutions. Additionally, every two years FATF holds a Financial Services Forum with representatives of the financial services sector and other businesses, to allow for public–private sector interface on matters of mutual concern.

One groundbreaking feature of FATF is that member governments are subject to peer review, a two-part process by which the group assesses implementation by member governments of the 40 recommendations. First, each FATF member conducts an annual self-assessment, using a standard questionnaire. Second, periodically members are subject to a process of mutual evaluation, involving a site visit by three or four experts from other member governments. The process of mutual evaluation has proved to be an extremely effective means of persuading governments to take meaningful steps to fill gaps in anti-money laundering regimes.

Largely as a result of awareness-raising activities undertaken by FATF, a number of FATF-style organisations have developed at the regional level, which organisations operate autonomously but coordinate activities with FATF itself. In the Asian-Pacific region, the Asia / Pacific Group on Money Laundering (APG), established in 1997, operates in a manner similar to FATF and, notably, in 2000 began a process of FATF-style mutual evaluation. The APG is supported by a secretariat based in Sydney, Australia, and includes 25 member governments: Australia, Bangladesh, Cook Islands, Fiji, Hong Kong, India, Indonesia, Japan, Macau, Malaysia, Marshall Islands, Nepal, New Zealand, Niue, Pakistan, Korea, Palau, the Philippines, Samoa, Singapore, Sri Lanka, Taipei, Thailand, the United States and Vanuatu. A number of additional governments in the region (Brunei Darussalam, Canada, Myanmar, and Vietnam), as well as certain inter-governmental organisations, participate in the APG as observers.[56]

Interpol

The International Criminal Police Organisation, or Interpol, today consists of 181 member states. Headquartered in Lyon, France, and coordinating many of its activities through National Central Bureaus in individual countries,[57] Interpol's mission, broadly defined, is to support law enforcement organisations throughout the world, in particular by facilitating the exchange of information and other forms of international cooperation, coordinating joint operational activities of member states, and developing and sharing expertise and best practices covering a wide range of criminal offences.[58]

With respect to IT crime, Interpol has recognised the need for law enforcement officials to acquire specialised knowledge and has developed international training courses, a handbook providing useful guidance for novice investigators working on computer-related crime, and a computer crime manual for more experienced investigators.[59] Interpol's general secretariat has also supported the formation of geographically-organised working groups comprising regional experts in computer-related crime who meet periodically to share experiences and develop best practices. The Asia-South Pacific Working Party on Information Technology Crime currently meets annually, most recently in October 2003, and has undertaken projects relating to the handling of digital evidence, forensic tools, and training.[60]

Interpol has also endeavoured to build close ties to existing regional structures in Asia, including ASEAN's Association of National Chiefs of Police

(ASEANPOL), in an effort to build on regional cooperation by facilitating the development of regional intelligence databases and the wide dissemination of data through Interpol's extensive telecommunications network.

In addition to its extensive work with individual governments and other inter-governmental organisations, Interpol has fostered an effective relationship with the private sector. One example is an effort beginning in 1995 to address the widening problem of payment card fraud. At that time, a working party consisting of police officials and representatives of the payment card industry met to address this issue and four years later Interpol formalised an agreement with a number of payment card companies to cooperate in the battle against payment card fraud. One particularly successful project, funded in part by the private sector, is the recent creation of a computer-based classification system for counterfeit payment cards. The system became operational in August 1999 and allows law enforcement officials around the world to retrieve forensic data based on technical examinations, as well as general intelligence. Payment card industry representatives working in the anti-fraud area will also have access to the otherwise closed system.[61]

As another example, Interpol has increased its focus on intellectual property-related crime, in light of the fact that such offences are increasingly carried out on a global scale by highly sophisticated and well-financed organised criminal groups. In collaboration with representatives of a wide range of industries and customs and police agencies, Interpol hosted an initial meeting of its Intellectual Property Crime Action Group in July 2002.[62] The structure of this private / public sector group reflects Interpol's recognition of the vital need for close collaboration between law enforcement and the private sector.

Consideration should be given to what further role Interpol could play (potentially in conjunction with other inter-governmental law enforcement bodies and industry representatives) in strengthening the international response to cyber-crime. One area of need is in the development of uniform forensic rules for the retrieval and analysis of computer data.

APEC

Founded in 1989 in Canberra, Australia, for the purpose of promoting economic growth among member states, APEC now consists of 21 member economies.[63] APEC is a consensus body that meets annually at ministerial level; during annual meetings, foreign and economic ministers define and allocate funds for APEC's various committees, an ad hoc policy group, ten specialised working groups, and other forums. Like many of the organisations discussed above, APEC has sought to prioritise its work in a way that will reflect input from private sector representatives.

APEC's orientation historically has been decidedly trade-related, but increasingly its members look to it as a vehicle for cross-border cooperation in enforcement affairs. Indeed, there has been considerable movement in that direction recently and APEC member economies should consider the utility of further broadening the organisation's focus. It bears noting that some of the major multilateral entities discussed above (e.g. the G7, the European Union, and the OECD) initially concentrated their efforts on economic issues but have proved to be effective forums for law enforcement coordination as well. Moreover, APEC's work over the past several years has included a number of areas relevant to cyber-crime enforcement in particular, including the following:

- An Intellectual Property Rights Working Group (IPEG):[64] Formed in 1996, IPEG has sought to enhance IP protection among member governments, such as by sharing information on existing protection regimes, studying effective enforcement measures, facilitating technical assistance, and promoting public education campaigns. In carrying out this objective, IPEG has involved private industry in relevant symposia and has posted on the APEC website a contact list of experts from the public and private sectors.
- An Electronic Commerce Steering Group (ECSG):[65] The objective of the ECSG, established in 1999, is to coordinate APEC-related activities in the area of e-commerce. Because of the private sector's leading role in the development of e-commerce solutions, the ECSG has sought to ensure industry involvement in all of the group's meetings. Thus far, the ECSG has not directly addressed law enforcement issues in an e-commerce environment, but the enforcement end logically connects to APEC's general interest in improving consumer trust and confidence in e-commerce. Further, the ECSG's increasingly detailed work in the areas of privacy and security in the online environment implicate law enforcement concerns.
- Sub-Committee on Customs Procedures (SCCP):[66] The principal aim of the SCCP is to simplify and harmonise customs procedures, partly in an effort to promote risk management techniques and enable customs officials to better target enforcement activities. Like many APEC entities, the group has welcomed the involvement of relevant private sector representatives. Additionally, the SCCP endeavours to coordinate its efforts with those of other inter-governmental organisations, such as the World Customs Organisation.

APEC leaders met in Mexico in October 2002 to discuss, among other matters, the threat of global terrorism and the importance of increasing the protection of global infrastructures. APEC members committed themselves to:

- Enact comprehensive cyber-security laws, on a par with existing international standards, particularly the COE Cyber-crime Convention
- Identify or create national cyber-crime units and international high-technology assistance contact points
- Establish institutions, such as computer emergency response teams, that exchange threat and vulnerability assessments and information.[67]

Recently, APEC's Telecommunications and Infrastructure Working Group has been most active in sponsoring projects to increase the ability of APEC member economies to more effectively address cyber-crime, including through greater intergovernmental and public–private sector cooperation. For example, in July 2003 the APEC Tel group hosted a useful five-day seminar on cyber-crime legislation and enforcement capacity-building which brought together dozens of experts from both government and industry.[68] The group has also surveyed the existing legislative regimes within APEC economies in relation to cyber-crime, with a view towards identifying gaps that need to be filled; this project may eventually lead to the development of model cyber-crime legislation.[69]

Possibilities for Enhanced Cooperation Among Jurisdictions in Asia

As expressed above, cyber-crime poses an immediate threat to the stability and security of all jurisdictions and requires an immediate and concerted response by governments, working together with affected industries as appropriate. Outlined below are proposed elements of a framework for effective regional cooperation in this area, taking into account existing models of multilateral cooperation that have proved successful in the context of criminal law enforcement; and a suggested plan for multi-phased implementation of these elements.

Elements of an effective cooperation regime

An effective regime for regional cooperation in combating cyber-crime should include, at a minimum, the following basic elements.

Criminalisation of offences

- Harmonisation of domestic legislation on cyber-crime (procedural and substantive), including at a minimum:
  - Measures to ensure the ability of domestic law enforcement officials to investigate cyber-crime effectively (e.g. authorising police to obtain preservation orders and to conduct searches and seizures in an electronic environment)
  - Criminalisation of the offences listed in the COE Cyber-crime Convention, as well as other common forms of high-tech crime
  - Sufficiently severe punishments to deter would-be offenders and ensure the availability of legal assistance and extradition.

Training and specialised personnel

- Adequate training and resources for relevant government officials, including police, prosecutors, and judicial officials. This should include:
  - Country-specific training programmes and the participation in global, regional and sub-regional training programmes that would facilitate the sharing of best practices. Consideration should be given to what contribution industry representatives might make to such programmes
  - Dedicated units in police agencies staffed by personnel with specialised knowledge in the area of cyber-crime and forensic computing, as well as the hardware and software needed for effective investigation
  - Specialised offices within justice ministries staffed by individuals familiar with the evidentiary hurdles and other unique issues that can arise in cyber-crime prosecutions.

Cooperation among police officials

- Developed and open channels of communication among law enforcement officials to facilitate coordination on operational matters and the sharing of information, to include where possible:
  - The posting of liaison officers
  - Active participation by national law enforcement officials in regional,

sub-regional, and global law enforcement organisations dealing with cyber-crime.

Mutual legal assistance and extradition

- A network of bilateral and / or multilateral agreements or arrangements providing for effective and efficient MLA in cyber-crime cases, to include:
  - The availability of assistance in the absence of dual criminality
  - An active central authority to coordinate all incoming and outgoing requests for assistance
  - A single point of contact available on a 24/7 basis to respond to requests for assistance in urgent matters involving high-tech crime
  - Measures allowing for the expedited preservation of particularly vulnerable types of electronic data
  - The possibility for the international sharing of the confiscated proceeds of cyber-crime
- A network of bilateral and / or multilateral agreements or arrangements providing for extradition in cases involving cyber-crime.

Regional forum

- A forum in which senior officials from the entire region can regularly exchange information on relevant legislation, best practices, and emerging trends and patterns, and can develop policies and practices to be implemented at national and regional levels.

Private sector involvement

- A mechanism for public–private sector interface on matters of mutual concern.

Preventive measures

- Public education campaigns.

Action plan for implementation

Putting the necessary structures in place to facilitate meaningful cross-border cooperation will require a phased approach. To be sure, the cyber-crime phenomenon is not susceptible to a quick and easy solution. However, governments in the region could adopt certain measures with relative ease and to considerable effect. Other steps will take longer to implement.

Near-term approach

Criminalisation of offences

- Share copies of existing domestic legislation relevant to cyber-crime (ideally by posting such information on the Internet).

Training and specialised personnel

- Incorporate cyber-crime-related issues into existing domestic, regional and sub-regional training programmes.

Cooperation among police officials

- Share information on appropriate points of contact for international law enforcement liaison on operational matters relating to cyber-crime.
  - o Where possible, individual agencies should post data on existing government websites
  - o Data for the entire Asian region might be posted on a single website, maintained and updated by an existing inter-governmental organisation (such as ASEAN or APEC) or perhaps by a non-governmental entity
- Increase near-term capacity of regional associations such as APEC and ASEAN to deal with cyber-crime.
- Increase involvement in Interpol.

Mutual legal assistance and extradition

- Share copies of existing domestic legislation relevant to international legal assistance (ideally, by posting such information on the Internet).
- Where necessary, establish a central authority for the handling of incoming and outgoing requests for assistance.
- Exchange information on central authorities, 24/7 points of contact, and other relevant officials (as with law enforcement liaison information, using the Internet where possible to make information available to specific countries and throughout the region).
- Relax sovereignty-based restrictions and other limitations on international cooperation, with a view to eliminating bottlenecks in legal

assistance practice and promoting the efficient collection and provision of evidence.

- Apply the broadest possible interpretation of existing agreements and arrangements (statute and treaty-based) to facilitate cross-border cooperation whenever possible. For instance, where a fugitive is sought for hacking or distributed denial of service attacks, and the applicable extradition treaty is a list-based agreement that does not expressly include such offences, extradition might still be granted if the crime could be properly characterised as one of the more traditional offences listed in the treaty (e.g. malicious mischief).

Regional forum

- Where appropriate, use existing structures and inter-governmental organisations to regionalise relevant work of other multilateral bodies (e.g. by endorsing and adopting statements of principles or action plans designed to promote effective international cooperation).
- Increase the near-term capacity of regional bodies such as APEC and ASEAN to address criminal law enforcement issues, with particular emphasis on cross-border cooperation and cyber-crime.

Private sector involvement

- Provide a forum for public–private sector interface on issues of mutual concern.
    - o As appropriate, invite industry representatives to attend relevant symposia or conferences or provide written input on matters under discussion
    - o Existing regional groups could develop private sector cyber-crime contact lists (to be posted on relevant websites).

Preventive measures

- Incorporate cyber-crime issues into existing public education campaigns.

Medium to long-term approach

Criminalisation of offences

- Harmonise criminal laws addressing cyber-crime (using the COE Cyber-crime Convention as a guide) and ensure that such offences are subject to penalties that take into account the serious nature of the offences.

Training and specialised personnel

- Create, and adequately resource, specialised cyber-crime units in police agencies and justice ministries.
- Institutionalise regular regional training programs, using existing multilateral organisations (e.g. UNAFEI, ASEAN, APEC).

Cooperation among police officials

- Promote the exchange of liaison officers.
- Dedicate additional resources to existing police organisations (such as ASEANAPOL and Interpol) to address cyber-crime.
- Consider the utility of creating a new pan-Asian association of law enforcement officials.
- Increase liaison among global, regional and sub-regional law enforcement organisations.

Mutual legal assistance and extradition

- Establish an effective network of agreements and arrangements on mutual legal assistance and extradition:
  - o Ensure that domestic statutes on international cooperation are sufficiently broad to cover cyber-crime
  - o Evaluate and, as necessary, update existing bilateral treaties to ensure that such agreements encompass cyber-crime and eliminate the dual criminality requirement for MLA
  - o Where necessary, establish new bilateral treaty relationships with key jurisdictions (within and without Asia), ensuring that such agreements are as broad as possible, provide for maximum flexibility, and are tailored to meet the need for rapid assistance in cyber-crime investigations
  - o Consider the utility of supplementing existing bilateral and multilateral agreements with regional or sub-regional conventions on cooperation.
- Sign, ratify, and implement the UN TOC Convention.
- As soon as possible, seek to join the COE Cyber-crime Convention.

Regional forum

- Strengthen the long-term capacity of regional and sub-regional bodies involved in law enforcement cooperation or, if appropriate, create an entirely new forum for the discussion of cyber-crime-related issues affecting the entire Asian region. One possible approach would be to expand the existing ASEAN model (discussed above) to establish, under the auspices of a broader regional organisation, subgroups or task forces staffed by senior government experts and dedicated to developing and implementing practical solutions to common problems.

Private sector involvement

- Expand the role of the private sector in new or existing regional organisations addressing cyber-crime:
  - o Develop government / industry cooperation principles
  - o Create government / industry task forces devoted to specific issues
  - o Work with industry representatives in developing communications networks that are reliable and secure but which preserve the ability of governments to fight high-tech crime
  - o Promote the development by industry of voluntary codes of conduct and standards.

Preventive measures

- Use all available forums to conduct public education campaigns.
- As necessary, tap available resources for capacity-building (e.g. though regional organisations providing technical assistance and / or the UN).
- Partner with industry in developing technological solutions.

Conclusion

Cyber-crime is among the greatest challenges facing law enforcement officials today, in large measure because no single jurisdiction, acting alone, can hope to meaningfully address the threat. To mount an effective response to this increasingly widespread form of criminality, governments must redouble efforts to further intergovernmental as well as public–private sector cooperation. Steps must be taken at the bilateral, regional, and global levels, and future action should fully reflect cooperation mechanisms that have proved successful in the past.

With regard to Asia in particular, there is no perfect vehicle for seamless cross-border cooperation in addressing computer-related crime. The Council of Europe Cyber-crime Convention remains the single comprehensive multilateral instrument in this area — and it holds the most promise as an effective global structure for cooperation. Even assuming there was international consensus for a truly global cyber-crime convention under UN auspices, it would take years to negotiate such an instrument and its terms would likely be weaker, and perhaps substantially weaker, than the COE Convention. For that reason, those states that are eligible to sign the COE instrument should actively recruit additional signatories from Asia and elsewhere and COE member states should apply a liberal approach when approving new countries for accession.

In the meantime, every effort should be made to increase capacity-building programmes to assist countries, especially those with economies in transition, in building an appropriate legislative framework, allocating sufficient resources, and developing sufficient technical expertise among justice and law enforcement officials to facilitate effective investigations and prosecutions. As outlined above, a number of bilateral and multilateral initiatives are already under way to achieve these ends but more needs to be done to bring these activities together, to achieve greater coherence and consistency in the outcome. APEC, because of its broad and geographically expansive membership, is probably the best vehicle to undertake this work despite the fact that it lacks the established bureaucracy and rule-making authority of other multilateral forums. It is promising to see both APEC's Electronic Commerce Steering Group and Telecommunications and Infrastructure Working Group increasing their activities in these areas. These initiatives, along with the work of other groups, must continue and indeed must accelerate if the international community is to keep pace with, and ultimately contain, new and increasingly pernicious forms of cyber-criminality.

15

The Council of Europe Convention on Cyber-Crime: A Response to the Challenge of the New Age

Peter Csonka*

The Council of Europe's Convention on Cyber-crime is a collective response by members of the Council of Europe (45 states) and some non-member states to the challenge of cyber-crime. It is the result of four years of intensive work by an expert committee set up in 1997, the Committee of Experts on Crime in Cyberspace (Committee 'PC-CY'), which was entrusted by the Committee of Ministers to follow up on previous Council of Europe (COE) recommendation policy documents without a binding nature — on computer crime and criminal procedure problems linked to information technology. The committee was particularly tasked to prepare a 'legally binding instrument', which in Council of Europe terms, means an international treaty.

The committee completed its work at the end of 2000 and worked in close coordination with the G8 and other international bodies on the draft Convention on Cyber-crime. The senior committee for criminal law policy at the Council of Europe, also known as the 'European Committee on Crime Problems', approved the final draft of the convention in June 2001. The council's political decision-maker, the Committee of Ministers, adopted the convention on 8 November 2001, and decided to open it for signature on 23 November 2001 in Budapest, on the occasion of an international conference organised there. On that day, 30 states signed the convention (the Budapest Convention), among which were 26 COE member states and four non-member states which had participated in the drafting process (United States, Canada, Japan, South Africa). At present the treaty has been signed by 37 states and ratified by eight and entered into force on July 2004.

Although consultations with prospective contracting states have revealed the difficulty of adapting domestic laws to the requirements of the convention, the treaty reached the threshold for activation in only 18 months.

During the process of negotiation, the convention received strong support from lawmakers and practitioners throughout Europe and beyond, but it has also been criticised on various grounds by a number of associations, particularly those active in the protection of freedom of expression, and also by representatives of certain branches of industry. As the contribution of the private sector and civil society to the prevention and control of cyber-crime is essential, it is important to explain what is the real purpose of the convention.

Challenges That Motivated the Convention's Drafters

Global networks and global crimes

As the world becomes increasingly dependent on global computer networks, users, whether private, corporate or government, realise how vulnerable they are to criminal intrusion and misuse. The Convention on Cyber-crime aims ultimately at protecting these networks from such intrusion and misuse. Computer networks deserve and need protection for several reasons: first, because over the past few years they have changed the world into a global information society in which there are virtually no longer any frontiers, either for their lawful use, such as for educational, scientific or commercial purposes, or for criminal misuse, such as for launching virus attacks against computer systems or for distributing paedophile pictures; second, because their implications are far-reaching in that virtually any kind of electronic information is now accessible to any Internet user anywhere in the world at any time (remote access, legal or illegal, to vast quantities of both official and private data stored by computer systems has now become completely unhindered); third, because computer networks bear the promise of a new era of online electronic commerce, offering services and goods, whose value may soon exceed hundreds of billions of dollars.

This world of virtual networks, which every user hoped would offer unprecedented benefits, is increasingly threatened by crime. Today's networks make it possible to distribute illegal content, such as paedo-pornography, computer viruses, or even information on how to build and use bombs, at a phenomenal speed and to a virtually unlimited number of users. These networks may be used to spy and steal confidential information that is often of great economic value, or to attack computer systems of governments or those of private companies from a distance in a totally anonymous fashion, actually or potentially causing considerable damage. The attacks may be, and law enforcement evidence suggests that they often are, perpetrated not only by young computer prodigies testing the limits of their skills but often, deliberately and maliciously, by professional hackers, cyber-terrorists or cyber-spies, hired and paid by corporations, organised crime or terrorist groups, and sometimes even by governments.

Since the 11 September 2001, the world has come to realise that some groups of people will not refrain from attacking the symbols of Western civilisation to further their goals. The violence of these groups may — and probably will — reach the Internet and computer networks soon, thus beginning a new type of confrontation, which will be difficult to win. Users, in particular governments, need to be prepared more than ever before to protect their computer infrastructure from this violence.

As Sussmann rightly noted:

> There is a revolution going on in criminal activity. It creates major problems for law enforcement in almost every part of the world — problems that have rarely been as systemic and pervasive. The revolution lies in the ways that networked computers and other technologies permit crimes to be committed remotely, via the Internet and wireless communications. A criminal no longer needs to be at the actual scene of the crime (or within 1,000 miles, for that matter) to prey on his victim. The possibility of an international element has been added to almost any crime, which means that cumbersome mechanisms for international cooperation can slow or derail many more investigations than ever before. Because everything from banks to phone systems to air traffic control to our military relies so heavily on networked computers, few individuals and institutions are impervious to this new and threatening criminal activity.[1]

Global crimes and local law enforcement

As the 'D-O-S' or 'denial-of-service' attacks on prominent commercial Internet sites and the dissemination of viruses such as the 'I Love You' virus brought into stark relief recently, computer-related crimes are international in nature. This means that important public safety issues must be considered by governments in their efforts to develop the Internet's power to communicate, engage in commerce, and to expand people's educational opportunities across the globe. It also means that secure networks depend to a large extent on the ability of governments to develop a coordinated response to criminal activities targeting or misusing computer systems. This response requires cooperation on three levels. First, national police and judicial authorities must have the legal tools and practices in place to give each other prompt mutual legal assistance in investigating and prosecuting computer-related crimes. Second, governments must enable direct collaboration between those government agencies entrusted with advancing the growth and security of e-commerce, and those charged with protecting the safety of the public. Finally, the private sector plays a crucial role in ensuring security and confidence in shared networks, and governments must work closely with industry at a variety of levels to respond to the problems associated with cyber-crime.

It is obvious that law enforcement is confined to national territories, and for most traditional crimes this principle is widely accepted and poses no problem. However, when investigating computer crimes, national borders become a real obstacle for law enforcement: while the Internet may be borderless for criminals, law enforcement agencies must respect the sovereignty of other nations. As a result, national authorities become increasingly dependent on cooperation with foreign counterparts. Unfortunately, differing legal systems and disparities in the law often present major obstacles in mutual legal assistance (MLA).

The failure of a country to criminalise computer-related offences is one such obstacle. When one country's laws criminalise certain activities on computers and another country's laws do not, cooperation in solving a crime and prosecuting the perpetrator may be impossible. That is, when a criminal weaves his communications through three, four, or five countries before reaching his intended victims, inadequate laws in just one of those countries can, in effect, shield that criminal from law enforcement around the world. Take the recent investigation of the 'I Love You' virus. International coordination would have proceeded more quickly and effectively had there existed common computer crime laws between the countries concerned, in particular in the country where the virus originated.

The Council of Europe has made, probably ahead of its time, a first attempt to harmonise substantive computer crime laws in 1989 by issuing guidelines to national lawmakers in its member states[2] and recommending that a minimum list of computer-specific offences be considered for ensuring a uniform European criminal policy in this area. This list includes the definitions of eight offences (computer-related fraud; computer forgery; damage to computer data or computer programs; computer sabotage;

unauthorised access; unauthorised interception; unauthorised reproduction of a protected computer program; unauthorised reproduction of a topography) and was supplemented by an optional list which contained four additional offences (alteration of computer data or computer programs; computer espionage; unauthorised use of a computer; unauthorised use of a protected computer program). In 1997, a report on the implementation of the guidelines concluded that insufficient harmonisation was achieved. As Kaspersen pointed out, 'there are member states which did not implement [the Recommendation] at all, whereas others only implemented a certain number of guidelines or did not follow the particular guideline in question'.[3] Kaspersen noted that significant discrepancies remained in member states' legislation and that a binding legal instrument, a treaty, would be necessary to enable effective international cooperation. In the absence of harmonised computer crime laws, investigations involving several nations are indeed bound to fail; for example, due to a lack of dual criminality (i.e. nations concerned do not have similar laws banning the conduct), a principle that governments must observe to obtain cooperation, whether MLA or extradition, from other nations.

High-tech crimes and old-fashioned law enforcement tools

As DiGregory reminds us, harmonisation of the laws defining criminal behaviour is essential but it is not enough:

> To enforce substantive computer crime laws, law enforcement authorities also need appropriate tools for detecting and investigating such unlawful activities. Many criminal cases today are investigated and solved on the basis of electronic evidence, which is highly volatile and perishable, and can be easily deleted or modified from half a world away. New technologies enable criminals to hide their identity through anonymous services, encrypt their communications, and commit crimes remotely from almost anywhere in the world. Thus, to the extent that existing investigative processes are tied to particular technologies, they may need to be modified or clarified to apply to emerging technologies and challenges.[4]

Computer criminals usually act remotely and often from great distances, through computer networks. Thus criminals may target or attack a computer or a system controlled by a computer (e.g. hackers disrupting a local phone service) or may use a computer to commit a 'traditional' crime such as fraud or theft (e.g. promoting bogus investments on a web-page). In addition, a criminal may use a computer in a way that is incidental to the offence but where the computer nonetheless contains evidence of a crime (e.g. drug dealers using personal computers to store records of drug sales and 'clients').

Frequently, to succeed in identifying such criminals, investigators must quickly follow a trail of communications from one point, such as a victim's computer in a computer hacking case, to the computer where the criminal is located, often by tracing the communication through a number of 'hops' in the communication chain. To trace this communication, law enforcement must often rely on historical transaction records — that is, stored records of the source and destination of a communication. To succeed, law enforcement must have the authority to compel ISPs or telecom operators to access or preserve log files, electronic mail records and other important evidence, and to do so quickly, before crucial information is altered or deleted. If the investigating authorities cannot quickly obtain this information from the providers and use it to match a crime with a source computer, the investigation may be frustrated.

When historical transaction records are not available, investigators may also try to trace a communication in real time — that is, attempt to identify a criminal while he is communicating or committing the crime. Tracing in real time can be very complicated, particularly where the communication traverses multiple providers. Many communication technologies are not designed to facilitate tracing. The victim's computer often only receives the address of the computer connected directly to it, not the address of the communication's source, and this address can be false or temporarily hijacked. Moreover, the infrastructure of the Internet does not normally provide an automated mechanism for identifying the true source. Therefore investigators will often have to contact individually each communications provider in the chain, to determine the source of the prior communication. In addition, when these investigations cross national borders, they can also cross time zones. This often means that it is night-time in at least one jurisdiction, and qualified personnel may simply not be available to respond in a timely fashion to requests for information. Unfortunately, when such personnel are not available, the tracing operation usually ceases and the opportunity to obtain the necessary information may be lost forever.

High-tech crimes and low-speed cooperation

In addition to harmonising substantive laws and empowering law enforcement with appropriate procedural authority, countries must develop new MLA regimes for investigating and prosecuting cyber-crimes. Because of the perishability of electronic evidence and the mobility of people, evidence must be gathered quickly. Existing MLA regimes between governments are generally slow and anticipate sharing evidence between only two countries, usually the victim's country and the offender's country. But when a criminal sends his communications through several countries, the processes for international assistance involve successive periods of time before law enforcement can reach data in those latter countries, increasing the chances that the data will be unavailable or lost, and the criminal will remain free to attack again. Thus it seems essential that governments consider new avenues and methods for cooperation between multiple countries and develop inter-governmental emergency networks so that investigators can communicate to other experts around the clock.

Governments need to realise that traditional investigative procedures — and particularly the often-cumbersome procedures that govern investigations at the international level — may not be adequate to meet the need in computer crime cases for immediate law enforcement action reaching beyond national borders. The irrelevance of borders is making some old crime-solving paradigms and practices obsolete. Likewise, the traditional international legal assistance regime often cannot accommodate requests for assistance that occur during a cyber-attack because responses cannot be handled in real time. Inefficient and overly bureaucratic instruments for MLA need to give way to more practical approaches, while the necessary guarantees for due process and other fundamental rights are maintained. They also need to accommodate the specific requirements of collecting and exchanging electronic evidence and presenting it at court. Such evidence may be scattered across several different countries; it can be deleted or altered with one click of a mouse and may be encrypted, but it will ultimately need to be authenticated in another country's court. This is a rather new situation for many nations.

Governments should also bear in mind that changes to evidence may result from a criminal trying to cover his tracks, or a system administrator routinely clearing old e-mails or other data from a company's servers. Whatever the case, critical evidence can be lost, long before an international request for assistance is ever transmitted. Traditional methods of obtaining evidence from foreign governments can include lengthy delays, as foreign legal processes, translations and diplomacy slowly proceed. Old modalities may not always be practical when considering new technologies. Therefore, when electronic evidence is sought, there may be a need for mechanisms such as a 'preservation of evidence request'. This implies that where there is a particular concern about the loss of electronic evidence, a country could make an informal international request that the data immediately be preserved. This could be accomplished in a number of ways, from having a telecommunications carrier or ISP copy and store a customer's data, to actually seizing a criminal's computer and securing (but not searching) it for a short period of time. Once data is protected from loss, expedited processes would provide the foreign country with formal documentation to authorise the issuance of a domestic search warrant or similar process, so as to obtain data disclosure.

Many of such procedural hurdles and problems in international cooperation were considered by the Council of Europe when it issued its second policy document on computer crime; that is, the Recommendation on procedural law problems relating to information technology.[5] The document was designed to supplement the previously adopted substantive criminal law guidelines with new policy guidelines to lawmakers on issues of procedural law and international cooperation in the area of computer crime. The new guidelines were based on the realisation that certain law enforcement powers, created for and usually applied in traditional investigations, need adapting to the specific nature of investigations in computer systems, both domestically and for rendering MLA. In particular,[6] they recommended that governments enable law enforcement authorities to:

- Search computer systems, seize electronic evidence therein and, when immediate action is required, extend computer searches to connected computer systems
- Adapt interception powers to the computer environment and make them available for computer crimes
- Collect traffic (transactional) data
- Ensure that seized electronic evidence is secured in an appropriate manner, for example, through a chain of custody
- Order a data-holder to submit specific data for the purpose of investigation and provide access information to it
- Impose an obligation on telecommunications providers to make their systems interceptable and for them to provide information on the identity of users for the purpose of investigations
- Ensure that seized and electronic evidence is available for MLA purposes and compatible with evidentiary requirements of foreign jurisdictions
- Ensure that technically literate and equipped personnel are trained for computer crime investigations and special units are set up
- Revise MLA arrangements and create a network of national computer crime contact points that can swiftly apply on behalf of foreign jurisdictions a wide range of investigative powers, including computer search and interception, and subsequently exchange electronic evidence.

Finally, the guidelines recommended that governments negotiate international treaties so as to create an unambiguous legal basis to conduct trans-border computer searches.

The implementation of this second set of guidelines has not yet been assessed, but most of its recommendations have now been incorporated into the Convention on Cyber-crime, which will require full compliance from contracting states. Similarly, the substantive law guidelines of 1989 have served as the main reference for the definitions of various computer crimes in the convention. Thus both policy documents were given a logical follow-up and will eventually be enforced as treaty obligations. Nevertheless, the time-lag between the first guidelines and the future convention, whose implementation will again take time, shows that laws and practices need a considerable amount of time to change, while technology does not. The challenges referred to above need addressing urgently. The Convention on Cyber-crime constitutes a first, pioneering effort to bring changes about, and in this sense I think I would give an affirmative answer to my own question in this paper's title.

The Convention on Cyber-Crime

The convention's aims

The Convention on Cyber-crime has three aims:

1. To lay down common definitions of certain criminal offences — nine are mentioned in the convention — for ensuring that relevant criminal legislations is harmonised at national level
2. To define common types of investigative powers better suited to the information technology environment, by ensuring that relevant criminal procedures are brought into line between countries; importantly, the convention also seeks to ensure that these powers are available not only for the investigation and prosecution of offences that it has defined but also of other offences committed by means of computer systems, or in relation to which there is evidence in electronic form
3. To determine both traditional and new types of international cooperation, to enable cooperating countries to put in place arrangements for the investigation and prosecution of the offences set forth by the convention, including the use of a network of permanent contacts.

The convention's structure

The convention contains four chapters: I Use of terms; II Measures to be taken at domestic level — substantive law and procedural law; III International cooperation; IV Final clauses.

Chapter II (substantive law issues) includes both criminalisation provisions and other connected provisions in the area of computer or computer-related crime: it first defines nine offences grouped in four different categories, then deals with ancillary liability and sanctions. The following offences are defined by the convention: illegal access, illegal interception, data interference, system interference, misuse of devices, computer-related forgery, computer-related fraud, offences related to child pornography, and offences related to copyright and neighbouring rights.

Chapter II (procedural law issues) — the scope of this goes beyond the offences defined in Chapter I in that it applies to any offence committed by means of a computer system or for which the evidence is in electronic form — determines first the common conditions and safeguards applicable to all procedural powers in this chapter. It then sets out the following procedural powers: expedited preservation of stored data; expedited preservation and partial disclosure of traffic data; production order; search and seizure of computer data; real-time collection of traffic data; interception of content data. Chapter II ends with jurisdiction provisions.

Chapter III contains provisions concerning general and computer crime-specific MLA as well as extradition rules. It covers traditional MLA in two situations: where no legal basis (treaty, reciprocal legislation, etc.) exists between contracting states, in which case its provisions apply; and where such a basis exists, in which case existing arrangements also apply to assistance under the convention. Computer-crime or assistance specific to computer-related crime applies to both situations and covers, subject to extra conditions, the same range of procedural powers as defined in Chapter II. In addition, Chapter III contains a provision on a specific type of trans-border access to stored computer data which does not require MLA (with consent or where publicly available) and provides for the setting up of a 24/7 network for ensuring speedy assistance among future contracting states.

Finally, Chapter IV contains the final clauses, which — with certain exceptions — repeat the standard provisions in COE treaties.

Criminal offences set forth by the convention

The first part of the convention concerns the introduction of harmonised criminal offences in the legislation of future contracting states, one expected result of which is to eliminate problems of dual criminality. Some of these offences have already been defined in significant detail by the first set of recommendations on computer-related crime, adopted in 1989.

Criminal offences set forth by the convention fall into four categories:

1. Offences against the confidentiality, integrity and availability of data or computer systems
2. Computer-related offences
3. Content-related offences
4. Offences involving the infringement of intellectual property and related rights.

Offences in the first category, of which there are six, all define criminal acts that target computerised information systems or data; their reprehensible nature is closely linked to the computing environment in which they take place. Although some of these offences may have an equivalent in the ordinary world (e.g. illegal access, or hacking, is comparable to violation of the home), others do not. Making these acts criminal offences is based on a clear criminal policy consideration to protect computer networks and the data they contain. The actual or potential damage caused by such infringements should not be underestimated: breaking into a computer system and introducing a virus can easily lead to the destruction of data or entire systems virtually anywhere in the world because of the interconnection of networks. To be considered an offence, however, these infringements must always be committed intentionally and unlawfully, that is, 'without right'. There are therefore acts, which if duly authorised and executed by public authorities (law enforcement, intelligence or judicial) or are accepted as lawful commercial practices, will not be considered a criminal offence under the convention. In this context, one needs to reassure representatives of industry that the convention expressly rules out criminal liability or other legal consequences regarding lawful practices (tests or hardware design) aiming to protect the security of computer systems.

Offences against the confidentiality, integrity and availability of data or information systems

By criminalising mere *illegal access*, that is, 'hacking', 'cracking' or 'computer trespass', drafters of the convention wanted to send a clear signal that this conduct is illegal in itself and needs to be prosecuted, particularly as it is considered in many jurisdictions as a kind of baseline offence: such intrusions may give access to confidential data (including passwords, information about the targeted system) and secrets, or to the use of the system without payment; they may even encourage hackers to commit more dangerous forms of computer-related offences such as fraud or forgery. Many national legislations already contain provisions on hacking offences, but the scope and constituent elements vary considerably. Certain countries apply a narrow definition or require additional qualifying circumstances. Under the convention, contracting states can choose whether to criminalise mere hacking or, alternatively, attach any or all of the qualifying elements listed in the illegal access provision, such as infringing security measures, special intent to obtain computer data, other dishonest intent that justifies criminal culpability, or the requirement that the offence is committed in relation to a computer system that is connected remotely to another computer system. The last option allows contracting states to exclude the situation where a person physically accesses a stand-alone computer without any use of another computer system. They may restrict the offence to illegal access to networked computer systems (including public networks provided by telecommunication services and private networks, such as Intranets or Extranets).

The provision on *illegal interception* aims to protect the right of privacy of data communication. The offence represents the same violation of the privacy of communications as traditional tapping and recording of oral telephone conversations between persons and applies this principle to all forms of electronic data transfer, whether by telephone, fax, e-mail or file transfer. The offence applies to 'non-public' transmissions of computer data. The term 'non-public' qualifies the nature of the transmission (communication) process and not the nature of the data transmitted. The data communicated may be publicly available information, but the offence is applicable if the parties wish to communicate confidentially. Similarly, the data concerned may be kept secret for commercial purposes until the service is paid, as in Pay TV. Therefore, the term 'non-public' does not *per se* exclude communications via public networks. In some countries, interception may be closely related to the offence of unauthorised access to a computer system. To ensure consistency between such provisions, countries that require proof of dishonest intent, or that an offence is committed in relation to a computer system that is connected to another computer system in accordance with the provision on illegal access, may also require similar qualifying elements to attach criminal liability to illegal interception.

The provision on *data interference* aims to provide computer data and computer programs with protection similar to that enjoyed by corporeal objects against the intentional infliction of damage. Conduct constituting the offence, such as damaging, deteriorating or deleting computer data, must involve a negative alteration of the integrity, or of information content, of data and programs. The input of data, such as malicious codes, viruses (e.g. Trojan horses), is also covered by the provision, as is the resulting modification of the data.

The provision on *system interference* aims to criminalise acts of computer sabotage. The offence covers the intentional hindering of the lawful use of computer systems, including telecommunication facilities, by using or influencing computer data. The text is formulated in a neutral way so that all kinds of system functions can be protected by it. The term 'hindering' refers to actions that interfere with the proper functioning of the computer system. Such hindering must take place by inputting, transmitting, damaging, deleting, altering or suppressing computer data. As opposed to data interference, the hindering of computer systems must be 'serious' to give rise to criminal sanction. Each contracting state needs to determine for itself what criteria must be met for hindering to be considered as serious. For example, a state may require a minimum amount of damage to be caused. The drafters considered as serious the sending of data to a particular system in such a form, size or frequency that it has a significant detrimental effect on the ability of the owner or operator to use the system, or to communicate with other systems (e.g. by means of programs that generate 'denial of service' attacks, malicious codes such as viruses that prevent or substantially slow the operation of the system, or programs that send huge quantities of electronic mail to a recipient to block the communications functions of the system).

The provision on *misuse of devices* establishes, as a separate criminal offence, some specific conduct, including production, distribution, sale and so on, related to access devices that are primarily designed or adapted for misuse. Devices that are designed and used for legal purposes are not captured. It was debated at length whether the devices should be restricted to those that are designed *exclusively* for committing offences, thereby excluding totally dual-use devices, but this was considered to be too narrow. Such a definition could have led to insurmountable difficulties of proof in criminal proceedings, rendering the provision practically inapplicable or only applicable in rare instances. The offence therefore requires a particular purpose, that is, intent to commit any of the other offences against the confidentiality, integrity and availability of computer systems or data, as defined in the convention. As the commission of these offences often requires the possession of means of access ('hacker tools') or other tools, there is a strong incentive to acquire them for criminal purposes, which may then lead to the creation of a kind of black market in their production and distribution. To prevent more dangerous consequences, drafters of the convention agreed to prohibit, at the source, conduct related to the production, distribution and sale of such devices, preceding the commission of other computer crimes. Further, the mere possession of such devices or access codes is also criminalised. However, contracting states will be able to accommodate local thresholds of criminalisation, in other words to require that a number of such items be possessed. The number of items possessed goes directly to proving criminal intent. It is up to each contracting state to decide the number of items required before criminal liability attaches. To reassure computer security professionals that tools created for the authorised testing, or the protection, of computer systems are not covered by the provision, a separate clause was added to exempt such legal devices, even though the concept is already contained in the expression 'without right'. For example, test devices ('cracking devices') and network analysis devices designed by industry to control the reliability of information technology products or to test system security are considered to be produced for legitimate purposes, and thus to be 'with right'.

Computer-related offences

Offences in the second category cover computer versions of two offences (fraud and forgery), which are usually perpetrated in the physical world and in traditional ways. Yet fraud or forgery can also be perpetrated by or through computer networks, which thus become the means by which the offence is committed rather than being its target. Both are basically manipulation-based conduct. The convention's drafters thought it necessary to make such conduct separate criminal offences because the definition of traditional forms — in most national laws — implies that they cannot be applied to acts perpetrated through computer networks; for example, in the case of computer-aided fraud, the element of deceit was considered to be missing and in the case of computer-aided forgery, the difference between an original and a copy seemed no longer to exist. Moreover, when fraud or forgery is committed through computer networks, a larger number of people are likely to suffer damage.

The inclusion of the computer version of these offences in the convention acknowledged the fact that in many countries certain legal interests are not sufficiently protected against new forms of interference and attacks. Indeed, with the arrival of the technological revolution, the opportunities for committing economic crimes such as fraud, in particular credit card fraud and the misuse of identity, have multiplied. Assets represented or administered in computer systems (electronic funds, deposit money) have become the target of manipulations like traditional forms of property. These crimes consist mainly of input manipulation, by which incorrect data is fed into a computer, or by program manipulation and other interference in the course of data processing. The aim of the provision on *computer-related fraud* is to criminalise any undue manipulation (including input, alteration, deletion, suppression of data as well as interference with the functioning of a computer program or system) in the course of data processing with intent to affect an illegal transfer of property. The aim of the provision on *computer-related forgery* is to create a parallel offence to the forgery of tangible documents. It aims to fill gaps in criminal law provisions related to traditional forgery, which usually require visual readability of statements, or declarations embodied in a document and which do not apply to electronically stored data. Manipulation of such data with evidentiary value may have the same serious consequences as traditional acts of forgery if a third party is thereby misled. Computer-related forgery involves the unauthorised creating or altering of stored data so that it acquires a different evidentiary value and the course of legal transactions, which relies on the authenticity of information contained in the data, is subject to a deception.

Content-related offences

The third category of offences, which concerns content, includes a number of acts related to child pornography. Considered by the convention's drafters as a real scourge of contemporary society and an object of international trafficking, the highest authorities of the Council of Europe have made dealing with this problem a top priority. The convention accordingly makes various acts, ranging from the possession to the intentional distribution of child pornography, criminal offences, so as to cover all stages in the chain of production and distribution. Other types of illegal content, such as racist propaganda, is not included among content-related offences, as the drafters of the convention and their governments failed to agree to do so. The issue was one of the most controversial matters in the negotiation process and, if no compromise could be reached in the initial text of the convention, it was mainly due to certain countries' interpretation of constitutional guarantees of free speech as a basis for legalising harmful and immoral information. The convention has since been supplemented by an additional protocol[7] on this question.

The provision on child pornography seeks to strengthen protective measures for children, including their protection against sexual exploitation.

By more effectively circumscribing the use of computer systems in the commission of sexual offences against children, the convention also has a modernising effect on the related criminal law provisions governing child pornography and obscenity. The provision criminalises various aspects of the electronic production, possession and distribution of child pornography. Most states already criminalise the traditional production and physical distribution of child pornography but, with the ever-increasing use of the Internet as the primary means of trading such material, it was strongly felt that specific provisions are essential to combat this new form of sexual exploitation and endangerment of children. Drafters of the convention shared the widely held belief that material and online practices involving child pornography, such as the exchange of ideas, fantasies and advice among paedophiles, could play a role in supporting, encouraging or facilitating real sexual offences against children.

Offences involving the infringement of intellectual property and related rights

The fourth category of offences involves the infringement of copyright and related rights through computer networks; for example through the large-scale distribution of illegal copies of work protected by intellectual property rights. In a way, this category is also linked to content, but content that is legal and protected. Such infringements of intellectual property rights, in particular of copyright, are among the most commonly committed offences on the Internet, causing concern both to copyright-holders and those who work professionally with computer networks. The reproduction and dissemination on the Internet of protected work, without the approval of the copyright-holder, is not only frequent but also affects a range of protected work including literary, photographic, musical, audiovisual and other creations. The ease with which unauthorised copies may be made through digital technology and the scale of reproduction and dissemination in the context of electronic networks made the drafters of the convention realise that it was necessary to include provisions on criminal law sanctions and enhance international cooperation in this field. Contracting states will be obliged to criminalise wilful infringements of copyright and related rights, sometimes referred to as 'neighbouring rights', arising from the agreements listed in the relevant provision of the convention (e.g. TRIPS and WIPO Copyright treaty), when such infringements have been committed by means of a computer system and on a commercial scale.

Procedural powers

The procedural part of the convention, based to a large extent on previous work on the subject by the Council of Europe (Recommendation No. R (95) 13 concerning problems of criminal procedure law connected with information technology), supplements the first part on substantive criminal law provisions. The procedural law provisions seek to ensure that law enforcement is able to cope with computer crime and reflect the recognition that, not only must substantive criminal law keep abreast of the new computer abuses, but so must criminal procedural law and investigative techniques. Equally, safeguards should be adapted or developed to keep abreast of the new technological environment and new procedural powers.

The procedural law of many countries still makes no allowance for the difficulties which law enforcement agencies encounter in applying to the virtual world investigative means designed for the physical, tangible world. Moreover, gathering, preserving and presenting reliable electronic evidence to the courts is a fairly new procedure and, in the absence of clear rules applicable to networks, this may well become a major obstacle in criminal investigations at both national and international level since the proof of a computer crime is very often electronic (e.g. digital images, viruses or codes). The convention therefore seeks to establish common rules concerning procedural powers, either by adapting some traditional procedural measures, such as search and seizure, to the new technological environment or by creating new measures, such as expedited preservation of data, to ensure that traditional measures of collection, such as search and seizure, remain effective in the volatile technological environment. As data in the new technological environment is not always static, but may be flowing in the process of communication, other traditional collection procedures relevant to telecommunications, such as real-time collection of traffic data and interception of content data, have also been included in the convention to permit the collection of electronic data that is in the process of communication.

The use of these procedures will make it possible to find and gather electronic evidence, whether it is related to the offences set out in the convention (e.g. child pornography) or to other offences (e.g. money laundering). The procedural-law section of the convention was made broader in its scope than the substantive-law section: for example, it will be possible to use the different types of investigative powers in any case where an offence is committed by means of a computer system or in which the evidence is electronic, even if the underlying offence is not defined in the convention.

The text concerns only specific criminal investigations and cannot be used, as some had suggested, to set up a widespread 'Orwellian' system of electronic surveillance. Undeniably, the convention will make it possible to seize data, or to oblige the person who possesses the data in question to disclose it, or to preserve data for the purposes of investigation, but the convention does not require and cannot justify the surveillance of personal communications or contacts by either service providers or law enforcement agencies, unless there is an official criminal investigation. All these provisions aim at permitting the obtaining or collection of data for the purpose of specific criminal investigations or proceedings. Drafters of the convention discussed whether it should impose an obligation on service providers to routinely collect and retain traffic data for a certain fixed period, but eventually did not include any such obligation due to lack of consensus.

In addition, drafters of the convention have included a large number of procedural guarantees, which are designed to prevent any abuse of the procedures that the convention defines. First of all, the text spells out that the introduction, implementation and application of the powers and procedures set out in the convention will be subject to the conditions and safeguards provided for by the domestic law of each party, having regard to the need for adequate human rights protection, especially as defined in the relevant international instruments (in particular the European Convention on Human Rights and the International Covenant on Civil and Political Rights). It also advocates that, before applying the measures envisaged, future contracting states should ensure that these are proportional to the nature of and circumstances surrounding the offence under investigation. Finally, the text stipulates, with regard to each procedure, that the relevant domestic conditions and safeguards must also be applied; contracting states will therefore be required to apply existing safeguards to investigations; for example making them conditional on authorisation from a judge or a senior government official (e.g. a minister), depending on the country concerned. It should also be realised that it would have been impossible to harmonise these procedural safeguards, if only at European level. However, the safeguards do exist in the domestic law of member states and are supposed to provide a similar level of human rights protection throughout the continent.

The convention deals with the following powers:

- Expedited preservation of stored computer data
- Expedited preservation and partial disclosure of traffic data
- Production order
- Search of computer systems
- Seizure of stored computer data

- Real-time collection of traffic data
- Interception of content data.

The powers of *expedited preservation of stored computer data* and *expedited preservation and partial disclosure of traffic data* are closely linked. Both apply to stored data that has already been collected and retained by data-holders such as service providers. Neither applies to the real-time collection of future traffic data or to real-time access to the content of communications. Nor do they mandate the collection and retention of all, or even some, data collected by a service provider or other entity in the course of its activities. The two preservation powers apply to computer data that 'has been stored by means of a computer system', which presupposes that the data already exists, has already been collected and is stored. The data in question may be illegal material (child pornography) or evidence of a crime (computer communications or transaction logs of a hacker). Determining the source or destination of these past communications can assist in identifying the perpetrators. To trace these communications so as to determine their source or destination, traffic data regarding them is required.

Both powers enable law enforcement to order or similarly obtain the expeditious preservation of specified computer data: the first preservation power is applicable when the data sought is likely to be particularly vulnerable to loss or modification but the custodian of the data is trustworthy, such as a reputable business, and the integrity of the data can be secured more quickly by means of an order to preserve it. For legitimate businesses, a preservation order may also be less disruptive to its normal activities and reputation than the execution of a search and seizure of its premises. This power does not mean that law enforcement has access to any of the data preserved: it only means that existing data will not be deleted until its disclosure is obtained. The second preservation power enables law enforcement to trace a communication back to its source, in particular where multiple providers were involved in its transmission, by obliging the data-holder to preserve and expeditiously disclose *some* traffic data so as to enable the identification of other service providers that were involved in the transmission of specified communications under investigation.

The power of issuing a *production order* enables authorities to compel a person in the territory of a state to provide specified stored computer data, or a service provider offering its services in the territory of the party to submit subscriber information. The data in question must be stored existing data, and does not include data that has not yet come into existence such as traffic data or content data related to future communications. Instead of requiring states to apply systematically coercive measures in relation to third parties, such as the search and seizure of data, it is essential that states have within their domestic law alternative investigative powers that provide a less intrusive means of obtaining information relevant to criminal investigations. This procedural mechanism will be particularly beneficial to third-party custodians of data such as ISPs, who are often prepared to assist law enforcement officials by providing data under their control, but who require an appropriate legal basis to release the data, thereby relieving them of any contractual or other liability for disclosing the data. The production order refers to computer data or subscriber information that is in the possession or control of a person or a service provider, and may only be imposed on persons in the territory of the contracting state, or on service providers offering their services in that territory.

The powers relating to the *search of computer systems* and the *seizure of stored computer data* are the computer equivalent of traditional search and seizure provisions in the tangible environment. With respect to the search for evidence, in particular computer data, in the new technological environment, many of the characteristics of a traditional search remain. For example, the gathering of data occurs during the period of the search and in respect of data that exists at that time. The preconditions for obtaining legal authority to undertake a search and the degree of belief required for obtaining legal authorisation to search are the same. But there are certain differences: first, the data is in intangible form; second, while the data may be read with the use of computer equipment, it cannot be seized and taken away in the same way as a paper record can; third, due to the connectivity of computer systems, data may not be stored in the particular computer that is searched, but such data may be readily accessible to that system through communication systems such as the Internet.

The *computer search power* in the convention is designed to ensure that data can be accessed and searched by the relevant competent authorities; search may concern data contained either within a computer system or part of it (such as a connected data storage device) or on an independent data storage medium (such as a CD-ROM or diskette). The power to *seize stored computer data* enables the authorities to seize or similarly secure computer data that has been searched or similarly accessed under the search power. It includes the power to seize computer hardware and computer data storage media. In certain cases, for instance when data is stored in unique operating systems such that it cannot be copied, it is unavoidable that the data carrier as a whole has to be seized. In the context of the convention, 'seize' means to take away the physical medium, on which data or information is recorded, or to make and retain a copy of the data or information. It also implies the use or seizure of programs needed to access the data being seized. Since the measures relate to stored (intangible) data, additional measures will be required to secure the data, for example 'maintain the integrity of the data' (i.e. maintain the 'chain of custody' of the data — the data copied or removed will be retained in the state in which it was found at the time of the seizure and remain unchanged during the time of criminal proceedings) or 'render inaccessible or remove those computer data in the accessed computer system'.

The most intrusive powers provided for in the convention are the *real-time collection of traffic data* and the *real-time interception of content data*. Both powers must be associated with specified communications transmitted by a computer system. Both powers enable the real-time collection or real-time interception of data by competent authorities or by service providers.

With the convergence of telecommunication and information technologies, the distinction between telecommunications and computer communications, as well as between their infrastructures, is becoming blurred. Thus the definition of 'computer system' in the convention does not restrict the manner in which the devices or group of devices may be interconnected. These interception powers therefore also apply to communications transmitted by means of any computer system, which could include transmission of the communication through telecommunication networks before it is received by another computer system. But the type of data that can be collected (or ordered to be collected) is of two different types: the first power concerns traffic data, the second content data. 'Traffic data' is defined to mean any computer data relating to a communication made by means of a computer system which was generated by the computer system and which formed a part in the chain of communication, indicating the communication's origin, destination, path or route, time, date, size and duration or the type of service. 'Content data' is not defined in the convention but refers to the communication content of the communication; that is, the meaning or purport of the communication, or the message or information being conveyed (other than traffic data).

Given the intrusive nature of real-time interception of content data, national laws often prescribe that it is only available in relation to the investigation of serious offences or categories of serious offences. Therefore, with respect to the interception of content data, the convention specifically provides that contracting states are only required to establish the measures 'in relation to a range of serious offences to be determined by domestic law'. However, the drafters were unable to agree on any obligation for states to include, as an exception, computer crimes in the national list of 'serious,' that is interceptable, offences. Thus the scope of application of this provision is to a large extent left to national discretion.

International cooperation

This part of the convention, in the eyes of many, is the most important because it makes it possible to implement the rapid and effective state-to-state cooperation required in computer crime or computer-related crime investigations and prosecutions. Where electronic evidence — which is very volatile by nature — is concerned, it is essential that law enforcement agencies are able to carry out investigations on behalf of other states and pass on the information with greater speed. In addition to traditional forms of international cooperation on crime (MLA and extradition), the convention stipulates that contracting states should apply the procedures set out in the procedural part of the convention as new forms of MLA (e.g. the seizure or preservation of data on behalf of another contracting state). Clearly, one of the fundamental objectives of the convention is to enable the application of common procedural powers specific to computer crime at an international level, through a range of cooperation channels, including existing MLA arrangements and also new avenues (the 24/7 network).

The convention makes clear that international cooperation is to be provided between contracting states 'to the widest extent possible'. The principle requires contracting states to provide extensive cooperation to each other, and to minimise impediments to the smooth and rapid flow of information and evidence internationally. The general scope of the obligation to cooperate stems from that of the procedural powers defined by the treaty: cooperation is to be provided in relation to the offences established by it, as well as to criminal offences related to computer systems and data and to the collection of evidence in electronic form of a criminal offence. This means that the convention is applicable either where the crime is committed by use of a computer system, or where an ordinary crime not committed by use of a computer system (e.g. a murder) involves electronic evidence.

The convention also creates the legal basis for an international computer crime-specific assistance network, a network (also referred to as the '24/7 network') of national contact points permanently and continuously available. As has been previously discussed, the effective prosecution of crimes committed by use of computer systems and the effective collection of evidence in electronic form requires very rapid response. Moreover, with a few keystrokes, action may be taken in one part of the world that instantly has consequences many thousands of kilometres and many time zones away. For this reason, existing police cooperation and MLA modalities require supplementary channels to address the challenges of the computer age effectively. The channel established by the convention is based on experience gained from an already functioning network created under the auspices of the G8 group of nations. Under the convention, each party has the obligation to designate a point of contact available 24 hours a day, seven days a week to ensure immediate assistance in investigations and proceedings within the scope of the convention. The establishment of this network is among the most important means provided by the convention of ensuring that contracting states can respond effectively to the law enforcement challenges posed by computer crime. This network will not replace but supplement the more traditional channels of cooperation.

Each national 24/7 point of contact is to either facilitate or directly carry out assistance, including the provision of technical advice, preservation of data, collection of evidence, the giving of legal information, and locating of suspects. Contracting states can determine where to locate the point of contact within their law enforcement structure, as the convention allows for flexibility in this regard: some may wish to house the 24/7 contact within the central authority for MLA; some may believe that the best location is with a police unit specialising in fighting computer crime Since the 24/7 contact is to provide both technical advice for stopping or tracing an attack, as well as such international cooperation duties as the locating of suspects, there is no one correct answer, and it is anticipated that the structure of the network will evolve over time. Among critical tasks to be carried out by the 24/7 contact, the convention authorises the ability to facilitate the rapid execution of measures if the 24/7 contact does not carry them out directly itself. For example, if a party's 24/7 contact is part of a police unit, it must have the ability to coordinate expeditiously with other relevant components within its government, such as the central authority for international extradition or MLA, so that appropriate action may be taken at any hour of the day or night. Moreover, 24/7 contacts must have proper equipment and must be able to communicate fast with other members of the network. Up-to-date telephone, fax and computer equipment will be essential to the smooth operation of the network, and other forms of communication and analytical equipment will need to become part of the system as technology advances. The convention also requires that personnel participating as part of a national team for the network must be properly trained in computer crime or computer-related crime and in how to respond to it effectively.

Finally, it has to be noted with respect to international cooperation that there are no plans, at this stage, for genuine cross-border investigations, such as cross-border searches into computer systems, because the negotiating states were unable to agree on such arrangements.

Conclusion

The Council of Europe's Convention on Cyber-crime is by no means a perfect instrument yet it is a very welcome pioneer. While it currently offers states a legal framework that reflects international best practice, it is also based on the understanding that, as information and communication technology evolves, it will need to adapt to new types of misuse. At the time of its drafting, consensus emerged between the drafters on the inclusion of the offences described above, but not on others. For example, identity theft, spamming, or terrorist threats were not regarded as major issues that should be included in the convention, even though contracting states may, by means of a review mechanism foreseen by the text, conclude one day that they need to.

Similarly, the convention does not always go as far as it could in furthering cross-border investigations. For example, trans-border network search has not been included because of serious concerns about sovereignty. Again, the contracting states may one day override this principle for the sake of effectiveness and speed.

What now matters is that countries that are entitled to ratify it do so as a matter of priority. Arguably, computer crime will not stop at the borders of future contracting states, and other states will also need to update their legal systems and enhance cooperation.

Ideally, the Council of Europe Convention should become a global instrument, reaching all nations that are willing and capable of joining the original group of contracting states, provided that they share the same objectives, put in place similar legal regimes and offer similar guarantees for human rights.

Attractive as global coverage may seem, however, it might just be too early for the Convention on Cyber-crime to embrace this universal dimension. The world may not be ready for it.

16

Human Security and Cyber-Security: Operationalising a Policy Framework

Julie Shannon and Nick Thomas

> Put bluntly, our accepted definition of the limits of national security as coinciding with national borders is obsolete.[1]
>
> The challenges of cyber-crime are enormous and immediate, and no agency or nation can realistically expect to deal with the problem alone. Thus, the role for ... law enforcement needs to be linked within the context of the actions of other justice sector partners, international initiatives, and new relationships with private industries to mutually protect critical infrastructure, manage demand, and keep our communities safe.[2]

The Internet is now truly a worldwide web. In almost every country, evidence of Internet penetration can be found. In mid-1981, there were just 231 Internet hosts, mostly located within the United States and Europe with a high proportion tied to government or academic institutions. By mid-2002, the number of hosts had exceeded 162 million, and could be found in every country.[3] Similarly in 1993, there were just 50 websites, again primarily in the United States. By 2000, over 350 million sites were registered.[4] This increase is particularly significant for the Asia-Pacific region: by 2004, nearly 236 million people in the region will have access to the Internet, compared with 221 million in Europe and 196 million in the United States.[5] As broadband penetration expands and ever more powerful computers and operating systems are developed, these numbers will only increase faster.

With this dependence has come a greater degree of openness. The need by different individuals and groups to exchange information quickly requires infrastructure that ultimately facilitates rather than restricts data flows. However, as has been demonstrated by the growing number of viruses, worms and Trojan horses, this cyber-structure can be used for ill as well as good. These attacks are inadvertently assisted by the lack of effective transnational regulatory or security structures. Where regulatory or security regimes have been emplaced, they tend to be specific to the site or nation-state. This creates problems for domestic law that is made even more difficult when cyber-attacks emanate from or traverse additional jurisdictions.

Human security emerged in the mid-1990s as an alternative to traditional (realist) conceptions of security, which were viewed as lacking in their ability to properly explain strategic situations, their causes and possible cures. Rather than view security as being solely the province of the state, human security diminishes the sovereignty of states. It posits that security is shared between the state, market and society, each of which has the capacity to provide security and to generate insecurity. To appropriately secure the state, therefore, requires a coalition of forces able to address security concerns outside the traditional state ambit.

However, this new form of security analysis has largely focused on insecurity in the real world, such as economic or food insecurity. This chapter argues that the forms that a cyber-attack may take and the mechanisms required to address it are similar in structure to mainstream human security issues. Accordingly, the implementation of human security models on cyber-security problems would lead to a better understanding of the problems as well as more appropriate methods of resolution.

Human Security: Origins and Relevance

The end of the Cold War questioned the underlying nature of what it meant to be secure. In both policy and academic realms, calls were made for a more inclusive model of security to be generated — one that could embrace the complexity of the new world order. In 1994, the United Nations published its Human Development Report entitled *New Dimensions of Human Security*. The report posited that security issues should be targeted at the level of the individual rather than the state. Although placed in a developmental context, the report was quickly adopted by international relations scholars as a model for understanding the post-Cold War security environment — one that could cope with multidimensional threats that did not emanate from a state nor were necessarily directed against state interests but which nonetheless detracted from the security of a state.

The new threats that human security addresses emanate, in part, from the globalisation of world affairs. Within this new international order, time and space have become compressed. Borders are no longer considered to be absolute delineations of a state's sovereignty and security. An event in one part of the world can have an effect in other, not necessarily geographically contiguous, areas.

This is especially true for cyber issues. Cyberspace does not merely compress time and space, it effectively unifies them. The speed of data transmission, and access to the target network, are the only limiting factors for cyber-attacks. Attacks against government systems, corporate networks or individuals can be launched from anywhere in the world. To make system protection and responses more difficult, cyber-attacks can be even more diffuse than those in the real world. The high interoperability of most computer systems means that system security is not limited to a single system under local control but can be made vulnerable by flaws in partner systems, or their partners' systems. Further, attacks can go through multiple countries, with any results redirected towards third-party countries.

This new model places a greater emphasis on proactive rather than reactive security. In essence, human security is a self-interested form of security. If security issues are interrelated and their sum is global, then the loss of security in one sector in one part of the world can be seen as detracting from the security of another part. Thus it is in all parties' interests to provide assistance to alleviate insecurity wherever it occurs, and to prevent such threats from reoccurring. Hence the development and operation of better security systems can discourage and prevent cyber-threats.

The holistic nature of human security requires a coalitional response to emergent and realised threats, whether they arise at the global, state or sub-state levels. In this model the role of the private sector and social organisations becomes critical to threat resolution. Corporations with knowledge of cyber-security are needed to complement government efforts. Similarly, social organisations such as citizens' groups or think-tanks allow for both the focused application of specialised capacities as well as the dissemination of information. In a negative sense, these two tiers can also be the origin of cyber-security threats — an aspect of globalisation that makes securing the state that much more difficult.

To assess the validity of the human security model to the problem of cyber-security we present and analyse a range of cyber-security case studies relating to threats at the global, state and sub-state levels. Following this, new forms of cyber-threats are offered and their implications examined.[6]

Cyber-security case studies

> Information technologies have revolutionised virtually every aspect of life in the past decade, affecting our Nation in ways as diverse as how business is transacted, to how our government functions, to the manner in which the military responds to crisis. Importantly, every critical infrastructure on which our security, our economy, and our way of life depend is linked to or reliant on the information infrastructure.[7]

From a security viewpoint the Internet is fundamentally flawed. It was designed to be an open system, with self-regulation by users and behaviour governed by trust. It was a utopian vision that did not take into account manipulation, exploitation or aggression. Thus what is required in addressing cyber-threats is a complete reconceptualisation of the Internet and its uses. Although it should not be assumed that cyberspace is an inherently harmful environment, care must now be exercised when linking new or existing systems to the Internet.

Reconciling the old vision with the new realities is the key challenge facing policymakers. Appropriate policies for combating the myriad cyber-security problems now emerging are often lacking because actors have yet to properly understand the security environment in which they are now placed. Moreover, the boundaries of cyberspace are not conterminous with the boundaries of the real world, and this makes the responsibilities for policy oversight difficult.

Nonetheless, some common issues have emerged, and the following case studies are an attempt to highlight some of them. The case studies are considered in terms of actors and their impact at the global, state and sub-state level. Security issues such as computer viruses pose entirely new security dilemmas and cannot be analysed within the framework of national sovereignty. Such concerns are discussed in the section on new threats. The implications of these case studies for policymakers will be analysed and possible frameworks for resolution suggested in the section following.

The global level

Programmes for developing national cyber-security systems are receiving increased military attention. It is estimated that more than 30 nations have developed aggressive computer-warfare programmes.[8] Nation-states such as Russia, China, Taiwan and the United States have openly announced investment in national programmes of asymmetric warfare, which include both offensive and defensive cyber-warfare tactics. These programmes essentially allow one state to launch a 'virtual' attack against another without the types of real-world engagement that usually characterise conflicts. The 'Moonlight Maze' and 'Solar Sunrise' cases draw attention to state-sponsored theft and espionage in cyberspace as well as to the effectiveness and use of legal and policy frameworks to manage these breaches of national security. In addition, new asymmetric threats to state security, recently highlighted by the events of 11 September, require nation-states to treat non-state organisations (NSOs) with offensive capacities effectively as equals. In the context of cyber-security, these threats involve NSOs using the Internet to acquire information and then launching an attack via cyberspace connections.

Moonlight Maze

> The Moonlight Maze case constitutes the largest apparent intrusion of Department of Defense networks to date. Beginning in 1998, hackers stole thousands of files containing technical research, contracts, encryption techniques, and unclassified but essential data relating to the Pentagon's war-planning systems. The Department of Energy, NASA, military contractors and military-linked civilian universities were also targeted.[9] Attacks appeared to come from the Russian Academy of Sciences, a government-supported academy with reported ties to Russian intelligence, which said the numbers were inoperative and denied any prior knowledge of the attacks.[10]

Official response to the Moonlight Maze attacks was disjointed and cooperation was slow to evolve among various US agencies, corporations and foreign governments. A 1998 presidential order made the FBI's National Infrastructure Protection Center the 'focal point' for collecting threat-related data. However, Justice Department approval is needed for passing this information to the president's cyber-security adviser. Meanwhile, the White House budget office instructed agencies to report Internet attacks to the General Services Administration.[11]

Solar Sunrise

> Solar Sunrise was a series of DoD computer network attacks that occurred from 1 to 26 February 1998. DoD unclassified networked computers were attacked using a well-known operating system vulnerability. At least 11 attacks followed the same profile on Air Force, Navy, and Marine Corps computers worldwide. Attackers obtained system privileges used to read

> password files, delete files and create 'back doors' for subsequent re-entry.[12] Attacks were widespread and appeared to come from sites in Israel, the United Arab Emirates, France, Taiwan, and Germany. Investigation finally led to one Israeli and two American teenagers. The Israeli National Police, working with US authorities, arrested Ehud Tenenbaum and charged him with illegally accessing US and Israeli government computers. The two American teenagers were charged and tried in a juvenile court.[13]

Alongside Moonlight Maze, Solar Sunrise brought attention to the fact that such intrusions pose real threats to national security. The attacks were widespread, systematic, and showed a pattern that indicated they might be preparation for a coordinated attack on the Defense Information Infrastructure. At the time, escalating tensions between the United States, Iraq and the United Nations caused concern that the breaches in security could be used to disrupt the flow of military information. As a result, the intrusion investigation was one of the largest ever conducted in the United States.[14] A standing Joint Task Force for Computer Network Defense was created, coordinated by the National Infrastructure Protection Centre. International cooperation was also effective, with strong cooperation between the US Department of Justice and the Israeli Ministry of Justice.[15]

Issues

These cases demonstrate how coordination among multiple government agencies is a crucial factor in developing a coherent approach to cyber-security. Moonlight Maze showed just how ill-equipped US federal agencies were for coordinating a response to this threat, with overlapping areas of responsibility. The lack of an immediate and harmonised response in this case should be understood not only from the newness of the threat but also from the mistrust between different federal agencies. This is not a problem exclusive to the United States, but occurs between bureaucratic departments and agencies in all states, at national as well as sub-state levels. As Solar Sunrise showed, cooperation can be more effective where there are clear lines of communication between the agencies and departments involved, supported by strong political will.

In a strategic sense, such cases demonstrate that 'an understanding of the critical infrastructure's threat environment is barely in its infancy'.[16] The necessity for increased communication across civilian and military organisations also brings its own risks, including a greater susceptibility to intrusion into network infrastructures, to manipulation of information resources, or to network attack: 'The requirement to operate across multiple security levels that are interoperable not only across the military services, but also with our Allies and coalition partners, and with unclassified entities within industry, government, and academia provides many avenues for exploitation and attack.'[17]

Trust also remains a key stumbling block in developing international coordination at this level. As with other security and intelligence activities, the intelligence gathered by a nation-state can reveal its strengths and limitations. Within a small circle of allies, partial or full information can be disseminated and cooperation sought. However, when nation-states outside this trusted circle are approached, there is little cooperation or information-sharing. This problem highlights a key nexus between the real world and cyberspace. Where lines of communication and trust have already been established, it is possible for nation-states to extend their cooperation into cyberspace. But the existence of a cyber-threat does not, in and of itself, necessarily push states into effective cooperation. The further development of confidence-building measures in both the real world and cyberspace is therefore crucial.

These types of cyber-attack raise new issues for international cooperation and legal recourse to action. The successful prosecution in the case of Solar Sunrise was in part due to the availability of clear evidence and existing avenues of cooperation between the governments. In contrast, the Moonlight Maze intrusions were 'distributed coordinated attacks', a style of penetration that is particularly effective at compromising existing defences — making it difficult for the victim's intrusion software to know that it is under attack as well as disguising the identity of the attacker. The nature and regularity of the attacks caused FBI officials to suggest that if not state-sponsored, then the attacks may at least have been state-allowed.[18] Due to the complex legal implications of this distinction, US officials claim the attacks were tracked only passively. Legal debate surrounds whether recourse to action such as a 'hack back', which has the potential to cripple intruder capabilities, could be construed as a possible transnational use of force.[19]

China and Russia have both expressed interest in some type of international controls on preventing such attacks. In the United Nations, the Russian Government has proposed the development of an international legal regime to combat information crime and terrorism. However, as the proposal was made through the UN General Assembly's First Committee, with a charter of disarmament rather than counter-terrorism, the action may have been directed towards curbing state-sponsored information warfare tactics, rather than targeting individual criminals.[20] Despite this, the UN General Assembly Resolution (53/70) on 'Developments in Information and Telecommunications in the Context of International Security' represents the beginnings of formal multilateral cooperation in this area.[21] There have been meetings subsequent to this resolution but no treaty has yet been agreed upon.[22]

While the previous focus of most nation-states was on limiting the capacity of other nation-states in their information-gathering or information-warfare capacities, the rise of organisations able and willing to use cyberspace to carry out real-world attacks on distant targets is a relatively new threat. Even before 11 September, the United States had begun to give serious attention to potential cyber-attacks on crucial infrastructure by other states or hostile groups. Part of the response has been the creation of the National Infrastructure Protection Council, a joint partnership between federal agencies and private industry, to prevent potential cyber-threats to national infrastructure. These infrastructures include telecommunications, energy, transportation, banking and finance, emergency services and government operations.

The role of state as either an aggressor or as a unitary defensive unit is challenged by cyber-security. As the state is necessarily broken down into components such as individuals and interest groups, it must look at organisations deemed threatening to security within the national borders. However, curtailing activities deemed threatening to national security can also negatively impact on individuals and civil society organisations within the state. As demonstrated by recent accounts of cyber-attacks by the Chinese government, this may take the form of attacks on organisations through espionage or the sending of viruses that can disrupt or destroy systems. In this case, organised virus attacks and evidence of hacking using Trojan horse programs on overseas-based dissident groups were traced to regional government offices in Mainland China.[23]

The primary weakness shown in these case studies is that the efforts to secure cyberspace at the global level has been reactive rather than proactive. Yet even when the threat has been identified, it has proved difficult to address it effectively. This seems to prevail even when there is an ongoing threat from an established protagonist. The studies above demonstrate the work still needed in the policy arena for developing an effective, proactive global strategy that can secure cyberspace.

State level

At the level of the state, the need for business and government to work together to provide regulatory mechanisms for cyber-crime is paramount. For crimes such as fraud and corporate data theft, cooperation often needs simply to be extended to cyberspace issues. Certain new forms of crime, such as data trawling, require additional types of legislation. Moreover, the new reaches of cyber-crime have made apparent a need for this cooperation to extend to areas of security that are traditionally the purview of the state. With national critical infrastructure, now as often handled by the private sector as by the state, the susceptibility of current security mechanisms to interference by cyber-criminals also requires government and business to work in tandem.

The Boden case

> In April 2000, the Maroochydore District Court in Australia convicted Vitek Boden of 30 counts of hacking into the computer-controlled sewerage system of the local council and deliberately releasing hundreds of thousands of litres of raw sewerage [*sic*] into public waterways. To sabotage the system, he set the software on his laptop to identify itself as 'pumping station 4', then suppressed all the alarms. During the intrusions, Boden had command of 300 supervisory control and data acquisition nodes governing sewage and drinking water. He was sentenced for 12 months for wilfully causing serious environmental harm, and also received a two-year sentence for several computer hacking and theft related charges.[24]

A subsequent call was made in Australia to develop programmes to study threats to critical infrastructure and its vulnerabilities. The Business-Government Task Force on Critical Infrastructure has now recommended the creation of a network among key public and private sector organisations to improve systematic and strategic responses to national infrastructure security and to examine the legislative framework for sharing relevant information.[25]

Online trading fraud in Korea

In 2002, South Korean police investigated a fraud that saw hackers break through a bank's security system to sell 5 million shares they did not own. Police later said they were attempting to discover how a hacker broke through firewalls at Daewoo Securities to sell the shares in Internet network provider Delta Information and Communications. The hacker disappeared, leaving Daewoo to settle the transaction. The hacker is believed to have stolen the password for an account held by Hyundai Investment Trust Management to undertake the 25.9 billion won scam.[26]

The orders for the Delta shares were traced to an online game room in Changchon-dong in western Seoul and the suspect was a former employee at a Daewoo Securities branch in Seoul.[27] Large South Korean investors stopped trading stocks online in response to the fraud, and share prices for Delta plunged. Pending an investigation, the regulatory Financial Supervisory Commission banned new orders and withdrawals at 39 accounts at 13 securities firms.

Issues

Cyber-security issues within the state further demonstrate the difficulty of confining cyber-crime to traditional security models. In a world with increasingly fewer borders, the impact of one actor on a range of others beyond the state is greater. The Boden case highlights the impact an individual may have on internal state security. In the Delta fraud, a state-based crime by an individual had a global impact on the nature of financial regulation. Potential crimes within the corporate sector may operate and be prosecuted at state level, but involve investment and backing from companies based overseas.

Statistics on the security of companies operating within the state begs for coordinated action among these varying actors. In the United States, the 2002 Computer Crime and Security Survey found that 90% of respondents had detected computer security breaches within the previous 12 months. The respondents were mainly large corporations and government agencies, including those concerned with critical infrastructure. Eighty per cent of respondents admitted financial loss as a result of computer security breaches.[28]

The need to ensure that technology companies give greater attention to security in the development of their products was highlighted by the Boden case. It is one of the few examples in which a digital control system has been used to deliberately cause harm. As nearly identical systems run in oil and gas utilities and many manufacturing plants, it demonstrates how vulnerable some sectors of a nation-state's critical infrastructure can be. The types of digital controls were not designed with public access in mind, and often lack even rudimentary security. Worryingly for policymakers, most of these systems are now connected to the Internet. Much of the technical information required to penetrate these systems is widely discussed in the public forums of the affected industries, and specialists note that the security flaws are well known to potential attackers. Indeed, in a recent international survey of Internet security, 70% of power and energy companies under review suffered at least one severe attack during the first six months of 2002.[29]

Despite this, trust between government and the private sector is a major obstacle in addressing security flaws. Public companies worry about the loss of customer confidence and the legal liability to shareholders or security vendors when they report security violations. The FBI has attempted to identify the most dangerous points of vulnerability in 5700 companies deemed essential to national security, but is facing considerable reticence within an industry at least equally concerned with access to information, privacy and regulation issues. Balancing these competing concerns is an ongoing issue and one where the law is still being developed.

Internet content liability and regulation issues are being addressed in the United States and Europe through a mix of direct legislation, industry self-regulation and third-party interventions.[30] It is likely that governments outside the EU will begin drawing up privacy laws in the next three to five years. While many businesses may still be state-based, the potential to create cyber-havens in states without adequate legislation means that this form of borderless crime must also be addressed at the regional level. The Asia-Pacific region has yet to develop these laws and it has been recommended that an industry-developed privacy code should be used in the interim. Given estimates that the e-business market in the Asia-Pacific will reach US$910 billion by 2004,[31] security of transactions must be addressed.

Recent surveys in Japan and South Korea suggest that the degree of distrust of the way Asian websites handle privacy is greater than the distrust in the United States and Europe. Current figures released for the Asian region suggest that as many as one in ten online consumer transactions may involve fraud, with similar rates likely for business and government.[32] As a result, the Asia Pacific Internet Association commissioned a study to explore the viability of self-regulation, and to outline a model code as well as a possible mechanism for self-regulation. Key proposals included the voluntary labelling of websites under the Internet Content Rating Association rating scheme.[33] This would protect users and provide guidelines for business in the event of security breaches like fraud.

South Korea has the world's highest proportion of high-speed broadband Internet users, and consequently some of the highest rates of cyber-crime.[34] The necessity for a code of practice that would standardise the kind of action taken, for example, in the Delta shares fraud is paramount; in Korea the public key infrastructure system should already allow for secure trading. However, Daewoo and many other South Korean brokerages use outdated security systems for online trading. To manage the Delta fraud case, brokerage firms made agreements to temporarily ban cash withdrawals from accounts that traded Delta stock on a large scale.[35]

These case studies further demonstrate that the supervision of online commerce overlaps with concerns over privacy. The use of the Internet for commerce evidently requires a strict regulatory regime, but this should not be one that breaches the privacy of the individual. In the absence of legislation, voluntary codes of practice may be one interim method for securing cyberspace for business. This may include some protection for individuals using transactions online. How the use of personal data may impact on the security of the individual is discussed in the next section.

Sub-state level

The widespread use of the Internet not only opens new avenues for attacks to state infrastructure and the military, but also places the individual user at risk. The mistaken uploading of personal data by corporations or governments, breaches of individual privacy through computer surveillance, or censorship of web contents are but three examples of the many challenges facing individual users. Those who use cyberspace to commit offences also face greater risks. The following case studies highlight three of these challenges — privacy, censorship and law enforcement. We argue that technology-neutral legal frameworks need to be developed to protect civil and political rights online, while respecting domestic cultural and political liberties.

Singapore individual privacy breach

> In April 1999, a Singapore law student filed a police complaint after an anti-intrusion program she installed indicated that someone with an account in the Home Affairs Ministry had hacked into her computer. It was revealed that the internal-security agency had secretly scanned 200,000 computers to trace a virus. SingNet, the Internet service provider, acknowledged that it asked the Ministry's IT security unit to scan its customers' PCs for viruses without their consent. SingNet is owned by Singapore Telecom, which is in turn 80%-owned by the government. The request to conduct the scan was reportedly made after the 6 March arrest of two youths who had hacked into 17 SingNet accounts.[36]

SingNet claimed the scanning did not 'enter' any PCs or unveil any personal data and also stated that it found 900 PCs infected with Trojan horse viruses that allow hackers to enter computers via the Internet and take almost complete control.[37] Regardless, public outcry over the incident led to an official apology from SingNet. As a result, the Infocomm Development Authority of Singapore issued guidelines on 7 January 2000 regulating the scanning of computers by ISPs (see Chapter 7 by Chan and Leong).[38]

Filtering of Internet content

> A 2001 Council of Ministers Resolution prohibits users within the Kingdom of Saudi Arabia from publishing or accessing certain content on the Internet. All Web traffic is apparently forwarded through a central array of proxy servers in the government's Internet Services Unit. In a recent Harvard study concerning the scope and effectiveness of these filtering mechanisms, connections were made to the Internet through proxy servers in Saudi Arabia. Out of approximately 60 000 Web pages tested, the authors tracked 2038 blocked pages. Such pages contained information about religion, health, education, reference, humour, and entertainment.[39]

The survey explored the effectiveness of the filtering mechanisms as well as the nature of the blocked pages. The authors concluded that 'the Saudi government maintains an active interest in filtering non-sexually explicit Web content ...; that substantial amounts of non-sexually explicit Web content is, in fact, effectively inaccessible to most Saudi Arabians; and that much of this content consists of sites that are popular elsewhere in the world.'[40]

Issues

The interface between governments and their citizens is one of the most keenly contested spaces in the cyber-realm. At the heart of this issue is the question of how far governments can go in protecting their citizens: a question unlikely ever to gain universal understanding and agreement. What is required instead is a contractual benchmark for cyberspace behaviour within each state. It may not be possible to identify such a benchmark quantifiably, given the widely varying socio-political differences, but some qualifiable measurements can be inferred.

In the Singapore example, an action was undertaken by a government agency supposedly in the best interests of its citizens. However, when the action was made public, both the agency as well as the corporation that made the initial request (in this specific case, majority-owned by the Singapore government) apologised and ceased action. It can therefore be concluded that in this instance the government exceeded its mandate and infringed on the civil liberties of its people.

Censorship is a more difficult matter to determine. The most frequent form of censorship occurs when the government blocks a website. Approximately 59 nation-states restrict public access to information by blocking Internet sites.[41] The Saudi Arabia study demonstrated the limiting of information on issues like womens rights, health and sexuality, and indicates state concerns regarding the scope of personal freedoms. The government cites the Qur'an as a basis for its action and describes its task with filtering as 'preserv[ing] our Islamic values, filtering the Internet content to prevent the materials that contradict with our beliefs or may influence our culture'.[42] In China, Internet filtering mostly occurs around news sites and indicates concerns over political subversion.[43] China has blocked access to the search engines Google and Alta Vista, and routinely blocks news sites such as the BBC, National Public Radio and Amnesty International.[44] It has also concluded agreements with search engines such as Yahoo! not to post any information offensive to the Chinese government.[45]

In comparing these two examples, a potential difference can be seen. While both countries actively censor material deemed harmful, in the case of Saudi Arabia the policy emphasis is on the state's role in the security of the individual, whereas in the case of China the emphasis is on the individual's role in the security of the state. This difference is shown in the way sites are filtered by the two governments. Attempting to access a restricted site in Saudi Arabia results in an 'access denied' message appearing on screen, alongside information concerning the blocking policy and a request form for the government to reconsider its block on the site. Attempting to access a restricted site in China, however, results in a 'host not found' message, leaving the user uncertain as to the cause of failure for the connection. Key word filtering and discarding of e-mails containing key terms is also used by the Chinese authorities, but without informing its citizens as to exactly what the terms are and what words are in the lists.[46] As a result, in the first instance a user knows what has happened and at the very least has a limited opportunity for corrective action, but in the second instance the user is unable to take action as the actual cause of the 'host not found' message is deliberately left unclear.

The development and acceptance of filtering and rating systems has slowed due to the complexity of debate surrounding such vital issues as the suppression of speech and the use of filtering in public libraries. ASEAN met in 1996 to discuss collaboration on finding ways to control expression on the Internet. Members cited the need to preserve cultural values as the impetus for the meeting. However, no common stance was found; the Philippines was concerned with censoring child pornography, while Thai representatives argued for freedom of expression.[47] As cultural values differ greatly within ASEAN, it is unlikely there will be complete regional agreement on content and censorship. Acknowledging these differences, the International Telecommunications Union for Asia and the Pacific argued, 'the issue is not regulating Internet content *per se*, but protecting vulnerable groups with technical apparatus or regulatory measures'.[48]

More broadly within Asian countries, there is a huge disparity in how governments penalise inappropriate use of the Internet. In China, violations of its regulations can lead to the death penalty or imprisonment for relatively minor actions.[49] In mid-October 2003, Luo Yongzhong was imprisoned for three years by the Changchun intermediate court in Jilin province for eight anti-government postings in chatrooms.[50] Since the introduction of the Internet in 1997, Vietnamese authorities have strictly controlled access to certain sites, following a rationale and regulatory system similar to that used in China.[51] In another case in late 2003, Vietnamese journalist and cyber-dissident Nguyen Vu Binh was sentenced to seven years' jail for espionage after criticising Viet Nam–China border accords, which were then e-mailed to other domestic groups as well as to lobby groups overseas.[52] In Myanmar, unauthorised use of a computer or a modem earns users up to 15 years in jail.[53]

The unfamiliarity of cyberspace can distort both threat perceptions and legislative remedies. Legislators and law enforcement officials have developed two options for protecting cyberspace and those who use it. The first option is to develop separate legislation for cyber-crimes, essentially creating a parallel legal system for these matters. The second option is to extend existing legislative safeguards to cover cyber-crimes.[54] On balance it can be argued that the second option is more proper as it does not privilege the role cyberspace might play in the commissioning of a criminal act.

In Asia, similar difficulties have arisen in enacting new legislation intended to protect citizens, but which in fact transgresses privacy and restricts usage. For example, South Korea introduced new legislation to tighten regulations and penalties on misuse and leakage of personal information in 2001. The section concerning an Internet Content Rating System raised so much public protest that the clauses related to the provision were deleted from the Act.[55] Civil rights groups protested that the rating system could be used by authorities both to raise censorship levels and to control information on the Internet.

These examples indicate the challenges facing states and their citizens in determining the appropriate use of cyberspace. In each of these examples a pre-existing issue has been complicated by the role of cyberspace. However, the development of cyberspace has also created a new class of threats, one for which existing modes of law enforcement and security regulation are, arguably, inadequate. This new threat from the use of cyberspace crosses all boundaries and has the potential to disrupt worldwide communications on an unprecedented scale.

New threats from cyberspace

The preceding sections on cyber-threats demonstrate the need to have coherent policies and operational systems at the global, state and sub-state levels. However, to a large extent the case studies we have drawn upon simply represent a new way of committing an established offence or attack. Where cyber-security events truly threaten to overwhelm or bypass national and / or global security infrastructure is when a multi-level threat emerges that requires coordination across a collection of states or international organisations and across a range of jurisdictions. The following two case studies highlight just such a transnational threat paradigm, one that requires a human security model to properly resolve.

The Chernobyl virus

> In 1999 the Chernobyl virus hit more than 650 000 computers in Asia. The virus disabled computers, destroyed programs and erased large amounts of stored information. Over 360 000 PCs were reportedly affected in China. The virus's Taiwanese creator, 24-year-old Chen Ing-hau, said he had wanted to cause mayhem on the mainland. Chernobyl also infected an estimated 250 000 PCs in South Korea. Chen was arrested but released without charge due to a lack of plaintiffs in Taiwan, where no infections were reported.[56]

Despite early alerts, countries lacking software protection in Asia and the Middle East were most badly affected by the Chernobyl virus. Government and financial institutions were particularly disrupted. In South Korea, government officials apologised for not taking more urgent action and estimated that US$250 million in damage had been caused.[57] China sustained damages of US$291 million and has subsequently begun to place more emphasis on the protection of computer networks. In the United States, private users without the level of anti-virus software protection used by businesses were the most affected.[58]

The 'I Love You' virus

> On the morning of 4 May 2000, the 'I Love You' virus began infecting computers around the globe. First detected in Asia, the virus quickly swept around the world in a wave of indiscriminate attacks on government and private sector networks. By the time the destructive pace of the virus had been slowed, it had infected nearly 60 million computers and caused billions of dollars in damage. Cooperation among law enforcement agencies around

the world led to the identification of the perpetrator, a computer science dropout in the Philippines. He was neither charged nor punished for his deeds because, at the time, the Philippine criminal code did not explicitly outlaw his actions.[59]

The widely publicised Love Bug virus caused an estimated US$8.7 billion in damage. Sent via an e-mail attachment that then mailed itself to other users in the victim's address book, it was the fastest-spreading computer virus ever created. The virus penetrated millions of computers, including those of the Pentagon, the CIA and the British Parliament. As a result of the incident, the Philippines immediately developed legislation addressing electronic commerce and computer hacking.

Issues

These two examples highlight the new potential danger posed by cyberspace. Whereas the previous case studies largely conformed to existing threats, but with a cyber-aspect, these threats go beyond such models to present a new threat typology. There are two aspects to this new threat type: magnitude and vector. These cases highlighted these aspects in different configurations. Each spanned the globe, affecting networks and individual computers connected to the three tiers. The threat vector also marks these cases as different from threats that have previously been charted. Both the origin and damage of the threats is largely virtual. In other words, they are aimed at the medium of interaction — cyberspace — rather than the theft of data, the destruction of property or the harming of an individual.

Virus transmitters are posing an increasingly serious threat to networks and systems worldwide. The economic impact of virus attacks on information systems around the world amounted to US$17.1 billion in 2000 — an increase from US$12 billion in 1999.[60] As viruses created by individuals or groups can impact on government, business and / or individuals anywhere, viruses can be seen as a truly transnational threat that can only be managed within a framework of human security.

Regional protection from virus attacks is sorely lacking; an estimated 25% of major companies in the Pacific Rim do not employ the use of virus protection on their systems.[61] Private users are further at risk, lacking the funds and access to technology for adequate system protection. Large companies have for many years installed firewalls, but comprehensive data security programs have only recently become commercially available to individual PC users. As a result, individual users are frequently the group most affected by virus attacks.[62]

In the absence of harmonisation of legal standards for the imposition of criminal liability for cyber-crimes, few virus perpetrators are found and prosecuted. Up to 500 new viruses are created and sent on Internet each month. The failure to prosecute the creators of the Chernobyl and Love Bug viruses demonstrates the need to develop domestic legislation that is harmonised to regional and / or global standards. Singapore, Malaysia, Japan, Korea, and the Philippines now have cyber-crime legislation, while many other countries in the region do not.[63] However, even in comparatively recently enacted legislation, attention is primarily given to the domestic situation rather the standards of other countries. This will only hinder future attempts at the transnational prevention and prosecution of cyber-crimes.

The 2002 Regional Preparatory Meeting in the Asia and Pacific Region for the World Telecommunication Development Conference placed a high priority on policy and regulatory issues and its implications in the information and communications technology sectors, and raised the question of how cyber-crime may be dealt with at the regional level.[64] The development and enforcement of regional regulatory frameworks faces considerable obstacles owing to technological disparities within and between regional states as well as different regulatory systems.

These issues show the potential threat that can be directed at cyberspace. If cyberspace is disrupted, then the essential medium through which the world functions breaks down. Viruses that use the lines of cyber-communications to spread at an exponential rate, or attacks that seek to prevent access to the Internet's core systems, present a new threat to security — not only because of the magnitude and vectors of such threats but also because threats at this level have not been previously witnessed, rendering policymakers ill-equipped to respond. Just as the existence of cyberspace has facilitated globalisation — reducing the concepts of time and space — the threats that emanate from this virtual realm can almost instantly affect the security of individuals, markets and nation-states everywhere. What these case studies have shown is the pressing need for the creation of proactive cyber and real-world policy regimes as well as an urgent need to develop mechanisms for rapid multi-jurisdictional responses to such threats.

Lessons Learned

The key lesson that emerges from the preceding case studies is the need for nation-states to develop appropriate safeguards to secure their critical infrastructure. There is a dearth of coordinated protection activities at the global, state, and sub-state levels. International organisations, nation-states and their core elements need to develop secure cyber-regimes across their areas of concern. Beyond such horizontal integration there is an urgent need to develop vertical coordination between these three tiers.

At the state and sub-state levels, this coordination is a matter of national policymaking. In the preceding analysis we have shown how much of the threat from, or effects of, a cyber-attack at these two tiers is still largely based on pre-existing patterns of criminal behaviour. Hence one of the surest methods of operationalising a coordinated national policy would be to recognise this, ensuring that existing legislative and security regimes 'are composed in a technologically neutral manner that would not exclude the prosecution of cyber criminals'.[65]

Transnational cyber-regimes offer one model for enacting policies to prevent sources of insecurity that have extended beyond a state's borders. Further, a range of possible alternative models have been developed by other groups, which also address transnational threats — such as that created by the UN Palermo Convention against Transnational Organised Crime or the work of the Financial Action Task Force. In both cases, nation-states are obliged to develop similar legislative and policy frameworks to combat transnational threats.

Conclusion

Human security is a new understanding of what it means to be secure. Rather than privileging the state as the sole holder of sovereignty, human security suggests that sovereignty is divided between the core elements of the nation-state — broadly categorised as the state, market and society. If sovereignty is so divided then, in a positive sense, it follows that the security of the nation-state is dependent on all of these elements being secure. In a negative sense, it equally follows that insecurity can arise from any of these elements. Such insecurity can be directed at any aspect of the nation-state. In a globalised world, insecurities can readily transcend national borders. In cyberspace there are few, if any, borders. Although this borderless environment is well suited for the transmission of information, as the preceding analysis has shown, it is also ideally suited for the broadcast of threats.

The threats from cyberspace are a mix of the old and the new. In the majority of cases, cyber-threats are old threats (such as espionage or theft) using new tools. Although either legislative amendments or new laws are required to address these threats, the broad legal regime remains the same.

The challenge for legislators and law enforcement officials is to ensure that, simply because a threat originates from cyberspace, the political system and its attendant civil liberties are not undermined. To meet this challenge, existing legislative and security regimes must be better integrated so that a 'whole nation-state' approach is used. Where these threats are transnational, multilateral cyber-policy regimes need to be developed.

New threats, however, present an unprecedented security challenge. The ability of a single individual, working in a physically detached area, to disrupt critical national infrastructure that can degrade the security of populations, markets, as well as one or more states, is a new security threat that can only be resolved by adopting a human security approach. The human security model provides for a preventive approach that allows any one of the three core elements of the nation-state to identify and resolve a cyber-threat. Due to its organisational and resource capacities, the state apparatus is likely to remain the locus of any responses to major cyber-threats. For other, lesser, responses individuals and groups are already spearheading threat alleviation measures — as happens when social organisations and corporations issue virus alerts and patches.

Cyberspace is not a utopian environment free of threat but neither is it a virtual hell. Rather, Janus-faced, cyberspace can be both — depending on the myriad desires and abilities of its users. Nor does it exist independent of the real world. Technological developments have seen cyberspace become the essential medium through which the world functions. Although the potentially anonymous nature of cyberspace transactions as well as the volume of information can make it difficult for legal and security regimes to react appropriately to real or potential threats, it is now clear that they have a justified need to do so. To develop such a regime that both reinforces legal codes while guaranteeing national security will require policymakers to draw upon the resources of the market as well as society. And in this, in building policy regimes that protect the core elements of nation-states as well as their critical cyber-infrastructure, human security models are uniquely structured to chart the way forward.

17

The Future of Cyber-Crime in Asia

Peter Grabosky and Roderic Broadhurst

Asia is an interesting and important region, indeed a crucial region, in which to observe the trajectory of digital technology and the criminal risks that accompany it. In some places, such as Singapore and Hong Kong, levels of connectivity are among the highest in the world. In the People's Republic of China, the rate of uptake of digital technology has been nothing short of stunning, as the Wong and Wong chapter in this volume illustrates. Information technology industries in places like Japan, Korea and Taiwan are world leaders; Malaysia and Thailand are committed to joining their ranks.

At the same time, there are Asian countries that have yet to benefit significantly from the digital revolution. For political and economic reasons, digital technology remains a relative novelty in countries like Myanmar, Laos, Mongolia, Cambodia and North Korea. This digital divide, as it exists in Asia, has a number of implications.

For those countries that have well and truly entered the digital age, progress is accompanied by risk. They have, within their borders, a greater proportion of potential victims and more potential perpetrators of cyber-crime. To the extent that techno-savvy offenders in foreign lands perceive these countries' information systems as attractive, the risk is that much greater. For these reasons, countries in the forefront of digital technology have begun to develop the legal and human resources appropriate to achieve security and prosperity in cyberspace. Substantive and procedural criminal laws, investigative skills, a vibrant information security industry, and mechanisms for cross-national cooperation are all hallmarks of those countries where economic security and cyber-security are inextricably intertwined.

By contrast, in countries for which the digital age has only just begun to dawn, circumstances differ dramatically. Commerce and infrastructure are less dependent on information technology, and there are fewer prospective cyber-victims and cyber-perpetrators. Laws and investigative resources are often inadequate to cope with terrestrial criminality, much less high-technology crime. To the extent that connectivity exists in these countries, the ability of prospective offenders to operate with relative impunity is that much greater. Not only are risks to the few existing domestic targets considerably higher, but risks to the more abundant targets in the region and indeed around the world are also real.

The chapters in this volume have provided an important overview of progress to date in the prevention and control of cyber-crime. In this concluding chapter, we seek to address two practical issues:

- What still needs to be done in terms of policy development?
- What research is needed to provide an evidence base for future policy?

In addition, we raise some additional questions about the role of the private sector in combating cyber-crime.

Policy Development

Jeff Bullwinkel mapped out ideal policy directions in his chapter. These include:

- The enactment of substantive and procedural laws adequate to cope with current and anticipated manifestations of cyber-crime
- The development of forensic computing skills by law enforcement and investigative personnel
- The achievement of a modicum of legal harmonisation in the region and indeed globally
- The creation of mechanisms for operational cooperation between law enforcement agencies from different countries: 24/7 points of contact for investigators, and mechanisms for mutual assistance in cyber-criminal matters generally.

Although Asia is and will remain a diverse region, its nations should continue to strive for the realisation of each of these goals. Given the rich diversity of legal traditions in the Asian region, it is unrealistic to expect uniformity in law, policy and practice. Nevertheless, this basic framework should serve as a roadmap for continuing efforts.

The most technologically sophisticated of Asian nations are already at the forefront of IT but face the new challenges that accompany the rapid development of compression and wireless technology. While it may be unrealistic to expect that all nations of the region will think alike in matters of law and practice in relation to content regulation, there is potential for wider consensus in matters relating to economic crime. And frameworks for cooperation in the investigation and prosecution of cyber-crime in Asia are now under construction.

Some of these frameworks are global in origin, and others more distinctively Asian as, for example, shown in Pavan Duggal's chapter on India's response to cyber-crime. As early as 1989, the Council of Europe published a study and recommendations addressing the need for new laws relating to computer crime. By the mid-1990s, as detailed in the chapter by Peter Csonka, the Council began developing a comprehensive Cyber-crime Convention. Several countries that do not belong to the Council participated in the negotiations that developed the Convention, including Japan, the United States and Australia. Asian observers who may be inclined to take a long-term view of policy development should note that the treaty took four years to negotiate and underwent more than 20 drafts.

Interpol established the Computer Crime Steering Committee in 1995 in an effort to rationalise and optimise regional responses to cyber-crime, and established four regions across the globe. In our region, the Interpol Asia–South Pacific Regional Working Party of IT Crime has been active since 1997. Among other projects, it has engaged in a survey of e-crime issues in the region; a survey of forensic and investigative tools used in Asia; and an assessment of Asian training strategies and facilities. The leader of this latter project was the Hong Kong Police. The activities of UNAFEI, discussed by Jeff Bullwinkel in his chapter, reflect the contribution that Japan is making to regional capacity-building in the area of cyber-crime control.

Other specific types of cyber-crime have elicited a wide international response. Given the global nature of cyberspace and its increasing use as a medium of commerce, regulators around the world must cooperate in the detection and suppression of market-related illegalities. The International Consumer Protection and Enforcement Network, a consortium of countries including Japan, Korea, Australia and New Zealand, conducts annual 'sweeps' of the World Wide Web in search of fraudulent sales pitches. Representatives of all participating nations search the Web for 'get rich quick' schemes and 'miracle cures' and report suspicious activities to authorities in the country from which the offending conduct appears to originate.

Through regional initiatives or overseas developments, the basic models of international cooperation, are there for adoption and adaptation to Asian conditions.

Evidence Base

The task of providing an evidence base for future policy development is challenging. Research on cyber-crime is in its infancy. Knowledgeable individuals and institutions, both in the public and private sectors, may for commercial, political or national security reasons be disinclined to share their wisdom with researchers. Information that finds its way on to the public record often may actually be misinformation or disinformation.

Despite these handicaps, it is important to develop a knowledge base, so we can begin to narrow the digital divide that exists in Asia today. Given the global nature of cyberspace, and the persistent risk of cross-border offending, a broader knowledge base will benefit the digital 'haves' as well as the digital 'have-nots'.

Country case studies, focusing either on individual incidents or on more general developments, can help raise public awareness of policy imperatives. The experience of the Philippines, whose substantive criminal laws were inadequate to respond to the 'I Love You' virus, was illustrative. The legislative 'patch' introduced in the aftermath of the incident may have stood the Philippines in good stead since then, but it was too late to apply to the alleged perpetrator, Onel de Guzman.

Similarly, case studies of individual investigations, successful or otherwise, can also be instructive. Success stories can help build confidence among new investigators, or among public officials generally in those countries that are on a steep cyber-forensics learning curve. 'Recipes' for success may also be useful for training purposes. The success of Operation Buccaneer, a large-scale international copyright piracy investigation, is illustrative. This coordinated international effort resulted in the execution of more than 65 searches in six different nations (see www.cybercrime.gov/ob/OBMain.htm, visited 11 February 2004).

Studies of unsuccessful investigations are no less important. Despite the fact that individuals or agencies do not like to dwell on failure, it is important to understand what went wrong, to reduce the likelihood of subsequent similar mishaps. Just as hospital staff meet in regular mortality and morbidity conferences, and aviation safety specialists analyse the circumstances of aircraft accidents, so too should cyber-crime specialists reflect systematically on cases that 'go wrong'. This information, too, can be useful for training specialists in cyber-forensics.

Other issues call out for comparative study. One of these might be the ways in which law enforcement agencies of different countries cope with evidence of possible criminal activity that may be encrypted. When evidence exists in a form that is not accessible to investigators, what do they do? Do they seek to mobilise decryption technology to 'break' the code (a strategy that has become much less effective given the widespread availability of strong encryption technology)? Do they issue, subject to judicial oversight, 'decryption orders' requiring assistance in rendering the evidence intelligible, with penalties for non-compliance? Do they use high-technology means of identifying encryption keys, such as keystroke logging devices or the technologies of remote search? Obviously, solutions will vary from country to country, depending on the rights accorded to suspects in criminal cases. But a comparative study could be useful as well as informative.

The ease of cross-border offending has posed new challenges for law enforcement agencies. It would be instructive to analyse some of the cases of cross-border offending that have come to official attention. Were 24/7 arrangements in place, and did they function as intended? Were the laws of the country from which the cross-border offending originated adequate to deal with the matter? Was there agreement or disagreement on the part of authorities of the two countries as to whether domestic prosecution was preferable to extradition? Was the outcome satisfactory to all parties?

The importance of bilateral and multilateral relationships to respond to cross-national cyber-criminality is the theme running through many chapters in this book. Tightening the web of relationships that was described in the chapter by Jeff Bullwinkel is a goal for all nations seeking security and prosperity in cyberspace. To monitor the progress towards this goal, periodic mappings of the 'density' of these relationships (including intelligence-sharing networks) would be useful.

The future of electronic commerce, in Asia and indeed, globally, depends on the continued confidence of current and prospective customers in the integrity and security of e-commerce systems. The chapter by Ivan Chiu reported research on public perceptions of e-commerce in the People's Republic of China. Observing trends in public confidence in e-commerce over time in one country is important. Similar research could be conducted on a cross-national comparative basis. Comparing findings relating to public confidence with actual levels of e-commerce can also be useful.

Statistics about the prevalence of computer-related crimes are notoriously poor. The most artful of cyber-crimes are not detected in the first place. Of those that are, many are never reported to police. Those proportionately few incidents that do reach official attention may be classified as generic offences such as fraud, and reference is rarely made to the technology applied to achieve the offence.

While it may be unrealistic to aspire to a situation of omniscience about the incidence of computer crime, this is not a ground for abandoning an attempt at useful measures of incidence. Rather than seeking a perfect picture, we should endeavour to build a mosaic, using hard evidence of events where that may exist, and approximations or estimates when nothing better is available. In any event, this task should be approached as systematically as possible, lest we be open to the criticism that we are inventing estimates, over-dramatising rare events or playing fast and loose with the truth. What might some of the components or fragments of an evidence-based surveillance system look like? They could perhaps include the following:

- Software and entertainment industries regularly estimate their losses resulting from electronic piracy. They will continue to do so, and should be encouraged to articulate fully the assumptions on which these estimates are based.

- Other strategies to complement official crime statistics include victim surveys. For example in many countries, large accounting firms conduct periodic surveys of their client base, or of industry generally, to determine the incidence and prevalence of computer-related crime that they have experienced. These should continue, but survey methods must be clearly specified if they are to meaningfully contribute to any 'overall picture'. Cyber-crime victimisation surveys therefore complement official statistics as a means of estimating the volume of cyber-illegality.

Not all reported cyber-crimes are prosecuted. There will be cases that do not receive police attention because of limited resources. Some investigations will founder because the complexity of the crime exceeds the technical capacity of law enforcement. Of cases that are referred for prosecution, prosecutors may themselves lack the ability to deal with them. Alternatively, evidence may be insufficient to sustain a prosecution. More complete knowledge about the attrition of cases from initial detection through to prosecution will point to where improvements in the administration of justice may be required.

Most incidents of cyber-crime do not proceed to conviction. Of those that do, we know little about the eventual sentences imposed. While it may be unrealistic to strive for consistency across nations in the sentences imposed on cyber-criminals, the reduction of disparity *within* countries is desirable given the transnational nature of offending. Systematic studies of sentencing can contribute to this goal and help clarify the role of deterrence-based responses to cyber-crime.

We know very little from any country about what constitutes aggravating or mitigating circumstances in cyber-crime cases. Some electronic pirates are in it for the money, while others do it for free. To what extent should motive matter, or should the financial loss to the copyright owner be the key factor in sentencing? In cases involving the release of a crippling virus, or a distributed denial of service attack resulting in thousands of dollars of down time and lost e-business, to what extent should it matter that the offender is a juvenile? What is regarded as an appropriate penalty in such cases?

Asian countries, no less than countries around the world, differ in terms of their policy priorities. For example, Keiji Uchimura's chapter illustrates the difficulties in Japan of enlisting private industry technical staff in the supervision of interception and the investigation of cyber-crime. These priorities are by no means constant and may vary over time depending on internal political and technological developments, and external exigencies. It would be useful to develop an overview of priorities in the Asia-Pacific region, and to observe how priorities change, both within individual countries and in such multilateral forums as the APEC high-tech group and ASEAN.

What are individual countries concerned about? What kinds of cyber-crime take precedence: hacking, fraud or theft of intellectual property? Are governments more concerned about infrastructure protection or child pornography? What explains the elevation or decline of an issue on the public agenda? Lobbying by the affected industries or a real increase in the underlying behaviour or international pressure?

Governments across Asia will continue to mobilise a variety of responses to cyber-crime; these will meet with varying degrees of success and entail costs. In times of fiscal restraint, it is important to ask which of these responses are most effective, and at what price. Whether the response to cyber-crime is driven by government agencies, by the private sector, or by some combination of the two, it will be useful to observe whether the response in question achieves its purpose without producing adverse unintended consequences, or 'collateral damage'. We noted earlier that there might be a tension between security and user-friendliness. A 'bullet-proof' system that turns off prospective clients may lose money in the long run. Filtering software that is overbroad may restrict access to legitimate sites. Limiting access to the Internet in order to discourage communication on behalf of political dissidents may also have the unintended consequence of inhibiting the development of electronic commerce. One could perhaps be forgiven for asking if there is a tolerable level of crime that we must endure to enjoy the maximum economic, cultural, educational benefits of digital technology. What tradeoffs are we prepared to make?

While government has necessarily driven much of the activity in response to cyber-crime, the private sector will play a crucial role in the prevention and control of crime in the digital age. To this we now turn.

Fostering Market Solutions

One of the more noticeable trends in contemporary public affairs has been the privatisation of state-owned assets. Governments around the world are shedding roles that were previously regarded as core functions; they are selling off assets that were once regarded as integral public property. And so it is that a great deal of national infrastructure — electric power, communications, transportation and financial systems — once owned by governments, now resides in private hands. Threats to this infrastructure are inimical to national security no less today than when these assets were public. As noted by Julie Shannon and Nick Thomas, securing this infrastructure has thus become a joint public–private responsibility.

When ownership and control of key assets are dispersed across a number of private institutions, challenges of co-ordination in furtherance of security are at least equal to those once faced by big government, where consistency and cooperation between agencies was often illusory. Private institutions may be ignorant of their vulnerabilities, or, if they are aware of them, they may be most reluctant to publicise this. Consequently, developing a coherent national programme of infrastructure protection becomes that much more difficult.

As noted in Laurie Lau's chapter, the information technology industry itself is largely private. Not only do industry giants such as Microsoft command resources and expertise that overshadow those of many nation-states, but other players in the global information industry also have significant roles. Even smaller companies, be they specialised information security firms or Internet service providers, are extremely knowledgeable. As Simon Bronitt and Miriam Gani observed in their chapter, private sector organisations are often ideally situated to prevent cyber-crime. They are also sometimes better placed to gather evidence of those crimes that are committed; in some cases they even provide expertise and resources to fund police investigations. Unilateral initiatives by the private sector show considerable promise. These include Microsoft's bounty on virus software writers, IFPI's general focus on deterring individual 'music pirates', and BSA's deployment of automated 'web crawling' software to identify bogus or illegal websites.

Collaboration between police and educational institutions can also be beneficial. The Hong Kong Police have developed a partnership with the Hong Kong University of Science and Technology to offer a professional diploma in computer forensics. The Centre for Information Security and Cryptography at the University of Hong Kong has developed DESK, which enables investigators to search for patterns in both Chinese and English, as well as to identify encoded or deleted files. The Korean Ministry of Information and Communication and KISA have also developed strong links with higher education institutions such as the specialist Information and Communication University and its Research Centre for Information Security. The potential for similar collaboration between law enforcement agencies and universities throughout the region is no doubt substantial.

The chapters in this volume by Lau and by Shannon and Thomas spoke of the 'governance' of cyberspace. By this was meant the various institutions, public and private, that exercise surveillance and control over one or more aspects of computing and communications. The state plays an important role, but there are many other players, both public and private. Indeed, the role of the private sector in the prevention and control of cyber-crime is arguably greater than in the domain of conventional criminality. It is certainly varied. Let us look at just a few of the ways in which private enterprise can become involved in the co-production of cyber-crime control.

In the first instance, systems can be designed to lessen their vulnerability to criminal exploitation. Cyber-crime is often facilitated by vulnerable software, much of which is designed with user-friendliness and convenience in mind rather than security. The common industry response is for manufacturers to structure their licence conditions to avoid potential liability, then to make 'patches' available as vulnerabilities become apparent later on. Whether market forces will eventually drive the widespread development of truly secure software remains to be seen.

Other information security technologies are becoming household words. Cryptography can help secure electronic commerce, while firewalls and other security technology can protect against hackers. Access controls can detect anomalous patterns of system use and raise the alarm about potential misuse. Biometric authentication technologies can guard against unauthorised entry.

Blocking and filtering technologies can help screen out undesirable content. Owners of intellectual property can create content that degrades when copied without authority or in violation of licence. In adopting such measures, commercial enterprises may be in a position to achieve more protection than poorly resourced law enforcement agencies can deliver.

Some may ask whether it is possible to harness market forces in furtherance of cyber-crime control. History, we believe, will answer this question in the affirmative. Half a century ago, motor vehicle manufacturers subordinated fuel efficiency, safety and vehicle security to such considerations as performance and style. Gradually government regulatory authorities imposed safety standards that were grudgingly accepted by industry. A few brave manufacturers sought to go beyond regulation, and actually market their products as safe and fuel-efficient as possible. They soon became market leaders. There are lessons here for those in the information industries of Asia, and the world generally.

Public–Private Collaboration

The degree of expertise residing in the private sector makes a degree of public–private collaboration in policing inevitable. We envisage three basic forms of relationship between the public and private sectors. Private interests may be required by law to assist government agencies; they may be engaged by government on a fee-for-service basis; or they may donate goods or services on a *pro bono* basis. Each of these has limits, which have yet to be fully explored in the context of cyber-crime. Each also has costs and benefits.

The first of these, *mandatory assistance*, refers to circumstances in which a private actor is required by law to assist government in some manner or other. For example, some countries require ISPs to assist in the identification and reporting of illegal content that comes to their attention, or to retain certain transaction details for investigative purposes.

The second is *commercial exchange*. Governments can rent or hire expertise to assist in one or more activities. Special expertise in forensic computing or cryptography may not reside within the ranks of police or other government agencies and therefore temporary engagement of private sector talent may be necessary.

The third form of relationship is that of *gift*. By this we mean private sponsorship of, or donations to, some aspect of the promotion of cyber law enforcement. Perhaps the most familiar manifestation of this is the assistance provided to public law enforcement agencies by the software, payment card and entertainment industries in response to electronic piracy and theft of intellectual property. Gift might also entail the *pro bono* secondment of specialised staff by private sector IT security firms to public law enforcement agencies.

Depending on the circumstances, each of these relationships would entail costs and benefits to the general public, the state agency, and the private actor involved. Ideally, the distribution of the costs and benefits will be equitable across the three sectors.

Requiring ISPs to retain large volumes of transaction data for lengthy periods of time can entail considerable expense. Nor may this approach be as effective as before, given the widespread adoption of anonymous stored value 'smart chip' and other untracked means of obtaining revenue. Taken to an extreme, this could have a chilling effect on a dynamic sector of the economy. Just how much of a burden should states impose on ISPs?

To what extent should states rely on contracting-in private sector expertise in forensic computing? Private sector salaries tend to be much higher than the salaries paid to public police, and over-reliance on private sector expertise can become prohibitively expensive. For reasons noted in the introduction, a degree of familiarity with digital technologies is now already essential for nearly all police. There may be an optimal level of police–private cooperation that will vary from country to country, and that will also change within a given country over time.

Those who suffer financial loss as the result of piracy or other theft of intellectual property may possess both the resources and the incentive to assist the government in the investigation and prosecution of such cases. Where governments lack the will or the resources to attend to these matters, industry co-production of enforcement may be the only alternative. When private interests offer their services in furtherance of a cyber-crime investigation, what safeguards exist to ensure that they themselves abide by the law? Should gifts (in the form of sponsorships and direct services) be explicitly or implicitly conditional? Is it possible for rich private interests to endow, in whole or in part, the computer crime squad of a poorly resourced national police agency? At what point does this support distort law enforcement priorities, such that police are acting for a private rather than the public interest?

It is not mere hyperbole to suggest that the environment of cyber-crime, in both the Asian region and globally, is constantly changing. Developing a body of knowledge about cyber-crime in Asia would be useful not just to future historians but also to contemporary policymakers. The periodic Asia Cyber Crime Summits convened by the University of Hong Kong constitute one forum for observing these changes, and help to set the agenda for law and policy that changing circumstances may dictate. A yearbook of Asian cyber-crime, which would chronicle important events, best practices and landmark cases for each of the countries of Asia, would be a valuable resource. Such a chronicle of major developments would not only provide a useful platform for policy deliberations in the Asian region but would help complete the bigger picture for those around the world who are confronting cyber-crime and its transnational scope.

Regardless of a given nation's trajectory into the digital age, cyber-crime will continue to pose challenges to the nations of Asia and to the region collectively. The challenges will be faced, and the responses crafted, by institutions of the state, the private sector, and individuals. Asia has seen increased sophistication in the forms of criminal activity and a shift towards profit-focused offences, especially fraud and deception-like offences. The involvement of organised crime is also apparent, especially in the exploitation of intellectual property through mass copyright infringement. One has also seen a notable increase in the virulence and sophistication of malicious code. This will require timely, substantial, and coordinated responses from CERT or equivalent agencies.

In response to consumer and market forces there has been increasingly coordinated action by the private sector against cyber-crime and in ways more complementary to government capabilities. There has been a shift away from 'alarm raising' by industry towards more collaborative action. Fortunately, the willingness and capacity of the private sector to protect its own assets have also increased. The private sector has begun to develop creative solutions to some the challenges of cyber-crime. In addition to providing technical support and information to state law enforcement agencies, they have begun to pursue civil law remedies with a view towards sending a deterrent message to prospective offenders.

Although recent years have seen a quickening of governmental and cross-national cooperation, there is still a long way to go. The lack to date of any systematic evaluation of the progress made in developing truly comprehensive forms of mutual legal assistance is itself telling. Action is necessary to map and assay the effectiveness of MLA in closing the gaps in the international legal system so crucial to combating computer crime.

Given the pace of technological change, the training and retaining of expertise requires continued investment. The parlous state of some law enforcement agencies in the region poses a continuing risk of cyber-crime safe havens. Doubtless the concerns of law enforcement agents will not be limited to those offences committed with or against computers. The associated involvement of digital technology will become no less prominent in 'ordinary' crime cases. Increasing connectivity means that IT in some form will soon be present at almost every crime scene.

Four issues continue to dominate the agenda of those seeking to control cyber-crime in Asia: the quest for a truly viable international law enforcement mechanism; the challenge of transnational criminal networks; the need for even closer private and public cooperation; and the continued need for research and training. Periodic assessments of regional developments, such as those contained in this volume, can help keep abreast of the rapidly evolving environment of cyber-crime.

Notes

Chapter 1

1. Victor Lo (Hong Kong Police) noted at the First Asia Cybercrime Summit (April 2001) that about 75% of cases in Hong Kong involved hacking and that this was about showing off and testing IT security rather than the pursuit of criminal enterprise. He and other discussants felt this would change as the opportunities presented by computer-related crime attracted innovative criminals.
2. For example, Hong Kong has an estimated 3.2 million residents on-line and is served by 56 ISPs. European Union computer-related crime trends also show that reported attacks on computer systems grew from approximately 1400 incidents in 1997 to just under 2500 cases in 1999. Similar increases have been observed for counterfeiting offences but computer fraud declined from 3000 cases in 1998 to 2250 cases in 1999, while computer assisted telephone service theft declined from over 7000 in 1997 to 4200 cases in 1999 — a trend also noted for recent Hong Kong data on computer crimes (Valeri 2001).
3. Figures cited from a 'Country Report' provided for the UN ESCAP Asia Pacific Conference on Cybercrime and Information Security, Seoul, 11–13, November 2002.
4. See www.police.go.th/crimewebpost/report/sum.php and summary country report by Surangkana Kaewjumnog, National Science Technology Development Agency, Asia Pacific Conference on Cybercrime and Information Security, Seoul, 11–13, November 2002. In 2001 there were about 3.5 million users and over 10 500 websites in Thailand and the number of users was expected to double by the close of 2002.
5. The new computer crime law is anticipated to take effect in late 2004 (personal

communication Ms. Surangkana Wayuparb, National Electronics and Computer Technology Centre, Ministry of Science and Technology) but as noted by Police Colonel Naras Savestanan (personal communication) the extent to which general police, as distinct from the small specialist unit already established, were equipped to handle computer-related crime remained a very significant challenge.

6. Comments by A M Natsir Amal, Ministry of Communication and Information, Republic of Indonesia, Asia Pacific Conference on Cybercrime and Information Security, Seoul, 11–13 November 2002.
7. Comments by Armi Jane R Borje, Commissioner, Philippines, National Telecommunications Commission at the Asia Pacific Conference on Cybercrime and Information Security, Seoul, 11–13, November 2002.
8. The TOC Convention came into force in September, 2003 (141 States and 16 parties have signed): see www.undcp.org/crime_cicp_signatures_ convention. html. The protocols in respect to trafficking in humans, smuggling in migrants and the illicit manufacture and trafficking in firearms have thus far attracted respectively 105, 101 and 31 state signatories.
9. As of July 2004 the Cybercrime Convention come into force after the minimum 5 ratifications (three of whom are by Council of Europe member states). As at 27 July 2002, 37 states have signed the Convention (including non-Council member states: Canada, South Africa and Japan). The 'First Additional Protocol to the Convention on Cybercrime on the criminalisation of acts of a racist or xenophobic nature committed through computer systems' has been signed by 22 states and awaits the necessary ratification: see http://conventions.coe.int/treaty/EN/projets/cybercrime27.htm; visited 9 August 2004.
10. The term 'regulatory' means in this context a contractual basis for rules of conduct and performance in contrast to 'mental intent' criminal laws and the associated higher thresholds of proof and reliance on custodial sanctions.
11. See for example the US Department of Justice (2000), 'Executive Order 13 133 Working Group on Unlawful Conduct on the Internet' — www.usdoj.gov:80/criminal/cybercrime/append.htm; European Council's treaty on cyber-crime (Csonka this volume and Csonka 1996) and the United Nations Secretary–General's 'Conclusions of the study on effective measures to prevent and control high-technology and computer-related crime'. For related analysis of the work of the European Union and the OECD see Valeri (2001).
12. UNAFEI, however, has activated training and related programmes. Further attention is likely and a number of states (for example, Singapore) and NGOs (for example, the Asian Development Bank and the Asian Crime Prevention Foundation) have promoted forums to raise awareness and improve cross-border cooperation on this issue.
13. Hong Kong is Vice-Chair of the UN group and participates in the NPA network: personal communication, Mr Victor Lo, Hong Kong Police
14. The Hong Kong Department of Justice established a dedicated mutual legal assistance unit in 1998. Five MLAT are in force and a further ten are under

consideration, although assistance to non-treaty jurisdictions can be offered subject to appropriate reciprocity. Hong Kong has 12 extradition agreements of which nine are in force and can cover computer offences. As noted by many commentators, formal channels are usually too slow to be effective and the authentication of evidence collected in other jurisdictions remains a problem.

15. For a cooler assessment of the European Union's efforts against organised crime: see Den Boer (2001). Despite the 1997 *Action Plan to Combat Organised Crime* (OJ 97/C 251/1) adopted by the Ministers for Justice and Home Affairs during the Dutch Presidency, differences between the policing institutions remain considerable. However, increased transparency and knowledge about one another's systems and recognition of the problem has led to re-organisation, improved resources and greater centralisation designed to improve cooperation amongst member states.
16. ASEAN comprises the following ten nations: Brunei Darussalam, Cambodia, Indonesia, Laos, Malaysia, Philippines, Singapore, Thailand, Myanmar and Vietnam: its meetings, coupled with the overlap among the 21 nations of the APEC forum, may yet hold out prospects for the development of a suitable mechanism for law enforcement coordination in the Asia Pacific region despite the primary focus on trade. In addition, Interpol regional meetings are held annually. The most recent, the 17th Asian Regional Conference, was held in Colombo in February 2002 and focused on terrorism.
17. The ACCORD followed the formalisation of the ad hoc meeting of the Special Senior Officials Meeting on Transnational Crime in Yangon (October 2000). Note also the increasing institutionalisation of cross-border cooperation on migration via the ASEAN Plan of Action on Immigration Matters.
18. China's largest portal Sina.com claims to be the world's fifth largest holder of e-mail accounts, with the 25 million-odd accounts, out of and estimated 570 million worldwide, ranking it the largest server of non-English e-mailers.
19. China now has about 50 million Internet users, ten backbone networks and 3 600 ISPs / ICPs. Although estimates of the numbers of Internet subscribers are difficult to verify, estimates placed the number around 33 million at the end of 2002 (MFC Internet Update 2002: www.mfcinsight.com, December). China's Internet population growth has been hampered by insufficient bandwidth and relatively expensive by-the-minute charges but this is expected to diminish as wireless applications and compression technologies become available.
20. PRC users are currently reported to spend an average 11 hours online a week: 40% on 'cultural activities': news, sports, movies and TV, IT, finance and literature and 60% on email and shopping. Nearly a third (32%) of users purchased goods / services online (source: PRC Ministry of Information Industry Vice-Minister Zhang Chunjiang: China Network Civilization Project Organizing Committee).
21. According to a CNNIC survey in 2001, 31.9% of the then 26.5 million net users purchased goods online in the previous year. Most Internet users are aged 20–30

years, and their payment ability is limited. Moreover, most surveyed Internet users were unsure if B2C would develop in the next two years. The CNNI report also noted that about two thirds of China's users, about 8 million people, are willing to try online shopping.

22. The PRC has launched a secure online financial services / e-commerce infrastructure run by the China Financial Certification Authority (CFCA). The CFCA issued more than 100 000 digital certificates in 2002 to corporate banking customers and Chinese stock traders.
23. Beijing's municipal Education Commission discovered through its survey that 20% of the city's secondary students primarily search out porn when surfing.
24. Philippe Bertrand (Visa Fraud Control, Asia-Pacific) reported that 400 cases of credit card fraud were noted in 2000 by Visa but difficulties of prosecution meant that only a fraction of cases went to court (cited in Broadhurst 2001).
25. Chinese Internet user profiles are similar to those found elsewhere in that professional, younger and urban populations are predominant. Many (30%) users have post-college level education, and half (49%) work in white-collar jobs. They typically use the Net to send and receive e-mail, chat, and seek information about health, community and education, and when shopping they normally buy theatre tickets, travel tickets, DVDs and VCDs. The Chinese Academy of Social Science's Social Development Research Center reported that China's Internet users average 27 years in age, 65% began surfing in 1999, 61% are male, 43% are students, 16% are managers, and 11% are science, education, culture or health workers.
26. Hui recommends developing hacking tools as a means to learn about them and staging 'laboratory' cyber attacks to help train investigators. Simple techniques such as creating document registries based on 'flags' (via # hash functions) help monitor intrusions and hacking.
27. The importance of the preservation of evidence and its connection with the need for harmonised procedures and laws is also necessary; see the guide from the USA National Institute of Justice designed to assist law enforcement and others who are responsible for protecting an electronic crime scene. 'Electronic Crime Scene Investigation: A Guide for First Responders' (NCJ 187736) at http://www.ncjrs.org/txtfiles1/nij/187736.txt.
28. Broadhurst (2001) reported Robert Yule's (IFPI) observation that there were an estimated 1.9 billion pirated units in circulation (DVD / CD, Internet and cassettes) worldwide. The introduction of recordable CDs / DVDs also facilitated the downloading of an estimated 25 million music files from the Internet. He also noted growing evidence that organised crime had moved into the production and distribution of pirated CDs.
29. Other examples include interpol's directory on art theft.
30. It took ten years to develop the Interpol credit card fraud classification scheme.
31. For the past three years, a specialised IP court in Thailand heard 3000 cases in which 98% of the accused pleaded guilty due to the emphasis placed on plea-

bargaining by the court in securing convictions. The Thai approach was to avoid tough penalties because higher penalties could encourage corruption of police (Mr Weerawit Weeraworawit Intellectual Property Department, Thailand cited in Broadhurst 2001)

32. Copyright holders, usually through industry bodies now directly invest in crime prevention and prosecutions. For example, Michael Ellis of the Motion Picture Association reported that they have helped in the past few years investigate and assist in some 4000 prosecutions of copyright violations in the Asian region.
33. Notably the Thai and Malaysia governments have actively encouraged IP industries especially in music products to reduce prices and co-operate more actively in promoting awareness of the costs of piracy on state and private revenue.
34. Internet piracy is not apparently clearly covered by PRC laws for distributed pirated works — although the view was expressed that a judicial interpretation has been issued for civil law breaches on the Internet.
35. The introduction of cyber-codes or unique identifiers for optical discs had been helpful in tracking factory sources but they also have been copied.
36. The Royal Malaysia Police (Mr Mohd Nawawi Ismail) noted that the *Copyright Act 1987* was ineffective and the recently passed *Optical Disk Act 2000* has yet to be fully assessed as operations had only been initiated from March 2001.
37. Personal communication Mr Mark Day and see: The Motion Picture Association Announces Expeditious Resolution of Two Landmark Civil Action Proceedings Concerning DVD Piracy in China (Encino, CA / Hong Kong) and, Motion Picture Association Announces the Successful Resolution of Six Civil Action Proceedings Concerning DVD Piracy in Shanghai (Encino, CA / Hong Kong).
38. Approximately 30 nations have passed specific laws criminalising computer-related crime. However, a large number have such laws in development or in process. Details of the relevant laws applicable for jurisdictions in the Asian region are reported by Urbas in this volume.
39. Summary drawn from remarks made by Mr R Sri Kumar, IPS, Inspector General of Police. India at the Asia Cybercrime Summit, April 2001, Hong Kong.
40. Comments of Victor Lo: Roundtable: Regional Law Enforcement Co-operation, Asia Cybercrime Summit, April 2001, Hong Kong.
41. There is an important role for professional associations and business corporations to play in fostering business ethics and contributing financial and other resources to public police, notably in the field of training. Many examples of effective partnerships between public police and private security occur; however, the form of assistance is often limited by commercial self-interest. The payment card industry's crucial contribution to Interpol's Universal Classification System for Counterfeit Payment Cards and their routine support in operational, training and computer support for public agencies is a good example.

Chapter 2

* This chapter is based in part on research conducted in collaboration with Dr Russell G Smith of the Australian Institute of Criminology, and Dr Gillian Dempsey of the University of Queensland. Michael Cook, Andrew Lester, Angela Leong and Catherine Stein provided valuable research assistance.

Chapter 3

1. See Don B Parker, 'Computer Crime'. In *Encyclopedia of Computer Science*, 4th ed., UK: Nature Publishing Group, 2000, pp. 349–53.
2. See Jiang Ping, *Jisuanji Fanzui Wenti Yanjiu* (Research into Computer Crime Problems), Beijing: Commercial Press, 2000.
3. See annual serial *Procuratorial Yearbook of China*, Beijing: Zhongguo Jiancha Nianjian.
4. See 'China Attaches Strategic Importance to IT Industry', *People's Daily Online*, at http://english.peopledaily.com.cn/200008/23/eng20000823_48843.shtml (visited 24 April 2002).
5. See 'President Urges Faster Development of Information Technology', *People's Daily Online*, at http://english.peopledaily.com.cn/200112/27/eng20011227_87579.shtml (visited 24 April 2002).
6. See 'Internet to Contribute More to China's Transformation', *People's Daily Online*, at http://english.peopledaily.com.cn/200111/27/eng20011127_85455.html (visited 24 April 2002). See also 'Connecting China Education Community to the Global Internet — The China Education and Research Network Project (20 April 1995)', at http://www.isoc.org/HMP/PAPER/077/html/paper.html (visited 15 January 2004).
7. See 'Evolution of Internet in China', CNNIC, at http://www.cnnic.net.cn/evolution.shtml (visited 27 February 2002).
8. Cheng Qi, '1999 Zhongguo Zhengfu Dashangwang' (1999 — The Year of E-Government in China), No. 10 *Fazhi Yu Jingji* (Legal System and Economy), No. 10, 1999.
9. See 'Survey Report On Internet Development In China', CNNIC, at http://www.cnnic.net.cn (visited 25 December 2003).
10. For a conference on the impact of IT on China's economical, social, and political development, see 'China and the Internet: Technology, Economy, and Society in Transition', international conference held at Davidson Conference Center at the University of Southern California 30–31 May 2003.
11. Chase and Mulvenon, *You've Got Dissent!*. http://www.rand.org/publications/MR/MR1543/ (visited 15 January 2004).
12. R O Keohane and J S Nye Jr, 'Power and Interdependence in the Information Age', *Foreign Affairs*, 77, 1998: 81–94.

13. Shanthi Kalathil, 'Dot com for dictators. (Internet use to challenge authoritarianism)', *Foreign Policy*, March–April 2003.
14. See study by Rong Huizhen, 'Diannao Wangluo — Wei Chengnian Ren Shishi Fanzui De Xin Meijia' (Computer Networks — New Media for Juvenile Crime), *Qingshaonian Fanzui Wenti* (Juvenile Crime Issues) 2, 2002: 12–15.
15. Yu Zhigang et al., *Wangluo Fanzui Dingxing Zhengyi Yu Xueli Fenxi* (Analysing the Nature of Internet Crime), Jilin: Jilin Renmin Chubanshe, 2001.
16. Wei Min, 'Diannao Shijie De Youling' (Phantom of the Computer World), *Jingcha Tiandi* (The Police Horizon), 50–51, 1994.
17. Ibid., p. 51
18. In historical context, before the maturing of economic reform, no one in China except a bank had any money. More significantly, no one used a computer except the government, particularly the banks.
19. Li Heng, 'New Faces of Cybercrimes', *Renmin Wang* (People's Daily Online), 11 April 2002, at http://english.peopledaily.com.cn/200204/11/eng20020411_93883.shtml (visited 15 January 2004).
20. Jiang Ping, *Jisuanji Fanzui Wenti Yanjiu*.
21. Ibid., p. 79.
22. Ibid., pp. 150–2.
23. Zeng Peiyan, 'Report on the National Economic and Social Development Plan, the Fifth Session of the Ninth National People's Congress, PRC, 6 March 2002,' Xinhua News Agency Online, 17 March 2002, at http://news.xinhuanet.com/english/2002–03/17/content_320000.htm (visited 15 January 2004).
24. See Premier Zhu Rongi, 'Government Work Report, the Fifth Session of the Ninth National People's Congress, PRC, 5 March 2002', *Xinhua News Agency Online*, 16 March 2002, at http://news.xinhuanet.com/english/2002–03/16/content_319108.htm (visited 15 January 2004).
25. The policy was endorsed by the Fifth Session of the Fifteenth CPC Central Committee meeting in 2001. See 'Jiang Zeming: Use law to protect and promote the healthy development of the internet' (Jiang Zeming: yunyong falu shouduian baozhang chujing xingxi wangluo jiankan fazhang), *China Police Daily Online*, 12 July 2001. http://www.cpd.com.cn/xxlr.asp?menulb=019 %D4 %DA %CF %DF %D0 %C2 %CE %C5&id =2465.
26. See Li Wenyan et al., *Jisuanji Fanzui Yanjiu*, pp. 5–6.
27. See 'Decision of the Standing Committee of the National People's Congress Regarding Comprehensive Control in Social Order and Security', issued by the NPC Standing Committee on 2 March 1991.
28. See 'Opinion on Further Improving Social Order Through a Comprehensive Approach', *People's Daily Online*, 19 November 2001, at http://www.people.com.cn/GB/shizheng/16/20011119/607800.html (visited 15 January 2004).
29. See 'Decision of the Standing Committee of the National People's Congress Regarding Comprehensive Control in Social Order and Security', issued by the NPC Standing Committee on 2 March 1991.

30. See *Zhonghua Renmin Gongheguo Fadian* (Laws of the People's Republic of China, Chinese–English edn), Jilin: Jilin Renmin Chubanshe, 2000.
31. William Yurcik and Zixiang Tan, 'The Great (Fire)Wall of China: Internet Security and Information Policy Issues in the People's Republic of China', University of Pittsburgh and Syracuse University (1996), at http://www.tprc.org/abstracts/tan.txt. n38. (visited 15 January 2004).
32. 'IT Sector Hails New Regulations', *China Daily*, 15 October 2000, at http://search.chinadaily.com.cn/isearch/i_textinfo.exe?dbname=cndy_printedition&listid=12441&selectword=IT%20SECTOR%20HAILS%20NEW%20REGULATIONS.
33. See 'Refreshing Your Understanding of the Internet', *China Daily*, 23 April 2002, at http://www1.chinadaily.com.cn/bw/2002–04–23/68055.html (visited 30 April 2002).
34. For text of China Internet Domain Name Regulations, see http://unpan1.un.org/intradoc/groups/public/documents/APCITY/UNPAN007466.pdf (visited 15 January 2004)
35. 'Websites to Play the Name Game', *China Daily*, 12 November 2000, at http://search.chinadaily.com.cn/isearch/i_textinfo.exe?dbname=cndy_printedition&listid=13638&selectword=DOMAIN %20NAME.
36. 'City Tackles Lawless Net', *China Daily*, 4 September 2000, at http://search.chinadaily.com.cn/isearch/i_textinfo.exe?dbname=cndy_printedition&listid=10757&selectword=CITY %20TACKLES %20LAWLESS %20NET.
37. One of the very first Internet police was established at Shenyang (Shenyang Municipality Public Security Bureau Communication's Office) over ten years ago.
38. Shanghai Internet Communication Safety Supervision Office (Shanghai Gonganju xingxi wangluo anquan jianchachu), 'Internet Police First Appears in Shanghai' (Wangluo jingcha zai Shanghai liangxiang), *China Police Daily Online*, 30 June 2001, at http://www.cpd.com.cn/xxlr.asp?menulb=019 %D4 %DA %CF %DF %D0 %C2 %CE %C5&id=2053.
39. See 'Wangluo Jingcha Shenshou Bufan' (Highly Competent Cyberpolice), *China Police Daily Online*, at http://www.cpd.com.cn, 11 April 2002 (visited 12 April 2002).
40. For example, in April of 2001, Yang Linhua and his wife set up a 'Chinese call girls' website full of pornographic materials to attract individual subscriptions and sponsors' advertisements. They made RMB35 000 in just six months. The couple was arrested and prosecuted in January 2002 by Shenyang police. See 'Purging Pornographic Materials from the Net, Calling upon the Sword of the Law' (Wangluo saohuang fuhuan falu zijian) *China Police Daily Online*, 8 February 2001, at http://www.cpd.com.cn/xxlr.asp?menulb=039 %C8 %CB %C3 %F1 %B9 %AB %B0 %B2 %B1 %A8&id=12058.
41. Net gambling is a growing concern to PRC police. The PRC has noted that net gambling is a worldwide phenomenon. In 1996 there were only 15 net gambling companies worldwide; by 1997 there were 50. The Yibo Wangluo Gongsi gambling company started in November 1997 and had a gross revenue growth of 5000%

in just one year. By the year 2000 the company was grossing US$15 million with 16 gambling sport events and doing business in 20 languages. In April 2001, Liaoning province public security broke up the nation's first net-gambling ring. See 'Gambling on the Net, the Black Current of the WWW' (Wangshang dubo, wangluo shijia de hechao), *China Police Report*, at 4939.shtml" http://www.china110.com/police/plzxjw/jfts/item/2001_11/574939.shtml (visited 20 February 2002).

42. Recently, the term 'electronic heroin' has been coined to depict the adverse impacts brought by the Internet, especially to young people, in an uncontrolled environment such as Internet cafés.
43. 'High School Student Died Abruptly When Playing Computer Online Game', *Xinhua News Agency*, 23 April 2002, at http://news.xinhuanet.com/it/2002–04/22/content_367495.htm (visited 23 April 2002).
44. 'Quanguo quti "wangba" lian wan jia' (Nation Suspended 20 000 'Internet Cafés'), *China Police Report*, 12 December 2000, at china110.com/police/policezt/item/2000_12/575498.shtml" http://www.china110.com/police/policezt/item/2000_12/575498.shtml (visited 20 February 2002).
45. 'China Cleans Internet Cafés', *People's Daily Online*, 20 July 2001, at http://english.peopledaily.com.cn/200107/20/eng20010720_75430.html (visited 23 April 2002).
46. 'Cultural Market to be Better Regulated', *China Daily*, 17 August 2001.
47. 'Young People Have Ethical Norms on Internet Conduct' (Qingshaonian yaoliao wangluo xingwei daode guifan), *China Police Daily Online*, 30 November 2001, at http://www.cpd.com.cn/xxlr.asp?menulb=039%C8%CB%C3%F1%B9%AB%B0%B2%B1%A8&id=8295 (visited 30 April 2002).
48. 'Education New Topic: How to Communicate with the Youth in Internet Age', *China Police Daily Online*, 15 April 2002, at http://www.cpd.com.cn/xxlr.asp?menulb=039%C8%CB%C3%F1%B9%AB%B0%B2%B1%A8&id=15387 (visited 30 April 2002).
49. 'No Security, No Healthy Development of Internet: Official', *People's Daily Online*, 3 November 2000, at http://english.peopledaily.com.cn/200011/03/eng20001103_54290.html (visited 30 April 2002).
50. See Jiang Ping, *Jisuanji Fanzui Wenti Yanjiu*, pp. 266–8.
51. See 'Chinese Youngsters Vow to Clean Up Net', *People's Daily Online*, 29 November 2001, at http://english.peopledaily.com.cn/200111/29/eng20011129_85583.shtml (visited 30 April 2002).
52. See 'Teen Hackers Told to Learn "Cyber-ethics", Obey Law', *China Daily*, 21 April 2000. http://search.chinadaily.com.cn/isearch/i_textinfo.exe?dbname=cndy_printedition&listid=4890&selectword=CYBER (visited 30 April 2002). ('The top US law enforcer has a message for teen hackers: The law is watching you. Speaking after Canada announced on Wednesday the arrest of a 15-year-old in connection with attacks on CNN's Web site in February, US Attorney-General Janet Reno made a call for children to learn "cyber-ethics."')

53. See 'Remarks of Attorney General John Ashcroft, First Annual Computer Privacy, Police and Security Institute (22 May 2001)', Computer Crime and Intellectual Property Section (CCIPS) of the Criminal Division of the US Department of Justice, at http://cybercrime.gov/AGCPPSI.htm.
54. See 'General Information — Cyber Ethics', Computer Crime and Intellectual Property Section (CCIPS) of the Criminal Division of the US Department of Justice, at http://cybercrime.gov/.
55. Felson, *Crime and Everyday Life.*
56. See 'Eight Ministries Joint Conference on Special Program to Keep the Internet Clean from Malevolent Information', *Xinhua News Agency*, 1 May 2002, at ERLINK "http://news.xinhuanet.com/newscenter/2002–05/01/content_379468.htm (visited 4 May 2002).
57. See M Farley, 'Electronic guerrillas breach blocks set up by the government to keep citizens from seeing unorthodox news and opinions on the Internet', *LA Times*, 1999, at http://www.gis.net/~cht/dissidents.html,
58. Lin Hai, a 30-year-old Shanghai software entrepreneur, was named China's first 'cyber-dissident', and was charged and convicted of providing 30 000 names to VIP References on 4 December 1999.
59. Research into and development of PKI has been pursued in China since 1999. See Han-she Che, 'For Construction and Development of China's PKI'. http://www.pki.org.tw/Schedule/020702/chs.pdf

Chapter 4

* The author dedicates this chapter to the memory of his mother who recently passed away.

1. http://www.ust.hk/itsc/y2k/
2. In this study, Beijing refers to the territorial boundary of the city of Beijing in the People's Republic of China. Also in this study, the author did not take Hong Kong and Macau into consideration.
3. http://www.nielsen-netratings.com/pr/pr_020422_eratings.pdf.
4. http://www.cnnic.net.cn/develst/2003–7/report2003–7.zip.
5. Commercial websites refers to websites of companies that only conduct business online only. Enterprise websites refers to websites of businesses that are conducted online and by other means. For further details of the classification between commercial and enterprise websites, please refer to http://www.cnnic.net.cn/tj/2.shtml for details.
6. Simply speaking, B2C refers to the online process of the flow of information, goods and services that target to the retail consumer. B2B refers to the online process of the flow of information, goods and services among companies, including the supply chain (Davis & Benamati 2003: 22). Besides B2B and B2C, there are other forms of e-business like B2B2C (business to business to consumer),

C2B (consumer to business) and C2C (consumer to consumer) (Turban & King 2003: 7) which are, however, beyond the scope of this study.

7. http://www.cnnic.net.cn/html/Dir/2003/11/22/1392.htm.
8. Yuang (2000) argues that most of the business websites in China cannot be regarded as e-business as they are still confined to the stage of displaying information of a company and its products.
9. There are some differences between hackers and crackers. Hackers refer to people who illegally invade other computers but do nothing to steal information from, or destroy or damage, the system in any way. Hackers invade other computers to see what is inside them. On the other hand, crackers illegally invade other computer systems and steal information from, or destroy or damage or get control over the operating system (Pfaffenberger 1997: 121, 224; Nader 1998: 143, 284). For the perception of safety and security when using computers, however, we should be aware of attacks from both hackers and crackers.
10. For details, see http://www.pricewaterhousecoopers.co.uk/extweb/newcolth.nsf/docid/IA47C7356C3D57AC85256AD1005834DI?OpenDocument.
11. http://www.mpinews.com/fprint.cfm?htm=htm%5C20020408%5Cta11441a%2Ehtm.
12. http://i.cmpnet.com/gocsi/db_area/pdfs/fbi/FBI2003.pdf.
13. http://app.singpao.com/20020409/international/99089_main.html.
14. http://www.mpinews.com/fprint.cfm?htm=htm%5C20031021%5Cta21205t%2Ehtm.
15. http://www.acpf.org/WC8th/AgendaItem2/I2PpTurnbullHK.html.
16. http://www.security.iia.net.au/downloads/grabosky.pdf.
17. http://www.auscert.org.au/Information/Auscert_info/2002cs.pdf.
18. http://www.cnn.com/TECH/computing/9901/26/clinton.idg/.
19. NK "http://www.cbi.org.uk/80256716004baae5/33a87f2eee41b54e80256803004f04e4/eff1596523e1653f" http://www cbi.org.uk/80256716004baae5/33a87f2eee41b54e80256803004f04e4eff1596523e1653f80256aaf00390135?OpenDocument.
20. http://www.security.iia.net.au/downloads/crime%20and%20security%20survey.pdf.
21. http://www.acpr.gov.au/pdf/Ecrime_Strategy.pdf.
22. http://www.year2000.gov.hk/english/index_2.html.
23. http://www.mingpaonews.com/20020107/t_gaa1h.htm. The United States government, for example, has used a lot of software from the Microsoft Cooperation, but is now paying more attention to the security of software, especially when Microsoft products are reported to have many security problems. Interested readers can refer to http://full.mingpaonews.com/20020118/t_tacl.htm for details.
24. The author would like to acknowledge the financial support provided by a research travel grant by the School of Humanities and Social Science at The Hong Kong University of Science and Technology.
25. The author assumed that the gender of the respondents did not affect the findings.

26. The author further divided postgraduate and undergraduate students into computer majors and non-computer majors. As a result, four groups were created, namely, postgraduate computer majors, postgraduate non-computer majors, undergraduate computer majors, and undergraduate non-computer majors.
27. hp://www.cnnic.net.cn/about.shtml" ttp://www.cnnic.net.cn/about.shtml.
28. http://www.cnnic.net.cn/develst/fa.shtml.
29. There was another explanation for the data on the method of payment for online purchasing in China. As far as the author was aware, credit cards were still not popular among Chinese. In view of this, among the payment methods, most e-businesses in China would provide an option of cash on delivery for their customers.
30. Digital government provides services through the Internet so that citizens can access the service 24 hours a day, seven days a week. The Chinese government, both central and local, remains at the stage of placing an informational homepage on the Internet for public surfing. Few public services are available on the Internet and 'digital governance' is yet to be established by the Chinese government. Digital government, however, is common in Western societies like the United States. In fact the government of Hong Kong is also promoting the idea of digital government, known as Electronic Service Delivery (ESD) (http://www.esd.gov.hk), to the public. Interested readers can refer to Dutton (1999) for further details.

Chapter 5

* An earlier version of this chapter was presented at the ANZSOC Conference, Brisbane October 2002. The David C Lam Institute for East-West Studies (LEWI), at the Hong Kong Baptist University, partially funded travel costs, for which the author is grateful. I also thank my wife Doris for her encouragement and support and Professor K B Chan and Dr Margaret Shaffer of the Hong Kong Baptist University, Dr David Wall and Professor Clive Walker of the University of Leeds and Ms Jane Cheung from LEWI, and Professor Carol Jones of the University of Glamorgan, UK, and the editors for their useful comments. Note that short title references in these notes refer to the bibliography at the back of the book.

1. F. Wong, 'HK edge in cyber trading', Hong Kong Standard Online (visited on 9 December 1999), para. 15, see http// www.hkstandard.com.
2. BBC News Online, see http://news.bbc.co.uk/1/hi/business/1248026.stm, visited 1 August 2002.
3. Lee, 'The Paradox of Political Economy', p. 309.
4. Ibid., p. 310.
5. Ibid.
6. Cf. ibid., p. 309.
7. Lau, *Society and Politics in Hong Kong*, p. 67.
8. Ibid., pp. 68–71.

9. Wall, 'Cybercrimes and the Internet', p. 2. See also Grabosky et al., *Electronic Theft*.
10. Wall, 'Cybercrimes and the Internet'.
11. See Wall, 'Insecurity and the Policing of Cyberspace'; Wall, *Crime and the Internet*.
12. See Levi, 'Between the Risk and the Reality falls the Shadow'.
13. See Parker, *Computer Security Management*.
14. Cheung, 'The Changing Political System', p. 45.
15. Ibid.
16. Ibid., p. 50.
17. Ibid.
18. See Hong Kong SAR Government website, http://www.info.gov.hk/gia/general/200310/22/1022185.htm, visited 24 October 2003, also see *SCMP*, 24 October 2003 edition; *MingPoa Daily (Chinese) Newspaper*, 24 October 2003 edn.
19. See Mueller, *Ruling the Root*, Chs 7–9.
20. See http://www.icann.com (visited 11 March 2003).
21. Digital 21 Hong Kong, *Building a Digitally Inclusive Society*, p. 23.
22. See http://www.info.gov.hk/citb/ctb/english/paper/doc/2004_D21_Strategy_consultation_paper_Eng.pdf, visited 22 October 2003.
23. Public Consultation on 2004 Digital 21 Strategy, Communications and Technology Branch, Commerce, Industry and Technology Bureau, Hong Kong SAR Government, 2003, para. 14, p. 6.
24. Charlesworth, 'The Goverance of the Internet in Europe', p. 59.
25. Ibid.
26. Council of Europe, Covention on Cyber-crime, Budapest, 23.XI.2001.
27. See D Wall, 'Maintaining order and law on the Internet'; see also Wall, 'Policing the Internet'.
28. Wall, Insecurity and the Policing of Cyberspace', p. 195.
29. Wall, 'Policing the Internet', p.164.
30. Ibid., p.163.
31. Ibid.
32. See http://www.linux.org.hk/, visited 17 August 2002.
33. See http://www.hktug.org/index.html, visited 17 August 2002.
34. Reiner, *The Politics of the Police*, p. 50.
35. Lau, *Society and Politics in Hong Kong*, p. 87.
36. Lau and Kuan, *The Ethos of the Hong Kong Chinese*.
37. Lau, *Society and Politics in Hong Kong*, p. 106.
38. Lau and Kuan, *The Ethos of the Hong Kong Chinese*, p.114.
39. See http://www.hkispa.org.hk/, visited 21 August 2002.
40. Wall, Policing the Internet', p. 165.
41. Cited in *The Times*, 31 March 2000, p. 7.
42. See K "http://www.iwf.org.uk" http://www.iwf.org.uk, visited 21 August 2002.
43. Wall, 'Policing the Internet', p. 166.

44. Johnston, *Policing Britain*, p. 130.
45. See http://www.hkpc.org, (visited 26 August 2002).
46. See http://www.ja.net/CERT/cert.html (visited 20 October 2003).
47. The figure is calculated from 7 million divided by 28 665 disciplined staff as stated in *2001 Hong Kong Police Review*, Hong Kong Police, Appendix 3.
48. Wall, 'Maintaining order and law on the Internet', p. 177.
49. R. Broadhurst, 'Crime Trends in Hong Kong', see http://hku.hk/crime/rb-crimetrends.htm, visited 12 December 2002.
50. Ibid., p. 2.
51. Ibid.
52. Ibid.
53. R Broadhurst, Summary Report: 2nd Asian CyberCrime Summit: Hong Kong University Council Chamber 5–6 November 2003, e-proceedings, p. 17.
54. Wall, 'Insecurity and the Policing of Cyberspace', p. 204.

Chapter 6

* This chapter is based on research conducted by the author at Cardiff University while seconded from the National Police Agency. It is drawn from a dissertation, supervised by Professor Michael Levi, focusing on the responsibilitisation of telecoms and financial industry for policing.

1. See Council of Europe (2001: paragraph 5).
2. The author concerned himself with the law by liaising with the telecoms industry and by focusing on the procedural details of due process of the Law.
3. For example, the *Interception Of Communication Act* (IOCA) 1985 in the UK and the Title III of the *Omnibus Crime Control and Safe Streets Act* of 1968 in the US.
4. Testimony of Hayashi, Norikiyo, the then Director-General of Criminal Police at Keisatsucho, before the Legal Committee, House of Councillors, 11 July 1999.
5. Testimony of Matsuo, Kunihiro, the then Director-General of Criminal Justice, Homusho, before the Legal Committee, House of Councillors, 6 July 1999.
6. Article 218 of the Criminal Procedure Code.
7. Articles 114 and 142.
8. 'Soshiki Hanzai Hoan no Yukue' (Organised Crime Bill's Whereabouts). *Mainichi Shinbun,* 21 May 1999, http://www.mainichi.co.jp/eye/feature/article/digital/55/55_4.html.
9. Article 12, paragraph 1 of the Interception Law.
10. Article 114, paragraph 2 of the Criminal Procedure Code.
11. Statement of Sasagawa, Takashi, a member of the House of Representatives, before the Legal Committee, House of Councillors, 29 June 1999.
12. Testimony before the Legal Committee, House of Councillors, 19 May 1998.
13. 'Tachiainin Keihi mo 'Jigyosha de'' ('Operators are' compelled to pay Tachiainin

costs), morning issue of *Asahi Shinbun*. 13 August 2000, http://www.asahi.com/tech/jiken/20000813b.html. However, the validity of the media's articles about the Interception Bill was questioned. Seko, Hiroshige, a lawmaker who had been employed by the common carrier (NTT), indicated (before the Legal Committee, House of Councillors, 13 July 1999), with evidence, the article's errors were grounded on prejudice.

14. Testimony of Matsuo, Kunihiro, before the Legal Committee, House of Councillors, 29 July 1999.
15. For example, the *Communication Assistance for Law Enforcement Act* of 1994 (CALEA) of the US places telecommunication providers under an obligation to be equipped with interception capabilities. Similarly in the UK, the *Regulation of Investigatory Powers Act* 2000 stipulates in article 12 that persons providing public telecommunications services are liable to assist with interception capabilities.
16. After two Annual Interception Reports reporting that no case was applied, the first productive report was submitted to the Diet in February 2003. It disclosed that four interception warrants for mobile phones were enforced for drug dealing cases in the previous year. See http://www.npa.go.jp/keiji/boujyuhouoku.htm.
17. Japanese police have obtained traffic data from telecommunication companies with court warrants.
18. See http://www.itu.int/council/index97/1997/135/135.html.
19. See http://www.etsi.org/.
20. Article 16 of the Convention on Cyber-crime: Explanatory Report. http://conventions.coe.int/Treaty/en/Reports/Html/185.htm.
21. See http://www.moj.go.jp/SHINGI/030324–2.html.
22. See http://www.npa.go.jp/safetylife/seiankis9/kobutu.htm.
23. See http://www.watch.impress.co.jp/internet/www/article/2002/0315/npa.htm.
24. Testimony of Tajima, Yoko, a member of the House of Councillors, before the Cabinet Committee, House of Councillors, 19 November 2003.
25. 'Keitai Denwa: Tokumei no Kyoki' (Mobile phone: an anonymous weapon), a morning issue of *Asahi Shinbun*, 26 April 2000, http://www.asahi.com/tech/jiken/20000426a.html.
26. Ibid.
27. Testimony of Yashiro, Eita, before the Budget Committee, House of Councillors, 25 April 2000.
28. 'Prepaid Shiki Keitai Denwa ni Kansuru Taiosaku' (Safeguard of Prepaid Mobile Phone). NTT DoCoMo, 5 May 2000, http://www.nttdocomo.co.jp/new/contents/00/whatnew0512.html.
29. Just as Garland (1996: 465) discovered the prototypical responsibilisation 200 years ago, controlling chaotic society in London aggravated by the rapid spread of capitalism.
30. Japanese interception has never applied to crimes other than drug-related.
31. See case studies above on both Japanese and British mobile phone operators.
32. There is at least an exception, the Japanese Interception Law.

33. The notion could not always be applicable. For example, again, paying the costs of Tachiainin (of the Interception Law) by the state might be problematic. Since watching the due process is an important role, payment of the personnel expenses by the party being overseen might be viewed as the emasculation of the Tachiainin.
34. See Duff and Marshall (2000: 33) for the difference between responsibilities and obligations.
35. See Manning (2000).
36. The service was privatised in 1985 (Hayashi and Tagawa 1994: 216).
37. http://www.iso.ch/.

Chapter 7

1. The following is a list of relevant websites:
   Centre for Information Systems Security, DSO National Laboratories.security.dso.org.sg
   Criminal Investigation Division, Singapore Police Force. http://www.spinet.gov.sg/aboutus/org/org_main_cid.htm
   Controller of Certification Authorities. www.cca.gov.sg
   Defence Science and Technology Agency. www.dsta.gov.sg
   DSO National Laboratories. www.dso.org.sg
   e-Celebrations Singapore. www.ecelebrations.gov.sg
   Infocomm Development Authority of Singapore. www.ida.gov.sg
   IDA Infocomm Security Campaign. www.ida.gov.sg/Website/IDAhome.nsf/fFrame?OpenForm&doc=@http://www.ida.gov.sg/Website/IDAcontent.nsf/dd1521f1e79ecf3bc825682f00045a340/9d12481c91154c1048256b1200150cbb? OpenDocument
   Information Technology Standards Committee. www.itsc.org.sg
   Institute for Infocomm Research. http://www.i2r.a-star.edu.sg/
   Monetary Authority of Singapore, Internet Banking Technology Risk Management Guidelines
   http://www.mas.gov.sg/display.cfm?id=2DE15130–3854–11D5–A686006008A60E7E
   Nation Infocomm Certification Centre. www.nicc.org.sg
   Nation Internet Advisory Committee. www.sba.gov.sg/sba/i_niac.jsp
   Netrust (Certification Authority). www.netrust.com.sg
   PKI Forum Singapore. www.pkiforumsingapore.org.sg.
   School of Computing, National University of Singapore. www.comp.nus.edu.sg/research/research.htm
   Singapore Academy of Law, Technology Law Development Group. http://www.sal.org.sg/svcs_rschLaw_tldg.htm
   Singapore IT Federation. www.sitf.org.sg
   SingCERT. www.singcert.org.sg

Singapore Customs, Strategic Goods Control. http://www.stgc.gov.sg/stgc/index_home.jsp
SPRING Singapore. www.spring.gov.sg
Tamasek Laboratories. www.temasek-lab.nus.edu.sg
TrustSg. www.trustsg.org.sg

Chapter 8

* We would like to thank Bec Jenkins, Michael Cook and Philippa Bergin for their research and editorial assistance, and Phil Drury, IT&C Unit of the Law Faculty, for explaining how computer systems really work. This research was funded by the ANU Faculties Research Grant Scheme, and is part of the wider research project examining the legal responses to terrorism funded by an Australian Research Council Discovery Grant (DP451473). With the kind permission of the respective publishers, this chapter is based on research and material published in 'Shifting Boundaries of Cybercrime: From Computer Hacking to Cyberterrorism' (2003) 27 *Criminal Law Journal* 303.

1. Aust, H of Reps, *Debates*, 27 June 2001, Hansard, p. 28641 (Darryl Williams).
2. Elder J, 'Cyber-Terrorism' (2001) *E-Law Practice*, Issue 9, p. 24.
3. Model Criminal Code Officers Committee of the Standing Committee of Attorneys-General, *Model Criminal Code — Chapter 4: Damage and Computer Offences*, Report (2001).
4. See Part 6 of the *Crimes Act 1900* (NSW), amended by the *Crimes Amendment (Computer Offences) Act 2001* (NSW).
5. On 26 September 2002, the Chief Minister presented to the Legislative Assembly of the ACT the Criminal Code Bill 2002, which includes cyber-crime provisions based on the Model Criminal Code. The *Criminal Code 2002* (ACT) came into force on 1 January 2003.
6. The Crimes (Property Damage and Computer Offences) Bill 2003 was introduced into the Victorian Parliament on 20 March 2003. The amendments to the Victorian *Crimes Act* thereby effected, commenced on 7 May 2003.
7. The trend towards uniformity is not absolute, however. The Northern Territory somewhat idiosyncratically amended the computer offences in its *Criminal Code* by passing the *Criminal Code Amendment Act (No. 3) 2001* (NT) which came into effect on 30 January 2002. The NT amendments effectively straddle the MCC and non-MCC regimes. While ss. 276C and 276D substantially mirror code provisions, ss. 276B and 276E have no Model Criminal Code equivalents and s. 222 (unlawful abstraction of confidential information from a computer) is retained from the previous legislative regime (see the tables below for further details). In introducing the Bill, the NT Attorney-General, Dr Toyne, made no specific reference to the Model Criminal Code but rather stated that the bill was 'the result of several months of consultation research into the developments of

national and international computer law' and that it 'fulfils the Northern Territory's obligation to assist in national and international efforts to control computer crime': Northern Territory Legislative Assembly, 2001, *Debates*, 17 October 2001.

8. Aust, H of Reps, *Debates*, 26 September 2001, Hansard, p. 31575 (Duncan Kerr). A wide definition of cyber-crime was adopted in Grabosky & Smith, *Crime in the Digital Age*.
9. See the discussion on these points by Urbas in 'Cyber-crime Legislation in the Asia-Pacific Region', pp. 58–9.
10. See the discussion in relation to fraud and forgery on the Internet, MCCOC, above n. 3, p. 100.
11. Aust, H of Reps, 27 June 2001, above n. 1, p. 28642.
12. AusCert, NSW Police and Deloitte Touche Tohmatsu, *2002 Australian Computer Crime and Security Survey*.
13. Ibid., p. 11.
14. Ibid., pp. 1, 5–6. This increase represented a doubling of the incidents reported in the previous survey in 1999.
15. Ibid., pp. 1, 7.
16. Ibid., p. 7.
17. See for example, Law Commission (Eng and Wales) *Computer Misuse*, Report No. 186, para. 3.35 and Attorney-General's Department, *Review of Commonwealth Criminal Law: Interim Report, Computer Crime* (Canberra, Australian Government Publishing Service, 1988) (Gibbs Report), para. 4.43.
18. AusCert, *2002 Australian Computer Crime and Security Survey*, pp. 1, 28.
19. Ibid., p. 1 with reference to Richard Power, *2002 CSI / FBI Computer Crime and Security Survey*, VIII(1) 2002.
20. Ogilvie, 'Cyber-stalking'. See generally, Oglivie, *Stalking*.
21. Many of the reported security incidents involving computers can be prosecuted as ordinary crimes. For example, one of the most frequently reported security incidents in Australia is the theft of laptops, which is manifestly a simple theft offence: see Austcert, p. 11. Likewise, the prosecution of computer fraud can effectively be dealt with by ensuring that existing fraud provisions extend to cover fraud perpetrated by means of a computer.
22. 'Telecommunications service' is defined as 'a service carrying guided or unguided electromagnetic energy or both' (s. 476.1). This definition is not limited to access via conventional phone lines but would probably include access via an intranet or wireless local area network. It is unclear whether this would extend to data accessed across optical fibre systems.
23. A. Steel, 'Vaguely Going Where No-one Has Gone: the Expansive New Computer Access Offences' (2002) 26 *CrimLJ* 72 at 73.
24. For an extensive analysis of computer related laws in Australia before 1988, see C Sullivan, 'The Response of the Criminal Law in Australia to Computer Abuse' (1988) 12 *CrimLJ* 228.

25. *Oxford v Moss* (1978) 68 Cr App R 183; *Stewart* (1988) 41 CCC (3d) 481. Discussed in Bronitt and McSherry, *Principles of Criminal Law*.
26. G Hughes, 'Computers, Crime and the Concept of "Property"' (1990) 1 *Australian Intellectual Property Journal* 154 at 158.
27. The definition of property in criminal damage offences is often narrower than those applied to theft offences; see for example, *Crimes Act 1958* (Vic), s. 96 (1) which confines 'property' to tangibles for the purpose of malicious damage.
28. *Cox v Riley* (1986) 83 Cr App R 54; *Re Turner* (1984) 13 CCC (3d) 430.
29. See Hughes, 'Computers, Crime and the Concept of "Property"', at 160.
30. See J McConvill, 'Contemporary Comment: Computer Trespass' (2001) 25 *CrimLJ* 220, who suggests that amending the definition of 'property' to include computer data would overcome the obstacles of applying theft and damage offences to computer crime. As Gordon Hughes has observed in relation to theft, however, 'stealing' data by copying still continues to present problems in relation to the requirement of an intention to permanently deprive; see discussion above, nn 26 and 29.
31. Section 222 of the Northern Territory *Criminal Code 1983* (NT) prohibits the unlawful abstraction of confidential information from any register, document, computer or other repository of information with certain states of mind. The NT is unique in protecting confidential information in this way.
32. Gibbs Report, above n. 17.
33. See *Crimes Act 1900* (ACT), s. 135K; *Criminal Code* (Tas), s. 257C. The equivalent offence in NSW was contained in *Crimes Act 1900* (NSW), s. 310 (now repealed).
34. Queensland Department of Justice, *Green Paper on Computer Related Crime and the Criminal Code of Queensland*, 1987, pp. 35–8.
35. See the discussion by Hughes, 'Computers, Crime and the Concept of "Property"' at p. 162. See Table 8.1 below for jurisdictions that have not legislated against unauthorised data modification.
36. *Stewart* (1988) 41 CCC (3d) 481 at 491–2 per Lamer J.
37. See, for example, the former section 309 of the *Crimes Act 1900* (NSW): 'a person who, without authority or lawful excuse, intentionally obtains access to a program or data stored in a computer is liable, on conviction before two justices, to imprisonment for six months, or a fine of 50 penalty units, or both'. The rest of the provision imposes greater penalty for access in the aggravating circumstances contained in the Commonwealth offence.
38. MCCOC, *Model Criminal Code*, p. 91.
39. See the discussion relating to crimes against the market in P Alldridge, *Relocating Criminal Law*, Ashgate, 2000, pp. 165–7.
40. MCCOC, *Model Criminal Code*, p. 94.
41. Ibid., p. 106.
42. For a detailed analysis of these provisions and their NSW counterparts, see the discussion by Steel, 'Vaguely Going Where No-one Has Gone'.
43. Ibid., pp. 92–3.

44. *MacLeod v Attorney-General (NSW)* [1891] AC 455 at 458–9 per Halsbury LC. The idea that the criminal law is 'territorial' in the sense of being bound to a defined geographic territory is considered to be a 'general thesis of the common law': *Thompson v The Queen* (1989) 169 CLR 1 at 33 per Deane J.
45. See Bronitt and McSherry, *Principles of Criminal Law*, Ch 2.
46. D Lanham, *Cross-Border Criminal Law*, FT Law & Tax Asia Pacific, 1997, p. 3.
47. Alldridge, *Relocating Criminal Law*, p. 142.
48. McConvill, 'Contemporary Comment: Computer Trespass', p. 227.
49. E.g. *Crimes Act 1900* (ACT), s. 3A; *Crimes Act 1900* (NSW), s. 3A which was replaced in 2000 by s. 10C, *Crimes Act 1900* (NSW) (geographical nexus), discussed in n. 61. See M Hinton and C Lind, 'The Territorial Application of the Criminal Law — When Crime is Not Local' (1999) 23 *Crim LJ* 285 at 287–8.
50. See for example, *Criminal Code* 1924 (Tas), s. 257F(1).
51. The tests of the majority were similar though expressed in different terms: Gleeson C J at 17 (real connection); Gaudron, Gummow and Hayne J J at 34 (sufficient connection); Callinan (real link). These formulations were influenced by the 'real and substantial link' test in Canadian law: *Libman* [1985] 2 SCR 178. In relation to a small number of offences, Victoria has adopted a real and substantial link test in preference to the territorial nexus test: s. 80A, *Crimes Act* 1958 (Vic). The Canadian test has the support of many commentators: M Goode, 'Two New Decisions on Criminal 'Jurisdiction': The Appalling Durability of Common Law' (1996) 20 *Crim LJ* 267 at 279–80.
52. In *Lipohar v The Queen* (1999) 168 ALR 8, Gaudron, Gummow, and Hayne J J held (at 41) that considerations of comity would have no bearing on relations between jurisdictions within a federal system: 'Within Australia, any rationale for the common law rule respecting comity between what became the States disappeared with federation'.
53. MCCOC, *Model Criminal Code*, p. 170.
54. *Lipohar v The Queen* (1999) 168 ALR 8 at 64.
55. MCCOC, *Model Criminal Code*, p. 242.
56. Aust H of Reps, *Debates*, 27 June 2001, Hansard, p. 28641.
57. This point was acknowledged in the Council of Europe, *Explanatory Report to the Convention on Cybercrime* (2001) para. 236: see URL, http://conventions.coe.int/Treaty/en/Treaties/Html/185.html, (viewed 9 October 2003). For a comparison between domestic and international conceptions of jurisdiction see Bronitt and McSherry, *Principles of Criminal Law*, p. 91.
58. Ibid., pp. 90–1.
59. Art. 22, ETS, No 185 (23/11/01). See Csonka, Ch. 15.
60. MCCOC, *Model Criminal Code*, pp. 245ff.
61. Bronitt & McSherry, *Principles of Criminal Law*, pp. 90–1.
62. Independently of the cyber-crime reforms in NSW in 2001 (see n. 4 above), the jurisdiction provisions were amended by the *Crimes Legislation Amendment Act 2000* (NSW). These amendments apply generally to all offences in the *Crimes*

Act: s. 10A(1). Under s. 10C, a geographical nexus exists when the offence is committed wholly or partly in NSW or when the offence has an effect that is felt in NSW. The ACT has followed the NSW approach, introducing similarly worded geographical nexus provisions of general application by way of Part 2.7 of the *Criminal Code 2002* (ACT). The NT has taken a somewhat different tack: computer offence-specific territorial nexus provisions formed part of the 2001 Act amending the NT *Criminal Code*; see n. 7 above. Under s. 276F, a territorial nexus exists where either the perpetrator performs the unlawful act within the NT or the computer affected by the unlawful act is in the NT. Victoria has followed the NT approach in terms both of substance and of adopting a computer offence-specific extraterritoriality provision: *Crimes Act 1958* (Vic), s. 247I. None of these jurisdictions have extended the extraterritorial application of their computer offence provisions beyond this.

63. The idea that cyberspace will emerge as a distinct legal space, generating its own laws and institutions, separate from 'real space law' was suggested in D. Johnson and D Post, 'Law and Borders: The Rise of Law in Cyberspace' (1996) 48 *Stanford LR* 1367.
64. See, for example, A Sofaer and S Goodman (eds), *The Transnational Dimension of Cyber Crime and Terrorism*, Hoover Institution Press, 2001, p. 2: 'A transnational response sufficient to meet these transnational challenges is an immediate and compelling necessity.'
65. C Reed, *Internet Law — Text and Materials*, Butterworths, 2000, p. 188. For a recent Australian text that succumbs to this fallacy, see Y F Lim, *Cyberspace Law: Commentaries and Materials*, Melbourne: Oxford University Press, 2002. Lim claims on p. 60: 'State and national borders are no longer relevant in cyberspace. The Internet lacks physical boundaries and communities and communications that exist on the Internet do not exist in any particular jurisdiction ... This anomaly poses a problem that current jurisdiction cannot solve.'
66. These points appear in Broadhurst, *Proceedings of the Asia Cyber Crime Summit*, p. 244.
67. Section 10.4, *Model Criminal Code* (self defence). See MCCOC, *Model Criminal Code*, pp. 108–11.
68. [1997] 3 SLR 922, at para. 52.
69 See S Bronnitt, 'Sang is Dead, Loosely Speaking — *R v Looseley*' [2002] *Singapore J of Legal Studies* 374.
70. For a review of these rules see O Akindemowo, *Information Technology Law in Australia*, LBC Information Services, 1999, Ch. 7.
71. Explanatory Memorandum, *Cybercrime Act 2001* (Cth), presented by Chris Ellison, 27 June 2001.
72. *Crimes Act 1914* (Cth), s. 3L(1).
73. *Crimes Act 1914* (Cth), s. 3LA.
74. Although not expressly authorised by the earlier Act, the process of taking a forensic image of the entire contents of the hard drive, upon which some evidence

may be contained, was held to be a lawful search in *Williams v Keelty* [2001] FCA 1301. The judge was persuaded by a forensic technician assisting police who testified that the alternative search for relevant files would have taken a week, and that simply 'copying a single file is probably the worst way of treating evidence from a computer' [50], see also [290–300].

75. *Crimes Act 1914* (Cth), s. 3L(1A).
76. *Klass v Germany* (1978) 2 EHRR 214; *Khan v UK* [2000] 31 EHRR 1016.
77. *Crimes Act 1914* (Cth), s. 3P(2).
78. For recent affirmation of the value of the right to remain silent, see *R v Swaffield; Pavic v R* (1998) 151 ALR 98 where the High Court held that using undercover police or informers to elicit confessions from suspects in unfair or improper derogation of their right to silence may justify the exclusion of that evidence: E Stone, 'Casenote: The Law of Confessions in Theory and Practice: Swaffield and Pavic' (1999) 3(1) *Intern'l J Evidence and Proof* 57. The Australian approach has recently been followed in Europe: see *Allan v UK* [2003] 36 EHRR 12.
79. The privilege originated as a means of protecting suspects from oppressive interrogation, but is now recognised as a basic human right protecting personal freedom and human dignity: *EPA v Caltex* (1993) 178 CLR 447. See also *Heaney v Ireland* (2000) 33 EHRR 264.
80. *Telecommunications (Interception) Act 1979 (Cth) — Report for the Year Ending 30 June 2001*, Canberra, 2001, p. 24.
81. For a recent review of the law in this area see A Ashworth, 'Re-Drawing the Boundaries of Entrapment' [2002] *Crim LR* 161. On the wider normative issues, see S Bronnitt and D Roche, 'Between Rhetoric and Reality: Sociolegal and Republican Perspectives on Entrapment' (2000) 4 *Intern'l J Evidence and Proof* 77.
82. For discussion of this concept, through which communities identify, demonise and criminalise individuals or groups, see Cohen, *Folk Devils and Moral Panics*, p. 9.
83. Dupont, 'Policing in the Information Age'.
84. Section 100.1 of the *Criminal Code* (Cth) defines terror acts as an action or threat of action done or made with the intention of advancing a political, religious or ideological cause and, additionally with the intention of coercing, or influencing by intimidation a government (including that of a foreign country); or intimidating the public or a section of the public.
85. For a recent article reviewing these provisions see G Carne, 'Terror and the Ambit Claim: Security Legislation Amendment (Terrorism) Act 2002 (Cth) (2003) 14 Public Law Review 13 at 14.
86. Summit Communiqué, 5 April 2002, http://www.nca.gov.au/content/MedRel/FinalSummitCommunique.pdf (viewed 10 October 2003). A significant outcome of the summit has been the preparation of a model law, to be enacted in all Australian jurisdictions, which will facilitate cross-border covert investigations in a range of areas including controlled operations and the use of surveillance:

Standing Committee of Attorneys-General and Australasian Police Ministers Council Joint Working Group on National Investigation Powers, *Cross- Border Investigative Powers for Law Enforcement* — Report, November 2003.

Chapter 9

1. For general information about the Japanese government's IT policies, see http://www.kantei.go.jp/foreign/policyindex_e.html.
2. http://www.kantei.go.jp/foreign/it/network/priority-all/index.html. The programme was revised in 2002, the revision being referred to as the 'e-Japan Priority Policy Programme — 2002'. The English version has not yet been released.
3. 2002 White Paper Information and Communications in Japan, Ministry of Public Management, Home Affairs, Posts and Telecommunications. http://www.soumu.go.jp/hakusyo/index.html.
4. See Figure 1.
5. See Figures 2 and 3.
6. For details, see V. 4. and the Annex.
7. The Penal Code (Law No. 45 of 1907), Art. 246–2: 'Except cases to which article 246 (Fraud) shall apply, any person who produces a false electro-magnetic record which represents acquisition, loss or alteration of property rights, by providing a computer used for the administration of another person's business with false information or command, or by putting such false electro-magnetic record in use for another person's business, acquires illicit profit or causes another person to acquire such profit shall be punished with imprisonment of not more than ten years.'
8. Ibid., Art. 161–2, para. 1: 'Any person who, with the intent to bring about improper administration of affairs of another person, unlawfully produces an electro-magnetic record which is for the use of the administration of such affairs and is related to right, duty or certification of fact shall be punished with imprisonment for not more than five years or with a fine of not more than 500 000 yen.' Para. 2: 'When the offence specified in para. 1 is committed against an electro-magnetic record which should be prepared by a public office or public officer, any person who commits such offence shall be punished with imprisonment for not more than ten years, or with a fine of not more than one million yen.'
9. Ibid., Art. 234–2: 'Any person who obstructs the business of another person by impeding the operation of a computer being used for another person's business fitting to the purpose of such use or letting such computer operate in a way contradictive to such purpose by destroying such computer or an electro-magnetic record for it, or by providing such computer with false information or command or by any other means, shall be punished with imprisonment for not more than five years or with fine of not more than one million yen.'
10. Ibid., Art. 258: 'A person who destroys or mutilates a document or an electro-

magnetic record in use by a public office shall be punished with imprisonment of not less than three months, nor more than seven years.'

11. Ibid., Art. 259: 'A person who destroys or mutilates a document or an electro-magnetic record of another which relates to a right or duty shall be punished with imprisonment of not more than five years.'
12. Ibid., Art. 163–2, para. 1: 'Any person who, with the intent to bring about improper economic administration of affairs of another person, unlawfully produces an electro-magnetic record which is for the use of the administration of such affairs and composes credit card or other payment card for cost or charge, shall be punished with imprisonment of not more than ten years or with a fine of not more than one million yen. The same shall apply to a person who unlawfully produces an electro-magnetic record which composes a card for withdrawal from a bank deposit.'
13. Generally, see the web-pages of the IT Security Office (Cabinet Secretariat). http://www.bits.go.jp/en/index.html.
14. Art. 22: 'In formulating measures on the formation of an advanced information and telecommunications network society, it is necessary to assure security and reliability for advanced information and telecommunications networks, protect personal data and implement other measures required so that people may use advanced information and telecommunications networks with a sense of security.'
15. http://www.bits.go.jp/en/kouhyou/0519action.html.
16. http://www.bits.go.jp/en/kouhyou/guideline.html.
17. http://www.bits.go.jp/en/kouhyou/cyber_terror.html.
18. The English version has not yet been released.
19. The English version has not yet been released.
20. See Figure 6.
21. Law No. 128 of 1999, http://www.npa.go.jp/hightech/fusei_ac2/ucalaw.html.
22. Art. 3 and 8.
23. Art. 4 and 9.
24. Art. 5.
25. Art. 6.
26. See Figures 2 and 3.
27. http://www.undcp.org/pdf/crime/a_res_56/121e.pdf.
28. http://www.apecsec.org.sg/whatsnew/press/PressRel_APECLeadersCounterTerrorStmt2002_261002.html.
29. Hong Kong, China, Indonesia, Korea, Malaysia, Philippines, Singapore, Thailand, India and Japan.

Chapter 10

1. http://www.nasscom.org/.
2. http://www.nasscom.org/it_industry/int_survey.asp.
3. http://www.nasscom.org/it_industry/internet_trends.asp.

4. http://www.srijith.net/indiacracked/stats/index.shtml.
5. http://www.mit.gov.in/itbill2000.pdf.
6. http://www.apnic.net/mailing-lists/s-asia-it/archive/2001/05/msg00017.html
7. http://www.tribuneindia.com/2002/20020728/ncr1.htm#3.

Chapter 11

1. A hash value of an electronic object, such as a computer file, is a binary string computed from all bits of that electronic object, and can be considered as a 'fingerprint' of that electronic object. The theory of hash value (Schneier, B. 1995. *Applied Cryptography,* Wiley and Sons, New York (2nd Edition)) supports the fact that if the hash values of two electronic objects are equal, then the two electronic objects are most likely equal. The hash value of other electronic objects such as a directory of files can be computed similarly.
2. Encoding for characters in Traditional Chinese.
3. Encoding for characters in Simplified Chinese.

Chapter 12

* This chapter is based on a paper initially prepared by the author while employed as a research analyst at the Australian Institute of Criminology (AIC) for the 1st Asia Cyber-Crime Summit held at the Centre for Criminology at the University of Hong Kong during 25–26 April 2001, and revised for the 2nd Asia Cyber-crime Summit held during 5–6 November 2003 (see http://www.hku.hk/crime). The author wishes to thank the organisers and sponsors of the Asia Cyber-crime Summit, Professor Peter Grabosky (RegNet ANU), the AIC research and library staff, and anonymous referees for helpful comments.

1. From Goodman & Brenner, 'The Emerging Consensus on Criminal Conduct in Cyberspace'. http://www.lawtechjournal.com/articles/2002/03_020625_goodmanbrenner.php, note 5, quoting Lev Grossman, 'Attack of the Love Bug', *Time Europe*, 15 May 2000; see further Infowar, 'Viruses': http://www.info-sec.com/viruses/viruses_1.shtml.
2. 'Philippine dropout to be charged for "Love Bug"', *New York Times*, 15 June 2000.
3. Goodman and Brenner, 'The Emerging Consensus', note 17.
4. *Electronic Commerce Act 2000*, s. 33(a).
5. For that matter, there is no consensus on whether this term is one word ('cyber-crime') or two ('cyber crime'). This paper uses the former to be consistent with legislative instruments such as the Council of Europe's Convention on Cyber-crime and the Australian Parliament's recently enacted *Cyber-crime Act 2001* (Cth).
6. Grabosky & Smith, *Crime in the Digital Age*, pp.14–17; see also Grabosky, Smith and Dempsey, *Electronic Theft*.

7. For a detailed analysis of the development of national computer crime laws in context see U Sieber, *Legal Aspects of Computer-Related Crime in the Information Society*, Comcrime Study prepared for the European Commission, Version 1.0, 1998, available at http://europa.eu.int/ISPO/legal/en/comcrime/sieber.html.
8. The terms 'Internet' and 'World Wide Web' are often used synonymously in public discussion, but there is a technical difference: the TCP / IP protocol that forms the Internet is amenable to various uses, only one of which is the Web. Other uses are e-mail, video and audio streaming, real-time chat services and so on: see K H Tan, 'Prosecuting foreign-based computer crime: International law and technology collide', Symposium on Rule of Law in the Global Village, 12–14 December 2000, Palermo, note 26.
9. See, for example, US Department of Justice, *The Electronic Frontier: Unlawful Conduct Involving the Use of the Internet*. Report of the President's Working Group on Unlawful Conduct on the Internet, March 2000: http://www.usdoj.gov/criminal/cyber-crime/unlawful.htm; and Smith & Urbas, *Controlling Fraud on the Internet*; also available on CAPA website: http://www.capa.com.my.
10. See Grabosky & Smith, *Crime in the Digital Age*, p. 91.
11. See Speer, 'Redefining borders'. Consider also recent developments involving ISP Yahoo! and the posting of material relating to auctions of Nazi memorabilia on sites it hosted: Carl S. Kaplan, 'Experts See Online Speech Case as Bellwether' *New York Times*, 5 January 2001: http://www.nytimes.com/2001/01/05/technology/05CYBERLAW.html.
12. See Heath, *Intellectual Property Rights in Asia*. http://www.intellecprop.mpg.de/Online-Publikationen/Heath-Ipeaover.htm.
13. See Clarke, 'Private enforcement of intellectual property rights in China'; Urbas, 'Public Enforcement of Intellectual Property Rights', also available at http://www.aic.gov.au/publications/tandi/tandi177.html.
14. See Goodman & Brenner, 'The Emerging Consensus', note 172.
15. See ibid., note 173.
16. For example, many of these substantive and procedural elements have been incorporated into recent Australian legislative reform in the *Cyber-crime Act 2001* (Cth). See also D E Thompson & D R Berwick, *Minimum Provisions for the Investigation of Computer Based Offences*, Report Series No. 129.1, National Police Research Unit, 1998. http://www.acpr.gov.au/pdf/ACPR129_1.pdf.
17. McConnell International, *Cyber Crime…and Punishment? Archaic Laws Threaten Global Information*, online report, 2000. http://www.mcconnellinternational.com/services/Cyber-crime.pdf. The basis used for comparison was a list of '10 different types of cyber-crime in four categories: data-related crimes including interception, modification, and theft; network-related crimes, including interference and sabotage; crimes of access, including hacking and virus distribution; and associated computer-related crimes, including aiding and abetting cyber-criminals, computer fraud, and computer forgery.'
18. OECD website: http://www.oecd.org/home.

19. Held in Vienna 10–17 April 2000, and endorsed by the General Assembly in December 2000. http://www.undcp.crg/pdf/crime/10_commission/resumed_session/14e.pdf.
20. http://www.unis.unvienna.org/en/news/2000/pressrels/cp388e.html.
21. See Goodman & Brenner, 'The Emerging Consensus', note 200 for details.
22. Full text at: http://conventions.coe.int/Treaty/en/Treaties/Html/185.htm.
23. As of July 2004, 37 countries had signed the Convention, including non-European members such as Canada, Japan and the United States, while eight have ratified, enabling the treaty to come into effect: http://conventions.coe.int/Treaty/EN/searchsig.asp?NT=185&CM =1&DF=
24. See http://www.coe.int/T/E/Legal_affairs/Legal_co-operation/Combating_economic_crime/Cyber-crime/Racism_on_internet/_Summary.asp#TopOfPage.
25. *International Crime Threat Assessment*, Report of a United States Government interagency working group in support of and pursuant to the President's International Crime Control Strategy, 2000, Chapter II: http://www.fas.org/irp/threat/pub45270index.html.
26. McConnell International, *Cyber Crime ... and Punishment? Archaic Laws Threaten Global Information*, online report: http://www.mcconnellinternational.com/services/Cyber-crime.pdf.
27. Added by the *Crimes Legislation Amendment Act 1989* (Cth).
28. See now s. 476.1 of the *Criminal Code Act 1995* (Cth).
29. Section 51(v) of the Constitution: 'postal, telegraphic, telephonic, and other like services'.
30. Section 9A was recently repealed with the enactment of the *Crimes (Property Damage and Computer Offences) Act 2003*).
31. Model Criminal Code Officers Committee (MCCOC) of the Standing Committee of Attorneys-General Australia 2001, *Model Criminal Code*, 2001, Ch. 4: 'Damage and Computer Offences' and Amendment to Chapter 2: 'Jurisdiction': http://www.law.gov.au/publications/Model_Criminal_Code/index.htm. In particular, New South Wales, Victoria, the Australian Capital Territory and the Northern Territory have fully or partially adopted the model provisions, with South Australia announcing similar amendments to be put before its Parliament in the near future.
32. Joint media release dated 20 August 2003: http://www.dcita.gov.au/Article/0,,0_1–2_15–4_116473,00.html.
33. *Spam Act 2003* (Cth): http://scaleplus.law.gov.au/html/pasteact/3/3628/top.htm.
34. D Clarke, 'Private enforcement of intellectual property rights in China', p. 33.
35. Chang et al., *China's Internet Policy and Legislation*.
36. Advertent or inadvertent disclosure of state secrets is also prohibited: http://www.bakerinfo.com/apec/chinaapec_main.htm#8 and http://www.bakerinfo.com/apec/chinaapec_main.htm#9.2 (Baker McKenzie).
37. Carr, 'India joins the cyber-race'.
38. Carr & Williams, 'Securing the e-commerce environment'.
39. Smith & Urbas, *Controlling Fraud on the Internet*.

40. Carr & Williams, 'Securing the e-commerce environment'.
41. For example, the Philippines' 'hacking or cracking' offence: s. 33(a) of the *Electronic Commerce Act 2000*.
42. For example, s. 246–2 of Japan's *Computer Crime Act*: intentionally obtaining a profit by introducing false information or wrong instructions into any computer system used in the course of business transactions.
43. An exception is s. 76 of India's *Information Technology Act 2000*.
44. The Philippines is an exception: s. 33(b) of the *Electronic Commerce Act 2000*.
45. *Computer Crime Act 1997*, s. 7: http://www.mycert.mimos.my.
46. Australian Commonwealth legislation makes maximum fines that can be imposed on a corporation five times the criminal fines applicable to individuals: s. 4B(3) of the *Crimes Act 1914* (Cth).
47. See C Buddle, 'Special team set up to tackle dramatic surge in number of computer offences', *SCMP*, 20 January 2000, p. 2.
48. National Police Agency: http://www.npa.go.jp/hightech/jyu_prog/pro_eng.htm.
49. *Korea Herald*, 'Law enforcement officers step up efforts to tame cyber crime', 17 November 2000.
50. See 'Cyber Crime Investigation Cell': http://cbi.nic.in/cyber1.htm.
51. Section 33(a): 'Hacking or cracking'.
52. For example, the Australian *Cyber-crime Act 2001* (Cth) provides for a six-month penalty for failure to comply with a magistrate's order to provide such information to investigating officials: see s. 3LA of the *Criminal Code* in the *Criminal Code Act 1995* (Cth) and s201A of the *Customs Act 1901* (Cth).
53. See, for example, in Australia: *Crimes (Overseas) Act 1964* (Cth); *Criminal Investigation (Extraterritorial Offences) Act 1987* (Cth); *Extradition Act 1988* and *Mutual Assistance in Criminal Matters Act 1987* (Cth).
54. *International Crime Threat Assessment*, see n. 25 above, Chapter II: http://www.fas.org/irp/threat/pub45270index.html (US Department of Justice).
55. Asia Law & Practice Ltd, *Intellectual Property Protection in Asia*; Gutterman & Brown, *Intellectual Property Laws of East Asia*.
56. International Federation of Phonographic Industries (IFPI) , *Music Piracy Report*, June 2001. http://www.ifpi.org.
57. http://www.IIPA.com.
58. IIPA report dated April 2002: http://www.iipa.com.
59. Section 51(xviii) of the Constitution.
60. Urbas, 'Public enforcement of intellectual property rights'.
61. Sanqiang, *Copyright in China*.
62. Note that this law now incorporates provisions of the *Supplementary Provisions Concerning the Punishment of Crimes of Counterfeiting Registered Trademarks* (22 February 1993; in force from 1 July 1993) and the *Resolution of the Standing Committee of the National People's Congress on Punishing the Crimes of Copyright Infringement* (5 July 1994).
63. Tsang, 'Anti-piracy Enforcement in Hong Kong'.

64. Note the legislative complications involved in *the Intellectual Property (Miscellaneous Amendments) Ordinance 2000* (No. 64 of 2000) and subsequent *Copyright (Suspension of Amendments) Ordinance 2001* (Cap. 568).
65. Sayers, 'Taming the Tiger'.
66. Vechayanon, 'Intellectual property rights enforcement'.
67. Williams, 'Effective IP enforcement'.
68. Microsoft Corporation 2001, 'Microsoft intensifies worldwide campaign against Internet piracy and criminal counterfeiting', media release, 2 April 2001: http://www.microsoft.com/presspass/press/2001/apr01/04–02InternetCrimePR.asp.
69. *Paris Convention for the Protection of Industrial Property 1883*
Berne Convention for the Protection of Literary and Artistic Works 1886
Rome Convention for the Protection of Producers of Phonograms etc. 1961
Convention Establishing the World Intellectual Property Organisation 1970 (WIPO)
Patent Cooperation Treaty (Washington, 1970)
Universal Copyright Convention (Geneva, 1952, revised Paris, 1971)
Geneva Phonograms Convention 1971
Trademark Law Treaty (Geneva, 1994)
Agreement on Trade-Related Aspects of Intellectual Property Rights 1994 (TRIPS)
WIPO Copyright Treaty 1996 (not yet in force).
70. China Daily Online, 'WTO entry boosts China's economy', at China.org (18 November 2002): http://www.china.org.cn/english/49058.htm.

Chapter 13

1. A Lo, '"Infected city" hoaxer likely to escape with a police warning', *SCMP*, 3 April 2003; A Lo, 'Obscure charge for alleged SARS prankster', *SCMP*, 14 May 2003.
2. Contrary to s. 161, Crimes Ordinance (Cap 200).
3. Pursuant to the Quarantine and Prevention of Disease Ordinance (Cap 141). SARS had only been placed on the list of infectious diseases on 27 March 2003. The prosecuting authorities admitted that this was possibly the first ever prosecution for this offence, although the Ordinance was enacted in 1936.
4. Discussion of the need for computer crime legislation began much earlier, in 1984, when a Working Group on computer-related crimes was formed within the then Legal Department (see para. 6, Legislative Council Paper No. CB(2)1187/99–00(04) (March 2000)). Data protection in a computer environment had also been discussed, with the setting up of a Working Group on data protection in 1983.
5. J Riley, 'Members of the local information technology industry believe the Computer Crime Bill shows a lack of understanding about the problems facing the industry', *SCMP*, 3 November 1992.
6. See The Prevention of Child Pornography Ordinance (Cap 579).
7. See The Interception of Telecommunications Ordinance (Cap 532).

8. See n. 23 below.
9. See HKCERT's homepage at http://www.hkcert.org/.
10. See Report at http://www.info.gov.hk/sb/eng/report/cr-rpt/report.htm.
11. Written and / or oral submissions were received from 46 different parties; for the full list, see Annex A to Legislative Council Brief (Ref. SBCR 14/3231/88 Pt. 21 (16.7.01)).
12. Set out as Annex D to Legislative Council Brief (Ref. SBCR 14/3231/88 Pt. 21 (16.7.01)).
13. Keynote Address at the IEE Sympsium on 'Internet Law in Hong Kong', 26 September 2003, para. 18. Available at http://md.iee.org.hk/Events/Presentation_Web/Keynote.pdf.
14. Ibid., para. 22.
15. Cf. the Council of Europe's Convention on Cyber-crime which uses the expression 'computer system', defined as 'any device or a group of interconnected or related devices, one or more of which, pursuant to a program, performs automatic processing of data' (Art 2).
16. See Recommenation 1.
17. 'Gain' and 'loss' are given extended meanings in sub-section 161(2), CO, which declares that they extend to include 'gain or loss in money or other property', whether temporary or permanent. Additionally, it is stated that 'gain' includes a gain by keeping what one has, as well as a gain by getting what one has not; and 'loss' includes a loss by not getting what one might get, as well as a loss by parting with what one has' (s. 161(2), CO).
18. See also *Li Man Wai v Secretary for Justice* (2003) FACC No. 6 of 2003, CFA, where this view of gain was accepted.
19. As to the appropriateness of community service as a sentence, see also *HKSAR v Choy Yau Pun* [2002] 4 HKC 309, CFI.
20. [2003] 2 HKC 1.
21. See also *HKSAR v Choy Yau Pun* [2002] 4 HKC 309, CFI.
22. At present, this list includes offences against the Theft Ordinance (Cap 210), along with incitement, conspiracy and attempt to commit such offences.
23. Draft Criminal Jurisdiction 0rdinance (Amendment of Section 2(2)) Order 2002; see further LC Paper No. CB(201324/02–03(01).
24. For definition of 'false' and 'making', see s 69, Crimes Ordinance; for definition of ' prejudice' and 'induce', see s. 70, Crimes Ordinance.
25. Section 16A(1) reads: '

    If any person by any deceit (whether or not the deceit is the sole or main inducement) and with intent to defraud induces another person to commit an act or make an omission, which results either — (a) in benefit to any person other than the second-mentioned person; or (b) in prejudice or a substantial risk of prejudice to any person other than the first-mentioned person, the first-mentioned person commits the offence of fraud and is liable on conviction upon indictment to imprisonment for 14 years'.

26. 'Deceit' means any deceit (whether deliberate or reckless) by words or conduct (whether by any act or omission) as to fact or as to law, including a deceit relating to the past, the present or the future and a deceit as to the intentions of the person practising the deceit or of any other person' (s. 16A(3), TO).
27. Originally, Ord. No. 1 of 2000.
28. 'Rule of law' means an Ordinance, a rule of common law or equity, or customary law: s 2(1), ETO.
29. For meaning, see s. 2(1), ETO.
30. Added by Ord. No. 80 of 1997, s. 63.
31. Article 9 stipulates that the following activities should be proscribed: (a) producing child pornography for the purpose of its distribution through a computer system; (b) offering or making available child pornography through a computer system; (c) distributing or transmitting child pornography through a computer system; (d) procuring child pornography through a computer system for oneself or for another person; and (e) possessing child pornography in a computer system or on a computer-data storage medium. Art 9(2) defines 'child pornography' as including 'pornographic material that visually depicts: (a) a minor engaged in sexually explicit conduct; (b) a person appearing to be a minor engaged in sexually explicit conduct; (c) realistic images representing a minor engaged in sexually explicit conduct.' According to Art 9(3), the term 'minor' shall include all persons under 18 years of age (though parties to the Convention may require a lower age-limit, which shall be not less than 16 years).
32. The Ordinance also: (i) added offences dealing with 'pornographic performances' involving a person under 18 to the Crimes Ordinance (see s. 138A); (ii) gave extraterritorial effect to a range of sexual offences under the Crimes Ordinance (see s. 153P, Crimes Ordinance); and (iii) criminalised the arranging or advertising of 'sex tours' involving children under 16 (see s 153Q, Crimes Ordinance).
33. See Gambling (Amendment) Ordinance (Ord. No. 12 of 2002).
34. For the meaning of 'infringing copy', see s 35, Copyright Ordinance.
35. Section 118(1) reads: '(1) A person commits an offence if he, without the licence of the copyright owner — (a) makes for sale or hire; (b) imports into Hong Kong otherwise than for his private and domestic use; (c) exports from Hong Kong otherwise than for his private and domestic use; (d) possesses for the purpose of, *in the course of, or in connection with*, any trade or business with a view to committing any act infringing the copyright; (e) for the purpose of, *in the course of, or in connection with*, any trade or business — (i) sells or lets for hire; (ii) offers or exposes for sale or hire; (iii) exhibits in public; or (iv) distributes; or (f) distributes (otherwise than for the purpose of, *in the course of, or in connection with*, any trade or business) to such an extent as to affect prejudicially the owner of the copyright, an infringing copy of a copyright work' [note: the words in italics were added by the Intellectual Property (Miscellaneous Amendments) Ordinance 2000 (No. 64 of 2000), but subsequently suspended by s 2, Copyright (Suspension of Amendments) Ordinance (Cap 568) until 31 July 2002 and then 31 July 2003.

36. Section 89 is essentially a codifying section, incorporating the prior common law relating to participation liability.
37. See *Report*, Ch. V, Recommendations 4–8.
38. See *Report*, Ch. X, Recommendation 37.

Chapter 14

* This chapter was initially prepared for consideration at the Asia Cyber-crime Summit (held in Hong Kong at The University of Hong Kong in April 2001). The views expressed in it are solely those of the author and do not necessarily represent the position of Microsoft Corporation.

1. Citations to the Cyber-crime Convention are to the final text of the instrument, produced in Budapest on 23 November 2001 (available at http://conventions.coe.int). As of this writing, 37 countries had signed the Cyber-crime Convention and four had ratified it. (The convention came into force July 2004: Editors.)
2. Additionally, on 7 November 2002 the COE's Committee of Ministers approved an optional protocol to the Cyber-crime Convention concerning the criminalisation of acts of a racist or xenophobic nature committed using computer systems (see http://conventions.coe.int/Treaty/EN/cadreprojets.htm).
3. As discussed below, police cooperation also exists at the multilateral level, through organisations such as Interpol, ASEANPOL and Europol.
4. For examples of such statutes in effect within the Asian region, see generally Australia's *Mutual Assistance in Criminal Matters Act* (1987) and *Extradition Act* (1988, amended in 1990); China's *Extradition Law* (2000) and *Civil Procedure Law*, Chapter XXIX (1990–92; Hong Kong's *Mutual Assistance in Criminal Matters Ordinance* (1997); India's *Extradition Act* (Act 34 of 1962); Japan's *Law for International Assistance in Investigation* (Law No. 69 of 1980) and *Law for Judicial Assistance to Foreign Courts* (Law No. 63 of 1905, as amended by Law No. 7 of 1912 and Law No. 17 of 1938); the Republic of Korea's *Extradition Act* (Act No. 4015, Aug. 5, 1988) and *Act on International Judicial Mutual Assistance in Criminal Matters* (Act No. 4343, Mar. 8, 1991); Malaysia's *Extradition Act* (Act No. 479 of 1992); New Zealand's *Mutual Assistance in Criminal Matters Act* (1992) and *Extradition Act* (Act No. 55 of 1999); Singapore's *Mutual Assistance in Criminal Matters Act* (Act No. 12 of 2000); Thailand's *Act on Mutual Assistance in Criminal Matters* (1992), and *Extradition Act* B.E. 2472.
5. In the criminal context, a typical scenario would involve a justice official seeking documentary or testimonial evidence for use in an ongoing investigation or judicial proceeding. As an initial matter, the justice official would petition a local court for an order issuing the letters rogatory, following which the request will be channelled through the foreign ministry of both the requesting state and the requested state, before the request ultimately is transmitted to an appropriate

authority in the requested state for execution. Once the requested evidence is gathered, it will be transmitted to the originating official via the same lengthy and circuitous route.

6. See, for example, Extradition Treaty Between the Republic of the Philippines and the United States, entered into force November 1996; Extradition Treaty Between the Republic of Korea and the United States, entered into force December 1999.
7. Additionally, because the cyber-crime phenomenon is a global problem requiring a global solution, all nations should, as a matter of priority, be working to harmonise criminal laws in this area.
8. In bilateral MLAT practice, the parties will in most cases be required to execute the request unless the request relates to a 'political offence' (e.g. belonging to a particular political party); the request relates to an offence under military law which would not be an offence under ordinary criminal law (e.g. insubordination); or the execution of the request would prejudice the requested state's security or similar essential interests.
9. See Treaty Between the United States and the Republic of the Philippines on Mutual Legal Assistance in Criminal Matters, Art 1.
10. The UN has developed useful model treaties on both extradition and mutual assistance in criminal matters (available at http://www.un.org.documents/).
11. See Art 36.
12. Ibid. at Art 37.
13. At the June 1996 summit in Lyon, G8 heads of state endorsed (and commended to all states) the Forty Recommendations and directed the Lyon Group to ensure active follow-up in implementation. See http://www.state.gov/www/issues/economic/summit/lyonsummary.html.
14. See Communiqué of Meeting of G8 Ministers of Justice and Interior, issued in December 1997 at Washington, DC (available at http://www.cyber-crime.gov/communique.htm).
15. Ibid.
16. The Statement of Principles and accompanying Action Plan are available at http://www.cyber-crime.gov/principles.htm and http://www.cyber-crime.gov/action.htm.
17. See Communiqué of Meeting of G8 Ministers of Justice and Interior, issued in October 1999 at Moscow (available at http://www.dfait-maeci.gc.ca/foreignp/g7/1999/moscow1-e.htm).
18. As another example of practical work undertaken by the G8, during the UK presidency in 1998, the Lyon Group produced a handbook on asset confiscation which includes, for each G8 country, a description of relevant domestic laws and information (including details on points of contact) on how to seek international assistance in connection with the seizure and confiscation of the proceeds or instrumentalities of crime. Jurisdictions in Asia could adopt a similar approach in sharing information on how to seek assistance in connection with cyber-crime investigations.

19. See, for example, press release on G8 Government / Industry Conference in Paris, May 2000 (available at http://194.25.60.123/www/de/aussenpolitik/friedenspolitik/g8/cyberspace/documents/paris-l); Press Release on G8 Government / Industry Conference in Berlin, October 2000 (available at http://www.mofa.go.jp/policy/economy/summit/2000/lyon.html); Kuriko Miyake, 'G8 Concludes Tokyo High-Tech Crime Meeting' (available at http://www.idg.net/english/crd_crime_548566.html) 30 May 2001 discusses a G8 government / private sector meeting in May 2001 to address a range of cyber-crime-related issues, including the distribution of illegal content and e-commerce security.
20. Also based in Vienna is the UNDCP and the Commission on Narcotic Drugs (CND). The UNDCP, which constitutes part of the UN Secretariat, provides leadership for all UN drug control initiatives and provides member states with technical assistance in their drug control efforts. The UNDCP also assists the CND in implementing the UN drug conventions, including the 1988 Vienna Convention. This provides for international cooperation in anti-drug efforts and establishes comprehensive measures against drug trafficking, including provisions against money laundering and chemical diversion.
21. The UN has prepared a manual on the prevention and control of computer-related crime, but the 1994 document requires updating. See *International Review of Criminal Policy*, Nos 43 and 44, 1994 (United Nations Publications, Sales No. E.94.IV.5).
22. The workshop, which was made possible through the support of UNAFEI, included discussion led by a panel of experts from governments, academia, and the private sector (including representatives from institutions in Australia, India, Hong Kong, and Japan).
23. See Tenth UN Crime Congress, 10–17 April 2000, Report of Committee II (United Nations Publications, No. A/CONF.187/L.10).
24. See Tenth UN Crime Congress, 10–17 April 2000, Vienna Declaration on Crime and Justice at para. 18 (available at http://www.uncjin.org/Documents/congr10/4r3e.pdf).
25. The TOC Convention (available at http://www.odccp.org/palermo/convmain.html) was drafted by an Ad Hoc Committee of government experts, including many representatives from the Asian region. The General Assembly approved the Convention at the Millennium Assembly in November 2000, and the instrument was opened for signature until 12 December 2002. See TOC Convention, Art 36(1). The TOC Convention entered into force in September 2003 (following the deposit of 40 instruments of ratification, acceptance, approval or accession).
26. Significantly, Art 5 requires signatories to criminalise conspiracy or association-type offences.
27. See Art 3(1).
28. See Art 2(a).
29. See Art 2(c).

30. See Art 3(2).
31. See Art 27(2).
32. The TOC Convention also has a freestanding article (Art 13) concerning international cooperation in the confiscation of proceeds of crime or instrumentalities used in the commission of offences.
33. Limiting language of this type is not overly surprising in a UN agreement as broad in scope as the TOC Convention, which reflects the extraordinary diversity of legal systems and cultural perspectives represented in the negotiations. Indeed, multilateral conventions commonly include many more safeguards than would be typical in a bilateral agreement. As illustrated above, the clear trend in bilateral MLAT practice is not to require dual criminality as a prerequisite for assistance. For that reason, wherever possible, countries in the region should seek to negotiate individual agreements with their most important partners in law enforcement.
34. See Art 16.
35. See Art 16(3).
36. See Art 29(2).
37. See Art 30.
38. See generally http://unafei.or.jp/.
39. See ASEAN Ministerial Understanding on the Organisation Arrangement for Cooperation in Legal Field, signed on 12 April 1986 in Bali, Indonesia (available at http://www.aseansec.org/politics/muclf86.htm).
40. See ASEAN Declaration on Transnational Crime, signed on 20 December 1997 in Manila, Philippines (available at http://www.aseansec.org/politics/adtc97.htm).
41. See Joint Communique of the Second ASEAN Ministerial Meeting on Transnational Crime, issued on 23 June 1999 in Yangon, Myanmar (available at http://www.aseansec.org/politics/jc_cri02.htm).
42. Ibid. at 2–3.
43. Ibid. at 3.
44. See Joint Communique of the Third ASEAN Ministerial Meeting on Transnational Crime (2001) issued on October 11, 2001 in Singapore (available at http://www.aseansec.or.id/5621.htm).
45. See http://www.europa.eu.int/scadplus/leg/en/lvb/133084.htm.
46. See http://www.europa.eu.int/scadplus/leg/en/lvb/133084.htm.
47. See http://www.europa.eu.int/scadplus/leg/en/lvb/114015b.htm.
48. See http://www.europa.eu.int/scadplus/leg/en/lvb/133055.htm.
49. See generally http://www.europol.nl/facts/en.htm.
50. Notably, Europol's mandate was recently extended to include the fight against cyber-crime. As an example of this activity, Europol hosted a seminar in October 2002 focusing on the increasing problem of child abuse on the Internet. See Europol Press Release dated 18 October 2002 (available at http://www.europol.eu.int/content.htm?news/prnew/en.ht.).
51. Ibid.

52. For general information on the OECD, see generally http://www.oecd.org/about/general/index.htm.
53. See OECD Press Release dated August 7, 2002 (available at http://www.oecd.org/EN/document/0,,EN-document-29-nodirectorate-no-12-33186-29,00.html).
54. For general information on FATF, see generally http://www.oecd.org/fatf/AboutFATF_en.htm.
55. FATF's secretariat has been moved to the offices of the OECD in Paris, and current members include Argentina, Australia, Austria, Belgium, Brazil, Canada, Denmark, Finland, France, Germany, Greece, Hong Kong, Iceland, Ireland, Italy, Japan, Luxembourg, Mexico, the Netherlands, New Zealand, Norway, Portugal, Singapore, Spain, Sweden, Switzerland, Turkey, United Kingdom, United States, the European Commission, and the Gulf Cooperation Council. A number of FATF-style regional organisations (discussed below) and other inter-governmental organisations dedicated in whole or in part to combating money laundering have observer status with FATF.
56. See generally http://www.oecd.org/fatf/Ctry-orgpages/org-apg_en.htm. Other FATF-like bodies include the Caribbean Financial Action Task Force, the Council of Europe PC-R-EV, the Eastern and Southern Africa Anti-Money Laundering Group, and the Financial Action Task Force on Money Laundering in South America.
57. National Central Bureaus, or NCBs, serve as the direct interface between each member state's police officials and the Interpol General Secretariat.
58. See generally http://www.interpol.int/Public/icpo/Guide.
59. See http://www.interpol.int/Public/TechnologyCrime/WorkingParties/Default.asp#steeringCom.
60. See http://www.interpol.int/Public/TechnologyCrimeWorkingParties/Default.asp#asi.
61. See generally http://www.interpol.int/Public/CreditCards/Default.asp.
62. See generally http://www.interpol.int/Public/FinancialCrime/IntellectualProperty/Default/.as.
63. For general information on APEC, see generally http://www.apecsec.org.sg/97brochureorganize.html.
64. See generally http://www.apecsec.org.sg/committee/intellectual_upd.html.
65. See generally http://www.apecsec.org.sg/workgroup/e-commerce.html.
66. See generally http://www.apecsec.org.sg/committee/customs_upd.html.
67. See USINFO East Asia Fact Sheet dated 29 October 2002 (available at http://usinfo.state.gov).
68. See http://www.apectelwg.org/apecdata/telwg/28tel/estg/telwg28-ESTG-09.htm for a detailed report on the workshop.
69. See http://www.apectelwg.org/apec/atwg/previous.html#12 for a link to the survey results.

Chapter 15

* This chapter is an updated version of an address given at the 1st Asia Cybercrime Conference April, 2001. At the time of the address, the author was a Senior Counsel at the Legal Department of the International Monetary Fund (IMF). He can be reached at pcsonka@imf.org. The views expressed here are personal and do not reflect those of the IMF, nor those of the Council of Europe, which was the author's previous employer. The author is grateful to the editors of this publication as well as to the organisers of the 1st Asian Cyber-Crime Summit, which provided the opportunity for presenting the following outline of the main policy objectives and legal provisions of the Council of Europe's Convention on Cyber-Crime, which was then only a draft. While the convention has since been adopted, at the time of the address it was not yet in force as only four states had ratified it.

1. Michael A Sussmann, 'The Critical Challenges from International High-Tech and Computer-Related Crime at the Millennium', *9 Duke J of Comp. & Int'l L.* 1999, p. 451.
2. Computer-related crime, Recommendation No. R (89) 9 on computer-related crime and final report of the European Committee on Crime Problems, Council of Europe Publishing, Strasbourg, 1990.
3. Implementation of Recommendation No. R (89) 9 on computer-related crime, Report prepared by Professor Henrik W K Kaspersen for the European Committee on Crime Problems, doc. CDPC (97) 5 (unpublished), Strasbourg, March 1997, pp. 104–6.
4. Remarks of Kevin DiGregory (former Deputy Assistant Attorney-General in the Criminal Division at the US Department of Justice in Washington DC) on 'Fighting Cybercrime — What are the Challenges facing Europe?' Hearing before the European Parliament, 19 September 2000.
5. Problems of procedural law connected with information technology, Recommendation No. R (95) 13 and Explanatory memorandum, Strasbourg: Council of Europe publishing, 1996.
6. For a detailed account, see Peter Csonka, 'Criminal procedural law and information technology: the main features of the Council of Europe Recommendation No R (95) 13', *Computer Law and Security Report*, 12 (1996) pp. 37–42.
7. With adoption of the first additional Protocol 'concerning the criminalisation of acts of a racist and xenophobic nature committed through computer systems', this gap was filled. The Protocol entails an extension of the convention's scope, including its substantive, procedural and international cooperation provisions, to offences of racist or xenophobic propaganda. Thus, apart from harmonising the substantive law elements of such behaviour, the Protocol aims at improving the ability of the Parties to make use of the means and avenues of international cooperation set out in the convention in this area. The Protocol was adopted by

the Committee of Ministers of the Council of Europe at its 111th Session on 7 November 2002 and was opened to signature in January 2003. It can only be signed and ratified by the contracting parties of the main convention.

Chapter 16

1. Jessica Tuchman Matthews, 'Redefining Security', *Foreign Affairs*, 68(2) 1989: 162–77.
2. Hamish McCardle, Jonathan Boxhall, Juan Ronderos and Rino Fransisco, *Cybercrime and its Effects on the Asia-Pacific Region*, CSACP Transnational Crime Working Group, 2001, p. 22.
3. Source: derived from data presented by the Internet Software Consortium (www.isc.org).
4. William Clinton, *The Struggle for the Soul of the 21st Century*, 2001 Dimbleby Lecture, 14 December 2001, London.
5. eMarketer, 'Asia-Pacific to have most Internet users', 6 September 2002; http://www.emarketer.com/news/article.php?1001580&ref=ed, accessed 17 September 2002.
6. We acknowledge that this three-way division is somewhat artificial and that there may be some overlap case by case between the three tiers. However, the case studies we draw upon can be *largely* identified as belonging to their assigned tier. This distinction is reinforced when we examine the new threats from cyberspace, which clearly cross all boundaries.
7. President's Committee of Advisors on Science and Technology, *White Paper on the Institute for Information Infrastructure Protection*, 11 July 2000, p. 1.
8. See for example, Admiral Chris Barrie, Chief of the Defence Force, 'Strategic Implications of New Technologies in The Asia-Pacific', paper presented to the ANZUS Anniversary Conference on the United States Alliance in an East Asian Context, University of Sydney, Australia, Saturday, 30 June 2001; and Doug Conway, 'Expert warns of "Cyberterror"', *Australian*, 23 September 2002.
9. James Adams, 'Virtual Defense', *Foreign Affairs*, May–June 2001.
10. Christopher C Joyner and Catherine Lotrionte, 'Information Warfare as International Coercion: Elements of a Legal Framework', *European Journal of International Law*, 12(5) 2001, available online at http://www.ejil.org.
11. Ted Bridis, 'Net Espionage Rekindles Tensions As US Tries To Identify Hackers Extracts', *Wall Street Journal*, 27 June 2001.
12. John Pike, 'Solar Sunrise', Global Security.org; http://www.globalsecurity.org/military/ops/solar-sunrise.htm.
13. Joyner and Lotrionte, 'Information Warfare as International Coercion'.
14. Vice Admiral Richard W Mayo, Director, Space, Information Warfare, Command and Control Office of the Chief of Naval Operations, *Information Technology: An Examination Of DoD Network Vulnerabilities*, 17 May 2001.

15. 'Israeli Citizen Arrested in Israel for Hacking United States and Israeli Government Computers', press release, 18 March 1998, http://www.cybercrime.gov/ehudpr.htm.
16. James Adams, 'Computer Security: Are We Prepared for Cyberwar?', Testimony before the Subcommittee on Government Management, Information, and Technology, Committee on Government Reform, 9 March 2000, http://www.house.gov/reform/gmit/hearings/2000hearings/000309.compsec/000309ja.htm.
17. Mayo, 17 May 2001, ibid.
18. Dion Stempfley, former Pentagon computer security analyst cited in Vernon Loeb, *Washington Post*, 7 May 2001, page A02, http://washingtonpost.com/wp-dyn/articles/A51965–2001May6.html.
19. For discussion and further references on this issue see Daniel Kuehl, Statement For the Joint Economic Committee, School of Information Warfare & Strategy, National Defense University, 23 February 2000, http://www.cdt.org/security/dos/000223senate/kuehl.htm.
20. Ibid.
21. See General Assembly Resolution 53/70.*Developments in the field of information and communication in the context of international security*, 53rd Session. Agenda Item 63. 4 December 1998.
22. See, for example, *Developments in the Field of Information and Telecommunications in the Context of International Security*, Private Discussion Meeting Hosted by DDA (Department of Disarmament Affairs] and UNIDIR [United Nations Institute for Disarmament Research) Room IX, Palais des Nations, Geneva, 25–26 August 1999.
23. Doug Narine, 'State hackers spying on us, say dissidents', *South China Morning Post*, 18 September 2002.
24. 'Aussie hacker gets two year sentence', ZDNet Australia, 31 October 2001.
25. Leif Gamertsfelder, 'Paltry figure allocated to shielding NII', *Canberra Times*, 20 May 2002.
26. Paraphrased from 'South Korea probes online dealing fraud', *BBC News*, 26 August 2002, http://news.bbc.co.uk/2/hi/business/2217584.stm.
27. Kim Yon-se, 'Daewoo Securities Employee Suspected in Delta Trade', *Korea Times*, 26 August 2002, http://www.hankooki.com/kt_biz/200208/t2002082618014743110.htm.
28. Computer Security Institute, 'Cyber crime bleeds US corporations, survey shows; financial losses from attacks climb for third year in a row', 7 April 2002, http://www.gocsi.com/prelea_000321.htm.
29. Riptech Inc. report cited in Michael Barbaro, 'Internet Attacks On Companies Up 28 Percent, Report Says', *Washington Post*, 8 July 2002, page E05, http://www.washingtonpost.com/wp-dyn/articles/A36498–2002Jul7.html.
30. As an example, the US directs the Internet Fraud Complaint Centre, while the UK is setting up the Centre for Cyber-crime Complaints, 'Calls for cyber-crime

database', *BBC news online*, 29 August 2001, http://news.bbc.co.uk/hi/english/business/newsid_1514000/1514215.stm.

31. Gartner Group survey, cited in Marianne Bray, 'Fraud hits one in ten Asian Internet deals', *CNN.com*, 20 March 2002, http://www.cnn.com/2002/BUSINESS/asia/03/20/asia.net/.
32. Australian Institute of Criminology, 'E-commerce fraud on the internet rarely reported', Media Release, 17 January 2002, http://www.aic.gov.au/media/2002/20020117.html.
33. Peng Hwa Ang, 'Code of Practice For Internet Content Self-Regulation', *Report to the Asia and Pacific Internet Association*, Nanyang Technological University, Singapore, http://www.apia.org/srexecutivesummary.htm.
34. Cyber-offences in South Korea, including slandering and financial fraud online, shot up 126% to 33 289 cases in 2001 from a year earlier, and totalled 39 482 cases in the first eight months of 2002, according to the cyber-crime centre under the country's National Police Agency, 34 'Interpol: Cyber-crime fight must be global', *Reuters*, 16 October 2002, http://news.zdnet.co.uk/story/0,,t283s2123975,00.html.
35. 'South Korea investigates online stock fraud', *Qinghai News*, 27 August 2002, http://english.qhnews.com/912/2002–8–27/18@112088.htm.
36. 'Singapore Government Scans 200 000 Users Computers', *Asian Wall Street Journal*, 6 May 1999.
37. 'How personal are personal computers?', *Far Eastern Economic Review*, 20 May 1999, http://www.feer.com/Restricted/99may_20/tech.html.
38. 'Singapore Issues Privacy Guidelines', *Straits Times*, 8 January 2000.
39. Jonathan Zittrain and Benjamin Edelman, 'Documentation of Internet Filtering in Saudi Arabia', Center for Internet & Society, Harvard Law School; http://cyber.law.harvard.edu/filtering/saudiarabia
40. Ibid.
41. Reporters Sans Frontières, 'Enemies of the Internet', March 2001, http://www.rsf.org/ennemis.php3.
42. Cited in Zittrain and Edelman, 'Documentation of Internet Filtering in Saudi Arabia'.
43. Noah Shachtman, 'Why Countries Make Sites Unseen', *Wired*, 18 July 2002; http://www.wired.com/news/politics/0,1283,53933–2,00.html.
44. Mike Musgrove, 'In China, Some Regain Access to Google Site', *Washington Post*, 13 September 2002; http://www.washingtonpost.com/wp-adv/advertisers/popunders/verisign_oct02.html.
45. David Lee, 'Multinationals making a mint from China's Great Firewall', *SCMP*, 2 October 2002.
46. Benjamin Edelman, 'When the net goes dark and silent', *SCMP*, 2 October 2002.
47. Ang Peng Hwa, ASEAN panel discussion participant, correspondence with Declan McCullough, http://lists.insecure.org/politech/1999/Nov/0051.html.
48. The International Telecommunications Union Regional Preparatory Meeting, Asia

and the Pacific, Policy and Regulation, Issue Paper for the World Telecommunication Development Conference, 2002.

49. For discussion of state regulations regarding the Internet see Human Rights Watch, 'Freedom of Expression and the Internet in China: A Human Rights Watch Backgrounder', www.hrw.org/backgrounder/asia/china-bck-0701.htm. Two Chinese cyber-activists, Hu Mingjun and Wang Sen, were sentenced to death for spreading anti-socialist writings. For two others, Ouyang Yi is awaiting sentence, and Li Zhi is awaiting trial for similar anti-state cyber-behaviour that also carries the death penalty.
50. 'China sentences another dissident for posting views on Internet', *Agence France Presse*, 22 October 2003.
51. Reporters Sans Frontières, 'Le Gouvernement Vietnamien Imite le Modèle Chinois de Contrôle de l'Internet', 7 August 2002, http://www.rsf.fr/article.php3?id_article=3307.
52. Stephen Collinson, 'US gives Vietnam a tongue lashing after cyber dissident jailed', *Agence France Presse*, 31 December 2003; and 'Vietnam: Cyber dissident jailed for seven years', *Global News Wire*. 5 January 2004.
53. Noah Shachtman, 'Why Countries Make Sites Unseen', *Wired.com*, 18 July 2002; http://www.wired.com/news/politics/0,1283,53933,00.html.
54. For a good summary of the challenges facing legislators see Graham Greenleaf, 'An Endnote on Regulating Cyberspace: Architecture vs Law?', *University of New South Wales Law Journal*, 21(2) 1998: 593–622.
55. 'Content Rating System to Filter Harmful Sites on Web', *Korea Times*, 14 April 2000, http://www.hk.co.kr/14_10/200004/t200004142221084A51108.htm.
56. 'How personal are personal computers?', *Far Eastern Economic Review*, 20 May 1999; http://www.feer.com/Restricted/99may_20/tech.html.
57. Chris Nuttall, 'Chernobyl Virus Causes Asian Meltdown', *BBC News*, 27 April 1999; http://news.bbc.co.uk/1/hi/sci/tech/329688.stm.
58. Robert Lemos, 'CIH is a Dodo', *ZD magazine*, 27 May 1999, http://news.zdnet.co.uk/story/0,,s2072074,00.html.
59. The President's Critical Infrastructure Protection Board, National Strategy to Secure Cyberspace (Draft for comment), September 2002, p. 49.
60. Computer Economics, cited at http://www.emcs.net/Protection/statistics.htm.
61. IDC Asia/Pacific statistics cited in Information Security Magazine, May 2001, http://www.infosecuritymag.com/articles/may01/departments_news.shtml#numbers.
62. 'How personal are personal computers?', *Far Eastern Economic Review*, 20 May 1999; http://www.feer.com/Restricted/99may_20/tech.html.
63. However, this may be changing. At the 9th ASEAN Summit (Phnom Penh, November 2002), Chinese and ASEAN leaders signed a joint cooperation agreement on non-traditional security. Among areas identified for more cooperation was cyber-crime. How this cooperation will be operationalised has yet to be clarified.

64. The International Telecommunications Union, Regional Preparatory Meeting, Asia and the Pacific, Policy and Regulation, Issue Paper, for the World Telecommunication Development Conference, 2002.
65. *Cyber Crime … and Punishment? Archaic Laws Threaten Global Information*, McConnell International LLC. December 2000, http://www.mcconnell international.com/services/CyberCrime.htm.

References

Note: this list covers only the text references in Harvard format found in Chapters 1, 2, 4, 6, 10 and 11. The other chapters have traditional references in their notes.

ABC News (2002), 'Man found guilty in Thailand's first case of cyber-defamation'. http://abc.net.au/news/newsitems/s642477.htm (visited 5 January 2004)

Aiziwa, K (2001), 'Current mechanisms for International Cooperation in Criminal Matters: Mutual Legal Assistance and Extradition, 24/7 Points of Contact Network, and Training in the Field of Computer Crime'. In Broadhurst, *Proceedings of the Asia Cyber Crime Summit*

Akdeniz, Y (2001), 'Controlling illegal and harmful content on the Internet'. In Wall, *Crime and The Internet*

Akdeniz, Y, C Walker and D Wall, eds. (2000), *The Internet, Law and Society*, Harlow: Longmans

Alvazzi del Frate, A (1998), 'Preventing crime: Citizens' experience across the world', *Issues and Reports* No 9, Rome: UNICRI

APIG (2003), Communications Data: Report of an Inquiry by the All Party Internet Group. London: APIG. Retrieved 21 March 2003 at http://www.apig.org.uk/APIGreport.pdf

Asia Computer Weekly (2000), 'Eye on North Asia: China Seeks New Law to Combat Cybercrimes' (2000), 6 November, p. 1

Asia Law & Practice Ltd (1996), *Intellectual Property Protection in Asia: Practical Strategies*, Hong Kong

Associated Press (1998), 'First cyber terrorist action reported'. Nando.net. http://www.techserver.com/newsroom/ntn/info/050698/info9_25501_noframes.html (visited 8 October 2000)

Associated Press (1999), 'Man guilty of Internet stalking'. http://www.bayinsider.com/news/1999/01/20/stalking.html (visited 1 July 1999)

Associated Press (2000), 'Microsoft Acknowledges Theft of Source Code'. The New York Times on the Web. http://channel.nytimes.com/aponline/technology/27MICROSOFT.html (visited 23 November 2000)

Associated Press (2001), 'Report: Bin Laden Uses Web to Plan Terrorism', CNN.com 6 February 2001. http://www.cnn.com/2001/TECH/internet/02/06/terrorists.internet.ap/index.Html

Associated Press (2002), 'China: Falun Gong Disrupts TV Signal'. http://vigilant.tv/article/2233 (visited 5 January 2004)

Australian Associated Press (2000), 'Man jailed for one of world's first spamming crimes'. http://it.mycareer.com.au/breaking/20001031/A17801-2000Oct31.html (visited 14 April 2001)

Bangkok Post (2001), 'Pianist could face music here before his extradition to US', 23 August, p. 7

Bauer, J. (1998), Testimony to the Subcommittee on Technology, Terrorism and Government Information, Committee on the Judiciary, United States Senate, 20 May 1998. http://www.securitymanagement.com/library/bauer.html (visited 10 February 2004)

BBC (2001), 'Attack on Japan ministry website'. http://news.bbc.co.uk/hi/english/world/asia-pacific/newsid_1252000/1252965.stm (visited 5 April 2001)

BBC (2002), 'Shanghai cybercafes shut down'. http://news.bbc.co.uk/1/hi/world/asia-pacific/1971153.stm (visited 22 December 2003)

BBC (2003), 'Computer viruses rampant in China', 21 October. http://news.bbc.co.uk/1/hi/technology/3210086.stm (visited 5 January 2004)

BCS Socio Technical Group (2003), 'Ebusiness Examined', *Computer Bulletin*, 45(2): 26–7

'Better Trade Flow Urged' (2001), *Asiainfo Daily China News*, 14 August, p. 1

BizAsia (2000), 'Asian Hacking War'. *BizAsia News*. http://www.bizasia.com/gen/articles/stand_art.htm?ac=B5YIZ-Q (visited 14 April 2001)

Blackman, A. (2003), 'Choking on spam: small businesses, easy targets for junk e-mail, start fighting back', *Wall Street Journal*, Classroom edn, December. http://wsjclassroom.com/archive/03dec/entr_spam.htm (visited 5 January 2004)

Blanchflower, M C (2003), 'Money Laundering: The advantages and disadvantages of Mutual Legal Assistance'. In Broadhurst, *Bridging the GAP*

Bloomberg News (1999), 'Man pleads guilty to loosing Melissa virus', 10 December 1999. http://seattlep-i.nwsource.com/business/meli10.shtml (visited 12 February 2001)

Bloomberg News (2001), 'Indian Techies Arrested in Bank Hacking Case'. http://news.cnet.com/news/0-1003-200-4602814.html (visited 31 March 2001)

Bowman, J. (2001), 'Security Warning as Net Crime Soars', *SCMP*, 22 February, p. 5

Braithwaite, J. (2000), 'The new regulatory state and the transformation of criminology', *British Journal of Criminology*, 40: 222–38

Broadhurst, R, ed. (2001), *Proceedings of the Asia Cyber Crime Summit*, Centre for Criminology, The University of Hong Kong

Broadhurst, R, ed. (2003), *Bridging the GAP: A Global Alliance on Transnational Organised Crime*, Hong Kong Police: Printing Department HKSAR

Broadhurst, R, ed. (2004), *Proceedings of the 2nd Asia Cyber Crime Summit*, Centre for Criminology, The University of Hong Kong

Bronitt, S, and B McSherry (2001), *Principles of Criminal Law*, Sydney: LBC Information Services, pp. 704–6

BSA (2002), Sixth Annual BSA Global Software Piracy Study. http://www.bsa.org/resources/2001-05-21.55.pdf (visited 1 August 2002)

BSA (2003a), Asia Pacific http://global.bsa.org/idcstudy/pdfs/Asia_Pacific.pdf (visited 22 December 2003)

BSA (2003b), Eighth Annual BSA Global Software Piracy Study. http://global.bsa.org/globalstudy/2003_GSPS.pdf (visited 22 December 2003)

Bullwinkel, J (2001), 'International Co-operation in Combating Cyber-crime in Asia: Existing Mechanisms and New Approaches'. In Broadhurst, *Proceedings of the Asia Cybercrime Summit Hong Kong*

Burn, J M, and M G Martinsons, eds. (1997), *Information Technology and the Challenge for Hong Kong*, Hong Kong University Press

Business Wire (2000), 'Malicious Virus Attacks Cost Organizations More Than $12 Billion in 1999'. http://www.info-sec.com/viruses/00/viruses_011400a_j.shtml (visited 12 February 2001)

Campbell, D (1999), 'Careful, they might hear you', *Age*, 23 May. http://www.theage.com.au/daily/990523/news/news3.html (visited 17 October 2000)

Campbell, D (2000), 'Big Brother is Back', *Sydney Morning Herald*, 29 August, Computer Section, p. 1

Carr, I (2000a), 'India joins the cyber-race: Information Technology Act 2000', *International Technology Law Review*, 4: 121–30

Carr, I, and K S Williams (2000b), 'Securing the e-commerce environment: Enforcement measures and penalty levels in the computer misuse legislation of Britain, Malaysia and Singapore', *Computer Law and Security Report*, 16(5): 295–310

Carter, D L (1995), 'Computer Crime Categories: How Techno-criminals Operate', *FBI Law enforcement Bulletin*, 64(7): 21–7

Casey, E (2000), *Digital Evidence and Computer Crime: Forensic Science, Computers and the Internet*, San Diego: Academic Press

Castells, M (1996), *The Rise of the Network Society*, Oxford: Blackwell

Cella, J J, and J R Stark (1997), 'SEC Enforcement and the Internet: Meeting the Challenge of the Next Millennium', *The Business Lawyer*, 52: 815–49

Chan, H (2001), 'Computer Forensics: A New Challenge to Crime Investigation'. In Broadhurst, *Proceedings of the Asia Cyber Crime Summit*

Chan, J M, P S N Lee and C C Lee (1996), *Hong Kong Journalists in Transition*, Hong Kong Institute of Asia-Pacific Studies, The Chinese University of Hong Kong

Chan, V P-K (1998), 'Tougher Laws for Hackers', *SCMP*, 2 July, p. 9

Chang, J T H, P Qu and I I H Wan, eds. (1999), *China's Internet Policy and Legislation*, Beijing: TransAsia Publishing

Charlesworth, A (2000), 'The Goverance of the Internet in Europe'. In Y. Akdeniz, C Walker and D Wall eds., *The Internet, Law and Society*, Harlow: Longman

Charney, S (2003), Remarks to the 2nd Asia Cyber Crime Summit, Centre for Criminology, The University of Hong Kong, 5 November 2003

Chase, M S, and J C Mulvenon (2002), *You've Got Dissent! Chinese Dissident Use of the Internet and Beijing's Counter-Strategies*, Washington DC: Rand

Cheng, J Y S, ed. (1982), *Hong Kong in the 1980s*, Hong Kong: Summerson Eastern Publishers

Cheung, A B L, (2002), 'The Changing Political System: Executive-led Government or 'Disabled' Governance', in S K Lau (ed.), *The First Tung Chee-Hwa Administration*, Hong Kong: Chinese University Press

Cheung, S (1991), *The Impact of Computer Fraud*, Business Research Centre, School of Business, Hong Kong Baptist College, Working Paper Series

China Daily Online (2002), 'China struggling to narrow digital divide', 18 May 2002. http://www1.chinadaily.com.cn/news/cb/2002–05–18/70183.html (visited 26 July 2002)

Clarke, D (1992), 'Private enforcement of intellectual property rights in China'. In *Intellectual Property Rights in China: Evolving Business and Legal Frameworks*, 10(2), National Bureau of Research Analysis, Seattle

Clarke, R (1998), Direct Marketing and Privacy. Paper presented at AIC Conference 'The Direct Distribution of Financial Services', Sydney, 24 February. http://www.anu.edu.au/people/Roger.Clarke/DV/DirectMkting.html (visited 24 October 2000)

Clarke, R, ed. (1997), *Situational Crime Prevention: Successful Case Studies*, 2nd edn, New York: Harrow & Heston

Cohen, S (1973), *Folk Devils and Moral Panics: The Creation of the Mods and Rockers*, London: Paladin

Cohen, S (1985), *Visions of Social Control*, Cambridge: Polity Press

Computer Economics (2002), Malicious Code Attack Economic Impact Update, August 31, 2001. http://www.info-sec.com/viruses/01/viruses_091901c_j.shtml (visited 24 July 2002)

Cook, B (1993), 'Expert Urges Changes to Computer Law', *SCMP*, 24 April, p. 4

Council of Europe (2001a), *Convention on Cyber-crime: Explanatory Report*. Retrieved 5 January 2002 at http://conventions.coe.int/Treaty/en/Reports/Html/185.htm

Council of Europe (2001b), *Convention on Cyber-crime*, European Committee on Crime Problems and Committee of Experts on Crime in Cyber-Space, Strasbourg. http://conventions.coe.int/Treaty/en/Treaties/Html/185.htm

Council of the European Union (1996), Council Resolution of 17 January 1995 on the lawful interception of telecommunication: Official Journal C 329, 4 November 1996, pp. 0001–0006. Retrieved 3 January, 2003 at http://europa.eu.int/smartapi/cgi/sga_doc?smartapi!celexapi!prod!CELEXnumdoc&lg=EN&numdoc=41996Y1104(01)

Crawford, A, ed. (2002), *Crime and Insecurity: The Government of Safety in Europe*, Cullompton: Willan Publishing

Csonka, P (1996), 'Council of Europe Activities Related to Information Technology, Data Protection and Computer Crime', *Information and Communications Technology Law*, 5: 177–90

Daily Yomiuri (2000), 'Fears of Cyber-Terrorism Mounting', 28 January, p. 3

Dato, K A (2000), 'Internet Related Crime and other High technology Crime'. Paper Presented at the 8th World Congress of the Asia Crime Prevention Foundation, Beijing, China, October

Davis, W S, and J Benamati (2003), *E-commerce Basics: Technology Foundations and e-business Applications*, Boston: Addison Wesley

DeGolyer, M (2004), 'How the Stunning Outbreak of Disease Led to a Stunning Outbreak of Dissent'. In C Loh and Civic Exchange, *At the Epicenter: Hong Kong and the SARS Outbreak*, Hong Kong University Press

Den Boer, M (2001), 'The fight against organised crime in Europe: A comparative perspective', *European Journal on Criminal Policy and Research*, 9: 259–72

Denning, D (1999), *Information Warfare and Security*, Boston: Addison Wesley

Denning, D (2000), Activism, Hacktivism, and Cyberterrorism: The Internet as a Tool for Influencing Foreign Policy. http://www.nautilus.org/info-policy/workshop/papers/denning.html (visited 16 March 2000)

Denning, D E, and W E Baugh Jr. (1997), *Encryption and Evolving Technologies as Tools of Organized Crime and Terrorism*, Washington DC: National Strategy Information Center

Diffie, W, and S Landau (1999), *Privacy on the Line: The Politics of Wiretapping and Encryption*. Cambridge MA and London: MIT Press

Digital 21 Hong Kong (2001), *Building a Digitally Inclusive Society*, Information Technology Services Department HKSAR, Hong Kong Government

Duff, R A, and S E Marshall (2000), 'Benefits, burdens and responsibilities: some ethical dimensions of situational crime prevention'. In A V Hirsch, D Garland and A Wakefield, eds., *Ethical and Social Perspectives on Situational Crime Prevention*, Oxford: Hart Publishing

Duggal, P (2000), *Cyberlaw in India: An analysis*, New Delhi: Saakshar Law Publications

Duggal, P (2000–2004), 'Brief Cases', weekly cyber-law interactive column published every Sunday in the *Economic Times*

Duggal, P (2002), *Cyberlaw: The Indian Perspective*, New Delhi: Saakshar Law Publications

Duggal, S (2001), India's First Cyberstalking Case – Some Cyberlaw Perspectives. http://www.cyberlawindia.com/2CYBER27.htm (visited 29 March 2001)

Dupont, B (2001), 'Policing in the Information Age: Technological Errors of the Past in Perspective'. In M Enders and B Dupont, eds., *Policing the Lucky Country*, Sydney: Hawkins Press

Dutton, W H (1999), *Society on the Line: Information Politics in the Digital Age*, Hong Kong: Oxford University Press

Edge Publishing (1999), Proliferation of Internet and Wireless Capabilities are Powering Piracy to New Levels – $112 Billion, 18 October. http://www.findarticles.com/cf_1/m0WUB/1999_Oct_18/56474251/p1/article.jhtml?term=piracy (visited 12 February 2001)

Edwards, O (1995), 'Hackers from Hell', *Forbes*, 9 October, p. 182

Europe Information Service (1999), Intellectual Property: Copyright Industry Unveils Anti-Piracy Plan, 6 March 1999. http://www.findarticles.com/cf_1/m0WXI/1999_March_6/54041290/p1/article.jhtml?term=piracy (visited 13 February 2001)

Evans, J (2001), Privacy group warns of e-mail wiretap. CNN.com, 5 February. http://www.cnn.com/2001/TECH/internet/02/05/email.wiretap.idg/index.html (visited 14 February 2001)

Evers, J (2000), Dutch ISPs to Pass Along Cyber-crime Costs, The Standard.com, 4 December. http://www.thestandard.com/article/display/0,1151,20571,00.html (visited 22 January 2001)

Farinordin, F (1996), 'New IT Legislation to be Tabled Next Year', *New Straits Times*, 29 November, p. 10

Felson, M (1998), *Crime and Everyday Life: Insight and Implications for Society*, Thousand Oaks CA: Pine Forge Press

Froomkin, A (1995), Anonymity and its Enmities, Journal of online law art. 4 http://www.wm.edu/law/publications/jol/95_96/froomkin.html (visited 10 February 2004)

Furnell, S (2002), *Cyber-crime: Vandalizing the Information Society*, Boston: Addison-Wesley

Garland, D (1996), 'The limits of the sovereign state: Strategies of crime control in contemporary society', *British Journal of Criminology*, 36(4): 445–71

Gaylord, M, and H Traver, eds. (1994), *Introduction to the Hong Kong Criminal Justice System*, Hong Kong University Press

Gilmore, W C (1999), *Dirty Money: The Evolution of Money Laundering Countermeasures*, 2nd edn., Strasbourg: Council of Europe Publishing

Goh, A (1996), 'Police Looking into Hacking of Govt Web Site', *Straits Times*, 10 December, p. 2

Gold, S (1999), BT Starts Switchboard Anti-Hacking Investigation. 11 January (Newsbytes). http://www.infowar.com/ (visited 23 December 1999).

Goodman, M D, and S W Brenner (2002), 'The Emerging Consensus on Criminal Conduct in Cyberspace', *UCLA Journal of Law and Technology*, 3

Grabosky, P, and R G Smith (1998), *Crime in the Digital Age: Controlling Telecommunications and Cyberspace Illegalities*, New Brunswick NJ: Transaction Publishers, and Sydney: Federation Press

Grabosky, P, R G Smith and G Dempsey (2001), *Electronic Theft: Unlawful Acquisition in Cyberspace*, Cambridge University Press

Grant, A, F David and P Grabosky (1997), 'Child Pornography in the Digital Age', *Transnational Organized Crime*, 3(4): 171–88

Gray, P (1991), *Psychology*, New York: Worth Publishers, Inc.

Grenville-Cross, I. (2003), 'Enforcement and Prosecution Strategies in the 21st Century: Combating Multi-jurisdictional Crime'. In Broadhurst, *Bridging the GAP*

Gutterman, A, and R Brown, eds. (1997), *Intellectual Property Laws of East Asia*, Hong Kong: Sweet & Maxwell

Hafner, K, and J Markoff (1991), *Cyberpunk: Outlaws and Hackers on the Computer Frontier*, New York: Simon & Schuster

Harrington, V, and P Mayhew (2001), *Mobile Phone Theft*, Home Office Research Study 235, London: Home Office

Hayashi, K, and Y Tagawa (1994), *Universal Service: The Principle of 'Fairness' in the Multimedia Age*, Tokyo: Chuko Shinsho

Heath, C (n.d.), *Intellectual Property Rights in Asia: Projects, Programmes and Developments*, Munich: Max Planck Institute for Foreign and International Patent, Copyright and Competition Law

Herrera, J (2001), 'International Aspects of Cybercrime'. In R D Clifford, ed., *Cybercrime: The Investigation, Prosecution and Defense of a Computer-related Crime*, Durham: Carolina Academic Press

Homusho (Ministry of Justice, Japan) (1998), *Hanzai Sosa no tameno Tsushin Boju ni Kansuru Horitsu An Kankei Shiryo* (Reference Data for 'Bill of Telecommunication Interception for Criminal Investigation'), Tokyo: Homusho

Hong Kong Security Bureau (2000), Inter-departmental Working Group on Computer-related Crime, Report. http://www.info.gov.hk/sb/cr-rpt/report.htm (visited 4 April 2001)

Howes, D (2001), 'E-Legislation: Law-Making in the Digital Age', 47 *McGill Law Journal* 39

http://app.singpao.com/20020409/international/99089_main.html

http://full.mingpaonews.com/20020118/_tacl.htm

http://i.cmpnet.com/gocsi/db_area/pdfs/fbi/FBI2003.pdf

http://www.acpf.org/WC8th/AgendaItem2/I2PpTurnbullHK.html

http://www.acpr.gov.au/pdf/Ecrime_Strategy.pdf

http://www.auscert.org.au/Information/Auscert_info/2002cs.pdf

http://www.cbi.org.uk/80256716004baae5/33a87f2eee41b54e80256803004f04e4/eff1596523e1653f80256aaf00390135?OpenDocument

http://www.cnn.com/TECH/computing/9901/26/clinton.idg/

http://www.cnnic.net.cn/about.shtml

http://www.cnnic.net.cn/develst/200201/doc2002-1.zip.

http://www.cnnic.net.cn/develst/2003–7/report2003–7.zip

http://www.cnnic.net.cn/develst/fa.shtml

http://www.cnnic.net.cn/tj/2.shtml

http://www.cnnic.net.cn/tj/rep2002.shtml

http://www.esd.gov.hk

http://www.mingpaonews.com/20020107/t_gaa1h.htm

http://www.mpinews.com/fprint.cfm?htm=htm %5C20020408 %5Cta11441a %2Ehtm

http://www.mpinews.com/fprint.cfm?htm=htm %5C20031021 %5Cta21205t %2Ehtm
http://www.nielsen-netratings.com/pr/pr_020422_eratings.pdf
http://www.pricewaterhousecoopers.co.uk/extweb/newcolth.nsf/docid/1A47C7356C3D57AC85256AD1005834D1?OpenDocument
http://www.security.iia.net.au/downloads/crime %20and %20security %20survey.pdf
http://www.security.iia.net.au/downloads/grabosky.pdf
http://www.ust.hk/itsc/y2k/
http://www.year2000.gov.hk/english/index_2.html

Hundley, R, and R Anderson (1995), 'Emerging Challenge: Security and Safety in Cyberspace', *IEEE Technology and Society Magazine*, 14(4): 19–28

Hynds, L (2003), 'Policing the Digital Frontier'. In Broadhurst, *Bridging the GAP*

ICC (2001), ICC Cyber-crime Unit. http://www.iccwbo.org/ccs/menu_cyber-crime_unit.asp (visited 4 April 2001)

Icove, D J (1997), *Collaring the Cybercrook: An Investigator's View*, IEEE Spectrum, June 1997

Iden, R L (2003), 'Cyber Crime: What's the Threat, the Challenge, and the Policing Response'. In Broadhurst, *Bridging the GAP*

Infosec.com (1998), Cyber-cash Making Money Laundering Easier, 8 December 1998. http://www.info-sec.com/commerce/commerce_120898a_j.shtml (visited 27 March 2001)

Inoue, M (1997), *Sosa Shudan to shiteno Tsushin/Kaiwa no Boju* (Telecommunications Interception and Eavesdropping as Investigative Tools), Tokyo: Yuhikaku

Institute for the Advanced Study of Information Warfare (2001). http://www.psycom.net/iwar.1.html (visited 4 April 2001)

Intellectual Property and Competition Review Committee, Canberra: Commonwealth Attorney-General's Department. http://ipcr.gov.au

Jamieson, A (2001), 'Transnational Organized Crime: A European Perspective', *Studies in Conflict and Terrorism*, 24: 377–87

Jiang Ping (2000), *Jisuanji Fanzui Wenti Yanjiu* (Research into Computer Crime Problems), Beijing: Commercial Press

Johnston, L (1992), *The Rebirth of Private Policing*, London: Routledge

Johnston, L (2000), *Policing Britain: Risk, Security and Governance*, Harlow: Longman

Johnston, L (2000a), 'Transnational private policing: the impact of global commercial security'. In Sheptycki, *Issues in Transnational Policing*, pp. 21–42

Jones, T, and T Newburn (1998), *Private Security and Public Policing*, Oxford: Clarendon Press

Joseph, M (2000), 'Both Sides Hacked Over Kashmir'. Wired News, 23 December. http://www.wired.com/news/politics/0,1283,40789,00.html (visited 31 March 2001)

Kasim, S (1996), 'Delay in Cyberlaws Implementation', *New Straits Times*, 2 December, p. 1

Keisatsucho (National Police Agency) (1996) *Heisei 8 Nen Keisatsu Hakusho* (White Paper on Police 1996), Tokyo: Keisatsucho

Keisatsucho (1999), *Heisei 11 Nen Keisatsu Hakusho* (White Paper on Police 1999),

Tokyo: Keisatsucho

Keisatsucho (2000), *Explanatory Notes to Punishment of Organised Crime and Control of Proceeds of Crime Law*, Tokyo: Keisatsucho

Kelley, J (2001), 'Terror groups hide behind Web Encryption', *USA Today*, 5 February 2001. http://www.usatoday.com/life/cyber/tech/2001–02–05-binladen.htm#more (visited 26 June 2002)

Khoo, B H (2003), 'Police Cooperation in Fighting Transnational Organised Crime: An Asian Perspective'. In Broadhurst, *Bridging the GAP*

Krochmal, M (2000), Distributed Denial Of Service Threat Grows. http://www.techweb.com/wire/story/TWB20000208S0016 (visited 12 February 2001)

Kwan, D (1999), 'Deputies Seek Safeguards on High Tech Trade', *SCMP*, 4 March, p. 8

Lanham, D, M Weinberg, K. E. Brown and G Ryan (1987), *Criminal Fraud*, Sydney: Law Book Co. Ltd

Lau, S K (1984), *Society and Politics in Hong Kong*, Hong Kong: Chinese University Press

Lau, S K (1988), *Basic Law and The New Political Order of Hong Kong*, Institute of Social Studies, Chinese University of Hong Kong, Occasional Paper No. 26

Lau, R W K (2002), 'Community Policing in Hong Kong Limits to Realizing a Vision'. In *The 3rd Annual Meeting of Asian Association of Police Studies Asian Policing in the 21st Century Proceedings*, Hong Kong

Lau, S K, and H C Kuan (1985), *Hong Kong After The Sino-British Agreement: Limits to Institutional Change in a Dependent Polity*, Institute of Social Studies, Chinese University of Hong Kong, Occasional Paper No. 9

Lau, S K, and H C Kuan (1988), *The Ethos of the Hong Kong Chinese*, Hong Kong: Chinese University Press

Lau, S K, and H C Kuan (1993), *Chinese Bureaucrats in a Modern Colony: The Case of Hong Kong*, Hong Kong Institute of Asia-Pacific Studies, Chinese University of Hong Kong, Occasional Paper No. 28

Lau, S K, and R P L Lee (1985), *The Birth and Growth of Academic Sociology in Hong Kong*, Institute of Social Studies, The Chinese University of Hong Kong, Occasional Paper No. 9

LeBlond, R, and Y P Lin (1997), 'Programs for Hacking Found Readily on Net', *Straits Times*, 30 May, p. 49

Lee, C C (2000), 'The Paradox of Political Economy'. In C C Lee, ed., *Communication Patterns and Bureaucratic Control in Cultural China: Power, Money, and Media*, Evanston IL: Northwestern University Press

Lee, S (2000), 'New Steps to Combat Hackers in Pipeline', *SCMP*, 15 June, p. 4

Lessig, L (1999), *Code and Other Laws of Cyberspace*, New York: Basic Books

Leung, P (1999), 'E-crime risks grow in region', *Business Asia*, 13 December. http://www.findarticles.com/cf_0/m0BJT/23_7/58358875/p1/article.jhtml?term=electronic+crime (visited 12 February 2001)

Levi, M (2001), 'Between the Risk and the Reality falls the Shadow: evidence and urban legends in computer fraud'. In Wall, *Crime and The Internet*

Li, D (2001), 'The Public and Private Law Enforcement Interface'. In Broadhurst, *Proceedings of the Asia Cyber Crime Summit*

Li Wenyan et al. (2001), *Jisuanji Fanzui Yanjiu* (Computer Crime Research), Beijing: Zhongguo Fangzheng Chubanshe

Lisker, J S (2001). 'Electronic Commerce Fraud: Risk Assessment and Prevention'. In Broadhurst, *Proceedings of the Asia Cyber Crime Summit*

Littmann, J (1997), *The Watchman: The Twisted Life and Crimes of Serial Hacker Kevin Poulsen*, Boston: Little Brown

Liu, J H, L Zhang and S Messner, eds. (2001), *Crime and Social Control in a Changing China*, Westport CN: Greenwood Press

Lizee, P P (2000), *Peace, Power and Resistance in Cambodia: Global Governance and the Failure of International Conflict Resolution*, Houndsmill: Macmillan

Lloyd, I J (2000), *Information Technology Law*, 3rd edn. London: Butterworths

Lo, A (1999), 'Computer Crime a Magnet for Teens', *SCMP*, 6 June, p. 2.

Lo, T W (1993), *Corruption and Politics in Hong Kong and China*, Buckingham: Open University Press

Lo, V Y-K (2000), 'Tracing and Tracking Suspects Across Computer Networks'. Paper Presented at the 8th World Congress of the Asia Crime Prevention Foundation, Beijing. http://www.acpf.org/WC8th/AgendaItem2/I2 %20Pp %20VictorLo %2C %20HK.html (visited 14 April 2001)

Luk, A (2001), 'Best Practice: Mechanisms for International Co-operation'. In Broadhurst, *Proceedings of the Asia Cyber Crime Summit*

McCardle, H, J Boxhall, J Ronderos and R Francisco (2000), *Cyber-crime and its Effects on the Asia-Pacific Region*, Council on Security Co-operation in the Asia-Pacific, Transnational Crime Working Group, Canberra

McDonald, J (2000), 'Cyber Pirates Plunder Asia's Internet Boom'. Fox News.com. http://foxnews.com/vtech/061200/pirates.sml (visited 30 March 2001)

Mail Utilities (2003), 'Millions of Computers in China Feared Infected by Internet Bug', 23 August, http://www.mailutilities.com/news/archive/154/2277.html (visited 5 January 2004)

Manning, P K (2000), 'Policing new social spaces'. In Sheptycki, *Issues in Transnational Policing*

Masterson, M (2000), Love Bug Cost Billions. http://cnnfn.cnn.com/2000/05/05/technology/virus_impact/ (visited 12 February 2001)

McKemmish, R. (1999), 'What is Forensic Computing?' *Trends and Issues in Crime and Criminal Justice*, No. 118, Canberra: Australian Institute of Criminology

McKinsey, K (2001), 'Shoppers Lost in Cyberspace', *Far Eastern Economic Review*, 164(7): 34–6

Morgan, M G (1981), 'Probing the Question of Technology-Induced Risk', *IEEE Spectrum*, 18(11): 58–64

Morgan, R, and T Newburn (1997), *The Future of Policing*, Oxford: Clarendon

Mostyn, M M (2000), 'The need for regulating anonymous remailers', *International Review of Law Computers & Technology*, 14(1): 79– 88

Mueller, M L (2002), *Ruling the Root: Internet Governance and the Taming of Cyberspace*, Cambridge MA: MIT Press

Murphy, D (2001), 'When Speed is King', *Far Eastern Economic Review*, 164(7): 36

Nader J C (1998), *Prentice Hall's Illustrated Dictionary of Computing*, 3rd edn, Sydney: Prentice Hall

Nielsen (2002), China Takes Prize for World's Second Largest At Home Internet Population as Numbers Reach 56.6 Million 22 April 2002. http://www.nielsen-netratings.com/pr/pr_020422_hk.pdf (visited 29 July 2002)

Newman, G (1999), *Global report on Crime and Justice*, UN Office of Drug Control and Crime Prevention, New York: Oxford University Press

Newman, G, and R Clarke (2003) *Superhighway Robbery: Preventing E-commerce Crime*, Devon, UK: Willan Publishing

Newman, K (1998), 'Phone Call Scams Skim off Millions', *New Zealand Herald*, 20 August 1998. http://www.infowar.com/ (visited 23 December 1999)

New Straits Times (1997), 'Expert to Look into Perak Website Hacking', 12 September, p. 10

Ng, Q M (1991), *Bureaucratic Response to Political Change: Theoretical Use of the Atypical Case of the Hong Kong Police*, Hong Kong Institute of Asia Pacific Studies, Chinese University of Hong Kong, Occasional Paper No. 2

Nikkei Weekly (2001) 'Legal Loopholes Favor Net Criminals: From Private Sector to Public at Large, No One is Safe from Onslaught of Anonymous Online Evildoers', 15 January.

Noble, R (2003), 'Interpol's New Approach: A Return to Basics'. In Broadhurst, *Bridging the GAP*

Nua.com (2000), 'Laos Tightens Control of Net Use'. http://www.nua.com/surveys/index.cgi?f=VS&art_id=905356137&rel=true (visited 1 August 2002)

Nua.com (2003), 'How Many Online?' http://www.nua.ie/surveys/how_many_online/index.html (visited 22 December 2003)

Ogilvie, E (2000a), 'Cyberstalking', *Trends and Issues in Crime and Criminal Justice*, No. 166, Canberra: Australian Institute of Criminology.

Oglivie, E (2000b), *Stalking: Legislative, Policing and Prosecution Patterns in Australia*, Research and Public Policy Series No. 34, Canberra: Australian Institute of Criminology. http://www.aic gov.au/publications/tandi/tandi166.html (visited 4 April 2001)

Opolot, J S E (1999), *An Introduction to Private Security: A Comparative Introduction to an International Phenomenon*, Lanham Austin & Winfield

Parker, D (1976), *Crime by Computer*, New York: Charles Scribner's Sons

Parker, D B (1981), *Computer Security Management*, Englewood Cliffs, New Jersey: Prentice Hall

Parker, D (1983), *Fighting Computer Crime*, New York: Charles Scribner's Sons

Parker, D (1998), *Fighting Computer Crime: A New Framework for Protecting Information*, New York: John Wiley & Sons

Pastore, M (2001), 'Asian B2B E-Commerce Approaches Quarter of World's Total', 5 April 2001. http://cyberatlas.internet.com/markets/b2b/article/0,,10091_735181, 00.html (visited 29 July 2002)

People's Daily Online (2000), 'China's First Computer Crime Suspect Extradited Back to China'. People's Daily Online, 13 January. http://english.peopledaily.com.cn/200001/13/eng20000113T204.html (visited 27 March 2001)

Pfaffenberger, B (1997), *Webster's New World Dictionary of Computer Terms*, 6th edn, New York: Que

Pollitt, M (2003), 'Digital Evidence in Internet Time'. In Broadhurst, *Bridging the GAP*.

Poon V Y K (2003), 'Cyber Crime: Challenges to the Enforcement of Intellectual Property Rights'. In Broadhurst, *Bridging the GAP*

Postiglione, G A, and J T H Tang, eds. (1997), *Hong Kong's Reunion with China: Global Dimensions of Hong Kong Becoming China: The Transition to 1997*, Hong Kong University Press

Rathmell, A (1997), 'Cyber-terrorism: The Shape of Future Conflict?' *Royal United Service Institute Journal*, October: 40–6. http://www.kcl.ac.uk/orgs/icsa/rusi.htm#who (visited 21 December 1999)

Recording Industry Association of America (RIAA), Anti-piracy website: http://www.riaa.com/Protect-Campaign-1.cfm

Reiner, R (2000), *The Politics of the Police*, 3rd edn, Oxford: Oxford University Press

Reuters (2001), 'Internet sex offer puts Malaysian husband in jail'. CNN.com/sci-tech, 4 April. http://www.cnn.com/2001/TECH/internet/04/04/malaysia.internet.reut/index.html?s=8 (visited 4 April 2001)

Reuters (2002), Internet Surge Ahead for Asia, but Limits Seen, 25 July 2002. http: //www.reuters.com/news_article.jhtml;jsessionid=DU0FO04O4 HAKA CRBAEZSFFA?type= internetnews&StoryID=1248991 (visited 29 July 2002)

Rigakos, G S (2002), *The New Parapolice Risk Markets and Commodified Social Control*, University of Toronto Press

Rioni, S G, ed. (1997), *The Politics and Economics of Hong Kong*, Cammack: Nova Science Publishers

Rosenau, J N (1992), 'The relocation of authority in a shrinking world', *Comparative Politics*, 24: 253–72

Sanchez, E (2002), 'Failure to Assure Security Seen Behind Slow Growth of Online Shopping', *BusinessWorld*, 2 July

Sanqiang, Q (2002), *Copyright in China*, Beijing: Foreign Languages Press

Sayers, K (2000–2001), 'Taming the Tiger: Towards a new intellectual property regime in Thailand', *Law Asia Journal*, 89–112

Schieck, M (1995), *Combating Fraud in Cable and Telecommunications*. IIC Communications Topics No. 13, London: International Institute of Communications

Schneier, B (1995), *Applied Cryptography,* 2nd edn, New York: Wiley and Sons

Schwartau, W (1994), *Information Warfare: Chaos on the Electronic Superhighway*, New York: Thunder's Mouth Press

SCMP (2002), 'Web expert jailed for phone scam', 7 March 2002, p. 8

Semple, K (2004), 'E-Mail Worm Snarls Computers Around Globe', The New York Times Online, 27 January. http://www.nytimes.com/2004/01/27/technology/27CND-VIRU.html (visited 28 January 2004)

Seneviratne, K (2000), 'Pressure on Pacific to Stop Money Laundering', Asia Times Online, 29 June. http://www.atimes.com/oceania/BF29Ah01.html (visited 29 March 2001)

Shehu, A Y (2001), 'Combating Cyber-crime: A Public / Private Sector Coalition in Asia'. In Broadhurst, *Proceedings of the Asia Cybercrime Summit*

Sheptycki, J W E, ed. (2000), *Issues in Transnational Policing*, London: Routledge

Smith, R, and G Urbas (2001), *Controlling Fraud on the Internet: A CAPA Perspective*, Canberra: Australian Institute of Criminology Research and Public Policy Series No. 39,

Smith, R G, Grabosky and G Urbas (2004), *Cyber Criminals on Trial*, Cambridge University Press

Smith, R E, I G Sarason and B R Sarason (1986), *Psychology: The Frontiers of Behavior*, Cambridge MA: Harper & Row

So, C Y K, and J M Chan, eds. (1999), *Press and Politics in Hong Kong*, Hong Kong Institute of Asia-Pacific Studies, The Chinese University of Hong Kong

Sofaer, A D, and S E Goodman, eds. (2001), *The Transnational Dimension of Cyber-crime and Terrorism*, Stanford KT: Hoover Institution Press

Software and Information Industry Association 2001, *Report on Global Software Piracy 2000*. http://www.spa.org/piracy

Speer, D L (2000), 'Redefining borders: The challenges of cyber-crime', *Crime, Law and Social Change*, 34: 259–73

Stallings, W (2000), *Network Security Essentials: Applications and Standards*, New Jersey: Prentice Hall.

Starr, C (1969), 'Social Benefit Versus Technological Risk', *Science*, 165 (19 September): 1232–8

Stephenson, P, A Kwan and D Ellis (2001), *Cyberlaw in Hong Kong*, Hong Kong: Butterworths

Sterrett, C, and A Shah (1998), 'Going Global on the Information Super Highway', *SAM Advanced Management Journal*, 63(1): 43–8

Stoll, C (1991), *The Cuckoo's Egg*, London: Pan Books

Sutter, G (2001), *A tale of two interception regimes: RIP v CALEA, a comparison*. 16th BILETA Annual Conference (9–10 April 2001). Retrieved 30 December 2002, at http://www.bileta.ac.uk/01papers/sutter.html

Tan, K H 2000, 'Prosecuting Foreign-Based Computer Crime, International Law and Technology Collide'. Paper presented to the Symposium on the Rule of Law in the Global Village, Palermo, Italy, 12–14 December. http://www.odccp.org/palermo/pdf/tan-paper.pdf (visited 14 April 2001)

Tan, O B (1994), 'Police Studying Setting up of Computer Crime Team', *Straits Times*, 24 July, p. 21

Tanabe, Y (2004), 'Inter-governmental Cooperation in Combating Cybercrime – UN Workshop on Crime Related to Computer Networks'. In Broadhurst, *Proceedings of the 2nd Asia Cyber Crime Summit*

Tendler, S, and N Nuttall (1996), 'Hackers Leave Red-Faced Yard with $1.29m Bill', *Australian*, 6 August, p. 37

The Hindu (2000), 'Engineer Held for "Cyber Crime"', *The Hindu*, 31 May, p. 13

Thomas, D, and I Loader (2000), *Cybercrime: Law Enforcement, Security and Surveillance in the Information Age*, London: Routledge

Thomas, N (1999), *Democracy Defined: Identity, Civil Society and Illiberal Democracy in Hong Kong*, Aldershot: Ashgate

Thomas, P A (2002), 'Legislative responses to terrorism'. In P Scraton, ed., *Beyond September 11: An Anthology of Dissent*, London: Pluto Press

Traver, H, and J Vagg, eds. (1991), *Crime and Justice in Hong Kong*, Hong Kong: Oxford University Press

Tsang, J (2001), 'Anti-piracy enforcement in Hong Kong'. In Broadhurst, *Proceedings of the Asia Cyber Crime Summit*

Tsuchiya, T (2001), *Degital jidai no gohoteki tsushin boju (Europe hen)* (Lawful interception in the digital age [Europe issue]). Chijo, November, pp. 14–20. Retrieved 6 May 2003 at http://www.glocom.ac.jp/project/chijo/2001_11/2001_11.pdf

Turban, E, and D King (2003), *Introduction to E-commerce*, Upper Saddle River, New Jersey: Prentice Hall

Turnbull, R G (2000), 'Internet and Other High-Tech Crimes: A Kong Hong Perspective'. Paper Presented at the 8th World Congress of the Asia Crime Prevention Foundation, Beijing, China. http://www.acpf.org/WC8th/AgendaItem2/I2PpTurnbullHK.html (visited 14 April 2001)

Urbas, G (2000), 'Public Enforcement of Intellectual Property Rights', *Trends and Issues in Crime and Criminal Justice*, No. 177, Canberra: Australian Institute of Criminology

Urbas, G (2001), 'Cyber-crime Legislation in the Asia-Pacific Region'. In Broadhurst, *Proceedings of the Asia Cybercrime Summit Hong Kong*

Valeri, L (2001), 'Europe and Cybercrime: Possible Lessons for Asia?' Paper presented to the 3rd Asia Development Forum, Bangkok, 12–14 June

Vechayanon, W (1998), 'Intellectual property rights enforcement and the role of the Intellectual Property Court in Thailand'. In *First Anniversary: The Central Intellectual Property and International Trade Court*, Thailand

Williams, M. (2000), 'Effective IP enforcement: Strategic approaches to countering software piracy', *Computers and the Law: Journal for the Australian and New Zealand Societies for Computers and the Law*, March: 32–8

Venditto, G (1996), 'Safe Computing', *Internet World*, September: 48–58

Wacks, R, ed (1993), *Police Powers in Hong Kong: Problems and Prospects*, The University of Hong Kong

Wahlert, G (1996), 'Implications for Law Enforcement of the Move to a Cashless Society'. In A Graycar and P N Grabosky, eds., *Money Laundering*, Canberra: Australian Institute of Criminology, pp. 22–8

Wall, S D, ed. (2001a), *Crime and the Internet*, London: Routledge

Wall, S D (2001b), 'Cybercrimes and the Internet'. In Wall, *Crime and the Internet*

Wall, S D (2001c), 'Maintaining order and law on the internet'. In Wall, *Crime and the Internet*

Wall, S D (2001d) 'Policing the Internet: Maintaining Order and Law on the Cyberbeat'. In Akdeniz et al., *The Internet, Law and Society*

Wall, S D (2002), 'Insecurity and the Policing of Cyberspace'. In Crawford, *Crime and Insecurity*

Wang, G W, and S L Wong, eds. (1999), *Toward A New Millennium: Building on Hong Kong's Strengths, Centre of Asian Studies*, The University of Hong Kong

Weber, M (1947) *The Theory of Social and Economic Organization* (transl. AM Henderson and Talcott Parsons, edited with an Introduction by Talcott Parsons), New York: Oxford University Press

Whitaker, R (1999), *The End of Privacy: How Total Surveillance Is Becoming a Reality*, New Press: New York

White House, (2000), International Crime Threat Assessment. http://www.fas.org/irp/threat/pub45270index.html (visited 15 February 2001)

Williams, M (2001), 'The Language of Cybercrime'. In Wall, *Crime and the Internet*

WITSA (2000) World Information Technology and Services Alliance Statement on the Council of Europe Draft Convention on Cyber-crime. Retrieved 26 December 2002, at http://www.witsa.org/ papers/COEstmt.pdf

Yeang, S C (2001), 'Curbing Attacks on Websites', *New Straits Times*, 14 January, p. 23

Yuang X (2000), 'Searching for Substance: The Reality of China's Internet Development', *Harvard Asia Pacific Review*, 4(2): 17–18

Zheng X F (2003), 'Organised Crime in Mainland China and its Counter-measures against Cross-border Organised Crime' In Broadhurst, *Bridging the GAP*

Index